D0221312

# OXFORD ENGLISH MONOGRAPHS

# THOMAS NASHE
# In context

LORNA HUTSON

CLARENDON PRESS · OXFORD
1989

*Oxford University Press, Walton Street, Oxford OX2 6DP*

*Oxford New York Toronto*
*Delhi Bombay Calcutta Madras Karachi*
*Petaling Jaya Singapore Hong Kong Tokyo*
*Nairobi Dar es Salaam Cape Town*
*Melbourne Auckland*

*and associated companies in*
*Berlin Ibadan*

*Oxford is a trade mark of Oxford University Press*

*Published in the United States*
*by Oxford University Press (USA)*



*British Library Cataloguing in Publication Data*

*Hutson, Lorna*
*Thomas Nashe in context*
*1. English literature. Nash, Thomas:*
*1567–1601*
*I. Title II. Series*
*828'.309*

*ISBN 0-19-812876-2*

*Library of Congress Cataloging in Publication Data*

*Hutson, Lorna*
*Thomas Nashe in context/Lorna Hutson.*
*p. cm. — (Oxford English monographs)*
*Revision of thesis (D.Phil.) — Oxford.*
*"Checklist of Nashe's writings": p.*
*Bibliography: p. Includes index.*
*1. Nash, Thomas, 1567–1601 — Criticism and interpretation.*
*I. Title. II. Series*
*828'.309—dc 19 PR2326.N3Z73 1988 88-10287*

*ISBN 0-19-812876-2*

*Typeset by Burns & Smith*
*Printed in Great Britain by*
*Biddles Ltd.*
*Guildford and King's Lynn*

For Jonathan Miles

## ACKNOWLEDGEMENTS

THIS monograph began as an Oxford D.Phil. thesis on Thomas Nashe's writings in their economic and social context. I am therefore most indebted to the Department of Education and Science for three years of graduate study, and to my doctoral supervisors, Emrys Jones and Glenn Black, for their stimulating criticism and patient encouragement at a very early stage. I would also like to thank Somerville College, and especially Katherine Duncan-Jones, who has been unfailingly kind and supportive. A year's research fellowship at Victoria University, Wellington, New Zealand, enabled me to rethink many of the assumptions in the thesis, and I would like to thank Don McKenzie, Brian Opie, and Linda Hardy for their interest and hospitality. From the first, Oxford University Press have been encouraging about the project, and I am grateful to them. Most of all, however, I have to thank Jonathan Miles for good-naturedly reading, criticizing, and typing the script in all its various obscure mutations from thesis to book.

L.H.

# CONTENTS

# ILLUSTRATIONS

Reproduced by permission of the British Library

# ABBREVIATIONS

*The Works of Thomas Nashe*, ed. R. B. McKerrow in 5 vols., with a supplement by F. P. Wilson, are cited in the text by volume and page number.

| | |
|---|---|
| *AESC* | *Annales: Economies, Sociétés, Civilisations* |
| *APC* | *Acts of the Privy Council* |
| *Cahiers E.* | *Cahiers Elisabéthains* |
| *CSPD* | *Calendar of State Papers Domestic* |
| *EC* | *Essays in Criticism* |
| *Ec. HR* | *Economic History Review* |
| *EETS* | *Early English Text Society* |
| *EHR* | *English History Review* |
| *ELH* | *Journal of English Literary History* |
| *ELR* | *English Literary Renaissance* |
| *ES* | *Essays and Studies* |
| *HLQ* | *Huntington Library Quarterly* |
| *JHI* | *Journal of the History of Ideas* |
| *MLR* | *Modern Language Review* |
| *MP* | *Modern Philology* |
| *N&Q* | *Notes and Queries* |
| *P&P* | *Past and Present* |
| *PBA* | *Proceedings of the British Academy* |
| *PMLA* | *Publications of the Modern Language Association* |
| *PQ* | *Philological Quarterly* |
| *RES* | *Review of English Studies* |
| *SP* | *Studies in Philology* |
| *TED* | *Tudor Economic Documents* (see Works Cited) |
| *TLS* | *Times Literary Supplement* |
| *TRHS* | *Transactions of the Royal Historical Society* |

# CHECKLIST OF NASHE'S WRITINGS

The list gives dates of registration and first publication, noting publishing difficulties and any complication created by official response. Information from *Works*, ed. McKerrow, vols. i–v; *Transcript of Stationers' Registers*, ed. Arber and articles by C. G. Harlow and C. T. Wright (see Works Cited).

| *Regd.* | *Title* | *Pub.* | *Notes* |
|---|---|---|---|
| 19 Sept. 1588 | *The Anatomie of Absurditie* | 1589 | |
| 23 Aug. 1589 | 'To the Gentlemen Students of Both Universities' | 1589 | A preface to Greene's *Menaphon* |
| Not regd. | *An Almond for a Parrat* | 1590 | Anti-Martinist propaganda commissioned by Bancroft |
| Not regd. | 'Somewhat to reade for them that list' | 1591 | Preface to pirated edn. of Sidney's *Astrophil and Stella* |
| 8 Aug. 1592 | *Pierce Penilesse his Supplication to the Divell* | 1592 | Regd. without Nashe's consent by R. Jones and pub. with conventional prefatory material, 1592. Subsequently repub., with plain title page and no apologetic preface to reader, by A. Jeffes, 1592 |
| 12 Jan. 1593 | *Strange Newes, of the intercepting certaine Letters and a convoy of Verses as they were going Priuilie to Victuall the Low Countries* | 1593 | Reply to G. Harvey's *Foure Letters and certaine Sonnets,* 1592 |
| 8 Sept. 1593 | *Christes Teares Over Jerusalem, whereunto is annexed, a comparative admonition to London* | 1593 | Another edn. pub. with cancel leaf for X3 and epistle to reader in 1594, after Aldermen's judicial proceedings against Nashe in Nov. 1593 |
| 17 Sept. 1593 | *The Vnfortunate Traveller, or The Life of Jack Wilton* | 1594 | |
| 30 June 1593<br>25 Oct. 1594 | *The Terrors of the Night or A Discourse of Apparitions* | 1594 | Regd. before Aldermen's proceedings, pub. in 1594 expressing gratitude to Sir G. Carey who took Nashe to Isle of Wight to escape Aldermen, Christmas, 1593 |
| Not regd. | *Have With You to Saffron Walden, or Gabriel Harvey's Hunt is Vp* | 1596 | A reply to G. Harvey's *Pierces Supererogation*, 1593 |

| | | | |
|---|---|---|---|
| 11 Jan. 1599 | *Nashe's Lenten Stuffe, containing the Description and first Procreation and Increase of the towne of Great Yarmouth in Norfolke: With a new Play never played before, of the praise of the RED HERRING* | 1599 | Regd. 'vpon Condicion that he gett yt Laufully Aucthorized' after government proceedings against Nashe for his play *The Isle of Dogs*, 1597 |

In June 1599 an order was given by Archbishop Whitgift and Bishop Bancroft that 'all Nasshes bookes and Doctor Harvyes bookes be taken wheresoeuer they maye be found and that none of theire bookes bee euer printed hereafter'.

| | | | |
|---|---|---|---|
| 28 Oct. 1600 | *A Pleasant Comedie, called Summers last will and Testament* | 1600 | Orig. written for Abp. Whitgift, 1593. Regd. in 1600 as 'A booke called SUMMERS last will and testament presented by WILLIAM SOMMERS'; no mention of Nashe |

# Introduction
## *Critical Contexts*

THIS book is about Nashe's writing, not his life, and the context it has tried to provide is deliberately not biographical. The facts known about Nashe's life are relatively meagre. He was born in Lowestoft in 1567, was a student at St John's, Cambridge, and in 1588 went from there to London where he wrote various works for publication and one play which, on performance, so scandalized the government that its author was forced to flee. Taking refuge in Yarmouth, he wrote one last work before all his writings were called in and prohibited by edict of the High Commission in 1599. By 1601 he was dead, aged not more than thirty-four. It is not known how he died, or where, or when.[1] These bare facts and uncertainties, apart from what can be gleaned from his writings, are the staple of Nashe's biography. However, since biographical interest in a writer is always in some measure a critical study of his life through his work and opinions, it has not proved difficult to flesh out this sparse biographical frame by recourse to Nashe's extant and published writings. In his case the temptation to do this is strong; much stronger than it would be, say, in the case of a critical study of Marlowe or Lyly. For Nashe seems always to be engaged in writing his life and opinions in an exceptionally intimate, physical manner. His published writings are always in the first person, an 'I' who is so disarmingly frank about the ongoing processes and hazards of writing that the act of composition itself becomes vividly present behind the printed words: 'now my penne makes blots as broad as a furd stomacher', he confides in the middle of a discourse on apparitions, 'and my muse inspyres me to put out my candle and goe to bed' (i. 384). This kind of authorial emergence from the text has less to do with an autobiographical impulse than it has with the author's insistent foregrounding of the writing process. So effectively does Nashe's writing convey a sense of the intractable materiality of words and the unpredictable nature of his own stylistic

[1] See McKerrow, v. 1–34; for important redating see C. G. Harlow, 'Nashe's Visit to the Isle of Wight and his Publications of 1592–4', and id., 'Thomas Nashe, Robert Cotton the Antiquary and *The Terrors of the Night*'.

enterprise that we come to imagine him continually present, like a precursor of Tristram Shandy, engaging even as we read with the animated unreliability of his own linguistic creations. Small wonder, then, that Nashe's texts should at times have been read in the manner of *Tristram Shandy* as a series of digressive progressions through the story of the author's own life and opinions. Charles Nicholl's biographical study is one such reading. 'Little', Nicholl remarks in explanation of his undertaking, 'has been written about the life and personality of the young man behind these pamphlets, surprisingly little for someone who steps out at us so vividly, and sheds such a casual, intimate light on his famous contemporaries.'[2] Yet, as Nicholl intermittently acknowledges, this vivid sense of presence pays tribute to the author's extreme stylistic self-consciousness. Nashe deliberately pursues just such an effect of intimacy, creating a sense of shared space by allusively invoking a contemporary locale, drawing on and intensifying current colloquialisms and discovering syntactical patterns which heighten the sense of a sentence without sacrificing the illusion of conversational spontaneity. Nashe's creative technique, as Neil Rhodes has explained, involves improvising from the familiar and the present; Nashe 'makes use of his immediate surroundings, gathering material from the tavern conversation or the contents of a kitchen', but the style is creative, he 'improves on the actually colloquial by inventing a quasi-idiom'.[3]

There is, however, a difficulty about yielding to the magic of this intensified evocation of literary London in the 1590s and inferring from it the circumstantial detail necessary to understand Nashe's life. For a critical impasse arises in which Nashe's texts themselves come to be interpreted and criticized in the light of the 'biographical' circumstances which they have been used to invent. The critical orthodoxy which explains Nashe's works as the commercially motivated expedients of a penniless but satirically gifted journalist is almost entirely based on the assumption that the carnivalesque text *Pierce Penilesse his Supplication to the Divell* (1592) is a kind of confessional autobiography. The assumption of journalistic pressure is, for example, built into Rhodes's sensitive criticism of Nashe's stylistic innovation. Rhodes argues that Nashe's colloquially based neologisms arise not from imaginative pressure, but 'because the writer is attempting to be super-colloquial, super-idiomatic. The journ-

[2] C. Nicholl, *A Cup of News: The Life of Thomas Nashe*, p. 7.

[3] N. Rhodes, *Elizabethan Grotesque*, p. 24.

alist must be the man on the spot; he must pick up the latest off-beat slang, even if it means making it up for himself.'[4] Assuming in this way that Nashe's creative transformation of a popular idiom is uniformly motivated by journalistic pressure (rather than assuming that the motives vary from text to text, so that the proverbially based, nourishing word play of *Lenten Stuffe* and the uncomfortable, disorienting puns of *The Unfortunate Traveller* serve different aesthetic and polemic ends) all too easily translates into a condescending reading of all Nashe's texts as ingenious responses to a commercial demand, even when such a reading neither questions what Elizabethan readers demanded, nor what their publishers regarded as commercial. This in turn produces the contradictory situation in which Nashe's texts, explicitly dissociating themselves from contemporary commercial writing and deploring the effects of commerciality, are ignored and their 'real' meaning discovered in the commercial interest assumed to have motivated them. Nicholl quotes Nashe's remarks about the infectious stink caused by the stale, used-up literary wares emanating from the commercial press (i. 239). The metaphors of bodily surfeit, vomit, and purgation which Nashe uses in this passage are part of his general association of poetic creativity with the imagery of festive, seasonal regeneration; but these Nicholl dismisses as 'tasteless' and 'kitchen-stuff rhetoric',[5] being interested less in Nashe's words than in the meaning he discovers behind the whole passage—the ironic 'reality' of its commercial motivation. This kind of criticism defeats the tribute to style implied by an impulse to explore the writer's personality, since it becomes incapable of accounting for anything in that style which distinguishes it from a hack production. Indeed, valuing Nashe's words primarily for their capacity to evoke an authentic, intimate impression of the milieu of the commercial writer of the Elizabethan period has a way of dispensing with the words themselves. When Nicholl considers the possibility of Nashe's having written a couple of mock astrological prognostications and decides that his authorship of these is, on the whole, unlikely, he concludes surprisingly that while such attributions themselves are questionable, 'the general conception behind them—of Nashe as someone knocking about the literary scene, ready to turn his pen to such hack formats as the "news from . . ." and the spoof-prognostication—is authentic enough'.[6]

[4] Ibid. [5] Nicholl, *A Cup of News*, p. 43. [6] Ibid. 82.

Such a general conception of Nashe, though highly questionable, can never be disproved by the self-fulfilling arguments which must result from both biographical and purely stylistic approaches to his texts. A broader context for reading Nashe needs to be supplied; we need room in which to get away from the chief recourse of this biographical and stylistic criticism, the assumption that Nashe's texts give us the journalistic repertoire of a single, personal voice. If we get away from the obligation to account for Nashe's writing in personal, biographical terms (his renowned hatred for Puritans, his 'temperamental' conservatism, for example) it becomes possible to argue that Nashe's versatile prose, with its exceptional sensitivity to the materiality of words, the plasticity of discourse, and the hazards of interpretation, is, far from being the vehicle of one histrionic personal voice, a parodic medium of dozens of public voices. Accentuating the properties and revealing the strategies of these public voices, Nashe's writing celebrates the dispersal of their discursive authority. The Elizabethan author–reader relation has its own conventional and often politically loaded voice, but it is not one to which Nashe's writing patiently conforms. His texts resist, for example, the habit of biographical and moral interpretation or the personal reference-hunting which have nevertheless persisted among his readers to the present day.

All this is not to say that there has not recently been excellent criticism of Nashe's style. But without the support of any sustained attempt to come to terms with each of Nashe's pamphlets as a distinctive, intelligently realized conception, stylistic criticism is all too easily absorbed back into the traditional ways of reading Nashe's personality through the texts. For while critics such as Neil Rhodes and John Carey have encouraged readers to be more attentive to local effects and ambiguities in Nashe's writing, they have at the same time actively deterred them from thinking about the texts as separate entities. 'Where Nashe failed completely was in accommodating his material to strong and abiding dramatic structures', writes Rhodes.[7] This determination not to read the pamphlets as entities is understandable in view of the biographical quicksands Rhodes wishes to avoid, but it leaves scholarship and reading at something of a standstill. Scholarship reacts, predictably enough, by paying attention to what conforms most to a generic prescription; the favourite texts for scholarly elucidation are the lyric 'Adieu Farewell Earths Bliss'

[7] Rhodes, *Elizabethan Grotesque*, p. 156.

(which fits into a long European tradition) and the narrative of *The Unfortunate Traveller* (which may or may not be a novel).[8] For readers the pamphlets remain, despite the stimulus of stylistic criticism, in a curious critical vacuum. What do they offer? They seem, for all their emotional flexibility and variety of texture, dislocated and pointless. Rhodes's remark about drama highlights the want of structure and human relevance which every reader must feel who appreciates Nashe's stylistic virtuosity for page after page in the pamphlets themselves rather than in the exhilarating isolation of excerpts under critical discussion. Yet Nashe cannot have intended that his pamphlets be read in quoted excerpts. That we find them otherwise inaccessible suggests not that we should hunt through them in an antiquarian fashion for biographical references (a way of reading mocked in the texts themselves) but that we should start considering the way in which an apparent shapelessness, a lack of continuity and coherence, might function as a politically and morally significant aesthetic in its own right.

Critics are in disagreement about the lack of formal or thematic coherence in Nashe's pamphlets. The older life-and-works approach found it useful to invoke the commercial pressures assumed by the 'life' to excuse the lapses of the 'works'.[9] With greater attention being paid to style, however, a strange transformation has occurred; what had traditionally been dismissed as incoherence or bad taste has been seized upon in critical discussion of Nashe's style as the 'flexibility' or 'instability of tone' that singles him out from the hacks and makes him worth reading. Appreciating the volatile effects produced by his uninhibited choice of metaphor, the critics of style have discovered a more intelligent writer than the Nashe who had emerged from critical accounts which were 'determined to wrench a uniform tone from every passage'.[10] But the messy shapelessness of individual texts and their lack of human relevance remains a problem. Indeed the problem has become unignorable, since this discovery of Nashe's intelligence means that he can no longer be excused as an irresponsible hack whose lapses in taste and moral feeling can be read as uncritical or expedient responses to a taste for crude sensationalism. However, the question has not been forced because, in an odd way, the old

8 R. Fehrenbach, 'Recent Studies in Nashe (1968–79)', p. 349.

9 McKerrow, v. 18; G. R. Hibbard, *Thomas Nashe: A Critical Introduction*, pp. 63–4, 151–5.

10 J. Carey, 'Sixteenth- and Seventeenth-Century Prose', in *English Poetry and Prose 1540–1674*, ed. C. Ricks, p. 378.

commercial-pressure argument has precluded it by implying that Nashe's virtuosity—his intelligent engagement on a technical level—was actually stimulated by the shoddiness of the sentiments he was marketing. If G. R. Hibbard can complain that Nashe was never 'wholly absorbed' in what he was saying, John Carey can reasonably reply that this was his salvation as an artist: 'It is in Nashe's resistance to "absorption" that his flexibility of response resides.'[11] C. S. Lewis earlier helped to prevent any sense of a problematic dichotomy between the coarseness of what Nashe seemed to be saying and the intelligence with which he had said it by suggesting that Nashe was actually provoked by commercial pressure into the unfettered exercise of pure technique: 'Paradoxically, though Nashe's pamphlets are commercial literature, they come very close to being, in another way, "pure" literature: literature which is, as nearly as possible, without a subject. In a certain sense of the word "say", if asked what Nashe "says" we should have to reply, Nothing.'[12] Neat as it is, this argument cannot be closely examined. Any writer so sensitive to the possibilities for producing disquieting, ambiguous effects by minute rhetorical alterations is unlikely to have a purely abstract and technical interest in doing so. Nashe must have intended to arouse in his readers the incompatible and self-scrutinizing responses that critics such as Rhodes have described. It becomes increasingly anomalous, as criticism goes on responding more sensitively to the ambiguities of Nashe's style, to maintain that these effects are merely the result of a technical virtuosity which the author himself was unable to control.

Of course, certain kinds of critical approach may benefit from this anomaly. The post-structuralist Jonathan Crewe has argued that the urge to render Nashe's texts coherent reveals more about the logocentric prejudice of the reader than it does about the possible intentions of the author. What Crewe identifies as the 'Nashe problem' amounts to the logocentric reader's inclination to resist acknowledging that in Nashe's texts the rhetoric is irreducible; the author is saying nothing. According to this thesis, all attempts to make sense of the heady profusion of possible meanings in Nashe's texts, from the splenetic responses written by Gabriel Harvey in the sixteenth century to the editions and annotations of R. B. McKerrow in the twentieth, become variations on an essentially logocentric urge to restore unity to the

[11] Ibid. 379.

[12] C. S. Lewis, *English Literature in the Sixteenth Century*, p. 416.

text.[13] The virtue of Crewe's position is that it does not shy away from the problems posed by a critical orthodoxy which asks readers to appreciate the intelligence of Nashe's style while ascribing its unevenness and want of proper feeling to the tastes of the hack writer's readership. However, if Crewe is right and an identifiable problem existed for readers of Nashe in the 1590s, it is surely misleading to select Gabriel Harvey as evidence of its typicality and continuity to the present day. For Harvey seems to have been remarkable among contemporary writers precisely because of his inability to appreciate the importance of Nashe's innovatory style. Nashe's more sensitive and even brilliant readers—Shakespeare, Jonson, and Donne, for example—did not find the tonal and thematic discontinuity of his style enough to thwart them from developing its very considerable creative potential. To these writers at least Nashe was aesthetically intelligible. His texts were saying something.

Even C. S. Lewis's persuasive argument that Nashe has ultimately nothing to say is suggestive of an intentional polemic, given what is now known about the importance ascribed by sixteenth-century humanists to the productivity of the literary text. It would have been difficult, given this educational context, for the most trivial poetry in print to say *nothing* to the resourceful sixteenth-century reader. Sixteenth-century attitudes to reading and writing were far from being a kind of modern logocentricism in an embryonic form. Quite different attitudes to the importance of discovering meaning in, or making sense of, the text are involved when the reader conceives of that text (as the humanists did) as a resource not just of latent significance but of latent moral and political power. Humanists looked on the reading of a poetic or fictional text less as the pursuit of logical or thematic coherence than as the discovery of materials for analogical reasoning and persuasion.[14] What may therefore appear to us, in reading Erasmus or Rabelais, to be an irreducible excess of rhetoric, confounding content in style and meaning in playfulness, may to a sixteenth-century reader have been signifying the text's easy mastery of the enormous communicative potential of classical literature. Consequently, if sixteenth-century readers were more concerned with the techniques for discovering and mastering the resources of such textual affluence than with pursuing the intention of

[13] J. Crewe, *Unredeemed Rhetoric: Thomas Nashe and the Scandal of Authorship*, pp. 1–20.

[14] See below, p. 45.

its immediate author, their response to the discovery that Nashe's texts say nothing—i.e. that they squander rather than make accessible the resource potential of figurative language—must have been very different from our own.

That there is a difference is plain in the very difference of metaphor. Whereas we complain that Nashe has nothing to say, that he tells us nothing, the equivalent sixteenth-century stricture would have been that his texts were 'prodigal'. The excess of rhetoric, or the expenditure of linguistic power, becomes scandalous in sixteenth-century terms not because it baffles readers, but because it is uneconomic. This in itself is highly suggestive with reference to reading Nashe, for it is the exaggeratedly physical nature of Nashe's writing, its habit of caricaturing and embodying its own rhetorical excesses, which has been singled out by Neil Rhodes as the hallmark of the Nashean style. Rhodes calls this style 'Elizabethan grotesque', identifying it with the yoking together of diverse and comically incompatible objects which is the basis of the grotesque manner in sixteenth-century painting. According to Rhodes, then, the solution to the problem of what Nashe might or might not be saying is stylistic, for he explains the tonal and thematic discontinuity of Nashe's texts partly in terms of a plastic aesthetic—a 'grotesque' relish for the physical heterogeneity of experience. Nevertheless, Rhodes goes on to concede that the moral and emotional ambivalence of Nashe's writing cannot be explained simply in terms of its insistent corporeality. He points out that writers strongly influenced by Nashe—Dekker and Middleton, for example—were able to render experience in a similarly comic and grotesque physical manner without reproducing Nashe's disquieting shifts of tone and attitude. These, Rhodes suggests, can be explained by the uncertainty of the sixteenth-century journalist's position in relation to his readers. Rhodes argues that the persona of the popular prose satirist, later developed by Dekker and Middleton, was Nashe's peculiar innovation. He was forced by the lack of an established persona into improvising from the available popular models, the figures of the preacher and the clown. Hence his equivocating uncertainty, his disturbing capacity to switch without warning from the accents of callous buffoonery to those of almost hysterical admonition; he reacts against his own excesses: 'the clown mocks the preacher, but the preacher terrifies the clown'.[15]

The question of Nashe's role as an author needs to be considered

[15] Rhodes, *Elizabethan Grotesque*, p. 52.

more broadly. If he knew his role to be experimental and unestablished when he set out, this is likely to be one of the things that his writing was conveying to his audience. His texts must have been involved in contentions with existing, inappropriate roles, and in anticipation of the risks and consequences of official misinterpretation. For official misinterpretation—censorship—was the most obvious check on experimenting with authorial roles in sixteenth-century England, and Nashe's relation to this political and social context has not been given enough attention. The idea of a preacher-clown dilemma formulates the options and pressures (as earlier critical assessments of Nashe have done) in terms of free commercial choice, but the most important forces motivating and restraining sixteenth-century writers were not commercial at all but political and pedagogical. The question of role needs to be put another way before it can be meaningful. We need to ask what the official position was concerning the status and function of figurative language in Elizabethan England. How was it justified? What decided whether a text was to be published? How did the published text signal to readers that it was acceptable? The humanists had put great emphasis on the value of classical literature as a political and educational resource; this may have posed problems for writers in the vernacular, who ran the risk of having their own compositions evaluated in similar terms.

On the whole it seems that the context in which Nashe's writings have been criticized has been either too limited or too broad. His 'works' have been used as hunting grounds for information about the London literary scene, while his 'texts' have been used for ahistorical speculations about the nature of rhetoric itself.[16] It is now time to place both, along with the 'literary scene', into the larger but still urgent and immediate context of sixteenth-century politics and education. What was expected of a young man possessed of formidable discursive ability emerging from the universities or the Inns of Court in the 1580s? How was he encouraged to think of employing his rhetorical and dialectical skills? Was the answer necessarily in writing and publishing, and if so to what end?

A valuable study by Richard Helgerson has already asked and answered some of these questions about Nashe's immediate predecessors—a literary generation which he christened the 'Elizabethan Prodigals'.[17] He shows that the writing of this genera-

16 Crewe, *Unredeemed Rhetoric*, p. viii.

17 R. Helgerson, *The Elizabethan Prodigals*.

tion—which includes Gascoigne, Whetstone, Sidney, Lyly, and Greene—is characterized by guilt, by the conscience that in writing fiction they are 'prodigally' wasting the time and talent which they should devote to the service of their country. As they all at one time or another find themselves developing fictive narratives or figurative analogies in a manner which seems to defy their professedly didactic intentions, they are all obliged to adopt a posture of repentance. This enables them to redefine the amoral tendencies of their writing as the prodigal experience of a misspent youth, which they claim to have set before the reading public for admonitory purposes. As Helgerson describes it, this pattern seems to set up obvious echoes with the themes of a work such as *The Unfortunate Traveller*, but Helgerson mentions Nashe only briefly. He sees Nashe's misogynist *Anatomie of Absurditie* (1589) as signalling the end of the prodigal era and ushering in the vogue for the new literary stance—that of the satirist—that would dominate the 1590s.[18] This decade represented a change in the assumptions governing the political aspirations of England's reformed and educated gentlemen. Whereas earlier writers of Elizabeth's reign tended to express feelings of guilt in publishing the 'prodigal' fiction which they claimed to be a self-indulgent evasion of political responsibility, their successors in the 1590s, denied access to political responsibility, made their frustration articulate in the form of satire. Thus the prodigals of the eighties were succeeded by the malcontents of the nineties—succeeded, that is, by men who were envious of state employment and critically satirical about the morals of those who seemed to be monopolizing it. From this thesis of Helgerson's we might expect to be able to classify Nashe among the malcontents and satirists of the nineties, but he will not fit so neatly. There is, after all, still the question of the 'Nashe problem'; if we can even suspect that Nashe's writings are not really saying anything, they clearly lack the ethical commitment, the rhetorical efficiency, of satire. Moreover, Rhodes's excellent analysis of Nashe's language demonstrates quite precisely how it differs from that of his satirical contemporaries; Nashe's writing is more grotesque, more involved, as Rhodes puts it, in the 'ludicrous diversity of the physical'.[19]

So Nashe is not one of the Elizabethan prodigals, although his writing has prodigal themes and he was clearly associated with them

[18] Ibid. 94.

[19] Rhodes, *Elizabethan Grotesque*, p. 49. See also S. Wells, 'Thomas Nashe and the Satirical Stance', pp. 1–17.

(his name is invariably linked, for example, with Robert Greene's). Nor can he, by virtue of his grotesquely physical and morally ambivalent style, be satisfactorily classified among contemporary satirists. Perhaps his writings mediate between the two literary modes, injecting a new mood of scepticism and satiric discontent into the old forms of repentant prodigality? That might explain, in part, his interest for contemporaries.

I shall eventually argue that the distinctive aesthetic and polemic coherence of each of Nashe's pamphlets can be best understood by analogy with the carnivalesque pastimes of pre-Reformation society in the model of dialogic, menippean satire. Like carnival pastimes, Nashe's pamphlets shape themselves by exaggerating the features of those discourses which would exclude and inhibit them; they transform drab contemporary restrictions surrounding the authorship and reception of printed texts into the exhilarating new resources of creative and interpretative freedom. To be in a position to show this, I have first to establish the nature of the restrictions on authorship and interpretation in the years just before Nashe began writing. This involves a series of chapters exploring the rather intricate links between England's economic recovery from mid-century crisis, the moral reformation which helped make that recovery possible, and the way in which attitudes to literature were affected by a reformed insistence that the exercise of reading contribute to the individual's provident control of circumstances. These will be followed by chapters on the significance of improvidence and pastime as an impulse in Nashe's writing, concluding with a consideration of Nashe's place in the classical, humanist and popular traditions of menippean satire. The second part of the book will be given over to the critical examination of individual texts in the light of what has been established.

# Part I : The Contexts

# 1

# Consuming Resources

## *Literature in Economic Context, 1558–1592*

THIS chapter will consider the curiously social and economic terms in which Elizabethan discourse discusses contemporary writing. Helgerson's book on the 'Elizabethan prodigals' has shown that the concept of prodigality operated powerfully in an ethical as well as an economic sense, and that the word was used in an ethical sense to express the anxious culpability of authorship in the 1570s and '80s. I want to suggest that there was a very close connection between the moral implications of 'prodigal' writing and the pragmatic, morally neutral sense in which 'prodigality' defined the waste of economic resources. In the farcical context of Nashe's writing a contemporary disinclination to distinguish between the moral and the economic senses of the word is frequently pilloried. In *Have With You to Saffron Walden* for example Nashe pretends to plead with his grave companions that they should not condemn his mock biography of Gabriel Harvey just because it will 'drink some inck, or prodigally dispend manie Pages that might haue been better employd' (iii. 55). This is obviously a joke; what is odd is the way in which, even in an admonitory mode, Nashe's effects seem to depend on an exploitation of physical and bodily resources, and this is what Rhodes, following Mikhail Bakhtin's innovatory criticism of Rabelais, has identified as the distinguishing feature of Nashe's 'grotesque' rendering of Elizabethan urban experience.[1] Nashe's grotesque depiction of social relations, however, for all its Rabelaisian qualities, differs from Rabelais in a way that is particularly revealing about Elizabethan society. For while Rabelais conceives of bodies as renewable organisms in a grotesquely growing and changing world, Nashe conceives of them as bodily material, part of society's expendable resources. Rhodes identifies an image from *Christes Teares Over Jerusalem* as an example of the 'purgatorial' side of Nashe's grotesque, where he is performing as preacher rather than as clown. The

[1] See M. Bakhtin, *Rabelais and his World*, trans. H. Iswolsky, *passim*; Rhodes, *Elizabethan Grotesque*, p. 16.

context is certainly an apocalyptic one; the destruction of Jerusalem by fire, plague, and famine figures as a lurid warning to sinful London, devastated by plague and threatened by invasion from Spain in the summer of 1593. Rhodes argues that the imagery of Gargantuan feasting, typical of the more benign, pastoral context of Rabelaisian grotesque, is inverted in Nashe's text where people start to consume one another. 'Ultimately', Rhodes puts it, 'people themselves, in one form or another, can supply most human needs—even road repairs.' He then quotes from *Christes Teares*: 'withered dead-bodies serue to mende High-waies with, and turne standing Quagmyres to firme ground (ramd full of their corses)' (ii. 59).[2] My argument turns on the precise way in which this image of Nashe's may be said to differ from similar imagery in Rabelaisian grotesque. It seems to me that an image in which decomposing bodies start to serve a useful social purpose (even for hyperbolic effect) is not quite the opposite of Gargantuan festivity, for it is not simply that the bodies are being tortured and consumed as they might be in a Boschian Day of Judgement but that they are being economically and resourcefully recycled. Society has collapsed, but Nashe is still turning bodies into social amenities, sinisterly promising improved communications and safer roads. Odd—yet this kind of imagery is not at all uncommon in Nashe's writing, comic or admonitory. In the same description of Jerusalem, for example, he expands on the theme that the Jewish people have foolishly built their houses on the sand, houses which are now about to topple. When they fall to the ground with a great crash, he says: 'The onely commodity they shal tithe to their owners will be (by their ouer-turning) to affoord them Tombes vnaskt' (ii. 47). Despite the fact that it is here not people but houses that are being destroyed, it is evident that the image is still following the same conjecturally economic development; the dignity of destruction is undercut by the notion of re-usability. Something, ceasing to be itself, starts being recycled, considered for its serviceable qualities in another project.

This imagery of recycling is not characteristic of the more organic web of Rabelaisian grotesque. In Rabelais, when a thing is destroyed or consumed or decomposed it contributes to some other life, some other new growth. We can compare Nashe's image of the withered dead bodies serving to mend highways with a technically similar but effectively different image of mutilation and bodily mutation in

[2] Rhodes, *Elizabethan Grotesque*, p. 46. I have slightly extended the quotation.

*Gargantua*, where dead bodies are choking a ford which Gargantua and his companions must cross on horseback. The positive orientation of this image is due to its humanist polemic against superstition—Gargantua persuades all his companions to ford the stream and not to be afraid of stepping on the dead bodies: 'The three others followed him without accident, excepting Eudemon, whose horse plunged his right leg knee-deep into the belly of a great, fat ruffian . . . And that horse—by a miracle of veterinary science—was cured of a ring-bone which he had on that leg, through contact with that great oaf's guts.'[3] Like Nashe's, this is an image of grotesque re-creation, which realizes the potential offered by dead and decomposing flesh. Nashe's context was of course admonitory, but this alone does not account for the difference of outlook conveyed by these two uses of bodily imagery. In *Gargantua* the dismembered body of the old, bad world (as signified by the great oaf's guts) is capable of contributing to the growth and nourishment of the new, living world, a world cured of narrow-minded superstition. There is a confidence, expressed in the anecdote's organic, folkloric magic, about the power of bodily growth and renewal, about things being destroyed and re-created in a new matrix. This is precisely the confidence that is lacking in Nashe's more ambivalent use of grotesque imagery.

Nashe's grotesque, we could say, is the grotesque vision of a society in which all material is potentially available for resourceful exploitation by some interest group. Birds, for example, are 'fethermungers' (iii. 203), thrifty creatures who manufacture plumage for themselves. In other contexts Nashe's tendency to see everything in terms of raw materials and resources provides him with a handy economic metaphor for artistic judgement. He condemns ineffectual, prolix writers in terms of the materials they consume. Cartwright, the Puritan polemicist, is suspected of having 'plodded through ten cart loade of paper, and bin the death of ten thousand pound of candels' (iii. 360). Gabriel Harvey is so lacking in economic sense that he 'makes no more difference twixt a sheet of paper and a full point, than there is twixt two blacke puddings for a pennie, and a pennie for a paire of blacke puddings' (iii. 36–7). People can be used up as easily, in Nashe's pages, as paper. In *Christes Teares* Nashe disposes providently of dead bodies and ruined houses; in *Lenten Stuffe* he calculates in human currency the cost of economic independence.

[3] François Rabelais, *Histories of Gargantua and Pantagruel*, trans. J. M. Cohen, p. 118.

Yarmouth prevents herself from 'going under' in both a physical and a financial sense by virtue of the herring industry, which defrays the expenses of maintaining a protective harbour wall. 'The red herring alone it is that counteruailes the burdensome detrimentes of our hauen, which every twelue-month deuoures a Iustice of peace liuing, in weares and banckes to beate off the sand' (iii. 174). The delicately maintained balance of the Yarmouth economy is expressed in curiously predatory terms, as if the red herring were scarcely generous enough to prevent the financial demands of the harbour wall from eating up the living of a justice of the peace. If this is grotesque, it is clearly different from a grotesque apprehension of humanity caught in a web of organic life in which all things are subject to seasonal growth and destruction. Indeed so pervasive in Nashe's writing are the economic rhythms of glut and scarcity, and so characteristic is his tendency to render a sense of fluent expenditure or costive thrift in sensational, bodily terms, that if we are to account for what is distinctive about Nashe's stylistic effects and tonal ambiguities, it seems plain that any purely aesthetic or purely rhetorical approach will be inadequate. I propose at this point to consider the Elizabethan economy and its determination of the ethical function of contemporary literature. For it does seem as though this peculiarly Nashean grotesque, relentlessly foregrounding the reduction of life to the resources of economic survival, might bear a more than incidental relation to the conceptual bases of Elizabethan economic policy. To say this involves more than suggesting that Nashe's writing 'reflects' contemporary economic concerns, for what requires consideration is the precise function of literary discourse in the ability of contemporaries to abstract and define a social problem as specifically 'economic', demanding an 'economic' resolution. The very idea of an effective economic policy in the sixteenth century implies a transformation of cultural values such as would have been inconceivable without the conceptual currency that humanism had drawn from classical literature. The ideal of European humanism, which sought to achieve social prosperity by educating society's governors in the mastery of this conceptual currency, finds an economic analogy in the specific direction taken by English humanism, for which the overwhelming obstacle to prosperity was the spectre of inflation. The educational programme of English humanism was bound up with the imperative of encouraging the nationwide mastery of material resources; specifically, with the patriotic motivation of self-interest in the undertaking of economic projects.

Readers of sixteenth- and seventeenth-century literature are likely to have come across economic projects as a phenomenon of courtly corruption, part of the fiscal feudalism—a general traffic in offices, titles, monopolies, and wardships—that bolstered the crumbling finances of the Stuart monarchs. Jonson's comedies are a rich source of transparently ludicrous projects: Sir Politic Wouldbe's device to detect plague on Levantine ships by means of sliced onions, for example, or Meercraft's schemes to make English wine out of raisins, and furnish the state with unadulterated toothpicks. Literary scholars are less likely to be aware, however, that the idea of the economic project, which came to be open to such scandalous exploitation just before the Civil War, had originally been conceived by resourceful statesmen of the sixteenth century as part of a policy to rescue England from the likelihood of economic disaster. Joan Thirsk has uncovered the link between sixteenth-century economic policy and the official encouragement of specific projects for the improvement and diversification of English manufacture; indeed her study has gone so far as to suggest that it was in the sixteenth century that England first began to develop in the direction of a consumer society, perceiving itself as a market for its own skills.[4] Her study reveals that behind the policy of economic recovery were the minds of such humanist statesmen and intellectuals as William Cecil (later Lord Burghley) and Sir Thomas Smith. These men gained their experience in office during the mid-century years of political and religious upheaval and phenomenal inflation; yet they were prepared, on the slender chance of political stability promised by the accession of Elizabeth I in 1558, to initiate a far-reaching programme of economic and moral reform. The first objective of their programme was to call a halt to the unregulated consumption by Englishmen of imported luxury wares from Europe. For, thanks to the opportunism of the English merchants and landlords, the technical advance in European manufacturing skills was having a disastrous effect on the English economy. Before the advent of the European-style consumer goods, England had been a subsistence economy; money was scarce, and men were content with very little in the way of furnishings or accessories to adorn their homes or persons; what they had was generally of the craftsmanship of their own or a neighbouring town. European goods changed all that, as Sir Thomas Smith noted in 1549:

[4] J. Thirsk, *Economic Policy and Projects: The Development of a Consumer Society in Early Modern England*, pp. 24–50.

What number first of trifles come hither from beyond the seas that we might either clean spare or else make them within the realm, for the which we pay inestimable treasure every year, or else exchange substantial wares and necessary for them, for the which we might receive great treasure? Of the which sort I mean glasses as well looking as drinking as to glass windows, dials, tables, cards, balls, puppets, penhorns, ink horns, toothpicks, gloves, knives, daggers, owches, broches, aglets, buttons of silk and silver, earthern pots, pins, points, hawks' bells, paper both white and brown, and a thousand like things that might either be clean spared or else made within the realm sufficient for us.[5]

English craftsmanship, full of 'deceits' and 'abuses', could not compete; everybody wanted cloth of Flanders dye, daggers of Spanish making, Italian glass: 'Not so much as a spur, but that is fetched out of the Milaners', wrote Smith.[6] The 'Milaners' or 'milliners' sold fancy goods originally made in Milan: haberdashers' shops were fast becoming outlets for foreign luxuries, and English journeymen haberdashers found themselves turned away by erstwhile master craftsmen, now turned merchants. The journeymen, however, were not the only sector to suffer. Importing such foreign merchandise involved the participation of English merchants and landlords (turning land from tillage to pasture) in satisfying a European demand for unwrought English wool and leather. One of the first writers to draw attention to the miseries being created by this commerce was the citizen Clement Armstrong. As early as the 1530s Armstrong explained in a series of documents how English merchants, finding a ready market at the Amsterdam staple for English wool and hides, exchanged these precious raw materials not for bullion but for manufactured wares, which they brought back to sell in London, thereby depriving the fullers, drapers, and leatherworkers who might have dressed and wrought wool and hides, the tenants and labourers whose tillage was lost by enclosure for grazing land, and the English handicraftsmen whose haberdashery wares lay unbought in their homes. 'Thus', wrote Armstrong, 'adventurers hath usid by bryngyng of straunge artificialitie owt of Flaunders to distroy all artificialite in England.'[7] The result was an unprecedented inflation which went on worsening

[5] *A Discourse of the Commonweal of this Realm of England* (1549) attrib. to Sir Thomas Smith, ed. M. Dewar, p. 63; see also M. Dewar, 'The Authorship of the "Discourse of the Commonweal" '.

[6] *A Discourse*, p. 64.

[7] 'A Treatise Concerninge the Staple and Commodities of this Realme', *c.* 1519–35, attrib. to Clement Armstrong, in *TED* iii. 105; see also S. T. Bindoff, 'Clement Armstrong and his Treatises of the Commonweal'; also 'William Cholmeley's Project for Dying Cloth in England, 1553', *TED* iii. 131.

through the reigns of Edward VI and Mary Tudor, despite protestations against enclosure and random, isolated attempts by civic bodies to cut down on the expenses of a traditionally ritualistic, hospitable social structure. At the accession of Elizabeth, however, policies were drawn up for consideration by Parliament which, to judge from the legislation of subsequent years, were the beginning of a sustained and deliberate programme to reverse the upward spiral of inflation once and for all. It was Sir Thomas Smith who explained what had been happening in the clear terms of economic exchange; England had been paying for the privilege of being deprived of its own productive potential. Many imported consumer goods were made by Europeans 'out of our own commodities . . . whereby they set their people awork and do exhaust much treasure out of the realm. As of our wool they make cloth, caps and kerseys, of our fells they make Spanish skins, gloves and girdles; of our tin, salts, spoons and dishes; of our broken linen cloth and rags, paper both white and brown.'[8] Smith understood as well as those that preached against enclosures what impulse it was that prompted merchants and landlords to break the codes of husbandry and traditional, guild controlled craftsmanship by participating in this European traffic of English raw materials: 'To tell you plainly, it is avarice that I take for the principal cause thereof', he wrote, 'but can we devise that all covetousness may be taken from men?'[9] His answer was to discover the virtue of avarice; individualism could be harnessed in the national interest. The solution lay in the conception of the project—individuals were to be encouraged, by government patents and grants of monopoly, to conceive viable projects for the manufacture of goods of a European standard out of English stuffs, using English labour. No longer would English wool, leather, tin, and offcuts go out of the realm to set strangers awork. Their wealth-creating potential would henceforth be recognized and the individuals who realized such potential would be rewarded. Patents were granted for the successful introduction of foreign techniques: for example a craftsman was given exclusive rights in 1565 for the manufacture of 'Spanish or beyond sea leather'.[10] Behind the idea of 'making within the realm' lay the exhilarating conviction that England could be solvent and self-sufficient. Since God had seen fit to bless the realm with resources of wool and leather, why should not English men learn, as one patriotically inspired projector wrote in

[8] *A Discourse*, p. 64

[9] Ibid. 118.

[10] E. W. Hulme, 'The Early History of the English Patent System', p. 125.

1553, to make these into, 'cloth and cappis, as fynely, truly and perfectly as any other nations shal be able to do'?[11] Of course this meant that people, as well as materials, had to start realizing their productive potential. Accordingly, much penal legislation, backed by propaganda and proclamation, was required to make the policy effective. In line with the 'considerations' drawn up and presented before Parliament in 1559, laws were passed to restrict the wearing of excessive foreign silks and velvets, the consumption of French wines and the purchase of haberdashery goods from beyond the sea. The encouragement of home industry took its penal form in laws passed enforcing the common people to wear English-made woollen caps on Sundays, or obliging them to grow hemp for the furnishing of sailcloth to the navy. Wednesdays and Fridays were added to the existing 'political lent' as days when meat-eating was prohibited to ensure a market for the emerging English fish industry.[12]

Proclamations were regularly issued to remind the population of its duties, while professional informers and unpaid justices of the peace were employed in tracking down and fining reluctant cap-wearers or hemp-growers, or those who persisted in the illegal consumption of meat. Where fines were tiresome to collect, bonds were taken for security. 'Thus the tailors were bound not to make "monstrous hosen" contrary to proclamations on apparel, alehouse keepers not to allow flesh to be sold on forbidden days, and retailers of wine not to sell new wine early in the season.'[13] It is important to remember that the laws and proclamations were invested with a *moral weight*. The necessity to practise thrift, to remain solvent, was impressed upon the people of England as a moral necessity. This becomes clear on an examination of the Elizabethan homilies, which systematically reinterpret the traditional deadly sins from a new economic vantage-point, waxing eloquent on the evils that spring from sloth and idleness and remaining discreetly low-key on traditional arguments against avarice, a sin which tends to occupy the lion's share of admonition in medieval homily.[14] Elizabethan homilies against gluttony and

11 'William Cholmeley's Project for Dying Cloth in England, 1553', *TED* iii. 131. For similar schemes see G. R. Elton, 'An Early Tudor Poor Law'; also 'Policies to reduce this realme of Englande vnto a prosperus welthe and estate (1549)', *TED* iii. 311–45.

12 'Considerations delivered to the Parliament, 1559', *TED* i. 325–30; for Sir Thomas Smith's role in these see S. T. Bindoff, 'The Making of the Statute of Artificers', in *Elizabethan Government and Society*, ed. Bindoff *et al.*, pp. 88–9.

13 F. A. Youngs, *The Proclamations of the Tudor Queens*, p. 44.

14 G. R. Owst, *Literature and Pulpit in Medieval England*, pp. 317–74.

drunkenness, against idleness, against excess in apparel, and on the benefits of a fish diet (i.e. the sanctity of fasting) were clearly composed in response to the exigencies of economic recovery. They are part of a programme of propaganda against the consumption of luxury imported goods, particularly manufactured goods. Among the true uses of fasting, Englishmen are asked to bear in mind 'the decay of towns nigh the seas' and the 'great commodities which may ensue' to the English fleet with the reduction of meat consumption.[15] Against excess in apparel the congregation is advised that it is 'foul and chargeable' being 'many ways hurtful to the state of the commonwealth, and also odious before Almighty God'.[16]

The need to inculcate more responsible attitudes and to enforce legislation against consumption of wine, meat, and manufactured goods was at its most acute in the 1560s and '70s, before the success of English projects had begun to make its alleviating presence felt. In 1560 Burghley noted: 'if the lawes for apparrell and taverns for excessyve abundance of wynes shall not be better observed, it is to be feared that the quantite of our english commoditees will be to small a great deale to answer the forrayn commoditees.'[17] Burghley's emphasis, we note, is on the economic imperative: England must learn not to consume more in the way of fancy foreign goods and delicacies than she produces in manufactured goods of her own. Yet the 'lawes for apparrell and . . . for excessyve abundance of wynes' are represented in the literature of the period as part of a moral debate, a debate in which literature itself occupies an ambivalent position.

Behind the attempt to reform the economy by transforming the basis of individual morality lies the humanist faith in the charismatic power of the printed word. Economic reform was seen as an inseparable part of a 'reformation of manners', that is, a reformation of habits of thought and behaviour, in which the paradigms of classical literature had a major part to play. This explains in part the pragmatism which characterizes the literary productions of the mid-sixteenth century. The most forward 'wits' of the 1540s and '50s were encouraged by their protestant-humanist patrons to engage in the translation of classical texts. These were not primarily *belles lettres*, but texts on such valuable subjects as military science, moral

[15] *The Two Books of Homilies Appointed to be Read in Churches*, ed. J. W. Griffiths, pp. 289-90. [16] Ibid. 308.

[17] 'Memorandum by Cecil on the Export Trade in Cloth and Wool, 1564(?)', *TED* ii. 45.

philosophy, the discouragement of sedition, or the education of governors.[18] The same pragmatic and educative bias continued to dominate literary production in the early years of Elizabeth's reign under the auspices of the leading patrons, Burghley and Leicester.[19] Original composition was not particularly encouraged; literary talent had to conform, to make some contribution to the concerted enterprise of producing responsible governors for a more responsible commonweal. In a letter of public apology to the High Commission for the ill-advised publication of his idle and lascivious fiction, George Gascoigne in 1573 acknowledged that poetry should indeed be employed in the propagation of a 'generall reformation of manners', rather than as an incitement to irresponsible and intemperate living.[20] The moral satires that emerged thereafter from his pen—*The Steele Glas* (1576), *The Droome of Doomesday* (1576), *The Glasse of Governement* (1575), *A delicate Diet for daintie mouthde Droonkards* (1576)—reveal how entirely seriously he and his patrons took this one contribution that new literature could usefully make to the state. Admonitory satire of this period concentrates on two aspects of economic reform. On the one hand, there is the satiric revelation of 'deceits' or 'abuses' in English methods of manufacture, such as we find in *The Steele Glas* or in Francis Thynn's *Debate Between Pride and Lowliness* (*c.*1570); on the other hand there is the castigation of unthrifty consumption of individual resources in irresponsible attitudes to drink, gaming, play-going, and sartorial ostentation that we find in satires like the *Diet for . . . Droonkards*, Edward Hake's *Newes Out of Powles Churchyarde* (1579).[21] Initially this literature of temperance and solvency was disseminated through the patronage system; Gascoigne's patrons were Lord Grey and the Earl of Bedford, while Hake enjoyed the protection of the Earl of Leicester.[22] From about 1577, however, publication of propaganda for the reformation of social morality was taken up by the civic authorities and reforming individuals.[23] In this wave of admonitory

[18] See C. H. Conley, *The First English Translators of the Classics*, pp. 21–2.

[19] See E. Rosenberg, *Leicester, Patron of Letters*; J. van Dorsten, 'Mr. Secretary Cecil, Patron of Letters'; and id., 'Literary patronage in Elizabethan England: The Early Phase', in *Patronage in the Renaissance*, ed. G. F. Lytle and S. Orgel.

[20] *The Complete Works of George Gascoigne*, ed. J. W. Cunliffe, i. 4.

[21] Ibid. ii. 171 and 465; Thynn, *Debate between Pride and Lowliness*, pp. 20–45. Hake, *Newes out of Powles Churchyarde*, sigs. DI$^{r}$–EII$^{r}$.

[22] See Rosenberg, *Leicester, Patron of Letters*, pp. 166–72, 280.

[23] See P. Collinson, *The Elizabethan Puritan Movement*, p. 208; W. Ringler, 'The

satire came Stephen Gosson's *School of Abuse* (1579), George Whetstone's *A Mirour for Magestrates of Cyties* (1584), John Northbrooke's *Treatise wherein Dicing, Dauncing, vaine Plaies or Enterludes . . . are reproved* (*c*.1577), and Christopher Fetherston's *Dialogue agaynst light, lewde, and lasciuious dauncing* (1582).

By 1584, the date of Philip Stubbes's encyclopaedic *Anatomy of Abuses*, admonition against deceits in English manufacture and the chastisement of intemperance and over-consumption of resources had lost none of its passionate vehemence but much of its urgency with regard to the economic situation. As the economic projects began to come of age there arose a need to come to terms with the concept of freedom rather than restrictive control of standards in English manufacture, and with the tolerance of consumption as a prerequisite for the existence of a consumer society. Controls and restrictions belonging to the period of cutting-back on imports and encouraging new projects had by this time begun to be exploited by the magistracy and aristocracy themselves in the form of monopolies and licences detrimental to the productivity of small manufacturing industries. However, Stubbes's *Anatomy*, regardless of such developments, reveals how the anti-prodigal discourse against the deadly sins of pride and idleness had acquired a momentum of its own. As his diatribe becomes inextricably involved in the description of those consumer goods he is concerned to condemn, Stubbes bears witness to the success of the economic projects. The society he describes is on its way to being a consumer society, but acknowledgement of this would involve endorsing prodigality and intemperance as the consumer demand on which productivity must henceforward depend. As yet, this was inconceivable. Consumer goods could be praised only from a manufacturing point of view, as the creators of productivity and solvency among individuals. Fine jersey stockings, for example, received contemporary praise for their productive benefits as part of an industry which had transformed the idle vagrants of Norwich into self-sufficient labourers.[24] From the consumption point of view, however, the story was different. Stubbes hotly denounced the newfangled intemperance of a society which rejected old-fashioned cloth hose for expensive knitted stockings, 'of *Iarnsey* worsted, silk,

First Phase of the Elizabethan Attack on the Stage, 1558–1579'; D. Norbrook, 'Panegyric of the Monarch and its Social Context under Elizabeth I and James I', D.Phil. thesis (Oxford, 1978), 51.

[24] Thomas Wilson, *The State of England Anno Dom 1600*, ed. F. J. Fisher, p. 20.

thred, and such like'.[25] The starching of apparel was a form of consumerism which provoked even stronger indignation than the sporting of fancy stockings. In 1615 Edmund Howes looked back to the early years of Elizabeth's reign with satisfaction, praising the demand for starched garments which in the 1560s not only stimulated the production of starch itself, but gave rise to such subsidiary industries as the manufacture of steel poking-sticks, used in the starching process.[26] Moralists and monopolists, however, felt it necessary to denounce starch, which was made from wheat, from the consumers' point of view as an immoral waste of the nation's food resources in the interests of vanity and display. Laundered ruffs created famine. According to Joan Thirsk, putting the question in this ethical way could only serve the interests of the Crown monopolists, since they used the moral argument against starch as an excuse to confine the trade to the better sort of starchmakers who could afford to pay fines, thereby ensuring them profitable returns from the undiminished demand for starched ruffs.[27] But according to Stubbes this longing for starch betokened the imminent moral and economic collapse of the nation. The devil's 'kingdome of great ruffes' was upheld by the idol starch as much as by the sin of pride which starch was supposed to signify. It was insolvency that would ultimately lead proud consumers to the devil, by the downward path of debt, Newgate and finally 'losse of their lyues at Tiburne in a rope'.[28]

Nashe focused on the ubiquity and utter irrelevance of this sort of moral satire when he wrote the ironically economic supplication of the bankrupt 'Pierce Penilesse' to the devil. The prodigal and idiotic Pierce applauds the moral fervour and anti-consumerism of contemporary literature: 'Wise was that sin-washing Poet', he exclaims, 'that made the Ballet of Blue starch and poaking stickes, for indeed the lawne of licentiousness hath consumed all the wheat of hospitalitie' (i. 181). Pierce's generous tribute brilliantly parodies the inadequacy of the sin-washing approach to the complexities of economic change. Consumerism typically figures as ostentation and vanity (the 'lawne of licentiousness') as though it were directly responsible for a

[25] *Philip Stubbes's 'Anatomy of The Abuses in England' in Shakespere's Youth*, ed. F. J. Furnivall, pt. I, p. 57.

[26] Edmund Howes, in John Stowe, *The Annales or General Chronicle of England*, p. 948.

[27] See Thirsk, *Economic Policy*, pp. 88–90; Youngs, *Proclamations of the Tudor Queens*, p. 146.

[28] Stubbes, *Anatomy of Abuses*, pt. I, pp. 52–3.

withdrawal from charitable habits associated with traditional pre-consumer economy (the 'wheat of hospitalitiy'), which is absurd, given the same moralists' readiness to condemn the all-consuming idleness which had also been a feature of 'hospitality' in the pre-Reformation organization of society. After all, it was the fact of producing and starching lawn ruffs, licentious or not, that defined the economic basis of moral reform and that would, ultimately, determine England's survival and prosperity.

By pointing out the hopeless inadequacy of such moralized formulations of contemporary economic relations, *Pierce Penilesse* (one might argue) anticipated the intellectual respectability of the consumer economy by a hundred years. At least it went so far as to suggest that thrifty citizens should not claim to be more productive of wealth than the gentlemen whose 'idle' activities afforded them such thriving business in term-time London.[29] There is no point, however, in representing Nashe as an economic theorist: his main concern in writing *Pierce Penilesse* was neither economic nor moral, but literary. He was concerned about the stagnation of contemporary literature under the continuing constrictive influence of the moral reformation. It seemed that any English poet who ventured to publish a composition that was not concerned to reform moral abuses would be stigmatized unless he excused the work as a piece of juvenile self-indulgence. By exposing the dated and inadequate economic basis of contemporary moral discourse, *Pierce Penilesse* was trying to argue seriously that it was time to recognize the wider intellectual contribution that poetic discourse had to make to the nation. Poetry, Nashe protested, should not always be reduced to the status of juvenilia: 'an Arte whereof there is no vse in a mans whole lyfe but to describe discontented thoughts and youthfull desires' (i. 192). The words 'no use in a man's whole life' are significant. For in the protestant-humanist scheme poetry was regarded as an educative instrument, a way of instilling in the younger scholar an emotional attachment to the discursive forms that would in later life be his chief source for gaining knowledge and power to influence others. A poet was not a man, but a boy composing verse exercises and, in imitation of classical models, 'a youth beguiled by the sportful fancy of love'.[30] This had to be a passing phase: the youth could not, to make sense of

[29] See F. J. Fisher, 'The Development of London as a Centre of Conspicuous Consumption in the Sixteenth and Seventeenth Centuries'.

[30] Helgerson, *Elizabethan Prodigals*, p. 6.

the educative scheme, spend the rest of his life composing useless poetry. Education prepared a young man to govern himself and his circumstances. As a result he became, in theory, a national resource, one whose wisdom and eloquence might enable him to contribute to the government and improvement of society at large. Moreover the poetry which in earlier years had been a part of study was in approaching manhood regarded as kind of threat to intellectual and moral maturity, the rock on which a man might founder, the siren whose voice might lure him to his doom. In order to ease their own consciences, perhaps, the lyric poets themselves devoted their poems to the setting out of such reflexive images of imminent destruction, images (in Nashe's words) of a mind wholly given over to 'discontented thoughts and youthfull desires'. Katherine Duncan-Jones has observed that whatever our impression of Sidney's poetic output (affected as we are by the romantic image of him as a poet/hero) might be, he himself would in all probability have regarded his lyric work as essentially vain and trivial, perhaps thinking of it as part of a technical preparation for some more serious undertaking of an epic nature. She writes:

> Most of the *Old Arcadia* poems have outstanding technical merit, using and stretching the language with a complex fluency unsurpassed by any poet of the period, Yet all are, by his own most exacting standards, *empty*. None offers us a picture equivalent to Aeneas carrying old Anchises from the flames of Troy, or Cyrus taking counsel in peace and war; the 'notable images' Sidney gives us, whether in Pyrocles, Philisides, Strephon and Klaius, or Plangus, are repeatedly of talents wasted and will-power sapped.[31]

Sidney's most exacting standards, in the *Defence of Poetry*, demand that poetry should body forth images of heroic *virtus* in action; yet his own poems most strikingly represent their protagonists' failure to attain *virtus*. The didactic potential which, he argued, could exalt poetry above history and moral philosophy, could belong (if his own verse was anything to go by) to epic alone. The lyric, conventionally devoted to the expression of personal desire, could bear no exemplary burden, and so must be largely irrelevant to the education of the *vir virtutis*—the man in full possession of himself.

Arguably, however, lyric poetry (since it played a part in the young governor's rhetorical education) could be defended for its powerful

[31] K. Duncan-Jones, 'Philip Sidney's Toys', p. 172.

negative example, as an instrument of warning. It was conceivable that the youthful reader, discovering how love wastes and ruins the lover and how the pursuit of such trivial pastimes exhausts the capacity for more honourable employment, might be dissuaded from making the same mistakes himself. This at least seems to have been a fairly well-received theory. In *The Anatomie of Absurditie,* for example, Nashe's earliest and most orthodox pronouncement on the subject, we find ourselves informed that lyric poems are in fact ethical guides which 'vnder fayned Stories include many profitable morrall precepts, describing the outrage of vnbridled youth, hauing the reine in their owne hands; the fruits of idlenes, the of-spring of lust, and how auaileable good educations are vnto vertue' (i. 27).

That Sidney's poetry can so frankly confess to being a waste of talent and a loss of time may be attributed to the fact that he was never in the position of having to rely upon it as self-advertisement, having to justify its didactic qualities for the purposes of publication. In this he seems to have had the advantage over the rest of the 'prodigal' authors of his generation. They, aspiring towards promotion and official recognition, felt it incumbent upon themselves to advertise their intellectual and discursive abilities by publishing such (juvenile) verses as they had written. As juvenilia were almost invariably songs and sonnets of dubious moral value, their authors were obliged to disguise them as best they could by presenting them as admonitions to tender youth. Gascoigne seems to have begun the trend by offering his *Posies*, suitably shorn of 'wanton speeches' and 'lascivious phrases', as 'a myrrour for unbrydled youth to avoyde those perilles which I had passed'.[32] Gascoigne's justification sounds feeble enough; even more implausible, however, are the protestations of George Whetstone, who claimed that the publication of his love poems would be edifying to readers who took care to read them as admonitions:

> Wherefore these toyes, who liste to read aright
> Shall fine *Loves woes*; now how to love I write.[33]

Our reaction to this is incredulity: how can Whetstone have expected to be taken seriously? There is something altogether strange about the way he packaged these 'toyes'; they are part of a collection of poems called 'the Garden of Unthriftinesse' yet they have, as Helgerson

[32] Gascoigne, *Works*, i. 5.
[33] George Whetstone, *The Rocke of Regard* (1576), ed. J. Payne Collier, p. 144.

noted, 'nothing to do with money'.[34] Whetstone's insistence on the financial providence of his poetic enterprise is striking. Helgerson dismisses the overtones of economic anxiety that infiltrate this and other prodigal publications as metaphors for a more general anxiety about wasting time, but this will not quite do. The parallels between literary and economic terminology throughout these decades are so precise as to warrant the possibility that their users had in mind some quite specific relationship between the two.

For example, we find the economic distinction between 'idle wares' and 'substantial goods' not just casually applied but exactly reproduced in the Elizabethan evaluation of literature. The distinction first came into effective being with Sir Thomas Smith's *Discourse of the Commonweal*. Thereafter it was the operative principle behind almost all the legislation, propaganda, and projection undertaken by Elizabeth's government on behalf of economic reform. Encouragement of projects, research into foreign production techniques, penal legislation against 'deceitful' manufacture, and customs duty on ready-made imports—all these strategies to make England economically self-sufficient were based upon the principle of exploiting commercial activity so that it created rather than consumed resources. Elizabethan proponents of economic projects clearly saw themselves as creating productive potential where none had previously existed. For example, when Robert Hitchcocke put forward a scheme in 1580 for the establishment of a fishing industry, he emphasized the advantage it offered in terms of employment to the idle vagabonds who would be required to man the fishing fleet: that 'lothesome monster Idelnesse' would be transformed into a national resource, by which 'this Realme hath clearely increased nyne thousande Marriners, more then was in this Lande before'.[35] Consumer products were identified as 'goods' or even as 'substantial goods' by virtue of the resources that they were able to create. England's raw materials, such as wool and leather, were 'substantial' not just because they had a commercial value but because they were able to 'set idle people on work' to create wealth, to employ England's labour in productive enterprise. Imported ready-made goods—especially haberdashery goods, highly wrought and using little in the way of raw materials—were 'idle wares' in that they simply consumed England's financial resources without contributing to her productive

34 Helgerson, *Elizabethan Prodigals*, p. 27.

35 Robert Hitchcocke, *A Pollitique Platt* (1580), sigs. A1$^r$ and A2$^r$.

capacity.[36] Consumer products manufactured in England occupied the ambivalent position of being 'goods' in their productive, labour-creating capacity, turning into 'idle wares' when they actually tempted consumers into making a purchase. Sir Thomas Smith gives a classic description of the seductive powers of idle wares on the unsuspecting consumer:

I have seen within these twenty years when there were of these haberdashers that sell French or Milan caps, glasses, daggers, swords, girdles, and such like, not a dozen in all London. And now, from the Tower to Westminster along, every street is full of them; their shops glitter and shine of glasses, as well looking as drinking, yea, all manner vessels of the same stuff—painted cruses, gay daggers, knives, swords and girdles—that is able [to] make any temperate man to gaze on them and buy somewhat though it serve to no purpose necessary.[37]

Evidently to Sir Thomas Smith the very act of making an unnecessary purchase could be defined as 'intemperate'. The resources that a man expends in idle purchase cannot be requited by any productive capacity in the wares he has gained. Whetstone implies a similar line of thought when he offers his love poems as proofs against the '*discommodities* of the *unnecessarie*'.[38] Even Sidney recommends his *Arcadia*, with its poetry of time wasted and will-power spent, to a sister who is asked to regard it as no better than a consumer of time: 'Read it then at your idle times . . .' he advises her, 'looking for no better stuff than, as in a haberdasher's shop, glasses or feathers'.[39] But if his own poetry is the epitome of idle consumption, the epic he envisages in the *Defence* is more than just productive in itself. It is capable, like substantial raw materials, of creating further productive resources: 'so far substantially it worketh, not only to make a Cyrus, which had been but a particular excellency as nature might have done, but to bestow a Cyrus upon the world to make many Cyruses, if they will learn aright why and how that maker made him.'[40] It seems that the notable images of epic poetry were not just incitements to virtue. They were somehow productive of a certain kind of virtue, that of being able to fashion the moral resources of others. A book devoted to the creation of the virtuous governor, Sir Thomas North's *Diall of*

36 See the distinctions drawn by Sir Thomas Smith, *A Discourse*, p. 63.

38 Whetstone, *Rocke of Regard*, p. i.

37 Ibid. 64.

39 Sir Philip Sidney, *The Countess of Pembroke's Arcadia*, ed. J. Robertson, p. 3.

40 'A Defence of Poetry', in *Miscellaneous Prose of Sir Philip Sidney*, ed. K. Duncan-Jones and J. van Dorsten, p. 79.

*Princes* (1557), makes the economic parallel explicit: poets who 'hinder through evil example good living' are set beside merchants who 'impoverish with unprofitable merchandise the people',[41] thus defining the productive virtues of North's publication by contrast with these idle, consuming wares. Gascoigne feared that the rumour that he had accepted money for the publication of his wanton poetry would exacerbate his offence in the eyes of the High Commission, for then he would have profited financially from the promotion of idle wares, and been 'not onely a craftie Broker for the utteraunce of garishe toyes but a corrupte Merchaunte for the sale of deceyptfull wares'.[42]

In *Euphues. The Anatomy of Wit*, John Lyly revealed the ethical ambivalence of the arguments that formed the staple of poetic discourse, observing that, at the service of youthful desire, they represented potential loss as much as potential gain: Euphues' wit could 'eyther breede an intollerable trouble, or bringe an incomperable Treasure to the commone weale'.[43] But if Lyly's *Anatomy* acknowledged the dangerous ethical ambivalance of rhetorical tropes, it managed simultaneously to obviate this danger by subjecting its essentially amoral discursive potential to a relentless discipline. Two years later, however, on completing the book's successor *Euphues and his England*, Lyly hit upon an expedient which overcame the ethical problem of wit. Writing separate prefaces for male and female readers, he continued to offer his text as a resource of moral discourse to the former, while to the latter he was happy to advertise it as a trifling item of unnecessary haberdashery: 'There is nothing lyghter then a feather, yet it is sette a loft in a woemans hatte, so that I am in good hope, though their be nothing of lesse accounte then *Euphues*, yet shall he be marked with Ladies eyes.'[44] This persistent denigration of wanton sonnets and love discourses in terms of consumerism is curious. It is almost as though the loss of temperance, the expenditure of resources on unnecessary, idle frippery was somehow equivalent to the expenditure of cerebral resources in the act of idle reading. Whetstone justified the disparagement of his 'honest' love poems as unthrifty because, as he explained, 'the exercise we use in reading louing discourses, sildome (in my conceit) acquiteth our

41 Sir Thomas North, *The Diall of Princes*, ed. K. N. Colville, pp. 3–4.

42 *Works*, i. 4.

43 *The Complete Works of John Lyly*, ed. R. W. Bond, i. 186.

44 Ibid. ii. 10.

paines, with any thing beneficiall unto the commonweale, or verie profitable to our selves'.[45] The 'exercise we use in reading' may use *us* up before we have anything profitable to show for it. In a 'general advertisement to the reader' Whetstone professes what seems to us an inexplicable concern with the financial improvidence of youth which is liable to tire 'his poore purse out of hart with prodigalitie' before he has learned 'any perfect order of spending'.[46] Temperance here is overtly equated with solvency, it is an order of spending. But its effects are vital: it is the 'hart' of the purse that is said to be in danger of exhaustion. Humanist education theory, interestingly enough, chiefly defined itself against scholasticism by its appeal to a man's heart, its ability, by uniting wisdom with eloquence, to build up a student's courage and resolution. To give a young student nothing but grammar, argued Elyot, 'mortifieth his corage'; the master was advised to 'set him in a fervent courage'[47] by eloquent persuasion of the delectation afforded by reading histories. Petrarch had long before argued against endless scholastic debates about the nature of virtue; the only way to know virtue is through that eloquence which can 'drive deep into the heart the sharpest and most ardent stings of speech'.[48] The danger of such delectably eloquent knowledge was that it could also be, in Sidney's words, 'heart-ravishing';[49] as capable, that is, of seducing and consuming the reader's courage as of making it steadfast and resolute.

Without wishing to press that particular point too far at this stage it seems fair to say that the heart which is in danger of being consumed by prodigality and/or the love of eloquence corresponds to something like the core of a man's being, the moral stamina that will eventually enable him to play a substantial role in the government and reformation of his society. The prodigal or bankrupt youth may be figured by an empty purse (as, for example, Nashe's Pierce Penilesse) because he lacks the inner substance with which to maintain himself and govern the commonweal. The connection between moral stamina and reading is as yet not quite clear, but even at this point we may be struck by the remarkable pragmatism of this formulation. Educa-

[45] Whetstone, *Rocke of Regard*, p. iii.

[46] Ibid., pp. i and viii.

[47] See W. J. Ong, *Rhetoric, Romance and Technology*, pp. 130–1; Sir Thomas Elyot, *The Boke Named the Gouernour* (1531), pp. 35–40, 44.

[48] 'On his own ignorance and that of many others', in *The Renaissance Philosophy of Man*, ed. E. Cassirer *et al.*, p. 104.

[49] Sidney, *Miscellaneous Prose*, p. 76.

tional and economic writings alike show an extraordinary lack of compunction about resolving beings—human beings—into potential 'substance'. A man's substance measures his capacity as a productive resource to the commonweal; his lack of it indicates his susceptibility to prodigal consumption. A great deal of mid-sixteenth-century literature, as John Dover Wilson pointed out, amounted to no more than amplification of the half-dozen words of the parable, 'wasted his substance with riotous living'.[50] Indeed, these very words were offered by Erasmus as the first topic sentence for amplification in the *De copia*.

The substance indicated by the biblical words was conveniently non-specific—financial, moral, or physical? Both Rabelais and Nashe exploited the comic possibilities of this: Rabelais's Panurge saved his own skin by prodigally throwing his bacon to the dogs, while the hero of Nashe's *Unfortunate Traveller* (who is at once a page boy and an embodiment of the printed page) escapes only with the greatest difficulty from an equally agonizing consumption of his substance. Falling bodily into the possession of bloodletting usurers and a flesh-eating courtesan, the page threatens to go the way of all gallants whom dice and harlots have consumed (ii. 304–16). Even if his heart's blood escapes being wrung out by the usurers, his flesh is ready to 'drop awaie in a consumption' being 'clean spent and done' (ii. 316) by the demands of sexual promiscuity. The substance of any printed page under the Elizabethan patronage system was of course totally identifiable with the interests of the state. The page existed as a serviceable entity, the exercise of reading which should be profitable to the reader and beneficial to the commonweal. What makes Nashe's pages so comically susceptible to consumption is the fact that they deviate from this norm; they refuse from the outset to be serviceable and indeed are offered by their author as waste paper to be consumed in various idle forms of wrapping and packaging: 'To anie vse about meat & drinke put them to and spare not, for they cannot doe theyr countrie better seruice' (ii. 207).

In *The Schoolmaster* Ascham observed it to be a general rule that quick wits are seldom 'fortunate for themselves or very profitable to serve the commonwealth'.[51] Nashe's page is an *unfortunate traveller* precisely because he is not profitable to serve the commonwealth,

[50] J. Dover Wilson, 'Euphues and the Prodigal Son', p. 339.
[51] Roger Ascham, *The Schoolmaster*, ed. L. V. Ryan, p. 22.

since the fortune of the individual is identical in Elizabethan terminology with his public role in the state. Unprofitable servants, Ascham continues, tend to 'decay and vanish, men know not which way'.[52] He clearly conceives of obscurity, the failure to get preferment and public office, as a kind of consumption of self. Such men 'vanish and decay' because they can no longer be said to exist as substantial and productive forces in the creation of the commonweal. Economic writings reflect exactly the same assumptions. Ascham's equivalent in the sphere of economic reform (although these realms are not really separable) must be William Cecil, Lord Burghley. Although we rarely hear his voice behind official proclamations on the subject of reform, the one known exception (a rather wordy injunction against excess in apparel) characteristically concentrates on the consumption of resources, making no distinction between the human and the financial:

THE EXCESS of apparel and the superfluity of unnecessary foreign wares thereto belonging now of late years is grown by sufferance to such an extremity that the manifest decay not only of a great part of the wealth of the whole realm generally is like to follow . . . but also particularly the wasting and undoing of a great number of young gentlemen, otherwise serviceable . . . who, allured by the vain show of those things, do not only consume themselves, their goods, and lands which their parents have left unto them, but also run into such debts and shifts as they cannot live out of danger of laws without attempting of unlawful acts, whereby they are not any ways serviceable to their country as otherwise they might be.[53]

Through the importing of unnecessary wares the nation's resources are exhausted, her store of bullion is depleted, her young gentlemen 'otherwise serviceable' are wasted and undone. Whether they 'consume themselves' or their revenues, 'goods, and lands which their parents have left them' is immaterial, since their serviceability as future magistrates depends on their being 'substantial' in every sense of the word. By idly consuming themselves men deprive the state of its resources; the exemplary Emperor Alexander Severus in Sir Thomas Elyot's *Image of Governance* is explicit in this respect, forbidding any Roman citizen to participate in circus games on the grounds that 'his body, beynge deade' would be 'nothynge profytable'.[54] Again, Nashe

52 Ibid.

53 *Tudor Royal Proclamations*, ed. P. L. Hughes and J. F. Larkin, ii. 381.

54 Sir Thomas Elyot, 'The Image of Governance', in *Four Political Treatises,* introd. L. Gottesman, p. 312.

produces a travesty of the self-consumer, portraying the youth of Gabriel Harvey as prodigally dissipated in the composition of English hexameters—'His braynes, his time, all hys maintenance & exhibition vpon it he hath consumed' (iii. 87). Even in pastiche of the prodigal theme, however, we encounter a phenomenon that is alien and difficult to understand. Why is there such preoccupation with the depletion of resources? Why is cerebral energy conceived of in this highly physical way, so that Nashe can write comically about 'consuming' the brain in writing poetry, and Whetstone, in all seriousness, about the 'exercise we use' in reading? Susan Sontag once made the provocative suggestion that nineteenth-century preoccupation with the disease of consumption might actually have been related to the enormous pressures of living in an early industrial economy. The physical condition of the consumptive embodied fears that the stamina of the individual might not be up to the demand of enterprise. It was a kind of 'proof' that 'energy, like savings, can be depleted through reckless expenditure. The body will start "consuming" itself, the patient will "waste away".'[55] It is easy to see how, in the context of the strenuous programme of social and economic reform undertaken in Elizabeth's reign, the figure of the prodigal might act as a focus for anxieties about not having the moral stamina or substance required to meet demands. Moral courage, like savings, might run out.

What remains unresolved in this picture is the part played by reading and poetic composition. If poetry is responsible for building up a store of moral courage, is it also responsible for exhausting it? Turning again to Ascham, we find a distinction between kinds of reading and writing, between poets and orators: 'the quickest wits commonly may prove the best poets but not the wisest orators—ready of tongue to speak boldly, not deep of judgement either for good counsel or wise writing'.[56] It cannot be the speaking/writing distinction that is important here, for Ascham transposes the more normal associations of speaking with oratory and writing with poetic composition. However, he goes on:

> Moreover, commonly men very quick of wit be also very light of conditions and thereby very ready of disposition to be carried overquickly by any light company to any riot and unthriftiness when they be young, and therefore seldom honest of life or rich in living when they be old. For quick in wit and

[55] S. Sontag, *Illness as Metaphor*, p. 62.

[56] *Schoolmaster*, p. 21.

light in manners be either seldom troubled or very soon weary in carrying a very heavy purse.[57]

What exactly distinguishes the wise orator from the poet so that the ready tongue of the latter, like ready cash, is too volatile to be retained as savings for a substantial old age? One senses a connection here with the Elizabethan predilection for the use of the word profitable in the context of reading. What constitutes the 'profitable' discourse of the wise orator? It is no use simply saying that it is didactic and moral, for that restates the question: how did the Elizabethans conceive of literature as didactic? Their persistent anxiety about the folly of idle reading suggests that their reading habits were nothing like ours. What we need to establish in the next chapter is exactly how these differed; we need to disclose, if possible, the potential profit to the reader which seems to lie concealed in the orator's ever-full purse.

[57] Ibid. 22.

# 2
# The Profitable Discourse of the Elizabethans

ASCHAM's distinction between the quick-witted poet and the wise orator seems to turn on the notion of discursive and moral solvency. The poet's purse is soon exhausted of its contents, whereas the wise orator appears always to have resources at command. As an image for the possession of discursive resources, however, the idea of the purse already defines wealth ambiguously in terms of expenditure. The advantage of bearing a purse is that it contains cash to defray unforeseen costs; at the same time this very readiness to meet emergency becomes a new form of susceptibility in the face of temptation. Translated into the terms of humanist education, the paradox seems to be that the young man who has been equipped by literature with the ready money of discursive ability is simultaneously rendered more susceptible to the expenditure of his talents in ways inconceivable to one without such a sophisticated improvising wit.

An ambivalent attitude towards the notion of ready money seems to be something which pedagogic discourse had in common with the discourse of economic and social reform. In the economically anxious early years of Elizabeth's reign, discourses tend to evaluate wealth in terms of its hidden potential, as though its manifestation could only signify expenditure and so poverty. Ascham implies that the expenditure of wealth denies the possibility of the future; prodigals 'decay and vanish'. Continuance into a material future is associated with the preservation of a full store, which in turn is associated with effective communication. Thus, for want of other wealth, Ascham bequeathes *The Schoolmaster* to his children as a store of vital resources: 'Seeing at my death I am not like to leave them any great store of living, therefore in my lifetime I thought good to bequeath unto them in this little book . . . the right way to good learning, which if they follow with the fear of God, they shall very well come to sufficiency of living.'[1] In the sense of income, of the guarantee of future resources,

[1] Ascham, *Schoolmaster*, p. 11.

living is set in opposition to the inevitable self expenditure of living within the present. Bright surfaces somehow lead men away from the cultivation of inner resources. We saw in Chapter 1 how, in an economic context, Sir Thomas Smith deplored the 'glitter and shine' of consumer goods which seduced otherwise temperate men into unnecessary expenditure while Burghley lamented how young men 'consume themselves' only because they are 'allured by the vain show' of ostentatious dress. The manifestation, or show, of wealth is invariably defined as vain because it indicates a future already dissipated, a gallant already spent and exhausted of his governing potential. That this applies to eloquence as well as to apparel we can infer from Nashe's statements on the subject in his earliest and most orthodox work, *The Anatomie of Absurditie*, a book which positively bristles with moralized examples of the folly of intemperance. Nashe berates young students for being so besotted with poetry that they 'forsake sounder Artes, to followe smoother eloquence, not vnlike to him that had rather haue a newe painted boxe, though there be nothing but halter in it, then an olde bard hutch with treasure inualuable' (i. 31). The conspicuous wealth of the 'newe painted boxe' discloses its true nature in the halter which indicates the future obliteration of the prodigal; only in the concealment of the 'bard hutch' can wealth really be said to exist. The revelation of substance becomes a contradiction because in revealing itself substance becomes expenditure and so prodigality. Concealment, however, defines wealth as productive potential; whatever is dark and hidden is as yet unfound out, unexploited: it remains as a store of living still on hand for the exigencies of an unpredictable future.

This way of evaluating wealth as productive potential has a strong affinity with the principles of oratorical training. The orator is always in the position of having to provide for the future: as Terence Cave wrote, 'the extempore moment is always, by definition, "ahead" '.[2] In Quintilian's *Institutio oratoria*, one of the texts on which the humanists based their teaching of the interdependence of wisdom and eloquence, the model . . . for the mental activity involved in providing for contingent demands on discourse is explicitly financial: 'In proportion as the speaker pays out what he has in hand, he must make advances to himself from his reserve funds'.[3] Considering the extent to which the education of Elizabethan youth was grounded in the

[2] T. Cave, *The Cornucopian Text*, p. 128.

[3] Ibid. 128, quoting Quintilian, *Institutio oratoria*, x. vii. 10.

performance of rhetorical exercises of imitation, invention, or improvisation, it seems plausible enough that concepts involved in the attainment of linguistic affluence should influence more general ways of thinking about the economy of the self. The most fundamental and difficult rhetorical skill, the ability to improvise a successful discourse, is defined by Cave as a kind of possession, a *habitus* or 'having'; the Latin word perhaps corresponds to the Elizabethan 'hability' or 'ability' which was similarly used in a rhetorical context to indicate mastery, discursive potential, 'a capacity which has been appropriated, is fully possessed'.[4] Oratorical improvisation seems to involve just the kind of tension between extremes of prodigality and provident concealment that we found problematic in Ascham's definitions of wit. In Quintilian's discussion of rhetorical improvisation Cave notes that

> the amassing of a treasure (reading, imitation, lexical accumulation, and the modes of figurative transformation) is considered throughout in the perspective of its eventual expenditure, that is to say, of mastery, the exercise of rhetorical power. The notion of 'having ready for production', 'having at one's fingertips'. . . is present from the outset in the negative image of the miser hoarding his treasure.[5]

This suggests that the definition of oratorical affluence involves not just hidden resources, but hidden resources which are ready for production. One is reminded, not irrelevantly perhaps, of *Tristram Shandy*'s lament for the eloquence of Greece and Rome, where the voluminous mantles of orators were capable of concealing such crucial resources as a tender infant, 'royally accoutred', which (given that the child's age had been exactly gauged for the purposes of oratorical production) might then be 'produced so critically that no soul could say, it came by head and shoulders'.[6] The point is that concealed riches are not assets to the orator or the entrepreneur unless they are also readily accessible. Erasmus writes in the *De copia* that the student must have the riches of his reading to hand, accessible as 'ready money', not hidden away, like those who 'hold a great many things in their minds, as though stored up in the earth, although in speaking and writing they are wonderfully destitute and bare'.[7] It is,

[4] *Cornucopian Text*, p. 126.
[5] Ibid.
[6] Laurence Sterne, *Tristram Shandy*, Penguin edn., p. 196.
[7] Erasmus, *On Copia of Words and Ideas*, trans. D. B. King and H. D. Rix (henceforward *De copia*), p. 89.

in a sense, the accessibility of the resources that contributes to their capacity to provide in emergency, which makes them into a 'great store of living' for the orator. In straightforward economic terms, too, the accessibility of cash was increasingly being recognized as a measure of its substantiality, its capacity to act as a storehouse of productive potential. 'Money', wrote Sir Thomas Smith, 'is, as it were, a storehouse of any commodity you would have.'[8]

The ideals of concealment and accessibility are nevertheless somewhat contradictory as yardsticks of value. Evaluating wealth according to its readiness for use carries with it the inevitable anxiety of expenditure and impoverishment. In Quintilian's *Institutio oratoria* this anxiety is frequently figured as a failure of stamina. The 'amassing of treasure' by preliminary study and exercise is recommended as a guarantee against the terrors of self-expenditure in performance: 'distress of harassing anxiety which wastes and fevers the orator who painfully corrects himself and pines away.'[9] The ideal orator is a man whose *habitus* is provident enough not to lay him open to such consuming fears; he is a man of substance, 'lord and master of all the resources of eloquence, whose affluence surrounds him'.[10] Nashe frequently gives us a sense of this terror of oratorical self-expenditure in a more or less palpable and exaggerated form. In *The Unfortunate Traveller* Jack Wilton claims to be in danger of exhausting his inventive capacity after extending a tribute of praise to his master, the Earl of Surrey, who has newly arrived on the scene: 'Let me not speake anie more of his accomplishments, for feare I spend all my spirits in praising him, and leaue my selfe no vigor of wit or effects of a soule to goe forward with my historie' (ii. 242). In the graver context of *Christes Teares Over Jerusalem*, Nashe adopts the persona of St Augustine to launch into a diatribe against the 'bodie-wasting industry' of oratory. The orator of the *Confessions* declares that he has 'wel-nie spit out al my braine at my tongues end this morning' (ii. 89).

All the same, there is more than just oratorical solvency involved in this Elizabethan preoccupation with profitable discourse. The idea of affording profit to the recipient comes into it too; after all, discourse is always supposed to be beneficial to the commonweal as well as to its author. We could say that to be profitable a discourse had always to be didactic, but problems arise when we try to reconcile our notion of didactic exposition with the concepts of concealment and resource

[8] Smith, *Discourse*, p. 111. [9] *Institutio oratoria*, XII. x. 77. [10] Ibid.

potential which are obviously inherent in the Elizabethan ideal of effective oratory. The idea of having a store of resources always ready for production is fundamental to the theory of rhetorical invention, and this aspect of invention is given most emphasis by Erasmus in the *De copia*. Indeed, the very notion of 'copia' and 'copiousness' as an ideal of discourse expresses more than anything else the vital importance of developing a richly inventive capacity, for as Cave remarks the word *copia* covers 'not only the notion of abundance itself but also the place where abundance is to be found, or, more strictly, the place and its contents: one of the particular senses of *copia* is "treasure-chest", "hoard", or "store"'.[11] What is especially interesting about this with reference to the question of didacticism is that at the beginning of Erasmus's handbook we find the prodigal bankrupt evoked as an admonition to those who have failed to be sufficiently copious in the very discourse with which they profess to teach the principle of copious discourse: 'a number of writers, having gone so far as to deliver precepts concerning this very thing . . . seem to have accomplished nothing else than, having professed copia (abundance) to have betrayed their poverty'.[12] Yet if we bear in mind the sense of *copia* as inventive ideal, involving the capacity to conceal and produce discursive resources, it is difficult to see how Erasmus could expect such a quality to be communicated in what we think of as a didactic fashion. (Erasmus's book itself of course is full of images of concealment and disclosure—the Silenus of Alcibiades, the merchant unrolling his carpet[13]—but these are not relevant here.) I suggest that in an educational system where the production of knowledge is inevitably part of a discursive process, all communication could be considered as more or less didactic. Rudolph Agricola wrote that: 'The aim of speech can never be simply pleasure as distinct from moving and teaching another. For all speech teaches . . . As far as invention goes, there is no difference between moving and teaching, for to move someone is to teach him as far as this is possible.'[14] What distinguished the didactic possibilities of copious discourse was its capacity to communicate not only its own argument but also a linguistic and figurative potential which might be exploited by the reader in inventing arguments of his own.

To illustrate this we might look at Nashe's *Anatomie of Absurditie*,

[11] *Cornucopian Text*, p. 6. [12] *De copia*, p. 11. [13] Ibid. 43, 101.

[14] W. J. Ong, *Ramus, Method and the Decay of Dialogue*, p. 103, quoting from Rudolph Agricola, *De inventione dialectica* (1518), Lib. II, cap. iv, p. 167.

a work which devotes itself almost entirely to making distinction between those discourses which afford profit to their readers, and those which are merely pleasant and prodigal ways of passing the time. The anatomizing of absurdity becomes a satirical exposé of the ways in which irresponsible readers and writers bankrupt themselves in dissipating the resources of learning and eloquence. As glittering apparel implies the vanity and inward insolvency of the gallant, so the improvidence of absurd authors is conspicuous to all in their vain publications, which surface in Nashe's image like hollow eggs:

> as an Egge that is full, beeing put into water sinketh to the bottome, whereas that which is emptie floateth aboue, so those that are more exquisitly furnished with learning shroude themselues in obscuritie, whereas they that are voide of all knowledge, endeuour continually to publish theyr follie. (i. 9–10)

Utterance in the form of publication lays claim, apparently, not only to fullness but to potency. These writers have pretended to be sources and begetters of discourse, they 'obtrude themselues vnto vs, as the Authors of eloquence and fountains of our finer phrases' (i. 10), while proffering only an impotent and empty flow of words, resonant as the tympany of a false pregnancy, the 'big' sound of a hollow drum (i. 10). Nevertheless, argues the author, their lack of potential as conveyors of eloquence might well be overlooked, did these publications offer any possibilities as storehouses of significant knowledge: 'Were that any Morrall of greater moment, might be fished out of their fabulous follie, leauing theyr words, we would cleaue to their meaning, pretermitting their painted shewe, we woulde pry into their propounded sence' (i. 10). Three different things seem to be established here: first it is assumed that publication implies a claim on the part of the author to teach or to be 'profitable' which, if unfulfilled, renders his discourse vain and absurd. Second, it is also taken for granted that one of the ways in which published discourse presumes to profit its readers is by offering itself as a source-book for the improvement of their own discursive capacities. Finally, it is conceded that this verbal criterion need not apply, provided some concealed 'moral' makes the text worth 'prying into'. If a published discourse fulfils none of these productive criteria and exists only on a superficial level of invention for the delight of the reader, Nashe feels justified in condemning it as a downright lie. Unproductive inventions abuse the authorized sources of learning by applying them to no instructive purpose: 'Histories of antiquitie' are 'belyed' and the moralizing potential of natural history, 'minerals, stones, and herbes', simply dissipated for the sake of ornament (i. 10). Nashe is not condemning the euphuism of *Euphues* itself, where the argumentative resources offered by the *exempla* of natural history were anatomized and displayed intact; he is objecting to the irresponsible application of euphuistic proofs in the interests of furthering romantic and lascivious narrative. Nashe sternly condemns the dispense of so much paper on 'loue passions' (i. 10) which gratify the reader's desire without generating either knowledge or the capacity for knowledge.

Throughout Nashe's *Anatomie*, poetic value is associated with the concealment and discovery of generative potential: the 'karnell' is discovered in the 'haune', 'fayrest and sweetest' grapes under branches, 'diuine . . . Philosophy' in 'blinde fables' and 'vnder the shaddowe of greene and florishing leaues, most pleasant fruite hidden in secrete, and a further meaning closely comprised' (i. 25–30). It is incumbent upon the reader, however, to realize this potential, and he is as liable as the author to fail, and to fall into the absurdity of improvident expenditure, particularly in the reading of erotic poetry where a wanton engagement with the enticing surface may render a youth inept to discover the poetry for his own purposes as valuable resource material: 'they that couet to picke more precious knowledge out of Poets amorous *Elegies*, must haue a discerning knowledge, before they can aspire to the perfection of their desired knowledge, least the obtaining of trifles be the repentant end of their trauell' (i. 30). What is most interesting here is the way in which *reading* itself may become a prodigal exchange of precious resources for glittering trifles; the reader, no less than the writer, may profess *copia* only to display poverty. We recall Whetstone's strictures against reading for pleasure; 'the exercise we use in reading louing discourses sildom (in my conceit) acquiteth our paines, with any thing beneficiall unto the commonweale, or verie profitable to our selves.'[15] What is this 'exercise' that needs to be compensated with profit? Nashe suggests that the reader should be poised to 'picke more precious knowledge' but he also seems to be concerned with gathering the resources of eloquence from 'the fountains of our finer phrases'. Both reading and writing are therefore providential exercises, concerned with amassing treasure, with acquiring a stock of materials ready for production. But this gathering is no mechanistic activity, the process of accumula-

[15] Whetstone, *Rocke of Regard*, p. iii.

tion itself involves imaginative expenditure, a version of the rhetorical procedure of finding out, discovering, or inventing the potential meaning concealed in any figure.

Marian Trousdale has explained how the Elizabethans 'produced' rather than 'consumed' the texts they read in this way, discovering in them the potential they required to meet their own discursive and practical needs. She quotes from 'A Compendious & Profitable Way of Studying', devised by a student born in 1583, which sets out just such a method of reading as the discovery or invention of resources:

> To reade over Homer 2 books with prying into all his sense, and the reason of the epethites, but not to lett anything pass unfound out . . . To note some Rhetoricall expressions, Description, or some very apt Simile, or a very applicative story, & the most choise morrall sentencess, & here a mans sense must direct him, when he considers how aptly such a thing would fitt with an exercise of his.[16]

Nashe gives us the impression that meaning was something beneath the rhetorical surface; 'leauing theyr words, we would cleaue to their meaning, pretermitting their painted shewe, we woulde pry into their propounded sence' (i. 10), but the student of 1583, concerned as he is with ancient texts, makes it clear that the picking out of precious knowledge is ideally inseparable from the rhetorical act of inventing or varying the text itself. 'Prying into the sense' of Homer involves discovering meaning in the epithets he uses; selecting 'choise morrall sentencess' involves keeping in mind one's own literary requirements. Ideally, then, everything amassed in such an exercise of reading will be as beneficial to the commonweal as it is profitable to the individual, since no distinction is made between the resources of knowledge and those of effective communication. We begin to appreciate what Sidney had in mind when he wrote that poetry could work so substantially as to 'bestow a Cyrus upon the world to make many Cyruses, if they will learn aright why and how that maker made him'.[17]

Crucial to this highly productive and provident concept of reading is the Renaissance concern with exemplum or example. In the *De copia* Erasmus sets out a model for the reading methods of generations of students, entitled 'On the Method of collecting *Exempla*'.

[16] Quoted from a seventeenth-century commonplace book, Folger MS Collection, v.a. 381, pp. 86–7, by M. Trousdale, *Shakespeare and the Rhetoricians*, p. 147.

[17] Sidney, *Miscellaneous Prose*, p. 79.

The plan is to have all the resources of future discursive invention at one's fingertips, in 'ready money'.[18] Erasmus has already defined *exempla* so broadly as to cover every conceivable discursive resource from epithets to full-blown narratives, and explained how these may be varied and transformed by all the usual rhetorical means—*similitudo, contrarium, comparatio,* hyperbole, epithet, *imago*, metaphor, or allegory.[19] What defines *exempla*, then, is neither their original literary function nor the new use to which they are adapted by the student but their existence as potential functions, their being ready, in all forms of discourse, for further production. Basically, Erasmus's method advises the 'picking out' or 'gathering' of potentially useful material and assigning it to some place—either a commonplace, or under the abstract heading of a vice or virtue—where it will be accessible at any time. This is extraordinary because it transforms the reading experience itself into a process of poetic or dialectical invention. One has, to some extent, to transform the nature of what one has read in order to assign it a place at all. One has to 'find it out', to pry into the sense of it, to moralize it. We see this clearly in Erasmus's dealing with the plurality of *exempla*.

> There are some which can be adapted not only for different, but even for opposite uses, and therefore should be noted down in several places. For example, if you should be treating the incurable cupidity of a miser, you would rightly adapt the fable of Charybdis. Likewise, if you were discussing insatiable gluttony, or the inexhaustable lust of a woman, the same fable would certainly be appropriate . . . [20]

Adapting *exempla* for various uses is both a provident act, in as much as it realizes the image's full discursive potential, and a licentious one, in as much as it suggests that meaning is produced by simply varying the text. The commonplace habit acknowledges this ethical ambiguity, justifying it pragmatically as a means of absorbing discursive power for future use. The student transforms the emotional impressions received from the text into the resources of a capacity to make an impression upon others. From this point of view, varying the text and locating images in a commonplace was a valuable way of stimulating the reader's memory and imaginative fertility. Erasmus points out that the method 'will also have the effect of imprinting

[18] *De copia*, pp. 87 ff.
[19] Ibid. 67 ff.
[20] Ibid. 90.

what you read more deeply on your mind, as well as accustoming you to utilizing the riches of your reading'.[21] The student thus turning reading experience into discursive ability is producing an inner self which, like an ever-full purse, is capable of transforming the demands of any emergency into discursive resources with which to meet it. Reading 'profitably' in the Elizabethan sense required the reader to engage in the active cultivation of discursive providence: the ability to invent aptly from the recollected treasures of reading.

Any kind of discourse, therefore, becomes a legitimate gathering-ground for the exemplary resources of one's own invention. As Erasmus writes:

> no learning is so far removed from rhetoric that you may not enrich your classifications from it. For from mathematics, which seems . . . remote, *simultudines* are taken. For example, a wise man, happy in his wealth, not dependent on any one else, constant and unmoved in his own virtue whatever way the winds of fortune blow, is compared with a sphere everywhere similar to itself.[22]

This applies (as we saw from Nashe's *Anatomie*) to the writings of contemporaries as well as ancients. Indeed, W. J. Ong writes:

> this is what poems and/or other 'inventions' were, *inter alia*—assemblages of commonplace materials . . . The Elizabethan anthology is typically presented . . . as a collection of materials to be used . . . The conceptual apparatus of 'flowers' and 'collecting' is tied in with the massive tradition of rhetorical invention . . . running back into classical antiquity and thence to the oral sources of literature.[23]

Moreover, this rhetorical method of gathering the honey from other men's flowers was by no means limited in application to more decorative types of composition. On the contrary, it was fundamental to the business of making one's ideas intelligible, and communicating them in an effective manner. The success of any policy, wrote Sir Thomas Smith in the *Discourse of the Commonweal*, is dependent on its recommending itself intelligibly and persuasively to others. He modestly describes his own discovery and solution of the economic

21 Ibid. 89. In the preface to his translation of Ovid's *Metamorphoses* Arthur Golding similarly writes that, by discovering or inventing the significance of fable, the reader helps to 'print it in his hart'. (*The Fyrst Fower Bookes of P. Ouidius Nasos Worke, intituled Metamorphosis*, sig. xiii $^{r}$–$^{v}$.)

22 Ibid. 90.

23 W. J. Ong, *Interfaces of the Word*, p. 179.

problem as being a discourse of the present situation which he has gathered and 'invented' like a posy from the wits of ancient writers:

And albeit you might well say that there be men of greater wit that have the matter in charge than I, yet fools (as the proverb is) sometimes speak to the purpose, and as many heads, so many wits . . . when every man brings in his gift, a mean-witted man may of the whole (the best of every man's devise being gathered together) make it as it were a pleasant garland and perfect to adorn his head with.[24]

Smith's application of a commonplace here ('quot capita tot sententiae') illustrates his method in action, but the gathering of verbal 'devices' involves more than just facilitating communication. It also involves, in Smith's case, a kind of dialectical invention; the application of exemplary resources to an existing and baffling situation in order to 'discover' it, to render it intelligible and ready for productive exploitation.

Appreciating this, we begin to make some real headway with Ascham's distinction between the quick wit who vanishes and decays through prodigality and the wise orator whose providence ensures him a great store of living. The idea of providence as an individual responsibility seems to have been a relatively new concept in sixteenth-century thought. Elyot defines it as a necessary virtue of the ideal governor, 'wherby a man nat onely foreseeth commoditie and incommoditye, prosperitie and aduersitie, but also consulteth and therewith endeuoureth as well to repell anoyaunce, as to attaine and gette profite and aduauntage'.[25] By virtue of his own providence a man would be able to overcome, or to make the best of, the unforeseeable reversals of fortune which would otherwise destroy him. He would be able, in Ascham's words, to prove 'fortunate' for himself and 'profitable' to the commonweal because of his ability to realize the potential offered by eventualities even when these were, to all appearances, highly unfavourable. Smith's *Discourse of the Commonweal* is in itself an excellent example of intellectual providence in as much as he, like Latimer, Lever, Crowley, Clement Armstrong, and other 'commonwealth-men' of Edward VI's reign, saw individual avarice as the principal cause behind the enclosures and uncontrolled imports and exports that were breaking down the old economic structure. Unlike the others, however, Smith had 'providence' enough to

[24] Smith, *Discourse*, pp. 11–12.
[25] Elyot, *Gouernour*, p. 99.

see how avarice itself might be exploited in the building up of an entirely new economic structure which would depend on the encouragement of individual enterprise through the enticements of privilege and protection.[26] Providence of this kind is the product of an extremely well-informed mind, able to see the resemblances and distinctions between one situation and another. Such soundness of judgement, according to the Elizabethans, came from accumulated experience, although they readily acknowledged that sufficient experience could not be amassed in the lifetime of a single individual. Life experience, however, could be supplemented by the experience gained in reading: 'for where it is denied man to live above a hundred years . . . by the benefits of learning he has the commodity of life of a thousand years, by reason he sees the events and occurences of all that time by books'.[27]

For the purposes of dialectical as well as rhetorical invention, material for proving knowledge had to be stored in the form of *exempla*, which comprised all the figurative language, the histories, the epithets and adages that might help to generate propositions with reference to any given situation. In its exemplary capacity poetry or figurative language is as important as any other kind of discourse for the development of the reader's providential qualities, his ability to participate in active life. Puttenham makes an extended claim for the place of poetic example in the developing of memory and judgement:

> There is nothing in man of all the potential parts of his mind (reason and will except) more noble or more necessary to the actiue life then memory: because it maketh most to a sound judgement and perfect wordly wisedome, examining and comparing the times past with the present, and by them both considering the time to come, concludeth with a stedfast resolution, what is the best course to be taken in all his actions and aduices in this world: it came vpon this reason, experience to be so highly commended in all consultations of importance, and preferred before any learning or science, and yet experience is no more than a masse of memories assembled, that is, such trials as man hath made in time before. Right so no kinde of argument in all the Oratorie craft doth better perswade and more vniuersally satisfie then example, which is but the representation of old memories, and like successes happened in times past. For these regards the Poesie historicall of all other next the diuine most

[26] Smith, *Discourse*, p. 118. See also A. B. Ferguson, 'The Tudor Commonweal and the Sense of Change'; G. R. Elton, 'Reform and the "Commonwealth-men" of Edward VI's reign', in *The English Commonwealth 1547–1640*, ed. P. Clark *et al.*, p. 37.

[27] Smith, *Discourse*, p. 27.

honorable and worthy, as well for the common benefit as for the speciall comfort euery man receiueth by it.[28]

It is by trying or proving new situations through the examples of times past, as Puttenham says, that a man realizes the potential stored in his memory which enables him to be of 'stedfast resolution' in taking any decision. In the ensuing discussion of historical poetry Puttenham makes no evaluative distinction between factual and fictional example and in his discussion of the rhetorical power of *exempla* Erasmus is equally unconcerned with such a distinction.[29] Both Erasmus and Puttenham define *exempla* as resources: for Puttenham they are the material of dialectical invention, comparative proofs of the present against the experience of times past, and for Erasmus they supply the material of rhetorical invention. As such, any distinction between their 'factual' and 'fictive' status is inconceivable. Lies are not lies in Renaissance literary theory unless they are also 'unprofitable'. The profitability of an example lies in its transformative potential, so that the generation of moral propositions from any given 'fact' is bound to distort that fact in the very process of validating it as 'true' and profitable to be remembered. Similarly, fictive *exempla* are capable of generating knowledge on any level, from plausible fact to allegorical fable. Like Puttenham, Sir Thomas Elyot defines history as example; 'The knowlege of this Experience is called Example, and is expressed by historie, whiche of Tulli is called the life of memorie'.[30] Cicero's much quoted dictum is perhaps alleged here less as support for the idea that history keeps alive the memory of great men, than in defence of Elyot's thesis that it is through the accumulation and application of *exempla* that a man's memory becomes a vital force. For Elyot history is not confined to the narrative of great deeds, nor indeed to narrative at all, but comprises 'all thynge that is necessary to be put in memorie' from the 'quicke sentences and eloquent orations' of governors to the natural properties of beasts and plants. Not even fiction is excluded from the category of history as example:

Admytte that some histories be interlaced with leasynges; why shulde we therfore neglecte them? . . . But if by redynge the sage counsayle of Nestor, the subtile persuasions of Ulisses, the compendious grauitie of Menlaus . . . We may apprehende any thinge wherby our wittes may be amended and our per-

[28] George Puttenham, *The Arte of English Poesie*, ed. G. D. Willcock and A. Walker, p. 39. [29] *De copia*, pp. 70–1. [30] Elyot, *Gouernour*, p. 280.

sonages be more apte to serue our publike weale and our prince; what forceth it us though Homere write leasinges?[31]

As Erasmus demonstrates in the *De copia* how several commonplaces of discourse may be generated from one exemplum, so Elyot turns figurative speech into *exempla* from which further propositions may be generated. Ending one of his chapters with a pithy sentence from Diogenes, he cannot refrain from observing how much potential knowledge is concealed in it:

What so perfectly expresseth a man as doctrine? Diogines the philosopher seing one without lernynge syt on a stone, sayde to them that were with him, beholde where one stone sytteth on an other; whiche wordes, well considered and tried, shall appere to contayne in it wonderfull matter for the approbation of doctrine, wherof a wyse man maye accumulate ineuitable argumentes, which I of necessite, to auoide tediousnes, must nedes passe ouer at this tyme.[32]

The words themselves retained in the memory store potential arguments which 'well considered and tried' in appropriate contexts of life and discourse will prove various kinds of knowledge. This provident ideal also manifests itself in the Renaissance preoccupation with the concept of *enargeia*, poetry as a 'speaking picture'. Hence the proliferation of mirror images within literary texts, the tableaux, painted shields, parenthetic descriptions and fables within fables which enable the characters to behold themselves, to moralize and invent a knowledge of their own circumstances. Elyot makes quite explicit the connection between recorded *sententiae* and vivid depiction in terms of the power each has to generate discourse. In his opinion, the nobleman's house should be a storehouse of stimulating *exempla*, visual and verbal:

concernynge ornamentes of halle and chambres, in Arise, painted tables, and images containyng histories, wherin is represented some monument of vertue, most cunnyngly wroughte, with the circumstance of the mater briefely declared; wherby other men in beholdynge may be instructed, or at the lest ways, to vertue persuaded. In likewise his plate and vessaile wolde be ingraued with histories, fables, or quicke and wise sentences . . . wherby some parte of tyme shall be saued, whiche els by superfluouse eatyng and drinkyng wolde be idely consumed.[33]

Elyot sees the capacity of images and sentences to quicken or stimulate the production of knowledge as in some measure compen-

[31] Ibid. 284. [32] Ibid. 52. [33] Ibid. 125.

sating for the idle consumption of time spent in feasting. Again, this recalls the prejudice against 'idle' reading, where time is spent in the pursuit of pleasure, without any compensatory development of the 'potential parts' of the mind. At last we begin to resolve the apparent paradox of defining profitable discourse as a discourse that can never be fully disclosed, that always conceals further inexhaustible resources ready for production. All rhetorical invention involves disclosure; the very definition of rhetoric is *discovery* of persuasive means. Even persuasive disclosure, however, may be condemned as 'lies' and 'idle' and 'unprofitable' in Renaissance terms if it is unworthy remembrance, if it is incapable of generating in the reader vital resources, concealed and ready for further invention. The substantial discourse of the wise orator, even if it is 'interlaced with leasings', will nevertheless be copious in rendering its topic sensible to the intelligence of the reader. Ill-advised discoursers, such as those who qualified for Nashe's *Anatomie of Absurditie,* are easily exposed by resourceful readers as lacking in exemplary force, unintelligible to the powers of memory and imagination. Their inventions stand condemned as lacking substance, 'a confused masse of wordes without *matter*, a Chaos of sentences without any profitable *sence*' (i. 10). The very opposite, in fact, of Elyot's wise sentence from Diogenes (quoted above), 'whiche wordes, well considered and tried, shall appere to contayne . . . wonderfull *matter* for the approbation of doctrine' (my italic).

The disclosures of narrative, which seduce the reader by the promise of novelty—what happened next—are invalidated by the criteria of profitable discourse. When Elizabethan writers condemn the publication of 'novels' they do not generally mean the sensationalism of news reports (which were usually moralized out of all factual pretence in any case). They are criticizing the prodigal waste of exemplary resources in discourse which can disclose nothing except itself, which is too particular to afford any knowledge of a more general application to the reader. In discourse, Elyot wrote:

> noueltie is not to be sought for, for therin ought not to be founden either singuler opinion, or thynge impossible, or contrarie to mens coniecture: but suppose that to be in herying moste gracious or pleasant, which beyng sowen in the mindes of other, maie assemble moste matter to the purpose.'[34]

[34] Elyot, *Four Political Treatises*, p. 29.

The most profitable discourse is that which enables the reader to generate knowledge, to 'assemble . . . matter to the purpose' so as to become an effective participant and communicator in society. Through exercise of profitable reading one appropriates the *habitus* which is most precious of all possessions, a mastery over events. Reversing the traditional concept of nobility as a purer kind of blood, the most inward proof of superiority, Elyot wrote that nobility was only the 'commendation, and . . . the surname of vertue' whose inner substance was ability, the 'hauynge and use of vertue'.[35] Virtue may here be taken to correspond less to Christian virtue than to Ciceronian *virtus*, an ideal which, as Quentin Skinner has explained, formed the basis for the humanist conception of the *vir virtutis*, the man fully in possession of his potential as a man.[36] The real significance of *virtus* emerges, as Skinner makes clear, in the context of man's relation to the unpredictability of his circumstances, which are seen as being under the auspices of the amoral *fortuna*, rather than divine Providence. *Virtus* defines itself as the ability to overcome the vicissitudes of *fortuna* to master events and make them realize themselves as potential wealth, as good fortune. The process of humanist education aims at developing man's ability to govern himself and his environment, so he may be as Skinner writes, 'a creative social force, able to . . . remake his social world'.[37] Those who can master *fortuna* and be 'fortunate for themselves' are therefore also the productive resources of government, 'profitable for the commonweal'. The *vir virtutis* stands as the ideal opposite to the prodigal: the one uses his inventive capacity to produce commodity for himself in spite of fortune, the other collaborates with fortune in the consumption of his prospects and himself. When in 1592 the Cambridge don Gabriel Harvey encountered the latest publication of a young writer so apparently down-at-heel that he was prepared to style himself 'Pierce Penilesse', the older man seems to have felt it his responsibility to offer some advice: 'Be thy resolute *selfe*,' he wrote, 'not the Slaue of Fortune . . . but the friend of Vertue . . . ', and 'Pennilesse is not his purse but his minde: not his reuenue, but his resolution' (my italic).[38] What Harvey could not condone was the way in which the author had failed to

[35] Elyot, *Gouernour*, pp. 129, 278.

[36] Q. Skinner, *The Foundations of Modern Political Thought*, i. *The Renaissance*, pp. 88–101.

[37] Ibid. 94.

[38] *The Works of Gabriel Harvey*, ed. A. B. Grosart, i. 97–8.

make the text itself a place for the trial and proof of productive knowledge of his own estate:

> He tost his imagination a thousand waies, and I beleeue searched euery corner of his Grammar-schoole witte . . . to see if he coulde finde anie meanes to relieue his estate, but all his thoughtes, and marginal notes consorted to his conclusion, That the worlde was vncharitable and he ordained to be miserable.[39]

Nashe's text has failed, by the criteria of profitable discourse, to 'assemble anie matter to the purpose'. Such pamphlets as this were nothing but 'nouvellets', Harvey complained, pandering to the appetite of 'idle creatures'.[40] Harvey's apparent inability to appreciate the parodic content of *Pierce Penilesse* may be no more than an indication of how out of touch dons can be with the racing pulse of London literary life, but it may also be a significant indication of the difficulties Nashe was up against when he set out to challenge old reading habits, and the expectations of profitable discourse.

[39] Ibid. 195.
[40] Ibid. 215.

# 3
# Publication
## *Credit and Profit*

IN the last chapter I suggested that Elizabethan readers were educated to expect a good deal from an encounter with a literary text. The exercise of reading classical literature involved varying the text so as to discover its working beauty as analogical potential for future use. To practise reading and writing was to furnish one's inner self and thereby to possess that self more fully and productively. Shakespeare's sonnet LXXVII illustrates this notion as it contrasts the gratifying illusion of fullness and self-presence discovered by gazing in a mirror with the apparently vacant stare of a blank page in a commonplace book:

> Thy glasse will shewe thee how thy beauties were
> Thy dyall how thy pretious mynuits waste,
> The vacant leaues thy mindes imprint will beare.[1]

The mirror which seems to be filled with presence and beauty discloses an imagery of emptiness and death:

> The wrinckles which thy glasse will truly show,
> Of mouthed graues will give thee memorie.

Blank pages, however, are filled with generative possibility for the future, inviting the mind to formulate discourse which, like a child both of and different from its parent, will provide future stimulus to engage the powers of discourse and reason:

> Looke what thy memorie cannot containe
> Commit to these waste blancks and thou shall finde
> Those children nurst, deliuerd from thy braine
> To take a new acquaintance of thy minde.
> These offices, as oft as thou shalt looke,
> Shall profit thee, and much enrich thy booke.

[1] William Shakespeare, *The Complete Works*, original spelling edition, p. 861. References to this edn. henceforward in text.

Shakespeare's full/empty contrast distinguishes the vanity of self-contemplation from the productivity of discovering the self as a progenitor of meaning through the related activities of writing and reading.

How did such a high regard for the educational effectiveness of varying the text affect the publication of original literary compositions in the sixteenth century? Relevant to this question is Shakespeare's contrast between mirror, dial, and book which plays on a commonplace of humanist pedagogic thought; that is, the notion of the book as a mirror capable of reproducing its idealized image in the reader destined to govern (North's *Diall of Princes* is an example). On to this notion English political thinkers projected their aspirations for the education of an entire governing class, of which each representative might be as socially productive and influential as a printed book. In other words, the discourse and behaviour of these governors would ideally affect others of inferior understanding in the same way that an instructive text creates in its readers the capacity for self-government. In 1531 Elyot envisaged a situation in which government office became the mirror or printed book that gave access and lent authority to the exemplary working of the governor's mind. He wrote that men who excel others in the 'influence of understandynge, and do imploye it to the detaynyng of other[s] within the boundes of reason, and shewe them howe to prouyde for theyr necessarye liuynge' are the men who deserve advancement to gouernment office, to be 'set in a more highe place than the residue where they may se and also be sene; that by the beames of theyr excellent witte, shewed throughe the glasse of auctorite, other[s] of inferiour understandynge may be directed to the way of vertue and commodious liuynge'.[2] There is here, of course, the notion of control and surveillance, but there is also a sense in which Elyot conceives the 'glass of authority' as a means of making the governor's mind visible and its providence influential, just as publication was a glass which made visible to contemporary readers the authoritative minds of the classical world. Elyot was emphatic about the link between government responsibility and discursive ability. In another discourse he anticipated a change in the social obligations of the English aristocrat; required in former times to protect his dependants with sword and spear, the knight of modern days would become an author of discourse and consequently

[2] Elyot, *Gouernour*, p. 5.

of social *mores*. Again, Elyot makes social elevation the medium of this discursive authority, 'by the meane of his dignite' the modern knight 'shuld more effectually with his learning and witte assayle vice and errour . . . hauinge ther vnto for his sworde and speare his tung and his penne'.[3]

In the early and middle years of the sixteenth century the dissemination of authoritative classical texts through translation and publication became closely associated with government and its qualifications. Translators tended to be young men from one or other of the universities or (as was more likely) from one of the Inns of Court. They practised the art of translation under the auspices of a patron who was likely to be an influential member of the government, with a protestant-humanist interest in the dissemination of learning, perhaps retaining some connection with a particular Inn.[4] His own youth, and the relative untriedness and inflexibility of the English language obliged each translator to characterize his undertaking as a working text, a kind of exercise which would both test and reveal his discursive ability for the future. At the same time, however, the authority of the original text fully justified its publication as a commodity for other students. So, for example, when John Dolman, translating Cicero in 1561, felt the need to defend the decision to publish against criticism of his youth and of the translation's want of eloquence, he argued that the bodily fitness and mental inexperience of his youth complemented the authority of the original text, so that translation enabled his soul to 'utter her force and vertue'.[5] The translator was thus in the happy position of being able to publish his discursive ability without having to identify the authority of the text as his own. He could dedicate his publication to an influential statesman, as John Studley did his translation of Seneca's *Agamemnon*, without claiming more for his version of the text than that by it 'yonge Studentes . . . myght take some commoditie'.[6]

This habit of justifying publication on the grounds that the original work is profitable and authoritative enough to lend its translation the value of a working text provided an ambiguous precedent for future authors. On the one hand it appeared to rule out the possibility of an

3 Id., *A Preservatiue Agaynste deth*, sigs. Aii$^{v}$-Aiii$^{r}$.

4 Conley, *The First English Translators*, pp. 38–40.

5 John Dolman, *Those Fyue Questions which Marke Tully Cicero disputed in his manor of Tusculanum*, sig. * 4$^{v}$.

6 John Studley, *The Eyght Tragedie of Seneca entituled Agamemnon*, sig. A* iv$^{r}$.

author offering his own compositions in published form as qualifications for government (unless, of course, they served a social and rhetorical function as epideictic or dedicatory material prefacing a more profitable text). On the other hand, the assumption that a text is rendered worthy of publication by its commodity or resource value ultimately begs the question of discursive authority inasmuch as it anticipates a readership intent on becoming able authors and discoursers. In 1570 Ascham's *Schoolmaster* registered with disquiet the increasing tendency of Englishmen to discourse freely on all matters of religion and government. For all his advocacy of words before matter, Ascham feared the consequence of independent thought upon discursive ability and in his usage the word 'discourser' became synonymous with a seditious determination to differ from the government's view.[7] The government policy on censorship gradually became more coherent and practicable in the course of Elizabeth's reign. As Sir Nicholas Bacon pointed out to the Queen in 1567, the bringing of foreign books into the country provoked 'mens minds to be at variance one with another, and diversity of minds maketh seditions'.[8] The government was at one with itself on the issue of censorship at this time since seditious literature was identified with a Catholic threat to the policies of reformation. The Stationers' Company (incorporated during the previous reign, in 1557) accordingly formed the basis of the Elizabethan censorship system, relying (in the spirit of contemporary economic policy) on the company's interests in defending its monopoly as a guarantee of its effectiveness in licensing new publications.[9] Not until the reforming interest began itself to overtake the government did any real threat to the system of literary patronage and censorship arise.

Humanist pedagogy, privileging as it did the productive potential of discourse, was always on the brink of suggesting that discursive authority was merely the effect of a dexterity with tropes and figures; except that poetry and fiction, the discursive kinds for which this suggestion most obviously held good, were traditionally exempt from the claims of authority and credibility.[10] It was, however, this very exemption, this licence, which made poetry and fiction so much more potentially productive in analogical terms than any other form of

[7] Ascham, *Schoolmaster*, p. 75.

[8] Quoted by D. M. Loades in an excellent analysis of Tudor press censorship, 'The Theory and Practice of Censorship in Sixteenth-Century England', p. 142.

[9] Ibid. 153.

[10] Erasmus, *De copia*, pp. 17, 70–86; Quintilian, *Institutio oratoria,* x.i. 28–30.

classical discourse. From this point of view poetry and fiction were highly profitable and exemplary, and the publication of translations was thereby justifiably patriotic. At the same time, however, it was imperative that such translation and publication should not appear to be promoting the productivity of the poetic fiction as a licence for diversity of opinion, or seem to be implying that discursive authority itself might simply be the effect of varying the text in question. In England this difficulty of reconciling the ideals of discursive productivity and political authority gave rise to instances in which the liberal spirit motivating the translation and publication of classical literature could seem to be internally contradicted by inhibitions on the reader's freedom of interpretation. This is interesting, because it seems to have been peculiar to England; from Terence Cave's account, French translators of the classics seem not to have had to come to terms with a similar division of commitment. Cave notes that from the prefaces of French and English humanists to editions of Homer, Virgil, and Ovid there emerges 'an image of an ideally rich work of literature, a living and inexhaustible paradigm of the humanist encyclopedia'.[11] As Cave goes on to explain, the inexhaustibility of such poetic texts 'is necessarily dependent on the conservation of their potentiality for the production of meaning and thus on the downgrading of the allegorical gloss. Once the *Metamorphoses*, for example, has been converted into a set of allegorical notations its significance becomes finite.'[12] In France this apparently led to the preparation of humanist translations which presented the texts in all their productive plenitude as unallegorized resources of meaning. In England, however, the humanist ideal of textual productivity was qualified by the practical politics of translation. In 1564, when Arthur Golding wrote from Cecil House offering his translation of the first four books of the *Metamorphoses* to the Earl of Leicester, he made it clear that he had been engaged in a patriotic and humanistic enterprise. Knowing that his patron has been 'woont to encourage them to proceede in their peynfull exercises attempted of a zeale and desyre to enryche their natiue language', he expects that the translation of Ovid's 'excellent deuises and fine inuentions' will find acceptance.[13] His preface to the

[11] Cave, *Cornucopian Text*, p. 175; Cave cites the preface to the humanist edition of Homer, *Copiae cornu sive Oceanus enarrationum homericarum* (Basle, 1558) written by the English Protestant Laurence Humphrey.

[12] *Cornucopian Text*, p. 176.

[13] Arthur Golding, *The Fyrst Fower Bookes of P. Ouidius Nasos worke intituled Metamorphosis*, sig. * i$^{v}$.

reader, however, cautions against its own justification of the imaginative productivity of poetry, at once explaining the sweet and subtle operations of metaphor, and denying the reader any such experience by providing every fable with a definite allegorical gloss.[14] Golding appears to be trying to provide readers who have not had the benefit of learning the operations of language through translation with the means to make use of the resources of figurative transformation while avoiding the inference that meaning itself can be changed in any material way by a trope or a figure. His solution to this exacting problem was to package the discursive productivity (which justifies, in patriotic terms, the translation of a poetic text) as definitive moral authority. Did Golding fear recrimination? The scholar Eleanor Rosenberg implies as much when she points out that after completing the translation of the *Metamorphoses* in 1567 he published no more poetry. Indeed, his later publications—a translation of Calvin's sermons, an exposition of the Gospels to be read in Church services, translations of Beza and Marlorat—suggest a stronger commitment to the control of meaning than they do to textual productivity.[15] We cannot now interpret Golding's motives; however, it is clear that both his cautious presentation of the *Metamorphoses* translation and his subsequent abandonment of poetry are indicative at some level of intellectual and political reservations about the desirability of publishing poetic fiction.

For all this reservation there remained, however, the precedent of justifying translation and publication as a serviceable commodity, both qualifying the author and furthering the patron's credit in the cause of reformation. A slight modification of this precedent justified the publication of an original composition in the hope that it might attract a patron. Such was the conjecture of George Gascoigne when he returned to England from the Netherlands in 1573, frustrated in his hopes of military advancement. Unfortunately, however, his book, *A Hundreth Sundrie Flowres*, which advertised on the title page both foreign poesies 'gathered . . . by translation' and native flowers plucked 'by inuention of our owne fruitefull Orchardes in England' was immediately seized on publication by the High Commission. Gascoigne's excuse for his presumption, in a letter to the High Commission prefixed to a revised edition, was that he had hoped, by

[14] Ibid., sig. * iii$^{r-v}$.

[15] E. Rosenberg, *Leicester, Patron of Letters*, pp. 158–9; see also L. T. Golding, *An Elizabethan Puritan*, p. 61.

employing print as a rhetorical device, to make disclosure of otherwise hidden discursive abilities. He had written and published 'to the ende that thereby the vertuous might bee incouraged to employ my penne in some exercise which might tende both to my preferment, and to the profite of my Countrey. For many a man which may like mine outwarde presence, might yet haue doubted whether the qualityes of my minde had bene correspondent to the proportion of my bodie.'[16] This defence relates Gascoigne's conception of the function of publication to that of the translators of the previous decade; the printed text becomes the space in which the aspiring governor both tries and discovers the virtues of his wit, offering to profit both himself and others. But Gascoigne's version is more narrowly self-advertising; he has transgressed by making the printed text the medium of original poetic invention.

The High Commission's objection to Gascoigne's book can be understood generally as an effect of the reformation of manners outlined in Chapter 1, and Gascoigne acknowledges in his apology that 'all ydle Bookes or wanton Pamphlettes' have been prohibited.[17] But there were more specific objections; a lack of prefatory material explaining the nature and purpose of the book had led to a scandalous contemporary application being made of Gascoigne's sophisticated short story *The Adventures of Master F. J.*[18] This points us to another difficulty for the would-be author of original fiction in the sixteenth century: an audience educated to read as if inventing resources applicable to their own circumstances would be liable to moralize and interpret the most innocent of texts. The author of fiction was thus caught in contradiction; his work was unprofitable and licentious if it could not yield any further meaning to the reader, but to the extent that any further meaning was open to contemporary interpretation by the reader the licentiousness of textual productivity was itself liable to be politically objectionable. Gascoigne's revised edition of 1575 cleared up the mystery and purged the wantonness of his original fictions, as well as including certain textual adjustments which might be compared with Golding's cautious delimiting of the text's meaning for unlearned readers of the *Metamorphoses*. For example, in revision, Gascoigne added pointed marginalia to the text of his translation of Ariosto's comedy, *The Supposes*. Where the original text in-

[16] Gascoigne, *Works*, i. 5.

[17] Ibid. i. 4.

[18] C. T. Prouty, *George Gascoigne*, p. 79.

vited the reader to identify the discursive virtuosity of the playwright with the plot's capacity to create and exploit opportunities for error (supposes), the addition of marginalia directs the reader towards a moral analysis of the perils of acting upon conjectures which are deceptive supposes. This alteration adapts the play for the purposes of social reformation inasmuch as it cautions against the equation of comic good fortune with the improvised responses of wit.[19]

Although even this revised edition of his poetic works was not well received by the High Commission, Gascoigne went on to gain patronage and recognition. But while his dedicatory epistles to the later works struggle to reconcile a posture of deference to his patron with the meaning of the humanist conception of the author as a governor in his own right by the influence of his mind, Gascoigne's actual discourses became more and more submissive, eventually abandoning altogether any claim to originality.

From Gascoigne's example we can see how the protestant-humanist respect for authorship exercised a double bind on sixteenth-century writers. Being obliged to claim for one's own text the status of a patriotic commodity meant being obliged to disclaim literary originality for fear of seeming to start a trend of licentious irresponsibility with the resources of meaning and interpretation. The situation was exacerbated by the policy of moral and economic reformation. As the demand for classical translation was satisfied, how were writers to serve the country and display their abilities without being original? The answer was even more assiduous attention to moral profit, and a more rigorous observation of the criterion that the author should be a transmitter of authoritative discursive resources. Gascoigne fulfilled his early literary promise in the patriotic translation of discourses on temperance; Lyly offered to students the compendious resources of wit arranged in the form of an admonitory fiction, to prove their own prodigal tendencies. Published discourses of the 1570s and early '80s are compiled or translated rather than authored: George Whetstone humbly announces himself in the *Mirour For Magestrates* (which is indeed derivative) as a mere transmitter of the profitable counsels of the Emperor Severus.[20] In-

[19] Compare the text of *The Supposes* in Gascoigne, *A Hundreth Sundrie Flowres* (1573), sigs. Bii$^{r}$– kiii$^{v}$ with that of *The Posies of George Gascoigne* (1575), sigs. Aii$^{r}$–Fiv$^{v}$.

[20] Whetstone, *Mirour For Magestrates*, sig. Avi$^{r}$.

evitably, this pressure on the printed text to serve as an instrument of social and moral reformation paralysed its capacity to furnish and stimulate the mind in the way that the humanists has originally intended. Thomas Izard observed that Whetstone's method of writing registers a change in the meaning of the rhetorical term 'amplification'. In 1553, when Thomas Wilson defined 'amplification' in his *Arte of Rhetorique*, the term was understood to involve the transformation of meaning in a text 'by changing a woorde'. For Whetstone, however, writing in the 1580s, 'amplification seems to mean the expanding and embellishing of a theme—chiefly by multiplying examples, citing instances, and repeating memorable sayings'.[21] This retreat into a mechanical fulfilment of the criterion of textual productivity was the only response possible for authors denied the chance of making their literary talent profitable by the accepted means of enriching the language with the living rhetorical plenitude of a translated classical text. At about this time, too, the industrious sector of society began to demand the educative benefits of classical discourse in an easily accessible encyclopaedic form; L. B. Wright's indispensable survey of this literature notes that 'the later years of the sixteenth century saw a multiplication of books of aphorisms, similes, flowers of rhetoric and history—a type of epitomized learning which scholars and educationalists for generations had urged upon all who sought the fountains of erudition'.[22] Publishers were quick to respond to the general reader's demand that literature be morally, socially, and economically useful and the prejudice against the idleness of fiction *per se* saw no signs of disappearing among this readership. Wright records a printer as late as 1625 responding to the demand for socially profitable reading matter by disguising a new edition of the *Decameron* as the '*Modell of Wit, Mirth and Eloquence*'.[23]

The inhibition on fictions which seemed to promote an idle, improvising reliance on fortune coupled with demands by patrons and reading public for a literature which would transmit classical *exempla* as discursive and moral authorities for the virtues of providence and solvency meant that in the 1570s and early '80s the conditions of authorship were best fulfilled by emptying one compendium of *exempla* into another, varying the text as little as possible. Whetstone's apparently far-flung and recondite examples in fact derive from a

[21] Izard, *George Whetstone*, pp. 152–3; Thomas Wilson, *Arte of Rhetorique*, sig. Kii^v^.

[22] Wright, *Middle Class Culture*, p. 147.

[23] Ibid. 404.

single encyclopaedia; Stephen Gosson's authoritative moral diatribes against the theatre contain sections copied verbatim from college lecture notes. Both these authors were patronized by the civic authorities, but the assumption that writing for publication was authorized by the wholesale transmission of *exempla* was not confined to any interested party. If John Northbrooke's polemic against pastimes contained whole pages of *exempla* lifted from authoritative compilations, so did the early fiction of the far from puritan Robert Greene.[24] The humanists' faith in *copia* and in the generative potential of the encounter between reader and text had been narrowed into a kind of retail trade of inert discursive resources.

In the course of the 1580s, however, some of the circumstances that had conspired to create such impossible conditions for the legitimate authorship of original fiction were temporarily alleviated. The concern with providence and solvency ceased to be a government priority and gradually became the preserve of the industrious sort. There were no longer any real grounds for the anxiety, prevalent in the '60s and '70s, that riotous living would consume all the witty young gentlemen eligible for office. The tone of Whetstone's admonition to the young gentlemen of the Inns of Court in the *Mirour For Magestrates* was beginning to seem inappropriate and old-fashioned. Authors such as Lyly and Greene found a way to write fiction without taking on the responsibility of transmitting moral and discursive authority, by addressing their books to female readers. Lyly's *Euphues and his England* (1580), Greene's *Pandosto* (1588) and *Menaphon* (1589) are comparatively free of the earlier compulsion to paralyse the narrative by moralizing its every turn of fortune.[25]

Nashe's arrival in London from Cambridge in 1588 coincided with what was apparently a new expansiveness towards the creation of contemporary literature. He responded to this by writing a preface addressed 'To the Gentlemen Students of both Universities' for the publication of Greene's *Menaphon* in 1589. The preface offered Nashe a pretext to conduct a spirited review of the state of English letters. Praising Greene for his adoption of an easy narrative style, Nashe went on to deplore the degeneration in English letters from the promising early purity demonstrated by Elyot, More, and later

[24] See for example Izard, *George Whetstone*, pp. 131–2, 157; Ringler, 'The First Phase', pp. 406–7; id., *Stephen Gosson*, p. 13; W. G. Crane, *Wit and Rhetoric in the Renaissance*, p. 121.

[25] See Helgerson, *Elizabethan Prodigals*, pp. 14, 77, 84–91.

Ascham to the contemporary state of stagnation in which authors appear to be mere retailers of classical and continental merchandise, taking up 'choise of words by exchange' from foreign suppliers, so that 'well may be the Adage, *Nil dictum quod non dictum prius*, be the most iudiciall estimate of our latter Writers' (iii. 313). Hidebound by the assumption that print exists to facilitate the transmission of profitable *exempla*, these latter writers can only 'pound their capacitie in barren compendiums' (iii. 318). Here, as in another preface written for a pirated edition of *Astrophil and Stella* in 1591, Nashe's concern to provoke the reader into responding to a purely aesthetic experience of the language inspires a caricature of contemporary moralized discourse as shabbily second-hand, or parsimoniously obsessed with making profitable use out of scrap, retailing 'the cinders of *Troy*, and the shiuers of broken trunchions' (iii. 332). The metaphor is a constant one in Nashe's writing. *Pierce Penilesse* opens his own idiosyncratic version of the topic of gluttony by revealing that the threadbare *exempla* of the excesses of ancient Rome are still the staple of English discourses on the folly of intemperance and riotous living: 'The Romaine Emperours that succeeded *Augustus* were exceedingly giuen to this horrible vice, whereof some of them would feed on nothing but the tongues of Phesants and Nightingales', the author begins, only to cheat the appetite for moralized sensationalism as soon as he has aroused it, 'whose exesse I would decypher at large, but that a new Laureat hath sau'd me the labor' (i. 199). The new laureate—probably Anthony Munday who had just translated a French treatise on Roman prodigality—has done the publishing trade in second-hand *exempla* credit enough, having 'performd as much as any Storie dresser may doo, that sets a new English nap on an old Latine Apothegs' (i. 199).

Up to this point Nashe's response to the conditions of authorship seems straightforward. The humanist reverence for the educational possibilities of the printed text had become extraordinarily restrictive and Nashe was conscious of its retarding effect on the development of a vernacular language capable of subtle and sophisticated expression. But Nashe's attempts to promote a general critical awareness of the restraint imposed by the exemplary imperatives of publication provoked a series of responses as anxious as that of the High Commission to the audacious Gascoigne in the 1570s; only this time it was less a question of moral and economic reformation in danger of being undermined than of the political threat being posed to the stability of the government by sceptical and independent discourses emanating from the press, openly questioning the authority of the established Church and State.

In this context 1588 was not after all such an auspicious year for Nashe to have embarked upon a literary career full of innovatory ideas about writing which must have depended entirely on the press for their realization. The Elizabethan censorship system, dependent as it was on the co-operation of the Stationers' Company, had been proving less efficient in dealing with offenders who wrote in the cause of ecclesiastical reformation than with the predominantly Catholic treason of the early years of the reign. In the 1560s a series of published tracts attacked the Church of England for not completing the Reformation; this kind of public assault on ecclesiastical institutions was continued through the '70s by the writings of Thomas Cartwright. The licensing system was clearly inadequate. Proposals were initially drawn up for its reform without involving the bishops, but in the event Archbishop Whitgift decided that the ecclesiastical surveillance of the press was essential. The Star Chamber Decree of 1586 transferred the responsibility of licensing books from the Stationers' Company to the Archbishop of Canterbury and the Bishop of London.[26] By 1588 Archbishop Whitgift and Richard Bancroft, soon to become Bishop of London, had already begun an energetic campaign against the voice of dissent when there appeared the first of a series of devastating attacks upon the bishops under the pseudonym Martin Marprelate. Martin addressed the ecclesiastical authorities with disarmingly confidential frankness and scepticism, borrowing and adapting his subversive, improvising style from the idiom of popular holiday festivity.[27] His pamphlets thereby focused the threat to political stability not only on the independence of the press, but, more important, on a special kind of discursive dexterity, foregrounding style. From the first, the principles of Tudor censorship had been founded on the assumption that books, like malicious rumours, stirred up dissension against the State by claiming that what they said was true; this invitation to the reader to be critically aware of style offered a new and subtler form of discursive threat. The bishops were at a loss how to reply until Richard Bancroft hit upon the expedient of employing secular authors to compose ironic responses on behalf of

[26] F. S. Slebert, *Freedom of the Press in England 1476–1776*, pp. 60–3.

[27] See 'Oh Read Over Dr. John Bridges' (1588), in *The Marprelate Tracts*, pp. 17, 29, 45–6.

authority. This was probably Nashe's first commission; he obliged by mimicking Martin's strategies in *An Almond for a Parrat* (1589) (iii. 337-76). But the bishops did not openly acknowledge their patronage of the anti-Martinists—Nashe, Greene, and Lyly—and in one sense the very success of their policy in employing such writers for their wit could only serve to emphasize the subversive potential of a sceptical style of discourse.

For all his critical independence in undertaking to write the preface to *Menaphon*, however, the Nashe who arrived in London from Cambridge in 1588 had fully intended to pursue a literary career under the auspices of patronage. Like Gascoigne before him he registered a composition with the Stationers' Company to be published in advertisement of his discursive abilities, but no discourse could have been less representative of wit or more stifled by the moralizing reflex Nashe professed to deplore than his bid for patronage, the *Anatomie of Absurditie*. All the signs indicate a work consciously conforming to the obligation to display discursive ability and transmit exemplary resources to the reader without allowing the deployment of tropes and figures to introduce any original turn to the thought. The book is uncharacteristically advertised on the title page as being 'compiled' rather than written by T. Nashe and it displays throughout considerable debts to other compilations of *exempla* (see *Works*, ed. McKerrow, vol. v., Suppl., pp. 1-7). The most lively reading in the whole brittle and tedious work is a gratuitous excuse to laugh at the miserable rhymes in *Bevis of Hampton*, which suggests that Nashe found stylistic criticism irresistible; on the whole, however, he manages to stick to the orthodoxy of protestant-humanist pedagogy, defending literature only to the extent that it is a productive instrument of ethical instruction. In the last lap of the *Anatomie* Nashe attempts rather woodenly to fulfil the ideal of youthful authorship as an exercise serving to profit the writer and his fellow students. 'To make vse of my *Anatomie* as well to my selfe as to others, I will prescribe as neere as I can, such a rule for Students that therby squaring their actions, they shall not be easily attached of any notable absurditie' (i. 42). But after a while he falters, conscious of being inappropriate: 'I know the learned wil laugh me to scorne, for setting down such Rams horne rules of direction' (i. 48). Nashe was simply incapable of carrying out the old-fashioned prescription with conviction; the learned were potential patrons but they demanded ability as well as conformity. He concluded lamely by desiring their pardon 'which may encourage me heereafter to endeuour in some other matter of more moment' (i. 49).

Whether it was the sprightly pedantry and conservatism of the *Anatomie* or the critical outspokenness of the preface to *Menaphon* which drew the author's talents to the attention of the bishops we do not know, but Nashe was certainly patronized intermittently by the learned ecclesiastical licensors of the press; initially in the campaign against Marprelate and then in a less controversial capacity, as the author of *Summers Last Will and Testament*, a show to entertain the Archbishop's household at Croydon in 1593. The point to note here, however, is that neither of these engagements offered anything like accommodation and protection enough to answer the manifold constraints that the patronage system itself continued to impose upon an author who wished to publish original and independently creative writing. The early years of Elizabeth's reign had focused government anxiety on the socially irresponsible attitudes promoted by unmoralized fiction. But in the final decade, haunted by the spectre of Spanish invasion and the fear that internal dissent fostered by Martinism and by the puritan press would be turned to the Spanish advantage (Nashe makes propaganda of this fear in *An Almond for a Parrat*, i. 343) the government discerned a new threat in the interpretative ambiguities of ironic discourse, satire and history. Masters of ironic discourse—Lucian, Rabelais, Aretino, and even Marprelate—became bywords for the subversive potential of satiric writing in the 1590s.[28] Nashe's writing life was almost entirely confined to the 1590s and his publications were from the very first inextricably involved both in reaction to the restrictive legacy of the reformation of manners and in constant anticipation of new and ingenious forms of censorious interpretation resulting from a post-Marprelate sensitivity to the subversive potential of all ironic discourse.

The first attempt to link Nashe's promotion of critical awareness in the general reader with a possible threat to political stability was a hostile notice of the preface to Greene's *Menaphon* written by the Revd Richard Harvey and prefixed to his *Theologicall Discourse of the Lamb of God and his Enemies . . . together with a detection of old and new Barbarisme, now commonly called Martinisme* (1590—McKerrow reprints the work's opening and concluding epistles in vol. v., appendix B, pp. 176–83). Richard Harvey was one among a

[28] See below, Chapter 10.

number of authors in the early 1590s who were claiming to detect in the aftermath of Marprelate the rise of new subversive freedoms being taken in the authorship and publication of discourse. He drew attention to the fact that new authors, such as this unheard-of Thomas Nashe, had the temerity to publish their own opinions, unsanctioned by the authority of a patron, indicating that their pronouncements in the field of literary criticism were the secular equivalent of Marprelatian discussions of how to reform the Church of England carried out in the subversive vein of Lucian or Rabelais (v. 178). Richard Harvey presumably did not know that Nashe had been one of the anti-Martinists, but one suspects it would have made little difference; his point—which the bishops themselves came belatedly to concede—was that critical discourse conducted in a spirit of sceptical irony should not be allowed access to publication.

Richard Harvey's insidious political interpretation of Nashe's critical enterprise marked the beginning of the notorious Harvey-Nashe quarrel (continued on Richard's behalf by his brother Gabriel) in which complex issues affecting authorship and publication—reader expectation, rhetorical self-advertising, the implications of patronage—were farcically played out in a series of extravagantly abusive pamphlets. Nashe initially attempted to dismiss Richard Harvey's insinuations by turning their author into an incidental joke on the topic of wrath in *Pierce Penilesse* (i. 195–7). However this tactic attracted its own misinterpretation in the form of response from Richard's brother, the Cambridge don Gabriel Harvey, who was in London on legal business in the summer of 1592. Gabriel Harvey had a more complex view of the political functions of ironic fiction and publication than had Richard. Privately, Gabriel Harvey admired Marprelate for the political effectiveness of his irony; publicly, his readiness to leap into the authorial breach and vindicate his defamed brother with a cunningly contrived detraction of Greene and Nashe entitled *Foure Letters and certaine Sonnets* (1592) is ample evidence of the extent to which he regarded the primary function of the press as that of politic self-promotion. More broadly, Harvey viewed 'rhetorical license'—that is, the licence of the orator to invent persuasive fictions and the power of the press to extend this licence by lending credit to such fictions—as a political weapon to be used in the service of an influential patron (his own attempt to serve the Earl of Leicester in this way, however, had the unfortunate result of offending the Earl of Oxford without really furthering the cause of the

Leicester faction).[29] From this point of view Harvey regarded Nashe as a potentially effective but politically incompetent talent; he simply could not understand why any considerable writer should choose to represent himself in the persona of a bankrupt fool thereby disabling the credit of his rhetoric against enemies such as Richard Harvey. Fiction and fictional personae should, according to Gabriel Harvey, be like the press itself, rhetorically subservient to the political effectiveness of the discourse in question. In 1579 Gabriel Harvey had made effective use of fictional prefatory techniques to facilitate the self-advertising publication of familiar letters between himself and Edmund Spenser without appearing culpably presumptuous.[30] He suggested repeatedly that Nashe make a more expedient use of his inventive ability in some similar enterprise, smoothing the way for some profitable or patriotic discourse. Nashe's ridicule of this inappropriate advice provoked Harvey into taking up the position originally adopted by his brother Richard, so that *A New Letter of Notable Contents* (1593) and *Pierces Supererogation* (1593) are full of insinuations that Nashe's brand of rhetorical licence, far from being politically ineffective (as he had suggested in *Foure Letters and certaine Sonnets*) was dangerously, Lucianically subversive. Paradoxically, this kind of attack helped Nashe to formulate discourses that would challenge the orthodox assumption that fiction and publication serve the rhetorical end of gaining credit and, through credit, political power. These discourses took the form of a fictional confession of a printed page, *The Unfortunate Traveller* and a reply to Harvey's assumptions about rhetorical self-presentation, *Have With You to Saffron Walden*. In the eyes of the authorities, however, there was no distinction between the political implications of Harvey's operation of the press and the conventions of published discourse in the interests of defamation, and Nashe's struggle to find within those conventions a space for a more freely imaginative form of discourse. Nashe's ultimate retaliation to the imaginative poverty imposed by censorship, *Lenten Stuffe*, was the last of his publications. In 1599 the bishops who had first employed Nashe's powers of irony gave order to ban the publication of all epigrams, satires, unlicensed English histories and plays, adding the explicit injunction that 'all Nasshes

[29] See V. Stern, *Gabriel Harvey*, pp. 39–47, 65–66, and, for Harvey's admiration for Marprelate, 183.

[30] Ibid. 59–65; Stern takes Harvey's disclaimers in good faith, but see *The Letter Book of Gabriel Harvey A. D. 1573–80*, ed. E. J. Scott, pp. 58 ff., 89.

bookes and Doctor Harveys bookes be taken wheresoeuer they maye be found and that none of theire bookes bee euer printed hereafter'.[31]

[31] *Transcript of the Stationers' Register*, ed. Arber, iii. 677.

# 4
# Festivity and Productivity

WE have seen how the need to inculcate responsible social attitudes through literature produced a schematically pre-fabricated or compendious style of discourse which could not but frustrate a writer whose special talent was, as was Nashe's, for improvisation. Prompted by his dissatisfaction with the costive, rhetoric-laden style of academic writing, Nashe initially located the opportunity for a more spontaneous creativity in the position of a commercial writer such as Robert Greene, who could respond flexibly to the market and, as Nashe wrote in the preface to *Menaphon*, 'hath liued all dayes of his life by What doe you lacke?' (iii. 314). Nashe soon found out, however, that the literary market place was as dictatorial in its demand for a providential moralizing style of discourse as the academic pedagogues had been. His solution was unequivocal; he identified the source of discursive plenitude with the figure of the carnival trickster who was also a spendthrift: Will Summers the wastrel, Pierce Penilesse the bankrupt, or such mock-patrons as the tavern-haunting Henry King, to whom *Lenten Stuffe* was dedicated (iii. 147–50). There is nothing particularly extraordinary in this identification of financial improvidence and plentiful wit. Not only was the association traditional, but it had, thanks to the humanist emphasis on discursive productivity, a newly acquired social and intellectual relevance. For the discursive productivity aimed at in the educational programme outlined by Erasmus in his *De copia* was based on the idea of the trope (the effective changing of word or phrase from one signification to another) which discovers new resources of meaning by transforming the figures of speech. Considered merely as an exercise pursued for the pleasure of discursive virtuosity, this capacity to produce meaning endlessly by means of figurative transformation becomes licentious and prodigal, and its tricksterish affinities become apparent. In Rabelais's *Pantagruel*, for example, it is the improvident trickster Panurge who is richest in languages and who, although unable to render to Pantagruel any account of how he has dissipated his enormous revenues, resourcefully discovers an inexhaustible wealth of arguments in defence of his own prodigality, merely by transforming the figurative terms appropriate to the discourse of thrift and solvency.[1] Such a dissipation of ingenuity in the pleasure of producing discursive variations for their own sake is a kind of linguistic festivity; hence its association with the hedonistic self-dissipation of the improvident trickster. The ideal writer and speaker, however, was supposed to have mastered this festive improvisatory facility as a means of serving his own productive ends. Erasmus's *De copia* aimed at schooling writers and speakers who were able to improvise, to exploit 'festively' such discursive opportunities as emerged in the actual circumstances of speaking, without abandoning themselves utterly to the pleasures of improvisation and (in a Panurgian way) losing sight of the scope and aim of the whole discourse. Such an ideal required a combination of disciplined preparation and tricksterish flexibility. Indeed, it was the preparative work of reading, imitating other authors, and gathering discursive resources which made effective improvisation possible, for preparation enabled the speaker or writer to depart effortlessly from his intended scope to take advantage of circumstantial opportunities to improve the discourse, returning to his original path without hesitation or loss. Quintilian wrote that improvisation was the crown of premeditative study, for 'although it is essential to bring with us into the court a supply of eloquence which has been prepared in advance in the study and on which we can confidently rely, there is no greater folly than the rejection of the gifts of the moment . . . our premeditation should be such that fortune may never be able to fool us, but may, on the contrary, be able to assist us'.[2] An element of tricksterish licence is suggested by the departure from prepared argument into the realm of inspired improvisation, for the trickster's good fortune relies on exploiting the opportunities latent in error and transgression. But provident foresight ensures that this error is calculated and remains merely an agency; where the trickster pays his tribute to fortune in festive self-dissipation the orator masters such festive opportunism as one of his many resources. The productive end of his discourse is thus not made a fool to fortune, though it is able to exploit all fortune has to offer.

A strikingly reflexive image of this discursive ideal, with its combination of providently plotted end and errant improvisatory means,

[1] Rabelais, *Gargantua and Pantagruel*, pp. 292–303.

[2] Quintilian, *Institutio oratoria*, x. vii. 5–6; see also Cave, *Cornucopian Text*, pp. 126–35.

had been newly made available to European thought in the humanist rediscovery of Roman New Comedy.[3] New Comedy differed most radically from the sacred or satirical traditions of European drama in its rhetorical exploitation of time. The popular satiric comedy of Europe had no interest in securing the conviction of the audience; it was subversive, provocative of scornful laughter. Sacred drama and the dramatized legends of romance, assuming faith in miracles and wonders, simply represented time in a linear sequence, chronicling the hero's or saint's life as it happened. But New Comedy disclosed events according to an artificial order of time, which exploited the rhetorical end of arousing desire in the audience, thereby reserving the power to satisfy this desire by the (otherwise unconvincing) contrivance of the happy end. In the sense that this happy outcome is the aim of the whole plot, comedy resembles the scope of a premeditated discourse. But just as discourse becomes effective by erring from its own premeditated path to take advantage of the benefits of fortune, so comedy, proceeding as it does by way of error to its fortunate conclusion, becomes an image of provident discursive festivity. The transgressive luck of the trickster is mastered by the plot as its chief rhetorical resource, since the deception of audience expectation and the exploitation of every possibility for error is an agency for arousing audience anxiety so as to secure conviction by the pleasure of relief.

In the humanist exposition of Terentian comedy to schoolchildren this analogy with the rhetorical mastery of resources was made explicit.[4] The comedies of Plautus, however, gave more scope for pedagogic disquiet, since in these the strategic deception of audience expectation was less easily identified with the provident mastery of plot resources than it was with the self-dissipating improvisations of tricksterish parasites and slaves. The parasites and slaves of Plautine comedy express a traditional tricksterish association of fortune with the generative ripening of seasonal time. Plautus's slaves become the errant agents of good fortune because their lives have no path, or because they are ready to discard the full purse in their keeping in order to receive the feast offered by the luck of the moment. Their commitment is to the facility of the action and, celebrating the outcome of their own festive virtuosity, they secure no productive end for themselves. But they dramatize most explicitly the fact that good for-

[3] See L. G. Salingar, *Shakespeare and the Traditions of Comedy*, pp. 69, 76–88.
[4] See J. B. Altman, *The Tudor Play of Mind*, pp. 133–9.

tune is the product not of cautious calculation alone, but of calculation combined with a flexible abandonment to the opportunities offered by the moment. In Plautus's *Pseudolus*, for example, Pseudolus unhesitatingly abandons the perfect plan 'stored up his chest' when a letter comes his way by chance, offering a wealth of unforeseen ways to achieve his ends. It is Pseudolus's self-mocking readiness to abandon his pretensions to providence and foresight that fills the moment so full of generative potential for him; the letter becomes festively inexhaustible, 'a perfect cornucopia'[5] offering everything he needs to get the mistress for his young master. All Pseudolus asks for himself, however, is freedom which, in tricksterish tribute to fortune, he dissipates on stage in drunken festivity. In the system of Plautine comedy time is seasonally generative; requiring in its exhaustion, the participation of a tricksterish festivity to disclose, or bring to birth its potential good fortune. In Plautus's *Menaechmi* it is the Syracusan twin's uninhibited abandonment to the opportunities for festivity offered by hazardous confusion in a foreign city which brings about the happy discovery of his twin; an identification which Shakespeare's adaptation of the play *The Comedy of Errors* (1594) significantly refuses to make.

For it was this very association of good fortune with the improvisatory abandonment of the trickster to festive opportunity which caused English educationalists to be distrustful of Plautine comedy and its Italian imitations. English pedagogues were inclined to prefer the extremes of cautious inflexibility dramatized by Dutch education drama, which translated the error-based plot of New Comedy into the context of the prodigal son parable, thereby identifying the deception of audience expectation with an admonitory image of the prodigal beguiled by his trust in fortune and ruined by parasites and slaves.[6] This English unease about the humanist advertisement of the social and discursive advantages of festive opportunism in urban life must be explained in terms of the government's need to combat customary attitudes of opportunistic improvidence among the people. Emerging from a predominantly natural economy in which money was rare, the English people tended to respond to the seasonal potential of time rather in the manner dramatized by Plautine comedy, identifying the security of future prosperity with a festive dissipa-

[5] Plautus, *Pseudolis*, II. 3. 670–4, in *Works*, with trans. by P. Nixon, vol. iv.

[6] See E. K. Chambers, *The Elizabethan Stage*, i. 238–9; C. H. Herford, *Studies in the Literary Relations of England and Germany in the Sixteenth Century*, pp. 152–64.

tion and redistribution of organic wealth. This improvising response to labour and its fruits was entirely appropriate to an economy of natural subsistence in which every harvest was a gamble dependent on the caprices of English weather.[7] But as artificial labour became economically significant, and the exchange of goods became more prevalent, opportunities for festivity increased, without being complemented by any internalized commitment to productive labour. The reformers who drew up and implemented the 1563 Statute of Artificers in an attempt to standardize the conditions of artificial labour, commented in 1573 that one of the reasons for non-observance of the statute was an utter lack among the people of any sense of obligation to provide for the future, or any compulsion to undertake regular work. Artificers, adapting the traditional opportunism of seasonal labour and festivity to the conditions of hire in towns, turned into shiftless urban parasites of the New Comedy variety:

> many of theim yf they worke one daye or weeke will playe twoe for it, wherby thei do not only earne less by their lawfull trades then else they should do, but also fall into lewde and excessive expenses and other vices . . . viz.:—hauntinge of ale howses, using of unlawful games, runninge and shiftinge from towne to towne . . . and so growe to such ydlenes that divers of theim cannot continewe at their occupacions, but practise to get thier livinges by unlawfull games, cosenages, deluding of mens wifes . . . . wher of great misery and encrease of Roges and vagabonds groweth.[8]

Such a hand-to-mouth lifestyle may have been appropriate to a people living at subsistence level when the surplus of goods was minimal, harvests uncertain, and money itself a rare sight. However, the 'decay of housekeeping'—that is, the turning over of much land from tillage to pasture—was commercially linked, as we saw, to an influx of foreign imports, so that as the sixteenth century progressed, Englishmen were aware of goods and cash being exchanged with increasing rapidity and ostentation.[9] Opportunities for 'play', previously dictated by the season, were being commercialized on an unprecedented scale. City life offered the plenitude and material well-being previously associated with rural festivity in the form of regular entertainment, feasting, drinking, sex, gorgeous apparel—all in such a context of commercial anonymity that the temptation to improvise a

[7] W. G. Hoskins, *The Age of Plunder*, p. 85.
[8] 'Memorandum on the Statute of Artificers, *c.*1573', *TED* i. 360.
[9] Hoskins, *Age of Plunder,* pp. 84–5.

living by participating in 'unlawfull games, cosenages, deluding of mens wifes' came to be regarded as a serious social threat.

Given this social context, it is hardly surprising that while Italian humanists sought to imitate and surpass the tricksterish comedy of Plautus and Terence, English protestant-humanists remained dubious about the results. Italian versions of New Comedy celebrate the dramatic scope offered by the commercial anonymity of urban life, emphasizing that the qualities needed to exploit such possibilities (the 'errors' and 'deceits' aggravated by disguise, discursive virtuosity, strategic arousal of expectation or anxiety, and so forth) resemble the dramatist's own techniques. Thus, for example, Ariosto's innovative imitation of Plautus, *La Cassaria* or *The Coffer* (1508), goes further than *Pseudolus* in identifying *virtus* (the successful overcoming of fortune) with flexible improvisation rather than with cautious calculation and providence. Ariosto insists on this point by having his veteran servant-trickster, Volpino, falter at a crucial moment, so that his promise to the young masters that they will have the girls in their arms by nightfall has to be fulfilled by another servant, Fulcio, who is inexperienced in plots and intrigue. Despite being nearly overwhelmed by the anxiety of having to take over from the masterly Volpino, Fulcio rallies and enacts a series of breathtakingly triumphant improvisations. His ingenuity is such that crises and obstacles themselves become his resources, the 'tributaries of his treasury', thus reversing the comedy's opening emphasis on the frustration of the young master, dying like Tantalus of thirst amid his father's inaccessible stores of merchandise.[10] Fulcio's hazardous negotiation of the passage from discipleship to aesthetic mastery is anticipated by the play's prologue, which draws attention to the hazards faced by Ariosto in attempting to prove Italian equal to the dramatic standards set by Plautus; the dramatist thus explicitly links the *virtus* of his own aesthetic achievement to the economic accomplishment of his tricksterish protagonist. But Ariosto felt no compulsion to represent Fulcio as economically provident; like Pseudolis before him, the Italian trickster acknowledges the collaboration of his *virtus* with the vicissitudes of fortune by celebrating fortune in a drunken spree. In this sense Ariosto's conception of the trickster is traditional; luck involves utter abandon and is incompatible with coffer-bound caution about the future. Ariosto's later play *I Suppositi* (1509) is interesting

[10] Ariosto, *La Cassaria*, v. iv. 150–60 in *Opere*, iv. 63.

because it appears not to identify the discursive *virtus* of the playwright quite so overtly with the deceptions of a single trickster; at a more sophisticated level of identification, however, it is clear that the good fortune of the outcome is causally linked to the opportunities for deception and conversational disclosure which are exploited as a way of life by the parasite Pasifilio, for it is Pasifilio's double-crossings that broach a plot solution in the form of a relationship that might otherwise have lain undiscovered among household secrets. Gascoigne's translation of this play was presumably well received at its first Gray's Inn performance in 1566, but, as we saw in the previous chapter, his revision of the printed text in 1575 suggests that the government had serious reservations about the public promotion of such Italian models of discourse and behaviour. Indeed, Gascoigne's next play, the *Glasse of Government* (1576), took pains to contrive an elegantly plotted action based, in the humanist manner, on deception, without identifying any economic good fortune in the outcome with such deliberate exploitation of opportunities for deception and disclosure as had constituted the 'supposes' of his last play. The *Glasse of Government* adapts the notion of deception-as-plot in the interests of moral and economic reform by identifying the action not with deception but with a magisterial detection of deception which brings about the downfall of the tricksterish young prodigals (for it is a 'prodigal son' play, and the witty young men are duly consumed by their riotous indulgence in commercial festivity). Whetstone's *Promos and Cassandra* (1578) is another of these magisterial detective plots, which self-consciously adapts the intrigue structure of the humanist comedy in the interests of moral reform, aware that the linear time of traditional English drama held no rhetorical power, and yet unwilling to identify such power with an Italian-style urban intrigue.[11] The stylistic enterprise of Whetstone's play can be linked to his treatment of the threat of commercial festivity in the *Mirour For Magestrates of Cyties,* where again he promotes the idea of magisterial detection of the deceptions and cozenages for which commercialized festivity—taverns, dicing houses, ordinaries—offered such ample scope in London, much to the loss of 'the Marrow & Strength of this happy Realme (I meane the Abilitie of the Gentlemen)'.[12] Whetstone deals with the opportunities for ex-

[11] See Whetstone's explanation of his aim to adapt Italian plot structure in the interests of English civic reform, *Promos and Cassandra*, sig. Aii$^{r}$.

[12] Whetstone, *Mirour For Magestrates*, sig. Aiv$^{r}$.

ploitation offered by dining houses and taverns rather than theatres, because theatres have, he explains, received enough civic attention in the last few years; but it was indeed the question of commercial theatre that condensed all the authorities' fears about the temptations of an opportunistic, improvising lifestyle for the unwary and their would-be deceivers. Commercial theatres, or inns in which plays were presented on a commercial basis, not only offered opportunities for dubious financial and sexual contracts; they actually represented such contracts as entertaining plots, their staple commodity being the deception of audience expectation. As early as 1574 (before the first commercial theatre was opened) the city fathers attempted to regulate commercial plays in inns because these created opportunities for financial exploitation of the poor and fond; thereafter they constantly linked their objections to the 'lascivious devices, shifts of cozenage' that plays might represent with the opportunities for exploitation that performances created for 'whoremoongers, coozeners, conny-catching persones', leading young men into 'vain & prodigall expenses'.[13]

The response of the magistrates in terms of the English adaptation of Italian humanist comedy is telling. On the one hand the deceits and errors which gave the comic ending its emotional conviction were central to the discursive power of which comedy was an image, on the other, representing power as the outcome of the deliberate exploitation of opportunities for error was emotionally and morally problematic unless the dramatist could make some admonitory distinction between provident and improvident manifestations of such opportunism. It is for this reason perhaps that, despite their appreciation of the aesthetic advance represented by Italian comedy, English sixteenth-century dramatists tend to exploit the exhilarating effects of intrigue with reservation, at least until the last decade of the century, as if trying to avoid associating the rhetorical achievement of a fortunate ending with the improvised deceptions required to bring it about. In Nicholas Udall's *Ralph Roister Doister* (1552) the intrigue which delays and delights the audience into anticipation of a comic ending swerves aside at the last moment to bestow the prize of the rich widow not on the improvising intriguers, but on a merchant called Gavin Goodluck whose steady providence has not been compromised by participation in the dramatic action. Shakespeare's *Comedy of*

[13] Chambers, *Elizabethan Stage*, iv. 317.

*Errors* (1594) adapts the plot structure of its Plautine model but allows the deceptions of the action to disclose good fortune as if of their own accord, without permitting any one of the deceived characters to participate festively in the opportunities offered by his or her errant situation. Indeed, it is remarkable how in Shakespeare's comedy the threat of insolvency is exploited to arouse an apparently gratuitous sense of identity crisis. In *Mother Bombie* (*c.*1590) Lyly similarly dissociates the good fortune of the denouement from the truant tavern-haunting slaves whose improvised deceptions effectively bring it about, for the titular Mother Bombie serves no other dramatic purpose than to foresee all, and the security of her provident knowledge foregrounds the dramatic providence of the plot itself.

It was not until 1598, and the first performance of Jonson's *Every Man in his Humour*, that an improvising participation in the festive opportunities offered by the commercialized leisure of contemporary London was overtly identified with good fortune brought about by a comic plot. In *Every Man In* Jonson elaborately ridicules the old-fashioned, admonitory image of commercialized urban leisure as the locus of prodigal corruption, crawling with parasites and thieves. Instead, his play offered both the urban reality and its fear-inducing moralized image as a hilarious, exhilarating source of entertainment and economic enterprise for articulate young men. The relation between wit and the city has changed; far from threatening to 'consume' him, the cultivation of a disreputable and opportunistic urban lifestyle becomes the mark of the young gentleman's social and financial providence. In this innovatory and specifically English version of humanist urban comedy, festivity is dramatized in all its overwhelming social and discursive potential as a plotless confluence of humours to be productively channelled and exploited by the ablest and most resourceful of the characters. Like Quintilian's affluent orator, Jonson's successful protagonist achieves his own ends by a combination of the self-mastery resulting from solitary premeditative study and a flexible social responsiveness to the gifts of the moment; a festive lifestyle offers him the opportunity of exploiting its sociable encounters and chance disruptions without threatening to immerse him totally. In *Every Man In* the exhilarating sense of opportunity offered by the urban confluence of heterogeneous languages, temperaments, weaknesses, and desires is reinforced by an imagery of flux and incontinence, as if the idle running on of tavern discourse and the impure mingling of bloods and linguistic registers were being divested of their old, pejorative associations with prodigal waste and promiscuous social loss to become (in the travestying figure of Cob the water bearer, for example) an extraordinary evocation of city life in the positive terms of its liquid assets—the refuse of kennels translated into an inexhaustible flow of overlooked social and financial opportunity. In the quarto of 1601 the city is Florence, not London, and the heroes' names—Prospero and Lorenzo di Pazzi—suggest the combination of discursive providence and tricksterish flexibility required to achieve the intended fortune, which in the closely guarded form of a wealthy merchant's sister is aptly named Hesperida. Jonson ensures that Prospero's emotional reserve makes his improvising witty eloquence compatible with long-term financial providence. Prospero and Lorenzo are able to enjoy and exploit the festivity of verbal incontinence, rendering down the obsessions, desires, and irrelevancies of their companions into a currency of humours with which to meet the contingent demands of their own plot. The 1601 quarto contrasts an older generation's cautious and outdated respect for the written text as a space in which to try and prove the productive resources of knowledge, with a younger generation's provident ability to discover the resources they need in the flow of action and conversation about them. Lorenzo senior is outraged by Prospero's dissipation of his discursive abilities in a conceitful letter inviting his son to town, but when the old man himself attempts to conceive a plot which will thwart his errant son his anxiety to preserve the integrity of thought as if it were a written text makes his plot an ineffectual labour of intention and reason.[14] Prospero, on the other hand, plays skilfully on the anxieties and desires of the people around him, thereby identifying his discursive providence with that of the dramatist Jonson himself. Both the dramatist and his creation display a consciousness that it is delay, the deception of expectation, that creates power by securing the emotions and anxieties of other people as 'humours' to be resourcefully channelled to productive ends. 'Wee'le prorogue his expectation a little', Prospero says when he hears that Lorenzo senior is in town. Where Udall in *Roister Doister* felt obliged to make a moral distinction between the providence of mercantile calculation and the expedient improvisations of dramatic intrigue, Jonson can emphasize the underlying similarity between the two modes of operation. His mer-

[14] Jonson, *Every Man In His Humour*, the quarto of 1601, II. i. 1–35, in *Works*, ed. C. H. Herford, P. Simpson, and E. Simpson, iii. 222–3.

chant Thorello, who bargains on the Exchange, reveals that he as well as Prospero knows the value of the emotional reserve which acts as a 'persuading spirit', channelling the anger or emotional weakness of others into the 'ready money' of compliance.[15] In a sense, the only difference between the merchant and the gallant in Jonson's play is that the latter is more resourcefully opportunistic, less likely to be hindered from his enterprise by any literature-induced anxiety about the prodigal loss and promiscuous devaluation of property (marital or financial) through the exchanges of commercialized urban festivity. Jonson's play marks the end of the moral distinction drawn between festive improvisation and solvent self-mastery by which Nashe was forced to deny himself the status of author and adopt that of improvident self-dissipating trickster. In Jonson's dramatic world (which was to form the basic of a distinctly English comedy of manners) participating in an improvised style of life and dialogic style of discourse (repartee) amid the opportunities for round-the-clock festivity offered by the metropolis becomes more sensationally productive than steady self-improvement by solitary reading or financial calculation; the tavern of *Every Man In* (appropriately called the 'Windmill' in the 1616 folio) offers a no less respectable opportunity for the productive channelling and financial exploitation of discursive exchange than does the nerve centre of urban prosperity, London's Royal Exchange itself.

Jonson's trickster gentlemen have absorbed the lessons of providence, and while they participate in worlds of urban festivity which they themselves may find time-wasting, distasteful, contaminating (*Bartholomew Fair* and the consumerized female social world of *Epicoene* are both ambivalently presented in this way) they strenuously preserve a sense of private self, resisting moral insolvency, precisely because they justify their participation in festivity by a productive exploitation of the resources it offers; they command the emotional and discursive flux it releases about them.[16] The achievement of such dramatic figures, reconciling as they do attitudes which had been mutually incompatible for half a century of pedagogic and propagandist discourse, is remarkable and extremely relevant to the ongoing transformation of economic attitudes in the seventeenth century. It is important to try and appreciate the depth of the conceptual change re-

[15] Ibid. II. iii. 221; II. iv. 143; and III. i. 4.

[16] See J. Haynes, 'Festivity and the Dramatic Economy of Jonson's "Bartholomew Fair" '.

quired to bring about a situation in which the discursive and social opportunities made available by a kind of festive insouciance—the improvising responses of wit—cease to be conceived as a threat to self-mastery and economic enterprise, and become its characteristic social properties. Reading Nashe in the context of this conceptual change enables us to understand how, by contrast, the improvisatory energy of Nashe's writing utterly resists absorption to any such productive end. Where Jonson makes the opportunities offered by festive gathering of people into a productive resource for certain witty individuals (just as on a commercial basis festivity inevitably becomes a resource of economic individualism) Nashe counters this tendency with an older, festive system of imagery in which discourse, people, and even time all resist being absorbed or exploited as productive resources because they are all conceived as existing in a vital, mutually generative relationship, capable of disintegration and decay. This system of imagery, traditionally associated with the promotion of fertility by the disintegrating agencies of laughter and mockery, was by no means obsolete or even ancient; it was as contemporary as the newer imagery of individualism. The extent and rapidity of the social change brought about by the humanist emphasis on individual providence and by a specifically English application of this emphasis to the urgent demands of economic recovery made enormous conceptual demands on Englishmen over little more than a generation. The social relations of a household economy, preserved in the discourse of popular festival, were neither absorbed by Nashe in Jonsonian style as the resources of individual productivity nor revived in the manner of Robert Herrick in a spirit of patrician nostalgia. Rather, their disruptive potential enables Nashe's writings, from *Summers Last Will and Testament* to *Lenten Stuffe*, to pit the changing discourses of moral and social values inconclusively against one another, making the moment of social transformation itself available for contemplation.

In her book on economic ideology and thought in the seventeenth century, Joyce Appleby includes a chapter on the poor considered as a productive resource.[17] That it was possible to conceive of the poor in this primarily economic way in the seventeenth century was, as we have seen, the result of a sixteenth-century discursive training which facilitated such resourceful transformative thought. It is both witty

[17] J. Appleby, *Economic Thought and Ideology in Seventeenth-Century England*, pp. 129–57.

and provident to conceive the causes and effects of economic adversity as discursive commonplaces—avarice, poverty—so as to be able to transform them into the resources of prosperity. Before the sixteenth century Englishmen would have been largely incapable of conceiving of people in terms of productive resources. But this discursive facility which enables the conceptual transformation of people into labour and resources had, as Appleby observes, social implications which remained concealed through the sixteenth and seventeenth centuries by an outward conformity to the older socio-economic relationship of lordship and service. Indeed, in England the transition from the feudal lordship-service relation to the capitalist relationship of individual and resources was so imperceptible that 'the categories of thought associated with capitalism appeared to the English as timeless forms imprinted on the very stuff of the human brain'.[18] Such an impression, of course, belies the sixteenth- and seventeenth-century situation, for, as Appleby insists, men could not respond positively to opportunities for further economic development without abandoning customary ways of holding and working the land. Ideological adjustment was required: 'the endorsement of new values, the acknowledgement of new occupations and the reassessment of the obligations of the individual to society . . . Before there could be new modes of behaviour, there had to be ideas to explain them'.[19]

The educational developments of the sixteenth century were responsible for encouraging the individual to become aware of the resource potential of the material and temporal environment as well as instilling in him a new moral obligation to provide for the future and to remain solvent. The premium on resourcefulness is evident in the specific direction taken by the economic policy of the Elizabethan government, which aimed at promoting national solvency through the issuing of incentives to enterprising individual projectors. A project was, as Joan Thirsk defined it, 'a practical scheme for exploiting material things'.[20] But the definition of 'things' here must be extended to cover temporal and human resource potential too. For financial profit was less essential to the worth of a project than its ingenuity—one could almost say its wit—in discovering concealed resource potential. Projectors were characteristically ingenious in their ability to realize the potential of material, temporal, and human resources which would otherwise be defined as idle (vagabonds, offcuts of

[18] Ibid. 8. [19] Ibid. 4. [20] Thirsk, *Economic Policy*, p. 1.

cloth, 'dead' or unproductive seasons of the year). J. U. Nef has pointed out that this preoccupation with the ingenious discovery of resource potential was peculiar to the development of the English economy: nothing like it was to be found on the Continent. It was at the end of the sixteenth century, he remarks, 'that men began to attach a value that was novel to inventive ideas whose only purpose was to reduce labour costs and to multiply production'.[21] Initially, as Joan Thirsk has shown, this premium on the exploitation of overlooked resources was linked to the reformers' concern over the wasteful exchange of valuable raw materials and the sacrifice of their productive potential for mere haberdashery items from overseas. They objected to paying for what it might profit them to produce within the realm, since fashionable and expensive items such as Spanish gloves were in fact made from otherwise unusable offcuts of leather. The earliest monopolies took the form of patents granting the right to individuals to gather material which would otherwise go to waste, rather in the way that the *De copia* style of education created wits which were capable of gathering and exploiting hidden opportunities disclosed by timely utterance. There were monopolies granted on the collection of 'lists, shreds and horns' and 'ashes and old shoes'.[22] Idle people became the equivalent to idle material in the resourceful projecting terms; John Spilman's paper-making monopoly granted him the right to employ vagabonds to gather rags from London streets. Seasonal time—which in the terms of a natural economy dictates the prosperity of human endeavour and continuance of human life—could now be conceived of as contributing to a productive human enterprise, such as Robert Payne's project for the manufacture of coloured woollen goods which proposed to exploit the enforced idleness of seasonal labour by having the woad cultivated and the wool dyed using the same employees at alternative seasons.[23] It is clear that although the project itself was a practical scheme, at the level of social relations it became a solvent of the conceptual structure of the traditional economic unit of the household which, whether manorial or belonging to a crafts guild, was based on ties of kinship and service, and prospered in accordance with the seasonal yield of non-transactable

[21] J. U. Nef, *Cultural Foundations of an Industrial Civilization*, pp. 60–1.

[22] W. H. Price, *The English Patents of Monopoly*, pp. 145, 151. See also Thirsk, *Economic Policy*, pp. 14–15.

[23] R. J. Smith, 'A Woad Growing Project at Wollaton in the 1580s'. See also Thirsk, *Economic Policy*, pp. 18–19.

land. The new economic unit was not the household but the individual whose life became central, not so much in terms of personal fulfilment as in the sense of an enterprise undertaken on society's behalf, a way of mastering the idle present and realizing its potential as a prosperous future. The need to adjust to a new concept of individual survival as a kind of premeditated enterprise to produce the future (rather than as an improvising collaboration with disintegrative and regenerative energies of seasonal time) emerges from endless sixteenth-century admonitions against improvidence and idle living. Shakespeare's sonnets contribute to this discourse, preoccupied as they are with the need to combat the devastating effects of time by labouring to produce oneself. Simply living is not enough; it is merely heading into 'the wastes of time'. One of the theses of the sonnets is a playful reversal of admonitions against prodigality and expenditure, arguing that apparent self-expenditure (in begetting children, or writing poetry) is in fact more provident than a retentive self-possession: 'For shame deny that thou bear'st loue to any, who for thy selfe art so vnprouident' (X). The teasing arguments of the sonnets depend throughout on an acceptance of the premise that what endures, what is productive for the future, is more valuable than prosperity beheld and enjoyed in the present; the poems consistently oppose the ephemeral outward wealth of the flowering rose to the distillation of the rose's scent, which becomes, because of its productivity for the future, a figure for substantial truth. True substance becomes that which is capable of producing and of being stored up to produce the future.

This privileging of future productivity over the prosperity of the present, insisting on the present as an illusion, an outward show, is typical of sixteenth-century discourse, as we saw from Nashe's contrast between the old bard hutch which concealed an invaluable treasure of future productivity and the alluring newly painted box, gaudily concealing nothing but futurelessness, the certainty of extinction (i. 131). In a land centred economy it is difficult to think of wealth in terms of storage and transaction, because the most valuable entity is the land itself which is less a possession than an environment. There are similar problems with the conception of storing, or transacting, time, since land and time together make up the generative environment that produces prosperity. We naturally talk about saving, wasting, or employing time, thereby expressing our sense that time exists as a material factor contributing to the success of our enterprise rather than that our enterprise (life) simply has its being in time. Medieval expressions of time, however, imply something more like the latter conception. Such phrases as 'pater noster wyle', argued E. P. Thompson, are characteristic of an 'attitude of submission and of nonchalant indifference to the passage of time, which no one dreams of mastering, using up, or saving'.[24] In traditional societies, according to Mircea Eliade, experience-laden time may only be 'accumulated' up to a certain point after which it becomes an intolerable and threatening burden which must be dissipated and renewed. Such a renewal may take the form of religious absolution, as in the Catholic tradition of the confession of sins, or it may take the form of an orgiastic ritual, such as is associated with the European Carnival.[25] Clearly there had always been a mercantile sector which made usurous transactions of time and a literate intellectual tradition which stored and made use of history. What was peculiar to the sixteenth century was a general diffusion of the idea that history and past experience were keys to survival in all the most practical spheres of life. The new idea that life was an investment of mental energy in the discovery of means to secure its own continuance and improvement must have had to struggle with the habits appropriate to an older way of life which acknowledged the necessity of destroying the impotent past as a ritualistic means of securing the fertility of the future.

The notion of providence as an individual responsibility, or even as a possibility open to the individual, was new in the sixteenth century. In writing on the moral virtues in the *Gouernour*, Elyot was careful to define the word providence: the concept was still strange in English. He identified it as a virtue proper to the individual, the capacity to exploit possibilities in order to determine as far as possible the outcome of one's labours. In a more traditional system of thought, however, dependence on 'providence' indicates almost the opposite. The providence of God forbids active exploitation of the environment in the interests of any individual; theoretically, landlords are stewards, distributors of God's plenty. When, in the early sixteenth century, this system was seriously disrupted by the changing patterns of trade which encouraged English landlords to become 'possessioners', exploiting land for grazing cattle and sheep, and enclosing commons, the reaction of mid-sixteenth-century preachers such as Latimer was

[24] E. P. Thompson, 'Time, Work Discipline and Industrial Capitalism', pp. 58–9.
[25] M. Eliade, *The Myth of the Eternal Return*, trans. W. R. Trask, p. 75.

to deplore the abomination of these 'vnnaturall lordes' who had upset the generative, distributive relationship of time and land, of lordship and service. The individual enterprise which Elyot would call providence was in this instance condemned by Latimer because it represented human interference in the providence of nature; 'monsterous and portentious dearthis made by man, not with standynge God doeth sende vs plentifullye the fruites of the earthe'.[26]

From Latimer's reaction it seems fairly clear that individual 'providence' had yet to be established as a moral responsibility. As yet there was no generally articulated doctrine that the individual has a social (and therefore moral) obligation to provide for himself. This doctrine was first established and widely disseminated in the sixteenth century; from aristocrats to artisans, young men were systematically taught the principle of regarding their lives as an expenditure to be balanced against an income that was not automatically self-renewing. England's Lord Treasurer wrote cautionary words to his son which give us some idea of how unassimilated were the basics of modern economic thought. Burghley proposes simple calculation as a check against the discomfort of insolvency: 'Beware that thou spend not above three of the four parts of thy revenue, nor above one-third part of that in thine house . . . For otherwise shalt thou live like a rich beggar in a continual want.'[27] For the middle classes the moral obligation to remain self-sufficient was spelt out in William Perkins's exhaustive instructions for devout and blameless living: 'Our riches must be imploied to necessarie vses. These are First, the maintenance of our owne goode estate and conditions.'[28] Even Nashe's idiosyncratically negative response to this kind of precept can only emphasize for us how new, how unassimilated, the imperative was. In 1593 he attacked the spreading of this new doctrine of providence: 'Ministers and Pastors . . . beeing couetous your selues, you preach nothing but couetous doctrine . . . That Text is too often in your mouthes, *Hee is worse then an infidel that prouides not for his wife and family*' (ii. 107).

The structure of the traditional household is intolerant of the conception of the individual as an economic unit with internalized anxieties about solvency and dreams of economic mastery, because its

[26] Latimer, 'The fyrst sermon of Mayster Hugh Latimer . . . before the Kynges Maiest.', in *Seven Sermons before Edward VI*, ed. E. Arber, p. 39.

[27] *Advice to a Son*, ed. L. B. Wright, p. 10.

[28] W. Perkins, *Works*, bk. iii, p. 148.

economy is dependent on the seasons. The source and continuance of prosperity is conceptually located in festivity, the distribution and consumption of wealth. The service traditionally rendered in return for the protection of lordship had etymological associations with festive distribution: the word lord in Old English is *hlaford* (loaf keeper), and servant is *hlafœta* (bread eater). But the providence of the loaf keeper is dependent upon the occasions of seasonal prosperity, and the obligations of mutual service were seasonally observed. There was no transaction of a quantity of benefits accorded by the lord against a quantity of rents and services rendered by the tenant, but 'a series of particular benefits was given in return for a series of particular renders, and the memory was preserved of the association of each benefit with the corresponding render'.[29] Gifts of food offered 'against Christmas', for example, suggest a sense of contributing to the feast as much as to the lord who would distribute it. Perishable wealth—food and drink—inevitably belongs to the time in which it is freshest and best consumed; hence, in the festive system of imagery, the ludicrous associations of stale or dried foodstuffs, such as stinking red herrings, or foods that are soon rotten, such as tripes and the innards that are used to make puddings. Before the drink trade began to be commercialized in the sixteenth century ale was a perishable festive drink; it could not keep and so was brewed specially by tenants for the occasions of communal feasting, hence the association in bride-*ales* and church-*ales*.[30] This conception of prosperity as occasional and ephemeral was utterly incompatible with the emergent discourse of economic individualism; in his comedy *Summers Last Will and Testament* Nashe exploits the possibilities of this incompatibility. Ver, the figure of Whitsun revelry, can make no account to the Summer Lord of how he has spent his wealth; he explains, nonchalantly: 'What I had, I haue spent on good fellowes; in these sports you haue seene, which are proper to the Spring, and others of like sort (as giuing wenches greene gownes, making garlands for Fencers, and tricking vp children gay) haue I bestowde all my flowry treasure, and flowre of my youth' (iii. 240–1). The discourse of temperance and solvency intervenes, trying to translate Ver into an admonitory *ex-*

[29] C. G. Homans, *English Villagers of the Thirteenth Century*, p. 258; see also M. E. James's excellent studies of social and conceptual change in the sixteenth century, 'The Concept of Order and the Northern Rising of 1569', and *Family, Lineage and Civil Society: A Study of Society, Politics and Mentality in the Durham Region, 1500–1640*, pp. 19–20, 183–7.

[30] Homans, *English Villagers*, p. 268.

*emplum*: 'A small matter. I knowe one that spent in lesse than a yere, eyght and fifty pounds in mustard and another that ran in det, in the space of foure or fiue yeere, aboue fourteen thousand pound in lute strings and gray paper'; but it is uttered by a fool (iii. 241). Ver's wealth was proper to the Spring, as the oxymoronic 'flowry treasure' beautifully suggests. Even more striking in Nashe's play is the conceptual challenge offered by the personification of Harvest, who calls attention to the distinction between mastery and the traditional conception of lordship when he reminds the possessive Summer lord that it is in fact the harvest time itself that occasions hospitality and distributes the feast. Harvest thus embodies the traditional conception of the lord as loaf keeper, both extending and debasing its social implications: 'I am the very poore mans boxe of pitie . . . there are more holes of liberality open in haruests heart than in a siue, or a dust-box. Suppose you were a craftsman, or an Artificer, and should come to buy corne of mee, you should haue bushels of mee; not like the Bakers loafe, that should waygh but sixe ounces' (iii. 261).

It is Harvest who feeds dependants and keeps open house: 'You obiect I feede none at my boord. I am sure if you were a hogge, you would neuer say so: for, surreuerence of their worships, they feed at my stable table euery day. I keepe good hospitality for hennes & geese: Gleaners are oppressed with the heauy burdens of my bounty: They rake me, and eate me to the very bones, Till there be nothing left but grauell and stones' (iii. 261). From Harvest's words emerges a link between the conception of the lord as the distributor of hospitality and the primitive notion of the festive lord or trickster, participation in whose disintegrating body revives the community or generates the possibility of good fortune. This latter implies a further link with Nashe the trickster-writer, who refers to his readers as his dependent god-children, to feast whom he has distributed all, unconcerned to reserve authorial credibility or to make the festivity of discourse serve a productive purpose, Jonsonian style.[31]

The traditional association of prosperity with the festive consumption of the gifts of the moment became unimaginable when the new obligations of individual solvency and productivity simply defined such a conception as 'waste' and 'excess'. Philip Stubbes in 1583 denied the festive conception of wealth altogether when he challenged the need to observe feasts on a communal and occasional basis. 'I

[31] See Nashe's remarks in *Lenten Stuffe*, iii. 225, and Ch. 5 below.

thinke it conuenient for one Freend to visite an other (at sometimes) as opportunitie & occasion offer it self', he wrote, 'but wherfore shuld the whole town, parish, village and cuntrey keepe one and the same day, and make such gluttonous feasts as they doo?'[32] Yet in the older way of thinking wealth was conceivable only as the moment of prosperity; communal consumption of the feast was a means of expressing and of evaluating wealth. Excess, too, was appropriate; of the gargantuan quantities of food and drink consumed at the harvest dinner of the carpenters' guild at Coventry in 1524 a modern historian remarks on what appears to be 'deliberate excess' at a time when the town's economy was seriously threatened.[33] No doubt the excess was deliberate, part of the heritage of practices involved in the traditional sense of 'economy' as 'keeping house'. Where wealth is perishable the conception of investment, transaction against the future, scarcely exists. The assumption is, rather, that liberal expenditure and festive consumption within the unit of the household guarantees prosperity and forms the basis of economy. Where a reformed commercial society stresses the dread of bankruptcy—the exhaustion of resources through over-consumption—traditional societies based on a natural economy emphasize the anxiety of rendering wealth sterile and infertile through hoarding, refusing to allow the disintegration and redistribution of material vitality. Thus the consequences of Harvest's imputed miserliness in *Summers Last Will* are automatically assumed to be the impoverishment of the generative earth:

> Haruest, heare what complaints are brought to me.
> Thou art accused by the publicke voyce,
> For an ingrosser of the common store;
> A Carle, that has no conscience, nor remorse
> But doost impouerish the fruitfull earth (iii. 259)

The social and religious ideals of a predominantly natural, subsistence economy were based on a seasonal understanding of wealth as regenerative through festive dissipation and distribution throughout the organism; that is, the household and its dependent neighbourhood. Thomas Lever, for all he abhorred monasticism, castigated the possessive individualism of the new style secular landlord by means of an almost grotesque image; new landlords

[32] Stubbes, *Anatomy of Abuses*, pt. I, p. 153.

[33] C. Phythian-Adams, *Desolation of a City: Coventry and the Urban Crisis of the Late Middle Ages*, p. 110.

absorb whole houses and neighbourhoods which the fat bellies of the monks had relieved through the dissipation and redistribution of hospitality. 'For yf ye were not starke blynd ye would se and be ashamed', preached Lever, 'that where as fyfty tunne belyed Monckes geuen to glotony fylled theyr pawnches, kept vp theyr house and relyued the whol country round about them, ther one of your gredye guttes deuowrynge the whole house and making great pyllage throughout the countrye, cannot be satisfyed.'[34] Festivity and hospitality are celebrated in seventeenth-century poetry as alternatives to an urban lifestyle where constant expenditure of resources is superficially more apparent than the concentration of financial opportunities; so Jonson congratulates Sir Robert Wroth on being able to leave an expense-incurring urban life to live at home with 'vnbought prouision blest'.[35] But where Jonson ingeniously figures the household economy with its festive conception of wealth as a resource to be mastered by the individual (it is the poet of 'To Penshurst' who suddenly emerges to absorb the feast he has made of it) Nashe tends rather to draw attention to the incompatibility of household and individual as moral and economic units. He brilliantly conflates the festive household and the individual struggling for solvency in the appropriately named landlord, Christmas, of *Summers Last Will and Testament*. As Christmas is both individual and household, the barred doors, the buttoned doublets fastening tight his home and body coalesce in a farcical exaggeration of the anxieties created by adjustment to the ideology of individualism. He glibly invokes all the arguments against hospitality: 'Gluttony is a sinne, & too many dunghills are infectious. A mans belly was not made for a poudring beefe tub: to feede the poore twelue dayes, & let them starue all the yeare after, would but stretch out the guts wider than they should be & so make famine a bigger den in their bellies than he had before' (iii. 285). For all his fear of unforeseen expenses Christmas is lavish in the distribution of classical *exempla* against prodigality: 'The scraping of trenchers you thinke would put a man to no charges. It is not hundreth pounds a yeare would serve the scullions in dishclouts . . . O it were a trim thing to send, as the *Romanes* did, round about the world for prouision for one banquet. I must rigge ships to *Samos* for

[34] T. Lever, 'A Sermon preached at Paul's Crosse, 13th Dec. 1550', in *Seven Sermons*, ed. E. Arber, p. 119.

[35] Jonson, 'To Sir Robert Wroth', in *Works*, ed. C. H. Herford and P. and E. Simpson, viii. 97.

Peacocks, to *Paphos* for Pigeons, to *Austria* for Oysters . . .' But the fool deflates this invalid rhetoric: 'O sir, you need not; you may buy them at London better cheape' (iii. 285–6). Christmas's house is a body sealed off ('I haue dambd vp all my chimnies', iii. 287), terrified of inadvertently releasing even its refuse as wealth. In bodily terms, as in the terms appropriate to a household economy, this behaviour is pernicious, impending vitality, impoverishing the neighbouring earth. Summer commands Christmas to 'breathe' his 'rusty gold' (iii. 287), recalling the imagery of the judgement day, in which the sin of avarice is associated with the decay and disease caused by the damning up of wealth. 'Your riches are corrupted' in the words of the Bible, 'Your gold and silver is cankered; and the rust of them shall be witness against you' (James 5: 2–3). In *Christes Teares Over Jerusalem* Nashe figuratively ascribed the putrefied air of plague-ridden London to the stagnant principles of economic individualism which invested in money and time, keeping 'gold and grain tyll it is mould, rusty, moath-eaten and almost infects the ayre with the stinche' (ii. 158).

Attitudes to servants were inevitably affected by the changeover from household to the individual and his resources. In the traditional household structure the lord did not master a labour force, but fed and kept house for numbers of kinsfolk and other dependants who rendered him various services and owed loyalty to his household and blood. A dialogue published in 1579 entitled *Cyuile and Uncyuile Life* revealed a complete transformation in attitudes towards the complex dependencies of the household. Urban life, with its demands on the individual's resources, transforms the dependent neighbour or godchild of the manorial lord into the employee of the substantial gentleman. The spokesman for what is traditionally understood by housekeeping and lordship contrasts the economics of his own household where 'hospitalitie is liberally kept, and many Children and Seruaunts daily fed, with all other commers' with that of his urban counterpart, whose criteria of solvency and efficiency demand that he keep 'no number of Seruaunts, but those that for necessary vses are imployable'.[36] Rationalizing the wastefulness of the traditional scheme, the country lord makes it quite clear that lordship is *defined* by a capacity to feed and keep house. The lord who lives meanly and privately erodes his own support, the devotion of his people. If he should 'bee no householder', the dialogue explains, 'nor

[36] *Cyuile and Vncyuile Life*, sig. EI$^{v}$.

keeper of seruaunts, you see that in his Countrey, neither the neighbours will loue him, nor y^e people do him reuerence'.[37]

The real assault on the traditional household conception of economy, of course, came about by the willingness of English merchants and landlords to participate in a European commerce which required English raw materials, and which produced inflation, unemployment and poverty, and a demand among Englishmen for imported consumer goods. The economic response involved devoting all the educational and discursive possibilities offered by humanism to the crucial task of conveying the idea that wealth is far from being regenerative, that resources run out, and that opportunities to be exploited are not part of a ripening seasonal time which demands festive celebration, but exist only to the extent that the individual who wishes to prosper by them is sober and solvent enough to look to their productive possibilities for the future. The future becomes the *locus* of prosperity, and the experience of prosperity as well-being is translated into the exhilaration of productive investment. Within the discourse of antiprodigal admonition, the plainness and simplicity of the traditional English householder became a nostalgic commonplace, somewhat in conflict with complaints against traditional excess.[38] But before this commonplace took hold of the imagination it was clear that the household style of economy, with its obligations of festive expenditure, was no longer viable. In 1539 Thomas Cromwell received a letter from the Mayor of Coventry explaining that the costs of hospitality for citizens and strangers over the period of Candlemas alone would have been sufficient for him to 'keipp his house half a yiere after'.[39] The households of the craft guilds were facing the same economic problems. 'At Corpus Christi tide', the Mayor continued, 'the poore comeners be at suche charges with ther playes & pagyontes, that they fare worse all the yiere after.'[40]

The century saw first massive cutbacks in traditional pastimes and housekeeping and then, more gradually, restraint on luxury imports and the beginning of a systematic policy to make England self-supporting in the manufacture of consumer goods. Thus in the course of the century there developed an increased awareness of the potential

[37] Ibid., sig. F4[4]; see also James, 'The Concept of Order and the Northern Rising'.

[38] See Smith, *Discourse*, pp. 20–2, 81–3.

[39] Phythian-Adams, *Desolation of a City*, p. 263.

[40] Ibid. See also P. Clark, *English Provincial Society from the Reformation to the Revolution*, pp. 39–44.

productive value of time and land; the entities 'time' and 'land' came to be seen less as vital creators of glut and scarcity than as inert resources to be invested in human enterprises which would guarantee future solvency or profit. Release of wealth on an unprecedented scale after the dissolution of the monasteries no doubt quickened a more general awareness of wealth in terms of quantitatively exploitable possibilities. In one anonymous treatise published at the turn of the century, we see how not only land, but also the other residual components of monasticism—time and labour—could be included in a calculation of potential resources for national solvency. The author makes such a calculation possible by considering all those who had previously been 'idly' occupied, as 'Monkes, chanons, fryers, chauntrypriestes, pardonners, heremites' and making these human resources equivalent to the temporal resources expended by the lay population in ritualistic activity: 'the tyme which the residue . . . did bestow in going of pilgrimages, in caruing painting & gylding of Images, in making of torches, and wax candels, in keping of so many supersticious holydays'.[41] Putting these human and temporal resources together, the author estimates the net result as being approximately a third of the total work resources (or man-hours) which the country might otherwise be expected to yield. Or, as he expresses it, 'as thogh the thyrd part of y^e men of this realm had then continuallye lyued in Idelnes as touching any necessary busines'.[42] Now that these man-hours have, by the dissolution of the monasteries, been diverted from 'idelnes and idell works' the author proposes that they be invested in the production of such necessary wares, 'all things ready made of iron, sope, rape oyle',[43] etc. as would make England independent of foreign imports.

At one level this treatise bears witness to a growing sophistication of economic awareness which manifests itself more generally in a new preoccupation with statistical calculation, both in the management of manorial estates (more to remain solvent than to realize profits) and as guides to economic policy. By the end of the century statistics are no longer a purely mercantile concern. J. U. Nef relates how in 1591 Lord Buckhurst confused the customs officers by asking for a year by year account of coal exports for the previous seven years. The officers misunderstood, returning a total for the seven year period with an

[41] *Pyers Plowmans exhortation unto the lordes knights and burgoysses of the Parlyamenthouse* (1549), sig. A4^r.

[42] Ibid.

[43] Ibid., sig. A8^{r-v}.

average: 'The distinction between the average traffic and the *rate of increase* was still meaningless to these customs officers', observes Nef, 'but the distinction was obviously clear to Buckhurst'.[44] Buckhurst of course was, like Smith, Burghley, Cobham, and others, a product of the mid-century humanist 'revolution' in education.

The breakdown of the household organization of the guilds, together with the movement of the aristocracy into business and civil service, resulted in traditional lordship being increasingly identified with mastery or employer-status. No longer a keeper of house and servants, the governor/lord now masterminded the investment of time, material, and labour in order to set people on work, securing their solvency and his profit. We can contrast Elyot's synthesis of old and new in his still organic conception of economic relations as mutual service and subsistence in the 'body lyuyng' of the commonwealth where 'the husbandeman fedeth hym selfe and the clothe maker',[45] or More's definition of the altruistically productive commonweal as 'one big household'[46] with the more radical vision of Thomas Smith, who shifted the crucial emphasis from one of mutual service in an organism to one of mutual endeavour in non-organic production: 'So in making of a house there is the master that would have the house made, there is the carpenter, and there is the stuff to make the house withal; the stuff never stirs till the workman do set it forward, the workman never travails but as the master provokes him with good wages, and so he is the principal cause of this housemaking.'[47] It is important, I think, to appreciate how neatly the intellectual providence of the entrepreneur or projector slotted into the old social paradigm of the lord as provider or bread giver. Thus Robert Hitchcocke's proposal for the establishment of a national herring fishery (which has already been quoted for the enthusiasm with which it envisaged turning the parasitical monster of vagrancy into a productive labour force) offered itself to readers as an act of intellectual hospitality, a 'feast' which would provide for the nation's future.[48] Real feasts fell into redundance as social expressions of prosperity; they were replaced by printed testimonies to the benevolence of the entrepreneur who 'set so many thousands awork'.[49] The synthesis of good housekeeper

[44] Nef, *Cultural Foundations*, p. 13.

[45] Elyot, *Gouernour*, pp. 1, 5.

[46] Thomas More, *Utopia*, trans. P. Turner, p. 85.

[47] Smith, *Discourse*, p. 96.

[48] Hitchcocke, *Pollitique Platt*, sig. ***r.

[49] D. C. Coleman, 'Labour in the English Economy of the Seventeenth Century', p. 280.

and provident employer helped to bridge a conceptual gap between the old socio-economic relations and the new. Thomas Deloney blended the ideals in the figure of his benevolent entrepreneur Jack of Newberry, a clothier who keeps good house for his servant-dependants as well as setting them on work. As in the old tradition, superfluity rather than efficiency signifies the prosperity of the household and the honour of its lord:

> Eachweeke ten good fat Oxen he
> Spent in his house for certainty.[50]

Nashe's social vision is remarkable for the way in which it rejects this kind of synthesis, indeed provokes awareness of its spuriousness. 'Lordship', translated into Smith's scheme of master, labour, and material, might as easily be equated with the raw material as with the capital; it all depends to which one attributes the stimulus of industry. Nashe foregrounds this ambiguity when in *Lenten Stuffe* he praises Yarmouth's commodity, the red herring, as the 'good Lord and master' of the people, a provident *pater patriae* who 'sets a worke thousands' (iii. 180) without apparently claiming the exclusive social and economic privileges of men whose government is as thriftily self-interested as their patronage rights are lordly. This Yarmouth red herring, however, turns out to be a fantastic, festive displacement of the London government, which is exclusive enough in its absolute monopoly of discursive interpretation and economic opportunity.

It has not been the aim of this chapter to argue that Nashe's texts advocate a return to the festive opportunism of a subsistence economy or even to suggest that it is possible to compare the quality of the social relations fostered by such an economy with those which answer the needs of possessive individualism. Joan Thirsk has argued convincingly that projects actually helped to keep up traditional social relations when they were undertaken by local lords and gentry to employ their impoverished tenantry rather than simply as a means to realize the resource potential of the anonymous 'poor'.[51] My interest has been in the conceptual and moral adjustments required to make such economic adaptability possible. I have set the old and new economic units of household and individual side by side in order to

50 *The Novels of Thomas Deloney*, ed. M. E. Lawlis, p. 27.

51 See J. Thirsk, 'Projects for Gentlemen, Jobs for the Poor: Mutual Aid in the Vale of Tewkesbury, 1600–1630', in Thirsk (ed.), *The Rural Economy of England*, pp. 237–307.

suggest how the new might have been conceivable in terms of the old, and how the humanist emphasis on improvisatory, discursive resourcefulness helped to conceal a conceptual transition by endorsing the opportunism associated with a tricksterish response to seasonal time, while transforming the moral and economic significance of such opportunism. The tricksterish capacity to turn all things to opportunity has its place in the development of a productive consumer economy; hence the English humanists' concern to incriminate tricksterish 'Italianate' literary forms which celebrated their own ingenuity without representing its long-term ends. English humanists needed to promote the association between providence, industry, and ingenuity that Elyot had made when he wrote that 'they that be called Industrious, do most craftily and depely understande in all affaires what is expedient, and by what meanes and wayes they maye sonest exploite them. And those thinges in whome other men travayle, a person industrious lightly and with facility spedeth, and findeth newe wayes and meanes to bring to effect that he desireth.'[52] One moral and literary effect of this was the development, at a popular level of a 'provident' form of the traditionally amoral 'Tyl Ulenspiegel' style of jest book; in this provident form, which began with Elizabethan coney-catching literature and became the staple mode of popular English criminal narrative, the tricksterish jests which invited the reader's irresponsible complicity could be invested back into the promotion of long-term economic responsibility by hanging the trickster as a criminal. On a more sophisticated literary and social level, English dramatists developed a 'humourous' style of intrigue comedy in which gentlemen might display tricksterish affinities with impunity since their apparently gratuitous indulgence in rowdy commercialized festivity was a socially sanctioned way of maximizing urban opportunities to secure longer-term good fortune. One of the reasons why Nashe's writing is so interesting in this transitional period is that it adapts tricksterish techniques in ways which resist these impersonally productive implications. Nashe conceives of discourse itself in the vital conditions of utterance, which, as soon as it tries to operate with productive anonymity, becomes 'stale', communicating this staleness to readers by seeming to disintegrate and mock itself, as if mediated by a fool. So it is that, in the historical moment of the inception of a provident literature of roguery, Nashe's

[52] Elyot, *Gouernour*, p. 100.

*Unfortunate Traveller* turns such a literature into a series of utterances which are already stale, informing against themselves. In order to understand how this comes about, however, it is necessary to consider in detail the significance of festivity and popular pastimes in Nashe's writing.

# 5
# Nashe and Popular Festive Pastime

I HAVE been arguing that humanist education, with its emphasis on the mastery of self and of circumstances through a mastery of literary discourse, helped to bring about changes in England's economic structure by encouraging more masterful, resourceful attitudes towards the material and temporal environment. What my argument needs at this point is some evidence for how people thought about time and its relation to their lives before education and reform affected their outlook. This is not something that literary sources are likely to provide. For the literature which describes traditional English life is almost inevitably written from the standpoint of reform. The meaning of customary ways remains obscure; to the reformer they are understandably nothing but 'idleness', a waste of resources. We have already seen how one anonymous writer in the 1550s could calculate the increase of man-hours available since the Dissolution, when people ceased to devote so much time to 'idelnes and idell works' and the 'keeping of so many supersticious holydays'.[1] According to John Northbrooke more than half the year had been taken up, in pre-Reformation days, 'in loytering & vaine pastimes, & in restrayning men from their hand labors'.[2] Pastimes are always dismissed by the reformers as idle and vain; indeed, apart from Elyot's attempt to extract profitable doctrine from the pastime of dancing (familiar to us through T. S. Eliot) there is no contemporary account of traditional pastimes which can help us to understand their positive significance as a social institution. Even when festivals are described in detail by contemporaries the aim is invariably to stimulate the urge for reform. The most detailed contemporary account we have, Barnabe Googe's *Popish Kingdom* (1570), is a translation from the German of Thomas Kirchmeyer or 'Naogeorgus', a Protestant whose zeal alienated him from Luther and drove him into exile in Switzerland. Impelled by his contempt for all popish rites and superstitions, he compiled an extensive account of

[1] *Pyers Plowmans exhortation*, sigs. A4$^{r}$–A8$^{v}$.
[2] Northbrooke, *Treatise*, sig. D54$^{r}$.

the popular festivities of the Catholic year. Googe's rendering is accordingly invaluable as detailed observation but negligible as means of access to the significance of popular festivity for the participants.

We know that despite contemporaries' use of the blanket term 'idleness', the feasts and pastimes of the pre-Reformation calendar took many forms and, we can safely surmise, fulfilled a variety of social functions. Late medieval England apparently saw no diminution but rather an increase in the amount of ritualistic and festive activity participated in by all levels of society.[3] This excess of expenditure on festival and ritual was cut back when the inflation that was to continue throughout the sixteenth century began.[4] In one of the ironic moments of his *Discourse* Sir Thomas Smith allows a merchant (whose irresponsible attitudes to import and export are in fact at the root of the inflation) to comment on the measures recently taken against the wastefulness of traditional life:

> such poverty reigns everywhere [he complains] albeit there be many things put down which beforetimes were occasions of much expense—as stage plays, interludes, May games, wakes, revels, wagers at shooting, wrestling, running and throwing the stone or bar, and besides that pardons, pilgrimages, offerings and many other such things—yet I perceive we be never the wealthier but rather the poorer.[5]

Smith's merchant gives us some indication of the pervasiveness and variety of the activities which filled peoples' lives for as much as half the year—activities which could hardly be described in our terms as useful or productive. Because it is not cast in the form of a polemic against the ideological threat of pastime, but rather as a neutral observation about the expense such a way of life incurred, Smith's list helps to bring home a sense of how arbitrary this enforced abandonment of ritual activity must have seemed to some. Pastimes might be outlawed but attitudes could not change overnight; in any case we know that holiday customs lived on among children and country people for centuries after society's governors ceased to be active participants. We must imagine the thinking men of the sixteenth century being intolerant of the disorder, the idleness, the lack of social responsibility fostered by traditional pastime, all the while appreciating its significance in a way which we can scarcely recapture. The duality of

[3] See C. Phythian-Adams, *Local History and Folklore*, p. 10; C. R. Baskervill, 'Dramatic Aspects of Medieval Folk Festivals in England', p. 29.

[4] Clark, *English Provincial Society*, p. 39.

[5] Smith, *Discourse*, p. 18.

this vision is perhaps expressed in the writings of such humanists as Erasmus and Rabelais, where an association is made between the conceptual freedoms offered by humanism (its rigour and rationality notwithstanding) and the licensed foolery of traditional pastimes unreformed by humanist thought.

None of this, however, helps us very much in thinking about how pastime might have shaped the consciousnes of time and wealth itself. Better than a text in this respect, perhaps, is Bruegel's famous depiction of the *Battle of Carnival and Lent*. In this painting the actual passage of time is visualized in the playing out of the seasons' pastimes round the village square. The comprehension of human existence in its temporal dimension enabled incompatible values to coexist in a state of comic (because perennial) antagonism to one another. This is clear in the domination of the picture by the struggle between the effigies of Carnival and Lent, and the division of the square into the various activities proper to either way of thinking. But, as Claude Gaignebet has explained, the square is not divided into two static halves. The different activities represented show that it is a calendar, stretching from Carnival back to Candlemas and from Lent forward to Easter.[6] Groups of villagers play the succession of pastimes that hasten the season on to its farcical demise at the approach of Lent. From Christmas to Candlemas there are processions of kings and lepers; the children celebrate by electing their own king; in February follow the games of Valentin and the wild-man Orson, with the election of the Carnival king, the celebration of a mock-marriage (a charivari) to the accompaniment of drinking and dancing. The regular personification of the season's pastime in the election, celebration and jubilant destruction of its own particular 'king' suggests something about the way in which pastimes shaped a general conception of time. Instead of being an inert resource, a supply of days or weeks, time becomes the effective agent of all activity.

Although Bruegel's painting represents the Netherlands and Googe's literary rendering of the same theme is translated from a German account, there is plenty of evidence to suggest that pastimes marked the turning seasons of the English year in a not dissimilar manner. The games we now regard as an amorphous body of children's playground amusements were once the occupation of a whole parish at particular times of the year. Historians and folklorists

[6] C. Gaignebet, 'Le Combat de Carneval et de Carême de P. Bruegel (1559)'.

have between them reconstructed a calendar very similar to the one Bruegel depicts, distinguishing the forms of misrule proper to Christmas, Epiphany and the New Year from the outdoor sports of Shrovetide, onward through Whitsuntide and the revelry of May games and Midsummer to the festivals of Harvest home, before the austere season of Advent anticipates once again the riotous succession of festivals after Christmas.[7] It is true that we hear more of Summer lords and May games and games of Robin Hood in England than we do of Carnival itself. But this need not prevent us from thinking of English pastimes as being 'carnivalesque' occasions. Robin Hood was a specially English version of the type of fool-lord that we associate with Carnival. His rule brought in the licentious 'order' of the greenwood just as other mock authority figures licensed misrule at Christmas or Carnival time.[8] Carnival itself is an occasion particularly rich in literary and historical allusions, but it makes sense, as Peter Burke writes, to think of every festival as 'a miniature Carnival because it was an excuse for disorder and because it drew from the same repertoire of traditional forms, which included processions, races, mock battles, mock weddings, and mock executions'.[9]

Presumably then, all the games and pastimes we read about in the sixteenth century carried more or less 'carnivalesque' associations for contemporaries, since they were especially indulged during times of general misrule, when playing the fool was allowed. Nashe's constant allusions to specific forms of pastime (he is often cited as a source by authorities on the history of children's games) certainly seem to charge his writings with an atmosphere of carnivalesque irresponsibility. His characters all seem to have a *penchant* for idle pastimes; Will Summers, of *Summers Last Will and Testament*, declares his passion for gambling at 'spanne Counter, or Iacke in a boxe' (iii. 279); Pierce Penilesse observes that antiquated ladies of fashion have complexions wrinkled deep enough to hide false dice and 'play at cherrypit' (i. 181); Jack Wilton, the narrator of *The Unfortunate Traveller*, comments that doctors may as well have played at 'shooe the Gander' (ii. 230—a Christmas game) for all the use they could be during the great sweating sickness. Equally futile in Jack's eyes is religious dispute; to him the theological differences thrashed out bet-

[7] A. R. Wright, *Moveable Festivals*; Phythian-Adams, *Local History*, pp. 21-5; Baskervill, 'Dramatic Aspects', p. 29.

[8] See D. Wiles, *The Early Plays of Robin Hood*.

[9] P. Burke, *Popular Culture in Early Modern Europe*, p. 195.

ween Luther and Carolostadius at Wittenberg are nothing more than a game of 'leuell coyle' (ii. 250—apparently from the French 'lever le cul', to shift the backside as in musical chairs). Contentiousness is generally caricatured by Nashe in terms of Shrovetide aggression: thus the controversial text of *Lenten Stuffe* excuses itself as a game of 'shettlecocke' (iii. 225) while the great literary scuffle with Harvey becomes a cock fight (iii. 30). Pastime even becomes a somewhat irreverent metaphor for poetic re-creation. In *Lenten Stuffe* Hero dreams that she and Leander are 'playing at checkestone with pearles in the bottome of the sea' (iii. 197). Originally played with knucklebones, the game here seems to temper the anticipation of the lovers' drowning with a delicate suggestion of the poetic sea-change wrought upon them by the divine muse of '*kit Marlow*' (iii. 195)[10]

Not that this preoccupation with pastime need in itself demonstrate anything new or significant about Nashe's poetics. After all, Sidney refers to pastime a great deal and, as Katherine Duncan-Jones observes, devotes his longest poem to describing the movements in a game of barley-break.[11] But Sidney is capable of making us conscious of pastime as a culpable waste (an exchange of talents for toys) even as he indulges in it; Astrophil's playful ingenuity is almost defiantly displayed, and the defiance is a response to a critical consciousness of the game as one in which 'my youth doth waste, my knowledge brings forth toyes'.[12] Nashe's attitude is just the opposite. His writings make pastime their positive term of value. Rather than using pastime as a pejorative metaphor for poetic activity, he refers to his text as the kind of game which licenses him to expose everyone else's pretensions about the profitability of what they are doing. In this perspective human endeavour is not seen from the vantage point of its aims and consequences (emphasizing the power of the individual in determining his own future) but from the vantage point of the experience itself, implicitly questioning definitions of profit and prosperity. Seen as pure inconsequential experience, pure pastime, frenetic human activity both mocks its own pretensions to achievement and derives

[10] For discussions of these games, 'spanne-counter', 'shoe the gander', 'cherry pit', and 'leuel coyle', see A. B. Gomme, *The Traditional Games of England, Scotland and Ireland*, i. 66, 329, and ii. 192, 210; J. Strutt, *The Sports and Pastimes of the People of England*, ed. J. E. Cox, pp. 270–94; Wright, *Moveable Festivals*, p. 28. For 'checkestones' see 'jackstone' (*OED*), the older form of 'jacks', which was probably originally played with knucklebones—see *The Colloquies of Erasmus*, trans. C. R. Thompson, 'Knucklebones or the Game of Tali', pp. 432–41.

[11] Duncan-Jones, 'Sidney's Toys', p. 169.

[12] Sidney, *Poems*, p. 174.

pleasure from that mockery in the form of an improvised game. The effect is rather like that of Bruegel's carnival crowd improvising their holiday procession out of the utensils of their working lives; Nashe improvises word games out of the materials of profitable significance.

The most extreme example of this is *Lenten Stuffe*. Here the experience of reading or writing is not referred to as a profitable gathering of knowledge, but as an improvised song and dance act, what the Elizabethans called a jig.[13] As spontaneous combinations of words, dance, and music, jigs were quintessentially celebrations made out of the materials of the moment. In *Lenten Stuffe* Nashe's professed subject is the gain brought to Yarmouth by the red herring, but his rendering redefines the very notion of prosperity as one of felt activity. It fits, then, that this prosperity should be expressed as a dance (which the Russian formalist Victor Shklovsky once defined as a walk 'constructed to be felt')[14] and that rhetorical divisions should be replaced by 'crashes' or bouts of dance music: 'on with our game as fast as wee may, & to the gaine of the red herring againe another crash' (iii. 183). Assonance plays with the words which would otherwise signify the evaluative intention of the oration ('game . . . gaine . . . againe'), thus mocking and frustrating the possibility of any sum total in celebration of the linguistic process itself. Gainful activity celebrates itself as game, revealing pastime as something more than just an evasion of productive activity, perhaps as a way of acknowledging the *experience* of wealth, which is beyond the expressive scope of calculation. Everywhere in Nashe's writing, the opposition between 'profitable knowledge' and 'toys' is broken down; edifying *exempla* become pretexts for play. At the beginning of *Summers Last Will and Testament* Nashe refers to the authority of Scipio and Laelius who 'by the sea side played at peeble-stone' (iii. 235). Cicero, Nashe's source, only says that they collected pebbles but in Nashe's text where serious endeavour is stripped of its consequentiality, an *exemplum* of idleness like this assumes the shaping power of an improvised game.

What is the source of this shaping energy? In Nashe's writing, as in traditional pastime, comic energy seems to spring from the pleasure of improvising a response to the very consciousness of ephemerality. Humanism, creating the possibility of control over the cumulative,

[13] C. R. Baskervill, *The Elizabethan Jig and Related Song and Drama*, pp. 9-11.

[14] Quoted by Ann Jefferson, 'Russian Formalism' in *Modern Literary Theory: A Comparative Introduction*, ed. A. Jefferson and D. Robey, p. 19.

long-term effects of human action, introduced a sense of responsibility for the future which rendered the old comic intimacy with ephemerality and bodily disintegration unnecessary and incomprehensible. So it is important for us, trying to understand the carnivalesque energy of Nashe's texts, to pay some attention to customary pastime as part of a seasonal cycle. This is not to be understood as a claim for the subversive potential of popular festive pastime *per se*, but as a means of understanding how a discourse derived from popular festive imagery and idiom could function as a challenge to the ideological assumptions behind the profitable reading of Elizabethan texts.

A comic apprehension of time as materially disintegrative becomes the shaping impulse of seasonal pastimes because the games themselves are responses to the sense of transition from one state of being to another. The English name for Carnival, Shrovetide, identifies it as marking the tide or approach of shriving, or purging oneself from carnal excesses. Barnabe Googe's rather clumsy verse makes the connection clear:

> Now when at length the pleasant time of Shrouetide comes in place,
> And cruell fasting dayes at hande approch with solemne grace:
> Then olde and yong are both as mad, as ghestes at Bacchus feast.

As late as Ash Wednesday, Googe exclaims, the riot continues, and the farewell to pastime demands its own mock-funeral, making an excuse for more pastime:

> Yet here no stay of madnesse now, nor end of follie is,
> With mirthe to dinner straight they go, and to their woonted playe,
> And on their deuills shapes they put, and sprightish fond araye.
> Some sort there are that mourning go, with lantarnes in their hande,
> While in the day time *Titan* bright amid the skies doth stande:
> And seeke their shroftide *Bacchanals*, still crying euery where,
> Where are our feastes become? Alas, the cruell fastes appere.
> Some beare about a herring on a staffe and loud do rore,
> Herrings, herrings, stinking herrings, puddings now no more.
> And hereto joyne they foolish playes, and doltish dogrell rimes,
> And what beside they can invent, belonging to the times.[15]

Googe draws attention to the improvisatory nature of festive invention; its products are 'belonging to the times'. He also indicates how

[15] Barnabe Googe, *The Popish Kingdome* (1570), sigs. O3ᵛ and P1ʳ.

the form of pastime is dictated by the impulse of riddance even to the extent of taking pleasure in bidding farewell to festivity itself. Games and ballads associated with the pre-Reformation calendar dramatize the seasons as a continuous farce involving the desecration, expulsion, and triumph of one ephemeral lord over another. A ballad of Mary Tudor's reign accuses Lent of driving out his predecessor, the anarchic and generous lord of Christmas: 'jentill Cristmas, with his myrry madnes/Thowe doyste hime exyle'.[16] All the seasons were thus conceived in antagonistic relation to one another, the young triumphing over the old, the lean over the fat, or the merriments of Carnival, Christmas, and summer combating the privations of Lent, Advent, and winter. The strife of Summer and Winter was as prominent as that of Carnival and Lent. Googe describes the summer as a boy dressed 'all in greene' and in 'youthful fine araye' challenging Winter 'clad in mosse' with hair 'hoare and graye'.[17] Austere Advent is cursed and sent on his way in carols that welcome Christmas, but Lent must be grudgingly brought in eventually to purge the excesses that continue through the days between Christmas and Carnival, 'Lenton stuffe ys cum to the towne', as Elderton's ballad says.[18] A constant, unbroken succession of seasonal combats and triumphs gives the very notion of change a comic, sceptical energy. The hierarchy of values is in constant oscillation; one day it is right to be excessive and eat and drink too much, the next it is right to fast and pray. Printed versions of pastimes suggest a broader consciousness of oscillation as interdependence; in *The debate and stryfe betwene Somer and Wynter* the old, defeated Winter reminds his younger antagonist that a succeeding winter will in course of time render him 'full lene', purging the summer surfeits that would otherwise be 'venymus' to the generative earth.[19]

If this driving out of one season by another is a central feature of seasonal pastime, then abuse itself is obviously essential to its creative energy. Combats apparently took place in the context of communal feasting, thereby highlighting the exuberant violation of material and ethical boundaries involved in both. The flyting and gargantuan

[16] '[W]o[e] worthe the[e], Lenttone', *Songs and Ballads chiefly of the Reign of Philip and Mary*, ed. T. Wright, p. 12.

[17] *Popish Kingdome*, sig. P2ʳ.

[18] W. Elderton, 'A newe ballad, entytled Lenton stuff', *Songs and Ballads*, ed. Wright, LX, p. 188.

[19] Anon., *The debate and stryfe betwene Somer and Wynter*, ed. J. O. Halliwell, p. 10.

feasting of the shepherds in medieval mystery plays seems to have this in common with the combats and junketings essential to traditional games of Robin Hood.[20] Shrovetide, though more usually associated with eating and drinking, was also in England the occasion of combative and aggressive games, such as cock-fighting, bear-baiting, tug-of-war and, as Alice Gomme writes, 'a contest, nominally that of a football match . . . in reality a fight between two sections of the town . . . the victors . . . announced by the joyful ringing of their parish bells'.[21]

Pastimes of rivalry and abuse characteristically polarized antagonits according to a hierarchical stratification (the old versus the young, the man versus the woman, the justice versus the thief) only to destroy the integrity of these polarizations as though they were seasonal oscillations. In the traditional May games or games of Robin Hood, the sheriff with his robes of office would be stripped and beaten by Robin, who was a version of the Summer lord, an outlaw and a buffoon. It did not follow from this, however, that Robin's holiday 'authority' resembled that of the sheriff; he remained a buffoon, a mockery-man to be sported with and humiliated by others.[22] The very notion of 'victory', of 'lordship' in the context of seasonal pastime, is defined by an inherent lack of integrity, an ambiguity of status. The 'chiefest man' at Christmas revels, is he who can 'finde out the fondest kinde of playes' according to Googe, and he is accordingly honoured with derision, for the children follow him 'crying foole'.[23]

Seasonal kings lack temporal integrity as well as integrity of status. Pastimes tend to centre on the passage of sovereignty, the succession of one king after another. Barnabe Googe and Philip Stubbes both make mention of pastimes in which the election of mockery kings (kings of Twelfth tide, lords of Summer) features as a distinct pastime,[24] while the impending death of the fool-king provides the pastime central to all carnivalesque ritual, the basis for trials, confessions, mock testaments, funerals, and so forth. In the Lincolnshire revels of 1601 a play called 'the Death of the Lord of Kyme' was

[20] F. M. Cornford, *The Origin of Attic Comedy*, pp. 70–100; Wiles, *Robin Hood*, pp. 32, 41–2; V. A. Kolve, *The Play Called Corpus Christi*, pp. 155–60. Throughout this chapter I am indebted to M. Bakhtin's *Rabelais and his World*.

[21] Gomme, *Traditional Games*, i. 134–7; Wright, *Moveable Festivals*, pp. 26–8.

[22] Wiles, *Robin Hood*, pp. 40–6.

[23] *Popish Kingdome*, sig. O4r.

[24] Ibid., sigs. O1v–O2r; Stubbes, *Anatomy of Abuses*, pt. I, p. 147.

played to 'make an ende of the Sommer Lord game'.[25] Middleton's *Inner Temple Masque* presents a whole series of holiday kings in various stages of disintegration and decay. The masque opens with the death of the Old Year who is reported to be 'full of diseases: he kept no good diet'. Thereafter it centres on the 'sickness' and decay of Kersmas, of Christmas, which coincides with the pastime of electing the Epiphany king and queen. The games of mock election, mock testament and mock funeral are conflated in Middleton's version:

> *D*[*octor*] AL. *Kersmas*['s]? Why, let me see;
> I saw him very lusty a' Twelfth Night.
> PLUM [porridge]. Ay, that's true, sir; but then he took his bane
> With Choosing King and Queen:
> Has made his will already, here's the copy.[26]

The presence of the doctor in Middleton's masque recalls the doctor of the mummers' play or the quack doctor of folk drama who magically revives and rejuvenates the old fool-king after his 'surfeit swell'd' death.[27] In Aristophanic comedy these motifs of seasonal rejuvenation and banishment are apparently present in the combat of agonist and antagonist. The 'bad' adversary is driven out with mockery and abuse by the 'good' adversary, who then becomes king. The adversaries are, however, essentially indistinguishable. They are in effect identical twins, and while the banishment of one is associated with dismemberment and destruction (a body torn and dispersed across the fields), the sovereignty of the other is associated with the not dissimilar process of 'concoction'; his rejuvenated body is recreated, as it were, from the dismembered body of his adversary.[28] Throughout Europe the personification and dismemberment of the season was the basis of festival. In Italy the effigy of an old woman was burnt at Epiphany; Googe mentions an effigy of Satan being smashed to pieces at Easter time, drenching participants with water. The trial and execution of Carnival was common on the Continent, and in England Lent was personified in Jack of Lent who processed to his execution and made his confessions, or was burnt or beaten in the form of a straw effigy dressed in rags and tatters. Straw or corn

25 N. J. O'Conor, *Godes Peace and the Queenes*, p. 114.

26 *The Works of Thomas Middleton*, ed. A. Dyce, v. 139, 141.

27 Cornford, *Attic Comedy*, p. 99; E. K. Chambers, *The English Folk Play*, pp. 23–33, 50–7.

28 Cornford, *Attic Comedy*, pp. 88–100, 148.

figures were also destroyed after harvest home.[29] (In *Summers Last Will and Testament* Will Summers wishes on the departure of Harvest that 'some bodie had had the wit to set his thatcht suite on fire, and so lighted him out', iii. 263.)

In Nashe's writings, interestingly, characteristically festive actions such as these appear to be present not only as isolated motifs but as the underlying shaping force of the composition itself. In *Have With You to Saffron Walden* the literary and ideological battle between Harvey and Nashe is represented as a carnivalesque antagonism; Harvey assumes the role of the disintegrating king whose season is up, 'tis time for such an olde foole to leaue playing the swash-buckler', (iii. 55). As Winter, in the seasonal strifes, declares it his task to rend and purge the overblown summer of 'venymus' matter which would otherwise stop the seasonal cycle and render time barren, so Nashe's *Have With You* devotes itself entirely to a verbal rending and re-creation of that corpulent 'bag-pudding' of rank material, 'dogs-tripes, swines liuers, oxe galls, and sheepes gutts' (iii. 34) which constitutes the substance of Harvey's garrulousness. Harvey's monstrous volume, 'swelling in dimension & magnitude aboue all the prodigious commentaries and familiar Epistles that euer he wrote' (iii. 36), reveals itself as nothing more than an infectious—because 'barraine'—hoard of rhetorical *exempla* which may as well have been 'stolne by the whole sale out of *Ascanius*, or *Andrew Maunsells* English Catalogue' (iii. 123). From a seasonal or carnivalesque point of view such literary insensitivity assumes the 'venymus' qualities of organic material which has not been allowed to disintegrate and decay; old formulations which refuse to abdicate their sovereignty over the living body of language. Accordingly, Nashe's own writing sets about to restore vitality to this stale accumulation of exhausted scraps of discourse by participating in it, breaking it up, 'dismembering' its discrete and portentous pronouncements and burying them in the spontaneous and irrelevant dialogue which results from this process. As phrases are torn out of Harvey's own discourse and grotesquely reassembled in Nashe's mock-oration and the wildly creative responses it provokes, Harvey's way of writing becomes a dummy, a scattered effigy which contributes as soil to the growth of new possibilities in language. The emphasis is on re-creativity, no matter how absurd. Nashe's fool-self, Pierce Penilesse, delivers Harvey's

[29] Burke, *Popular Culture*, pp. 185, 193; *Popish Kingdome*, sig. Q1$^{r-v}$. For Jack of Lent see *The Diary of Henry Machyn, 1550–63*, ed. J. Gough Nichols, p. 33; Wright, *Moveable Festivals*, pp. 39–40, 186.

words to his companions to stimulate their own creativity, rather than to invite criticism. 'Since you can make so much of a little', he cries, gratified at the witty reception of a ludicrous phrase, 'you shall haue more of it' (iii. 51).

This festive action of grotesque verbal dismemberment and re-creation resurfaces in the biographical portrait of Harvey in the form of the recurrent carnival motifs of rags and cast-off clothes. As represented in mock-oration and mock-biography the 'Gabriel Harvey' of *Have With You to Saffron Walden* is a collection of scatterings, he simply lacks the autonomy, the 'self-possession' which expresses meaning in discourse, or determines events in biographical relation. In material terms this mock-Harvey possesses nothing, but makes creative use of everything; ingeniously improvising the resources of life out of what circumstances happen to fling his way. He contrives a black velvet suit to advance himself at court by unpicking the old velvet saddle that someone has been kind enough to lend him (iii. 74). Discarding material as irresponsibly as he purloins it, this Harvey 'is neuer wont to keepe anie man longer than the sute lasteth that he brings with him', preferring to cast him off immediately and to 'get one in newe trappings' (iii. 97). Instead of providing copious and exemplary material—the rational deeds and resolutions that were the staple of biography—Nashe's 'life' of Gabriel Harvey presents experience as a series of cunningly improvised pastimes. The strategic Machiavellism which gives coherence to Harvey's actions as they are represented by Harvey's own writings here translates itself into innocuous foolery; the ambitious Italianate courtier 'in his blacke sute of veluet' has degenerated into indiscretion, and been gathered up as an effigy ripe for re-creation: 'such another pretie *Iacke a Lent* as boyes throw at in the streete' (iii. 94).

Clearly in the mock-biography, as in the mock-oration, the action of *Have With You* is creative rather than satirically reductive. There is no 'exposure' of the victim Harvey by the 'truth telling' satirist Nashe. On the contrary, true to festive dissolution of opposites and antagonists, *Have With You* presents both Nashe (as Pierce Penilesse) and Harvey (as Gorbuduck Huddleduddle, Gobin a grace ap Hannikin etc.) as a couple of foolish tricksters ('ordinarie Iesters that make sport', iii. 18) who proceed to violate all the limits of language and behaviour, rendering themselves incoherent and absurd for the delight and recreation of spectators (iii. 30). Nashe specifically declares that he and Harvey will disintegrate bodily, 'consume our selues' in the course of a festive combat designed to 'recreate and enkindle' the 'decayed spirites' of the people (iii. 30). Thus while Nashe appears to resemble the seasonal victor—successful youth against age, or Robin Hood overthrowing the officious sheriff—it immediately becomes apparent that this 'victory' involves the sacrifice of his own credit and coherence; the effective power of his own discourse is dispersed in the recreation of Harvey's. Similarly, while Harvey is evidently mocked and made a fool of in Nashe's biographical portrait of him, the Harvey that emerges from *Have With You* is more like an engaging jest-book hero than the flayed victim of a corrective satire. Like the traditional stage Vice, or the primitive trickster whose creative and destructive acts are performed inconsequentially for the diversion of his audience, 'Gabriel Harvey' is alternatively sly and foolish, unconscious of and unrelated to the norms of his society. Pierce Penilesse absolves him of any malicious intent against the nobility; but as one who 'talks idlely all his life time' (iii. 65), the 'poore tame-witted silly *Quirko*' may 'euen to talke treason . . . be drawn vnwares, and neuer have anie such intent, for want of discretion how to manage his words' (iii. 49). The primary accusation against Harvey is not that he is proud or ambitious or pedantic, but simply that he is 'idle' and 'fond'; the emphasis throughout is on the creative ingenuity with which he contrives to remain so; from bribing his tutor with Latin verses in beautiful italic script 'to get leaue to playe' (iii. 60) and filching inordinate amounts of extra bread '*vnder pretence of swearing by it*' (iii. 69) through the debauchery of a youth spent composing English hexameters, Gabriel Harvey is revealed to have devoted his entire life to the gratification of an excessive penchant for playing the fool. It seems clear, then, that various features of English popular festive ritual—its ageing fool-lords, torn and scattered effigies, merry combats and licensed tricksters—play a significant part in the text of *Have With You to Saffron Walden*. Indeed, the text's very title suggests the festive expulsion of an antagonist, a game of driving the old fool back to the confines of Saffron Walden, where he can no longer blight the London community of professional writers.

Up to now I have been drawing mostly on Bakhtin and Cornford in my comments on the significance of English holiday pastimes, but at this point it is helpful to turn to Mircea Eliade's more general formulation of seasonal ritual in the *Myth of the Eternal Return*. His specific concern with changing perceptions of time leads Eliade to analyse the seasonal 'expulsion of sins, diseases and demons'[30] in traditional communities as expressions of the abolition of accumulated guilt-ridden time rather than as straightforward promotions of fertility. By his account the observance of violent saturnalian rituals at New Year, Carnival, Midsummer, and so on is evidence of a community's desire to disrupt the sterile ongoing of time in a salutary annihilation of the past, a violation of old boundaries, customs, and taboos. So the adoption of a world-upside-down perspective in all things is part of a creative process of confusion, an exchange of static and accepted forms for the heady and alarming profusion of deformity which introduces the possibility of endless alternatives to the way things usually are. It is, he writes,

> a regression into the mythical period before the Creation; all forms are supposed to be confounded in the marine abyss of the beginning . . . Enthronement of a carnival 'king', 'humiliation' of the real sovereign, overturning of the entire social order . . . and hierarchy, 'orgy', chaos. We witness, one might say, a 'deluge' that annihilates all humanity in order to prepare the way for a new and regenerated human species.[31]

The regenerative efficacy of carnival humiliation and decay derives not from creative intention, but from unconscious transgression and excess, as natural generation requires the dissolution of all outside walls, skins, and borders which seal off and prevent regrowth, the mingling of the seed in the earth. Aside from his direct social experience of popular festivity, Nashe would have been familiar with the striking examples of chaotic, carnivalesque interregnum portrayed by Ovid. Twice in the first book of the *Metamorphoses* flood or conflagration devastates the worn-out world. Universal deluge produces a world-upside-down where chaos reigns, anchors are cast in fields, and wolves found swimming among sheep (or, in Nashe's bizarre version, an aged cripple is found using his crutches as oars, i. 29). As the flood recedes, a licentious golden age is introduced by the spontaneous engendering of monsters. The fertility of the world is thus renewed by the annihilation of contour and form.[32] Nashe was imaginatively drawn to this Ovidian image of the carnivalesque regeneration of the world. In *The Terrors of the Night* he describes dreams as a spontaneous mental engendering of monsters, a kind of carnival 'humiliation' or purgation of the images and projects which

[30] Eliade, *Myth of the Eternal Return*, p. 54.

[31] Ibid. 57.

[32] Ovid, *The Metamorphoses*, trans. M. M. Innes, pp. 37–40.

tyrannize over our minds in the day-time. The uninhibited operations of the nocturnal imagination become, in this context, an analogy for the animate chaos which preceded the creation of the world: 'No such figure of the first Chaos whereout the world was extraught, as our dreames in the night', Nashe notes, for in dreams 'all states, all sexes, all places are confounded and meete together' (i. 356).

Whether cerebral, social, or mythical, this carnivalesque chaos derives its creative power from the withdrawal of intention and purpose, the erasure of boundaries and contours. Thus, in farce, the cunning trickster who mocks the old buffoon, and the old buffoon whose body is beaten and torn into a thousand pieces, are not so much interdependent combatants as the dual aspect of a single carnivalesque action, the action of animate uncreation. The effigy or buffoon is the old world in a process of dissolution in which its material elements escape the confines of their accustomed form. Dispersed, the material content which made up a world now reassembles itself in accidental configurations—the ephemeral and haphazard grotesques of carnivalesque 'art'. The creative capacity of both the old fool and the cunning trickster is derived from this chaotic, comic dissolution, for the trickster is, as Kerényi put it, 'the spirit of disorder, the enemy of boundaries'.[33] It is by the agency of the trickster that the body of the old world is grotesquely re-created as a collection of cast-offs, an effigy world, but the trickster at the same time possesses no integrity, dispersing all his own being in the mocking dissolution of the past.

It is well established that all carnivalesque ritual involves the breaking down of boundaries, material and conceptual, social and territorial. The participation of the trickster in the form of the fool-lord Robin Hood, or the mocking, shrewish wife, or the man-woman dancer of the traditional plough plays is evidence of an urge to transgress all limits, even the limits of sex.[34] The function of the trickster, as Kerényi wrote, is 'to add disorder to order and so make a whole, to render possible within the fixed bounds of what is permitted, an experience of what is not permitted'.[35] At festival time, society extends its hospitality specifically towards those elements by the exclu-

[33] K. Kerényi, 'The Trickster in Relation to Greek Mythology', in *The Trickster: A Study in American Indian Mythology*, ed. P. Radin, p. 185.

[34] E. K. Chambers pointed out that English folk plays invariably included parts for a fool and a 'Man-Woman, that unquiet spirit for whom there is no obvious function, but for whom a place always has to be found', *English Folk Play*, p. 153.

[35] Kerényi, 'The Trickster', p. 185.

sion of which it normally defines itself. A Christmas proclamation of the medieval city of York declared that 'all manner of whores and thieves, dice players, carders, and all other unthrifty folke, be welcome to the towne, whether they come late or early, att the reverence of the high feast of Youle'.[36] The authorities of Lincoln proclaimed safety from the law to every citizen 'in gam sportis to goo or doe what hym pleys'.[37] At midsummer and harvest festivals social and hierarchical boundaries were broken down as the lord or mayor presided in the capacity of 'housekeeper', distributing plenty, while social inferiors were feasted with superiors. The antagonism and rivalry expressed in seasonal pastimes is another manifestation of the violation of behavioural boundaries, licensing the expression of latent hostility between neighbours or neighbouring communities. According to historians popular festive games express a special awareness of territorial boundary: in Shrovetide football the victors were not those who launched the ball into the opposition's goal, but those who carried it back to their home territory; tug-of-war manifests a similar preoccupation with boundary and identity. Breaking down boundaries (social and territorial) was also expressed in the annual trespass into the greenwood to gather branches for Robin Hood, while the boundaries between the proud sheriff and the outlaws of Nottingham are broken down by the madness or 'grene wode' that enters the sheriff as he dons the greenwood livery.[38] Seasonal festivity, then, provides opportunities for the dissolution of existing contours and the violation of authorized, apparently coherent structures. No one, however, emerges intact from the effects of participation in festivity, least of all those who play the fool to instigate it. This is one of the contradictions inherent in the notion of drawing on the tricksterish energy of carnival for the shaping of a coherent discourse; it explains why Nashe was obliged to sacrifice the authority and integrity of his rhetorical voice for the sake of being able to turn other discourses into the material of carnival mockery. It also explains why, unlike the poetry of another highly print-conscious author, Jonson, Nashe's printed texts do not express any concern that a stupid reader will destroy their integrity by being unable to comprehend the author's intention. Jonson assumes that it is the task of any reader taking an author's book in hand to possess himself of that author in the act or

[36] Phythian-Adams, *Local History*, p. 23.

[37] Baskervill, 'Dramatic Aspects', p. 31 n.

[38] Phythian-Adams, *Local History*, pp. 19, 26; Wiles, *Robin Hood*, pp. 19, 47.

reading and understanding. Nashe's assumption is very different; based on the popular festive model of the (dying) seasonal lord electing his successor, or facing trial before fellow fools, Nashe's texts address a readership which, like themselves, must be understood to lack integrity, since all—authors, texts, readers—are being re-created in a sceptical, laughing encounter. This is dramatized in *Have With You*, which translates Nashe's interpretation of Harvey (or vice versa) into a critical encounter between Harvey's book, Nashe's authorial reactions, and the responses of imagined sceptical auditors. Other Elizabethan writers give the impression that the reading public is relatively submissive in its reception of the printed word; in Nashe's writing we hear the echo of popular laughter. Of one notorious astrological prediction Nashe writes: 'I am sure it is not yet worne out of mens scorne, for euery Miller made a comment of it, and not an oyster wife but mockt it' (i. 289). If his writings bore people, Nashe assumes that they will find the creative stimulus they were looking for by taking the author apart and re-naming him with 'a hundred newe tytles of Idiotisme' (i. 192). In his texts, the right to name is not reserved to those in authority: 'euery Boy' may sing 'ignominious Ballads' of respectable moneylenders (ii. 103). In Yarmouth, it is the 'carterly Hoblobs thereabouts' who 'concoct or digeast' the respectably historic name of the place ('Cerdick Sands', after the Saxon lord Cerdicus) into the more amusingly relevant 'Sarding' or 'fucking' sands (iii. 161); Nashe identifies with these locals in their response to authority, since like them he makes the naming-power of others yield him imaginative stimulus and nourishment.

It is for this reason, and not for lack of inspiration, or for any commercial dedication to novelty, that Nashe's pamphlets are so relentlessly topical, so devoted to the handling and mishandling of contemporary voices, contemporary fashions of discourse. For it is these other styles of discourse that must be cast into the role of the old, blighted, and rotten world, made into a festive antagonist to be violated and broken down with mockery for the recreation of author and reader. This too accounts for the pugnacity (often mistaken for satirical venom) with which Nashe assaults his chosen topics. The violence is, in fact, essential to his carnivalesque purpose of breaking down intractable or threatening modes of thought and forcing them to yield material pleasure (imaginative stimulus, or laughter; often figured by Nashe as nourishing food). In *Have With You* Nashe breaks down Harvey's book, with all its inhibiting assumptions about authorship and publication, to 'recreate and enkindle' readers and professional writers; in *Lenten Stuffe* the threat of political interpretation is figured in the hostile element of the sea, which is materialized as a carnival buffoon, and forced to yield up red herrings for the replenishment of readers and authors who have been starved by the 'short boord-wages' (iii. 145) imposed by political censorship. Just as *Have With You* is suffused by the atmosphere of festive combat (Nashe's war-cry, for example, is the May-lord's 'heigh for our towne greene' while he goes about to pour ink on the 'barrain' scalp of his antagonist, iii. 20), so in *Lenten Stuffe* a whole series of aggressive rivalries are set—despite the 'lenten' of the title—in the context of Yarmouth's great autumn feast lasting from Michaelmas to Martinmas. Autumn fairs and church ales traditionally provided opportunity for reconciliation and 'neighbourliness . . . between communities';[39] in Yarmouth this meant extending hospitality to the town's ancient adversaries the Cinque Ports, with whom normal relations consisted of such 'confusion, discords, outrages . . . as perhaps were never before known . . . between any two communities in the British dominions'.[40] In *Lenten Stuffe* Nashe exploits the coexistence of rivalry and hospitality in Yarmouth's festive relations with the Cinque Ports. It is one of a number of incidental rivalries—between Yarmouth and Lowestoft, Sestos and Abydos ('townes that like Yarmouth and Leystoffe were stil at wrig wrag', iii. 195), the birds and the fishes, the English and the French navies—which figure the pamphlet's general concern with the struggle to salvage identity from the threat of total engulfment and obliteration. Nashe's own circumstances at the time of writing make the question more than metaphorical, and the reader's uncertainty as to whether all this violence is a life and death matter or merely a festive game is deliberately kept up by a constant switchback between images of play and bloodshed. Nashe's use of the word 'bloody' tricks us into mistaking the merry antagonism of the seasons for a real aggression in the contrast between fishmongers and their 'bloudy aduersaries, the butchers' (iii. 183). Contrarily, the festive epithets applied to the Saxon invader Cerdicus, who is described as 'maylord or captaine of the morris daunce', temporarily distract us from the deadly implications

[39] Phythian-Adams, *Local History*, p. 26.

[40] C. Parkin, *The History and Antiquities of Yarmouth*, pp. 249–81 (quotation at p. 251).

of the merriments in which he 'reueld here and there with his battleaxe' (iii. 161).

By encountering the threats of official misinterpretation, or the inhibitions of authorial convention, in the form of carnival antagonists, Nashe makes them accessible to laughter, thereby stimulating the creativity of readers and future authors. He occasionally draws attention to the tricksterish self-sacrifice that this involves for himself—in the open gesture of the festive fool-lord towards his readers, at the end of *Lenten Stuffe* for example, 'no more can I do for you than I haue done, were you my god-children euery one' (iii. 225), or in his declaration at the beginning of *Have With You* that he is ready to sacrifice his credibility and turn jester to re-create the exhausted imaginations of readers about Paul's Churchyard (iii. 30). Like Falstaff, he distributes the body of his own discourse as the material from which to make laughter: 'I am not only witty in my selfe, but the cause that wit is in other men' (2 Henry IV, I. ii. 5–9). His writing is nothing if not resourceful. It draws upon itself, materializing its own metaphors, parodying its own procedures, just as Falstaff, fast dwindling toward his lenten purgation, is ready to make fun of his own decay: 'A good wit will make vse of anything; I will turne diseases to commoditie' (ibid. I ii. 249–50). At the same time, however, this kind of resourcefulness eventually yields to exhaustion, having 'consumed' itself. All Nashe's pamphlets exhaust themselves and their topics in this way; at the end of *Lenten Stuffe* Nashe finds his conceit 'cast into a sweating sicknesse' (a consumption) which threatens to turn into a carnival pyre ('a hote broyling saint Laurence feuer', iii. 226), reminding readers that turning diseases to commodity can be a risky business.

Nevertheless, as Bakhtin has shown, carnival imagery identifies defilement and decay with laughter as the agent of regeneration. In the symbolism of Carnival, what was distant, sealed-off, and authoritative about the past is brought low and mingled through laughter and abuse for the recreation of the present. The unsavoury end-of-season leftovers have to be defiled by curses, their effigies smeared with filth. Gaignebet notes that fishwives were told to empty their barrels on the last day of Lent, and shit on the leftovers.[41] In English carols and ballads the season is sent packing with curses and execrations. One ballad sends Lent to the devil with 'Many a knave

41 Gaignebet, 'Le Combat', pp. 337–9.

after him for to crake his crowne',[42] while several Christmas carols begin by abusing and humiliating Advent:

> FAREWELL Advent and have good day
> Christmas is come, now go thy way.
> Get thee hence! What dost thou here?[43]

These games of mocking riddance, expulsion, and burial (like the Ash Wednesday search for vanished Shrovetide feasts, or the Netherlandish game of burying the alleluia during Lent[44]) suggest a model for the rhythms of Nashe's texts, particularly for their irreverent and abusive handling and riddance of topics. Even in *The Terrors of the Night* (not otherwise a particularly carnivalesque text) when Nashe wants to abandon a particular topic—the theme of Iceland—he takes leave of it as though it were winter: 'Farewell frost . . . farewell *Island*, for I haue no more to say to thee' (i. 360). In *Pierce Penilesse* the sequence of moral topics is like a succession of festive games of riddance. Parodic exaggeration turns satire into self-mockery; Pierce takes irreverent leave of his own excessive invective when he moves on from the moral theme of wrath to that of gluttony: 'Come on, let vs turne ouer a new leafe, and heare what Gluttonie can say for her selfe, for Wrath hath spet his poyson, and full platters do well after purging' (i. 199).

One of the purposes of indulging in carnival excess is to be able to clear the air, to turn over a new leaf. Nashe uses the phrase again when he describes what he hopes will be the outcome of his 'cock-fight' with Harvey's book in *Have With You* (iii. 30). Nashe's mockery was motivated by more than the paid comedian's desire to raise a laugh. Its aim—to break down old restrictions into the material of present freedom and pleasure—was based directly upon the experience of popular festive pastimes.

42 '[W]o[e] worthe the[e], Lenttone', *Songs and Ballads*, ed. Wright, p. 21.
43 *Ancient English Christmas Carols*, ed. E. Rickert, p. 54.
44 Gaignebet, 'Le Combat', p. 340.

# 6
# Nashe's Literary Theory

Now the question arises: when did Nashe abandon the protestant-humanist notion of reading for profit to pursue his own 'festive' notion of reading as a recreative purgation of received images and ideas? Surprisingly enough the answer seems to be at the very beginning of his career, even while he was busy sifting the provident profits of poetry from its licentious abuses in the didactic *Anatomie of Abuses*. From the start Nashe seems to have formed an intensely physical conception of poetic activity, and of the activity involved in mentally 'discovering' the poetic resource potential of a text while reading. However, in the preface written for the publication of Robert Greene's *Menaphon* (published about the same time as the *Anatomie of Abuses*) this physical conception of poetic activity includes a strikingly festive concern with the notion of fertility and regeneration through the pleasure of mockery. In this preface Nashe simply ignores the moral and provident criteria so central to the *Anatomie*, and formulates the crisis of contemporary literature as one of threatened sterility. He argues that an easy commerce of prefabricated tropes has been substituted for real poetic activity; new images and ideas can no longer be generated from texts so sterile and tropes so exhausted. All English authors have become translators and compilers, offering the reader nothing but 'barren compendiums' (iii. 318).

Nashe had a reason for insisting on the sterility of texts loaded with 'Ouids and Plutarchs plumes' (iii. 312) and other wares from the literary pawnbrokers. He meant of course to extol by comparison the easy, unpretentious style of Greene's *Menaphon*. But he goes about this in an extraordinary way. He suggests that reading Greene's book will be like participating in a carnival of the intellectual senses, a salutary and pleasurable purgative for eyes and ears 'surfeited vnawares . . . with the lauish of our copious language' (iii. 314). Mental comparison of Greene's easy style with the 'ouer-racked Rhetoricke' of the literary retailers will not only 'expell the infection of Absurditie' but will be a pleasurable experience in itself, like carnival laughter; 'ouer-racked Rhetoricke' will become the 'ironicall recreation of the Reader' (iii. 314).

Nashe does not say that in itself Greene's writing style possesses tricksterish characteristics, capable of turning a more sententious discourse into a literary grotesque, a source of critical pleasure. The tricksterish or carnivalesque process of re-creation begins with the comparison which Greene's new style sets up in the reader's mind. In the act of comparing styles, the old mode of discourse, which still clings to its old pretensions of authority and meaning, will reveal its irrelevance, will be perceived by the reader for what it is—a parody of itself. The reader will, as it were, 're-invent' the old style in his own mind as a caricature-style, the image of a cast-off mode of discourse which merrily invites the mockery of all who encounter it.

It is important for us to appreciate just how great is the creative capacity and freedom attributed by Nashe to the reader of any discourse. Reception of language is in itself for him a creative act, part of the creative process. From this conception of response to discourse as a process of creation or of grotesque re-creation arises the very notion of discourse as self-parodying which is so central to Nashe's work. As Nashe imagines the reader or hearer of a discourse to be engaged in conceiving (or 'conceptualizing') its style to the point of re-creating or caricaturing that style by exaggerating its characteristics, so his own writing often takes the form of enacting the characteristics of another's 'way of writing' until these acquire the aura of self-mockery and draw upon themselves the implied laughter of the author in the ironic comparisons of successive styles.

The notion of styles parodically enacting their own characteristics, or of styles embedded within styles, is perhaps most clearly exemplified in dramatic form where the 'voice' and the discursive style are easier to distinguish so that the central aesthetic function of parody becomes more evident. In *Summers Last Will and Testament* Nashe makes a mockery of the play's conventional, heavily moralized, euphuistic prologue by representing it as being his, the author's, invention, but delivered by a fool, Will Summers. The prologue itself is so heavily freighted with similes and sententiae that one critic has hypothesized it to be parodic re-writing of a play originally written by Lyly.[1] What Nashe is doing here, however, is not writing a parody of an actual piece of writing by Lyly, so much as presenting the outmod-

[1] M. Best, 'Nashe, Lyly and *Summers Last Will and Testament*'.

ed style itself for the 'critical recreation' of the audience. The pretentious words of the prologue have been deprived of the authenticating support of their author in their mediation by an uncomprehending clown. He handles them as the remnants of a worn-out communicative currency, refusing to play the game and 'understand' the elaborate code of values they bring into play. The terms of his extempore abuse are explicitly festive and organic; the prologue is full of old, stale, infectious formulations: 'Ile shewe you what a scuruy *Prologue* he had made me, in an old vayne of similitudes' (iii. 234). Here 'scuruy' is not emptily derogatory; it has all the connotations of disease and blight which in festive terms are associated with the impotent pretensions of the past. In a characteristically festive manner Will Summers invites an audience not merely passively to 'hear' the prologue, but as 'good fellowes' to 'giue it the hearing' so that they may 'iudge' its author in a carnival trial by mockery and laughter throughout the show which follows (iii. 234). In a sense, then, the 'style' becomes the hero or victim of a dramatic trial conducted by the imaginations of the audience or readers; indeed, this is the case with all Nashe's works. He characteristically provokes awareness of a literary style or styles and invites us to judge its fitness for the articulation of certain forms of experience by presenting the 'image' of that style as the hero or victim of a semantic drama. As Will Summers proposes that the audience should conduct a trial of the author's prologue, so the whole of *Have With You to Saffron Walden* centres around the trial and re-creation of Harvey's sententious obsolescence. Harvey's book, as Rhodes notes, is endowed with a 'notional humanity' through Nashe's grotesquely physical conceptualizing of its pedantry.[2] This 'vnconscionable vast gorbellied Volume' (iii. 35) is animated into 'speaking' for itself, in the selected highlights delivered by one fool (Nashe as Pierce Penilesse) to his audience of 'good fellowes' who are gathered to 'giue it the hearing'. Grotesquely embodied and defiantly pleading in its own incoherent defence, Harvey's book releases the stale intelligence of its congested apophthegms, dramatizing their semantic possibilities in the encounter with the spontaneous mockery of a fictional audience.

Those parallels between Nashe's parodying poetic and the 're-creative' experience of time in a pre-literate festival-oriented society suggest that the much remarked extempore quality of Nashe's writ-

[2] Rhodes, *Elizabethan Grotesque*, p. 42.

ing is actually based on a challenge to the assumptions of protestant–humanist poetics. As literary artefacts Nashe's pamphlets have tempo rather than structure; they draw their vitality *ex tempore*, from the wealth afforded by the passing moment. Although they seem satiric, they are incapable of becoming morally corrective because they are constantly in the process of reviewing themselves, turning their own excesses into the subject of new 'ironicall recreations'. As such, Nashe's writings are obliged to sacrifice any pretension to the humanist prerequisite of eloquence (the capacity to provide instruction and meaning for the future) because they exist merely in this combustible encounter of two antagonists, verbal material and tricksterish time. Nashe's 'festive' art therefore organizes itself in opposition to the dominant aspects of the humanist ideal of eloquence. First, it deliberately lacks the integrity to persuade, convince and so teach the reader. Second, in breaking up semantic formulations it refuses to ensure provision of memorable meaning for future use by the reader. Fundamentally, all Nashe's writings challenge this identification of eloquence with persuasion and providence by conceiving festively of time and of human endeavour and refusing to acknowledge the humanist conception of time and personal talent as being investments in a patriotic enterprise. This is not to say that all Nashe's writings are saying the same thing; each is shaped differently according to the specific constraints imposed by this more general moral ideal of eloquence. Aesthetically, each is formed in response to specific constraints upon the freedom of the artist. *The Unfortunate Traveller* is about how the freedom of the 'page' (printed discourse) is inevitably sacrificed under the contemporary system to the interests of persuasive rhetoric or providential history; *Have With You* is concerned with the related problem of differentiating between a published fiction and the rhetorical projection of the self; while a work like *Summers Last Will and Testament* simply defends the right to 'waste' verbal material and to 'play' with precious time.

The obvious next move at this point would seem to be the exploration of each of Nashe's major writings in its separate context; but before we can proceed to that one further question arises. How can Nashe's anti-humanist literature of 'festivity' be placed in the sixteenth-century tradition of literary *festivitas* of which the humanists (notably Erasmus) were primary exponents? Clearly we need to put Nashe's carnivalesque aesthetic into its literary as well as its popular–festive context. For while it is possible to argue (from the preface to *Menaphon*) that Nashe assumed the reader's freedom and capacity to experience any kind of literature in a carnivalesque or festive way, there remains a perfectly valid distinction to be drawn between the carnivalesque experience of literature in its mocking reception by the reader, and literature which anticipates this kind of reception by deliberately lacking integrity in the first place. Literature of this latter kind is always to some extent involved in mocking the integrity or 'truth' of value systems and systems of meaning whether these systems be mythical, philosophical, or linguistic. Rarely is the focus of mockery so exclusively verbal and rhetorical as we find it in Nashe's writing, but then Nashe wrote at a time when the system for producing discourse (as it operated within the conventions of publication and patronage) was practically as pre-eminent a creator of social values as any mythic or philosophical system had ever been. Given the social and moral powers theoretically attributed to the command of discourse, Nashe's conception of responsive reading as a way of re-creating oneself through impotent discourse is perhaps not so eccentric an idea as it seems. What we must concern ourselves with at this point, however, is not Nashe's own concept of reading as a recreative experience, but the existence of literature which was recreative or disintegrative within itself.

A tradition of disintegrative literature exists in what has been called the 'Lucianic' tradition; that is, the genre of menippean satire as it was inherited from the ancients and employed by such humanist writers as Erasmus, More, Rabelais, Ulrich von Hutten, and Cornelius Agrippa.[3] It is difficult to define what constitutes the essence of menippean satire, but the very fact that the genre's ancient exponents (notably Varro) associated the word *satura* with a sense of plenitude and diversity, such as belongs to a sacrificial feast, or to the grotesque stuffing of entrails such as puddings or sausages, suggests a connection with the Nashean conception of 'festive' pastime as the re-creation of the past in a grotesque feast of material and temporal potential. In an interesting discussion of the name and origin of the literary form of *satura* Michael Coffey quotes from Diomedes the grammarian:

[3] The 'Lucianic tradition' is discussed by D. Duncan in *Ben Jonson and the Lucianic Tradition*. On Menippean satire see M. Coffey, *Roman Satire*, pp. 149–201; M. Bakhtin, *Problems of Dostoevsky's Poetics*, trans. R. W. Rotsel, pp. 92–8; F. A. Payne, *Chaucer and Menippean Satire*.

> *Satura* takes its name . . . from a full dish which was packed with a large number of varied first fruits and offered among primitive people to the gods in a religious ritual and called *satura* from the abundance and fullness of the material . . . It may also be derived from a certain kind of sausage which was filled with many ingredients and according to Varro called *satura* . . .[4]

The 'genre' of menippean satire was characterized from ancient times by its lack of generic integrity; Coffey states that its essential feature was the introduction of verse into prose narrative.[5] It was a medley, an 'admixture of genres and their reciprocals'[6] in which critical awareness of the limits of one mode of expression was encouraged by its incongruous juxtaposition with another. Both in ancient menippea and in the menippean works of the humanists, aesthetic form and vitality is provided not by structure and coherence, but by the activity of the 'trickster' which breaks down barriers and juxtaposes what ought to be kept separate. To speak metaphorically of writing as 'tricksterish' in this way may seem remote and condescending, but in fact the most learned menippean satirists seem to have been perfectly aware of the links between their sophisticated irony and the antics of the primitive trickster. More defends Erasmus's *Praise of Folly* in figurative terms, likening its rhetorical strategy to the recreative irresponsibility of the stage dysard. 'That boke of Moria', he writes, 'doeth in dede but ieste vppon the abuses of suche thynges, after the manner of the dysours parte in a playe.'[7]

The trickster thus functions both as the means by which discourses are provocatively mishandled and offered for reassessment and (because of the fool's inability to assume control of the discourse which he mishandles) as a way of dissociating this subversive operation from the work's author, the unconscious idiot as it were patronizing and licensing the highly conscious authorial purpose. This is, of course, the convention appealed to by Erasmus in answering those who had been offended by Folly's criticism. Rather should people be offended by Folly's praise, he argued: 'there is merit in being attacked by Folly, for when I made her the narrator I had to maintain her character in appropriate style.'[8] This menippean strategy of

[4] Coffey, *Roman Satire*, pp. 13–14.

[5] Ibid. 172.

[6] B. A. Babcock, 'Liberty's a Whore: Inversions, Marginalia and Picaresque Narrative', in *The Reversible World*, ed. Babcock, p. 100.

[7] *The Confutation of Tyndale's Answer*, ed. L. Schuster *et al.*, *The Yale Edition of The Complete Works of St. Thomas More*, viii, pt. 1.

[8] Erasmus, *Praise of Folly*, pp. 60–1.

being 'authorized' by licence lies behind Nashe's elaborate game of 'countenancing' his own pamphlets through abusive, mock-dedicatory epistles to such unorthodox patrons—fools, devils, barber surgeons, and capering drunkards—as will in each instance serve to negate the conventions governing that specific kind of publication within the Elizabethan patronage system. At once the relationship between Nashe's mock patrons and the personified 'Folly' of Erasmus suggests that the characteristics of menippean satire (its propensity to employ tricksterish protagonists, to parody and transgress generic conventions, to indulge in dialogue with itself, and to embody the objections of its opponents) are here being employed by Nashe as a creative response to the limitations of the contemporary literary system. If Nashe's art has menippean features, then, these cannot be superficial considerations of style or tone; they must be essential elements whose aesthetic and intellectual nature (in relation to the popular festive rituals previously discussed) needs to be explored.

# 7

# Nashe, Mock-Testament, and Menippean Dialogue

IF the notion of literature being 'festive' is to imply anything more specific than a certain link with seasonal revelry, it has to be defined in more precise terms. For my purposes here it will do to define festive or carnivalesque literature as literature that is disingenuously, ironically inefficient; that is, literature that transforms its rhetorical conventions and strategies into the comically palpable objects of literary experience. There is no reason why such ironic reflexivity should not be labelled 'festive' with reference to sixteenth-century writers, since they evidently associated literary irony with the festive experience of occasions like Carnival. The links between Nashe's writing and the fat-versus-lean aspect of popular festivity have been discussed by Rhodes, but it seems to me that this aspect of the Carnival–Lent opposition is not central. More important for understanding Nashe's place in the development of festive literature during this period are the implications of the festive disintegration of the fool-king, the comic transference of his sovereignty to the underworld. In the early part of the sixteenth century, when the Reformation was in its first strength, the festive concept of the fool-king's death was widely adopted in humanist writing as a figure for intellectual liberation, an exuberant occasion for revealing the breakdown of an old, corrupt system of values.[1] In this of course the humanists had literary as well as ritualistic precedents, for they looked back to the 'threshold' dialogues, or the dialogues of 'news from the underworld' which had been made so popular by Lucian. Closer to the ritualistic celebration of the fool-king's death, however, was another literary offshoot. This was the dying fool's last will and testament—a form which offered similar opportunities for ironic revelation in the itemization of absurd bequests from an old tyrant to his heirs. Nashe's pamphlets are indebted both to the dialogic genre of 'news from the underworld' and to the grotesque 'dismemberment' of authority which takes place in

[1] See Herford, *Literary Relations of England and Germany*, pp. 24–33, 50–65; Bakhtin, *Dostoevsky's Poetics*, p. 95.

the mock-testament. This, I take it, is why Nashe's pamphlets have been so difficult for critics to place generically. They do not belong to any genre, indeed, they force contemporary genres into a dying confession of their authority over readers.

Lucianic dialogues, reporting slyly on the sordid truth about gods and great men in the underworld, share with festive mock-testaments a topical, colloquial, and freely confessional idiom. But while both derive this idiom from the carnivalesque celebration of the fool-king's death and disintegration, the mock-testament occasionally retains further links with its ritualistic origins in its comic development of the notion of dismemberment. The fool not only confesses through his last will and testament; he actually takes himself to pieces, bequeathing merriment in the revelation of his impotent, dispersed body. It is tempting to distinguish mock testaments from netherworld dialogues along these lines, and to suggest that the dialogue places more emphasis on the ironic revelation of fraudulent ideas, whereas the testament derives pleasure from exploiting the redundant, comic material that is revealed in the death of an old system of Truth. Truth takes leave as a carnival effigy whose working parts become embarrassingly visible to all as it loses the illusion of autonomy and coherence that once assured its unquestioned authority. Thus one might argue that Fielding's Lucianic device of pairing letters written by Thwackum and Square to Allworthy at the end of *Tom Jones* (bk. XVIII, ch. iv) reveals the men's fraudulence dialogically, like an ironic confession from the underworld, whereas another eighteenth-century novel with carnivalesque affinities—*Tristram Shandy*—bears more resemblance to a grotesque testament, cluttered as it is with the effigies of impotent, authority-claiming discourses.

Leaving the eighteenth century and returning to the sixteenth, however, we find this distinction between ironic dialogue and grotesque dismemberment to be simply meaningless. Erasmus's *Praise of Folly* is a mock-encomium, a piece of ironic rhetoric, yet as its generic precedents Erasmus cited both Seneca's netherworld confession of the death of the Emperor Claudius (the *Apocolocyntosis*) and the grotesque will and testament of the pig Grunnius Corocotta.[2] What is more, the motif of the 'true confession from the underworld' figured in English festive pageantry as a vehicle for social and political satire.

[2] Erasmus, *Praise of Folly*, p. 57. For a reproduction of the testament of Grunnius Corocotta, see P. García de Diego, 'El Testamento en la Tradición'.

Henry Machyn's diary of the 1550s records a festive procession in London in March 1552 when Jack of Lent's wife had to read out his confession in a comic attempt to save him from execution.[3] In the 1540s particularly we hear of Catholic institutions participating in their own festive funerals, both in print and in pastime. Roy and Barlow dramatized the comic death and burial of the Mass in their book *Rede me and be nott wrothe*, and in 1547 Bishop Stephen Gardiner wrote to Protector Somerset complaining that people were taking religious reform into their own hands with the publication of ballads of 'Jack a Lents Testament' celebrating the death of Lent and satirizing other ecclesiastical institutions. Lent, Gardiner claimed, was 'buried in rime' and 'Steuen Stockfish bequeathed, not to me, though my name be noted'.[4] Obviously in this particular ballad Jack of Lent's seasonal leftovers (the uneaten herring, stockfish, etc.) were being 'bequeathed' in a politically loaded gesture against the upholders of Lent as an institution. It is clear from this that the public creation and dismemberment of carnival effigies has essential links with the discrediting confessions of threshold dialogue. Generic antecedents of both kinds seem to lie behind the conception of Nashe's *Unfortunate Traveller* which introduces itself at once as confessional narrative and as the grotesque testament of its own textual integrity. The introduction offers the story as 'certaine pages' of waste paper which have been bequeathed to the public by a dead 'king of Pages' whose body lies apparently whole and 'entombed' in the authoritative 'Acts and Monuments' of its printed history (ii. 207–8). Opening the book, however, to hear '*Iacke Wilton* tell his owne Tale' (ii. 208) is to witness the gradual disclosure of the history's lack of integrity and authority; an experience which implicates the reader in its mocking reflection of his own expectations.

The idea of the worthless bequest is central to the menippean confession or the mock-testament. It signifies the disinterestedness of the speaker, his lack of any proprietorial impulse, any motive for claiming to possess the truth, or for trying to convince anyone that he does. In one instance Nashe, in a letter to readers, 'bequeathes' an answer to his critics, leaving it to them as his 'last will and Testament' (ii. 186). Evidently this does not mean that he thinks he has silenced or satisfied his enemies, but rather that he is anxious to rid himself of the

3 Machyn, *Diary*, p. 33.

4 See William Roy and Jerome Barlow, *Rede me and be nott wrothe*, ed. E. Arber; Baskervill, *Elizabethan Jig*, p. 47.

absurd issues they have raised by handing responsibility back to them. The mock testament is characterized by this gesture of abandon, this abdication of the responsibility of power and of the need to keep up appearances. There is a kind of pleasure in giving up possession of oneself and one's belongings; in the satiric *Testament* of Jyl of Brentford, for instance, Jyl is frank about handing her body and goods to the earth, 'for they be his'.[5] Losing self-possession, power and worldly inheritance is a relief, for it also means shedding responsibility for the crimes of the past. This is why fools like the drunkard of *Colyn Blowbols Testament* and the Catholic devil in the *Wyll of the Deuyll and Last Testament* are so ready to return the sordid paraphernalia of their past to their living disciples. Recipients of bequests accept them as a form of mockery, a gift that implicates the receiver in the incriminating and uninhibited confession which the testament discloses. 'First', says the devil, 'I geue and bequethe to pope Phelix, all suche superstitious & idle holydayes, as he inuented', then, more cynically, he goes on, 'Item, I geue my Chastitee to the Cleargy'.[6] Colyn Blowbol leaves 'alle the londys and possessions' that he has in Southwark (i.e. the stews) to Sloth and her gracious sisters.[7]

The confessions of the dying fool would seem from this to correspond to the disintegration of his once vital and effective body. Both actions are ways of articulating the moment when a system ceases to be taken for granted by everyone as the inevitable 'way things are' and begins to look awkward and arbitrary; what was invisible and powerful becomes an embarrassing heap of redundant material. If we are talking about literature, the effective system is a genre which depends on the acceptance of various conventions for its beauty and its credibility. Deliberately violating these conventions is a way of drawing attention to their materiality, of making them 'confess' or 'bequeath' strategies originally designed to gain aesthetic power over the reader. In effect, then, menippean literature is the grotesque testament or the dying confession of conventions that it appears to mishandle. It is a foolish, incompetent representative of its chosen genre, one which ingenuously reveals to the world all its artistic secrets. Barred from entering into the illusion created by literary experience, the reader is obliged to come to terms with the literary

[5] Robert Copland, *Jyl of Brentford's Testament*, ed. F. J. Furnivall, pp. 8–9, 11.

[6] Anon., *The Will of the Deuyll and Last Testament*, ed. F. J. Furnivall, pp. 20–1.

[7] 'Colyn Blowbols Testament', *Remains of the Early Popular Poetry of England*, ed. W. C. Hazlitt, i. 100.

devices that force themselves on his consciousness. For example, if we read *The Unfortunate Traveller* as the mock testament of a page which acknowledges its economic dependence on the court (ii. 209) we can see how the text refuses to comply with the conventions of courtly patronage and press censorship, and obliges the reader to encounter the literary forms through which these conventions are observed as an incoherent clutter of diverse and densely physicalized discourses. The whole book is a medley of decadent styles, as rich and yet profitless as the 'rich offals of bases, of helmets, of armor' (ii. 278) left by the Earl of Surrey to the disappointed heralds after his devastating performance at the tournament.

Once we adopt this perspective, reading Nashe's writing as foolish testaments to moribund literary conventions, rather than as incompetent essays in those conventions, we are well on our way to appreciating what his texts have to tell us. Up to now, critical discussion of Nashe's work has tended to founder on the question of its internal discontinuity and our uncertainty of the author's intention. Strangely enough, even application of the latest deconstructive approaches, with their sensitivity to rhetorical free play, seem scarcely to have affected the critical account of Nashe:[8] we are still told that his writing tends to suffer from insufficient authorial control, that it is at once distressingly flippant and callously moralistic and that it inevitably goes too far, transgressing the bounds of humanity and taste. These characteristics are still present, but they become aesthetically intelligible once we cease to assume the integrity of Nashe's rhetorical and satirical voice. Ethical satire is certainly a rhetorical genre, and as such requires us to look for some consistency in the satirical stance of the speaking subject; after all, the effectiveness of the genre depends upon the satirist's ability to convince us that his partial vision is somehow true. Nashe, however, is rarely trying to convince us of anything of the sort. His writing, far from expressing his 'own' satiric viewpoint, tends to treat satire as merely one among many pragmatic and socially useful modes of discourse, to be caricatured accordingly. His writing is (largely) not rhetorical in the sense that it is not using figures of speech to persuade the reader; on the contrary, it abdicates the responsibility of rhetoric to convince and gain the reader's credit,

[8] Jonathan Crewe (*Unredeemed Rhetoric*, p. viii) admits that he is using Nashe to make a point about the issues raised by the presence and availability of rhetoric for a Renaissance author; he does not suggest that Nashe's writing might itself have been dealing with these issues.

offering instead to juxtapose rhetorical strategies and socially operative forms of discourse in such a way as to make it seem quite astonishing that they should ever have exercised power over anybody.

Take *Pierce Penilesse*, for example. This is a work most often described in terms of a Juvenalian re-working of medieval commonplaces, warmed-over social themes. Nashe, according to Hibbard, 'repeats the charges which preachers, poets and pamphleteers have been making since the fourteenth century'. Inheriting 'two traditions of satire, the classical and the medieval', Nashe 'marries them to each other'.[9] In fact, of course, it is the very impotence of ethical satire—both homiletic and Juvenalian—that *Pierce Penilesse* sets out to mock. Far from being a work of moral satire on economic themes, it is the last will and testament of such tired old patriotic satires, a confession from the underworld of the pragmatic economic bias behind the high-toned moral discourse which continues to uphold the interests of courtly monopolists and businesslike publishers.[10] Thus the seven deadly sins format is not a throwback to medieval satiric practice as critics have thought, but a parody of the way in which contemporary official discourse, with its exhortations to observe the political Lent and to eschew gluttony and idleness, claims a universalized moral authority for the advancement of specific economic interests. Here there is at least one precedent in popular literature, in William Elderton's ballad of *A New Merry News* (which Nashe refers to twice as the 'parliament of noses'—i. 256 and iii. 177). This ballad, like *Pierce Penilesse*, parodies the official discourses of economic control—restraint on the import of wine in particular—and relies entirely for its shape on the shape given to it by such official forms as the supplication for economic grievances, the commission of search and enquiry, the punishment of offenders, or the establishment of a licensed company. All these, of course, are made to work in reverse: people are punished for not having red noses, and the penalty is enforced drinking; the official discourse of restraint is thus turned inside out to promote licence.[11] Nashe's *Pierce Penilesse* is as shapeless as Elderton's ballad, proceeding as it does by the mockery of one official voice after another. At times the commonplaces of moral and economic discourse are spoken by Pierce himself, in which case, as in

[9] Hibbard, *Thomas Nashe*, pp. 64, 76. See also J. Peter, *Complaint and Satire in Early English Literature*, pp. 132–3; O. J. Campbell, *Comicall Satyre in Shakespeare's 'Troilus and Cressida'*, pp. 21–34.

[10] See below, pp. 172–96.

[11] William Elderton, 'A New Merry News', *Fugitive Tracts*, ed. W. C. Hazlitt, no. ix.

Elderton's ballad, these forms are reversed and emptied of their original meaning (as when Pierce demands rent for the devil's 'tennement of his purse' (i. 165) or berates him for allowing himself to be called a 'bastard' by atheists (i. 172). At other times the moral authority of commonplace discourse is brought into a grotesque physical relationship with the exposed motivations of its specific utterance. On the whole it is not so much social types that we encounter in Nashe's writing as effigies of certain forms of speech. The physical description of a familiar type slides imperceptibly into a caricatured version of his speech in a way that is quite new in English prose. Thus we have, for example, the spoilt bankrupt heir, who takes refuge in the swagger that he is ready to 'teare the gold out of the Spaniards throats, but he will haue it, byrlady' (i. 171), or the wrathful justice who 'makes Newgate a Nowne Substantiue, whereto all his other words are but Adiectiues' (i. 187–8). What is notable about this technique is the way in which the ethical pretensions of discourse are undermined by being given localized utterance. Morally authoritative forms of speech appear not so much hypocritical as harmless and incompetent; the very opposite, in fact, of rhetorically convincing satire.[12]

*Pierce Penilesse* has been linked with the vogue for Juvenalian satire in the 1590s, but it stands apart from this vogue precisely because it is in prose, and prose is more capable than poetry of accommodating and objectifying the various accents and forms of contemporary discourse, even to the extent of typographical parody (of dedicatory epistles, marginal comments, etc.). This is why Nashe's pamphlets have appeared shapeless to critics in the past; their shapelessness is parodic virtuosity. Units as loose and formally unconstraining as the 'pamphlet' and the familiar prose period are capable of mediating any literary form the author chooses to represent; even lyrics are not exempt, as we see from the pastiche love poems of *The Unfortunate Traveller*. These lyrics are in fact not quite pastiche; their poise is such that two of them found their way into *Englands Parnassus* presumably as compositions for straightforward imitation (iv. 276 and 280). Nor, however, are they expressions of Nashe's satiric 'viewpoint' (as compared, for example, with the polemic against sonnets and elegies in the first satire of Everard Guilpin's *Skialethia*).[13] They are, rather, images of the lyric form,

[12] R. C. Elliot, *The Power of Satire*, pp. 49–87.

[13] Everard Guilpin, *Skialethia*, ed. D. Allen Carroll, p. 59.

rendered ambiguous by the implications of context, by their ability to function within the cynical economy of Jack's narrative. For the lyrics cannot really be separated from the narrative in which they are embedded; they are mediated on a level with other images of persuasive rhetoric, giving readers a sly glimpse of the farcical social operations of exalted literary discourse. If this sounds esoteric to us, we can be sure it was less so to readers familiar with a society in which print and rhetoric were the media of politics and patronage, the instruments whereby power relations were formed and the reformation of social values established. Nashe's pamphlets dramatize the operations of the media, making fun of a society for which all material was loaded with rhetorical potential. Every garment, every word, every gesture is forced to take part in the transactions of bestowing praise and receiving credit—whether the parties involved are readers, patrons, publishers, or learned classical authorities. Parody, or the repetition and distortion of the rhetorical gesture, becomes Nashe's surest way of emptying it of power and restoring it to readers as unintelligible contortion—pure gesture, pure pleasure. The absurdity that is already latent in fashionable or officially authoritative discourse is merely helped into prominence by being stylized as gesture, a mock version of itself. When Harvey, for example, attempts rather clumsily to compliment Sir Philip Sidney's style with the declaration that it is 'fine Greece and the finest Tuscanisme in graine', his self-advertising incompetence reveals itself when Nashe recasts the phrase 'in the verie style of a Dier's signe' on the page:

> HEERE WITHIN THIS PLACE IS ONE THAT DIETH
> ALL KINDE OF ENTELECHY IN FINE GREECE, AND
> THE FINEST TUSCANISME IN GRAINE THAT MAY
> BEE, OR ANY COLOVR ELSE YE WOLD DESIRE, AND SO
> GOD SAVE THE QUEENE (iii. 50)

When, in *The Unfortunate Traveller*, Jack accuses Tabitha the courtesan of using 'mocke holy-daie iestures' (ii. 258) to try and persuade him in her favour, we realize that these are the gestures of which his own narrative is made up. And so it is with most of Nashe's texts; they are not made of significant, satiric gestures directed against a target, but are composed of ineffective holiday gestures, parodic revelations of the social and rhetorical strategies of contemporary literary form.

The holiday gestures of the fool, pleasurably divesting repressive sign-systems of their everyday authority, are obviously comparable to the fool's characteristic fondness for nonsense speech, for babble, the only purpose of which is to re-appropriate the instruments of meaning and distinction as source of material comfort and pleasure. Nashe's rhetorical personae declare their affinity with the popular festive fool, or the 'Vice' of the Tudor interlude,[14] by their predilection for such gratuitous wordplay, which even at its most sophisticated seems to retain links with a festive dynamic of dismemberment and grotesque re-creation. Nashe's foolish speakers seem to have food and dismemberment on the brain; their puns constantly transform significance into the recollection of nourishment or the anticipation of violent destruction. Will Summers, for example, interprets the command to dispatch as a batch (of freshly baked bread); Jack Wilton transforms the sergeant's mace (symbolic of his power to arrest and punish vagrants) into a spice, and then puns on his 'own' cue as an actor, turning it into 'cue' meaning a portion of food (ii. 225).

As a reflex of his expression, this preoccupation with nourishment indicates the precarious ephemerality of the fool's linguistic existence. It is only by punning, or pounding at verbal materials in this way that the fool is able to participate in language which constructs itself explicitly to deny him. Rabelais made the position clear when he created Panurge as the essential spirit of all that was being denied and excluded in the vast accumulation of humanist wisdom on the theme of anti-prodigality. As well as ingeniously turning this rhetorical material inside-out in his resourceful praise of debts, Panurge actually manages to secure his own survival when threatened by a pack of ravenous hounds by acting out a prodigal defiance of the humanist proverb against 'throwing one's bacon to the dogs'. Had he not in this episode seized the chance of making a pun and reversing the proverb's meaning in the act, dogs would have eaten the prodigal instead of his bacon.[15] Taking the words of wisdom literally enables folly to exist in its very teeth; for a moment Rabelais allows himself to deny in Panurge the very essence of the humanist equation of the resourceful

[14] On the link between the morality Vice and the popular festive fool see F. H. Mares, 'The Origin of the Figure called "The Vice" in Tudor Drama'.

[15] Rabelais, *Gargantua and Pantagruel*, pp. 214–18; on 'throwing bacon to the dogs' as prodigality, p. 292.

orator with the wise and provident man. A less learned but just as illuminating example of the fool's linguistic expedience occurs in an exchange from Thomas Lupton's morality play *All For Money* (1578). The Vice, Sinne, encounters Money, who demands to know whether he comes of ancient stock. Sinne nonchalantly replies:

> The last stockes I was in was euen at Bamburie
> They be worme eaten which shewes them ancient to be:
> If they were mine because they be so olde,
> I would burne them in winter to keepe me from the colde.[16]

Sinne's misunderstanding strategically avoids his having to define himself by the value which Money (inevitably) attaches to the notion of 'ancient stock'; the concept is taken literally and its hierarchical character mocked in Sinne's materialization of ancient stock as an obsolete instrument of repression, one which will afford recreation for the fool when it is carnivalesquely destroyed, i.e. burnt, 'to keepe me from the colde'.

Nashe's fools likewise ensure their own survival within a hostile linguistic environment by turning the impositions of metaphor into material for their own wordplay. This, for example, is the source of the frustration which fills the dialogue between Summer and his Stewards in *Summers Last Will and Testament*. Unable to articulate their own offerings in the linguistic terms of Summer's demands, the stewards are forced to re-create his words (as puns, as snatches of songs) in ways which will accommodate and affirm their ephemeral values. The text of *Lenten Stuffe* exists by virtue of its efforts to re-create the hostile reception of its words as the nourishing source of its creative energy. The sea which is always threatening to overwhelm and engulf Yarmouth corresponds to the anticipation of political censorship which inhibits the artist and makes nonsense of his aesthetic power. In *Lenten Stuffe* both become ambiguous sources of nourishment in the image of the red herring, a monster of meaningless, but action-packed, verbal procrastination, whose only purpose is to gain time and space in which to play a little with the threat of extinction. The pamphlet is therefore full of ambiguous images of hunters which turn into food and vice versa; Plautus's fishermen which emerge from the sea 'wel washed and salted' like the fish they fail to catch when

[16] Thomas Lupton, *A Moral and Pitieful Comedie Intituled All for Money*, sig. C4[r].

they 'sneake home to bed supperlesse' (iii. 224) or Leander 'sodden to haddocks meate' having had his own 'belly full of fishbroath' in the Hellespont (iii. 197–8). Like Panurge surviving by throwing his bacon to the dogs, the text of *Lenten Stuffe* spins itself out of the tale of its unravelling, squandering proverbial significance in the energetic verbal pursuit of evasion. We have a page-long digression on the decision not to include a praise of Yarmouth by comparison with other ports which derives its densely-packed activity from the physical animation of metaphor, desperately avoiding a metaphoric 'deeper' significance. It reads like a cartoon-fantasy of the imagination in action:

I had a crotchet in my head, here to haue giuen the raines to my pen, and run astray thorowout all the coast townes of England, digging vp their dilapidations, and raking out of the dust-heape or charnell house of tenebrous eld the rottenest relique of their monuments, and bright scoured the canker eaten brasse of their first bricklayers and founders, & commented and paralogized on their condition in the present, & in the pretertense; not for any loue or hatred I beare them, but that I would not be snibd, or have it cast in my dishe that therefore I prayse Yarmouth so rantantingly, because I never elsewhere bayted my horse, or tooke my bowe and arrowes and went to bed . . . Mutch brainetossing and breaking of my scull it cost me, but farewell it, and farewell the Baylies of the Cynqueports, whose primordiat *Genethliaca* [nativity] was also dropping out of my inckhorne . . . (iii. 167)

Proverbs which are meant as metaphors for cerebral activity—the 'digging up' of historical records, the 'braintossing', skull breaking, giving reins to the pen or baiting the horse—are here invested with an apparently gratuitous physical pugnacity. The ostentation of such resourceful side-tracking has a characteristically festive ambiguity; the interpretative hostility which it is trying to elude is also the source of its existence, its linguistic invention. All this *Lenten Stuffe* has in common with all figures of carnival celebration which, down to the simplest of puns, inevitably rely on the paradox of deriving their 'nourishment' from the anticipation of destruction. Nashe's animation of metaphor is related to the impulse that fashions the carnival effigy: both personify and animate in order to beat up and destroy invisible constraints. In all literature which has popular festive affinities the destructive, iconoclastic energy of the pun or curse which 'dismembers' words and bodies is compensated for by the creative energy of personification which makes dismemberment possible. A ballad which expresses everyone's disgust at the deprivations to be endured because of Lent derives its comic energy from the process of embodying and cursing a physical effigy of Lent, binding it and beating it out of the town:

> Now ys pace [Pacques: Easter] even cum, and he ys reddé bowen
> [bound]
> For to tayke his leave, the devyll might him drowen!
> On a skalde mare backe to ryd owt ath towne;
> Many a knave after him for to crake his crowne,
> With payne;
> . . . I pray the dyvell breake his necke,
> That he cum no mor agayn.[17]

This cursing of hunger by embodying and dismembering it has literary precedents too: Plautus makes the parasite Ergasilius curse a hungry day by threatening to tear out its eyes.[18] Both the hungry parasite of Plautine comedy and the traditional cursing and driving out of Lenten abstinence are worked into the comic cursing of authorial deprivation in Nashe's *Lenten Stuffe*; the insatiable sea of criticism is grotesquely personified, so that Yarmouth fishermen can use their oars to beat out its brains (iii. 183) in the resourceful pursuit of herring.

It seems that in the sixteenth century the mock testament was recognized as having affinities with the satirical energies of the pun and the curse, particularly in its articulation of dismemberment as a nourishing, vitalizing process. An early recipe book entitled *Wyl bucke his Testament* goes so far as to present itself as the bequest of a dying buck to the novice cook. Anticipating those helpful diagrams that divide sheep and cows into butchers' joints, Wyl bucke divides himself up, item by item, in disinterested anticipation of the several dishes his body will provide. To prevent his 'blood' and 'guts' from going stale, for example, he advises that they be given to the pudding wife, who will turn them into a 'morsell for a kinge'.[19] What seems odd is the merry abandon with which the buck, erstwhile festive lord, bequeaths himself to provide the meat for the feast. This frankness, however, is not uncharacteristic; it is part of the ambiguity of being the king of any carnivalesque sport or feast. We find it again

[17] '[W]o[e] worthe the[e], Lenttone', *Songs and Ballads*, ed. Wright, p. 21.

[18] Plautus, *The Captives*, III. ll.464–8, in *Works*, i. 506–7. Nashe recalls this play in *Lenten Stuffe*, iii. 154, identifying himself with the hungry parasite Ergasilius.

[19] J. Lacy, *Wyl bucke his Testament*, sig. A2$^{r}$.

in another ballad of the 1550s, which celebrates the transformation of the sour crabapple into the king of the feast, cider for all:

> Thus I, Jack Sawse, do mayk my laste wyll . . .
> When the tanner hathe grownde my frut in his myll,
> I bequethe my lyccore to the whole conggregacion.[20]

From the confessional or grotesque testament as it survives in these festive (or 'feasting') contexts, it is a short step to the netherworld dialogue of Lucianic tradition. The essential identity of these forms was certainly obvious to Nashe who, in a letter to a friend in 1596, compares Harrington's *Metamorphosis of Ajax* first unfavourably to 'Gillian a Braynfords [Wi]ll in which she bequeathed a score of farts amongst her frends' (v. 195) and then to the scatological 'lastwords' (v. 196) of the Emperor Claudius in Seneca's *Apocolyntosis* or the *Ludus de Morte Claudii*. Seneca's netherworld dialogue was in at least one edition of 1515 bound up with Erasmus's *Moriae Encomium*[21], and Nashe would have been totally familiar with the distinctive features of the genre—its foolish untrustworthy speakers, its world-upside-down perspective, its frank revelation of social injustice—from the Lucianic dialogues and colloquies of Erasmus which he and his contemporaries read at school.[22].

At about the time that Nashe started producing his own highly individual work in this Lucianic tradition there appeared a number of less distinguished netherworld dialogues, mostly vehicles for topical comment on the contemporary publishing scene. Examples are the netherworld trial of the coney-catching author Robert Greene in *Greenes Newes both from Heaven and Hell*, and Henry Chettle's resurrection of various netherworld speakers in his satirical *Kind-Hartes Dreame*. Chettle's *Dreame* resembles *Pierce Penilesse* in its technique of parodying official discourse against moral and economic abuses. It conducts a spirited defence of the commercial theatre against the official argument that players encouraged idlers and unthrifts by bringing the recently dead Tarlton back to life to impersonate a brothel-keeper who has fallen on hard times. Predictably, the brothel-keeper appropriates all the official arguments against the

20 'Fyrst when thow, nature', in *Songs and Ballads*, ed. Wright, no. LIII, p. 171.

21 *Erasmi Roterdami Moriae Encomium & Ludus L. Annae Senecae de Morte Claudii Caesaris* (1515).

22 See T. W. Baldwin, *William Shakespere's Small Latine & Lesse Greeke*, i. 129–30, 287–8. See also *The Colloquies of Erasmus*, trans. C. R. Thompson, pp. 133–46.

players, whose immoral 'idleness' can then be blamed for the decline of his own 'thrifty' business.[23]

Chettle's use of the authorities' own words against the players as a form of reflexive criticism is entirely typical of this genre. The official position is never overtly criticized, never tried by externally applied standards; it is merely given scope to represent itself, to reproduce its own words in the netherworld context. Self-condemnation becomes inevitable as the figures of parodic repetition make the strategies of self-praise (carefully concealed in the original argument) visible to all. In *Greenes Newes both from Heaven and Hell* it is Greene's own fictional creation, the product of his own words, who speaks back to him and gets into heaven, leaving his author behind.[24]. The trial of Harvey's book in *Have With You to Saffron Walden* consists of hearing Harvey's words 'fram' d . . . in his owne praise and apologie' (iii. 42). This resembles the kind of farcical self-indictment that one finds in such Lucianic dialogue as *The Double Indictment* and is closely related to the rhetorical genre of mock encomium in which, as in Lucian's *Phalaris*, self-praise turns insidiously into self-condemnation.[25] Their liability to misinterpretation made Lucianic strategies of this kind inappropriate to the reforming needs of the early Elizabethan period, so we find few examples of the netherworld trial before the 1590s, although an exception might be made for Francis Thynn's *Debate Between Pride and Lowliness* in which the examination of the respective abuses of Pride and Lowliness in consumption rebounds in a sceptical trial of various abuses in Elizabethan manufacture.[26]

The element of trial is obviously pervasive in the concept of menippean literature as literature in which the integrity of genre and style is violated, and one genre is called upon to comment on or to 'try' another. For a literary work to play the trickster to itself, to put itself

[23] Henry Chettle, *Kind-Hartes Dreame* (1592), ed. G. B. Harrison, pp. 40–2. See also [Barnabe Rich?], *Greenes Newes both from Heaven and Hell*, ed. R. B. McKerrow, and, for a discussion of these sixteenth-century threshold dialogues, B. Boyce, 'News from Hell: Satiric Communications with the Netherworld in English Writing of the Seventeenth and Eighteenth Centuries'.

[24] *Greenes Newes*, p. 17.

[25] *The Double Indictment* is in Lucian, *Satirical Sketches*, trans Turner, pp. 166–95; Phalaris and other famous examples in the same genre, *The Fly* and *The Parasite* (mentioned by Erasmus in *Praise of Folly*), are in Lucian, *Works*, trans. Harmon, i. 2–31, 82–95, and iii. 235–317. For mock-encomium in general see T. Burgess, *Epideictic Literature*, pp. 157–66; A. S. Pease, 'Things Without Honor'.

[26] Francis Thynn, *The Debate Between Pride and Lowliness* (1570), ed. J. Payne Collier.

on 'trial', it must foreground the ways in which significance is mediated in different kinds of discourse. It must, as Bakhtin writes, present its utterances in 'various degrees of parody and objectivization'.[27] This is what happens in *The Unfortunate Traveller* (1593) where the page itself is personified as a master parodist and a carnival king ('sole king of the cans and blacke iackes, prince of the pigmies, countie palatine of cleane straw and prouant', ii. 209). The printed page thereby becomes the explicit mediator of innumerable alien discourses, different styles, genres, and types of utterance whose pretensions to integrity are mocked by the materializing effect of Jack's narrating mimicry. The style of a discourse becomes a more or less palpable substance; the harsh Tudor didacticism of the Earl of Surrey's wonted discourse is characterized by his having 'a mouth out of which was nought wont to march but sterne precepts of grauetie & modestie' (ii. 245). As well as 'palpabrizing' or making effigies out of various styles, Jack's endless mimicry has the effect of emphasizing stylistic incongruity by juxtaposing one genre with another, or interrupting one narrative style with the insertion of another more colloquial.

The discordant effects resulting from this transgression of generic and stylistic boundaries have provoked reactions varying from Agnes Latham's view that *The Unfortunate Traveller* is self-consciously about style, a 'satire on literary themes and modes' to G. R. Hibbard's opposite account of the work as the product of a hack responding uncritically to the public's demand for variety and sensation. More recently, critics like Ann Rosalind Jones and Margaret Ferguson have emphasized the free play of irony within the text as a positive feature in itself, a way of calling into question the possibility of integrity in rhetorically based discourse.[28]

It seems to me that this free-wheeling irony, along with what has been characterized as its 'picaresque' qualities, are features which place *The Unfortunate Traveller* in the Lucianic or menippean tradition. Here again Nashe scholars have been condescending; Hibbard, for example, criticizes the careless nineteen-year lapse between the battle of Marignano and Jack's witnessing of the Anabaptist rising in

27 *Dostoevsky's Poetics*, p. 97.

28 A. Latham, 'Satire on Literary Themes and Modes in Nashe's "Unfortunate Traveller" ', pp. 89-90; Hibbard, *Thomas Nashe*, pp. 175-6; A. R. Jones, 'Inside the Outsider: Nashe's *Unfortunate Traveller* and Bakhtin's Polyphonic Novel'; M. Ferguson, 'Nashe's *The Unfortunate Traveller*: The "Newes of the Maker" Game'.

Munster.[29] But Jack's ability to defy normal chronological and spatial boundaries relates him to other menippean tricksters who have descended to Hades, or flown up to Olympus. 'Like a Crowe that still followes aloofe where there is carrion,' says Jack, 'I flew me ouer to *Munster* in *Germanie*' (ii. 232). The inference seems to be that nineteen years presents no obstacle to the carrion-hunting moral historian (the narrative is here following and implicitly criticizing Lanquet's *Chronicle*), so that this page, like Icaromenippus, is a trickster who has conveniently sprouted wings to witness the strategies of moralizing chronicles.

Jack's extensive travels, like his protean powers of mimicry, ensure that the narrative page of *The Unfortunate Traveller* is a space in which, regardless of chronology, famous discoursers, tyrants, and rebels of history can encounter parodic images of one another. Into the already eminent assembly of Thomas More, Erasmus, Agrippa, and Henry Howard, Earl of Surrey, Jack thrusts Cicero in the very act of pleading his notorious defence of parricide, *Pro Roscio Amerino* (ii. 252). The fantasy of being able to encounter great men and to challenge the authority of their examples, lives, and opinions is apparently typical of Lucianic dialogue: Lucian in the Elysian Fields, for example, tells us that he finds 'no sign of Plato' but is significantly informed that the great philosopher 'had gone to live in his *Republic*, where he was cheerfully submitting to his own *Laws*'.[30] Lucian's gesture ironically unites the image of the man with that of his ideas only to give each the lie. The sceptical effect is similar to that produced by Jack's comparison of Erasmus and More, two exemplary ironic discoursers, in *The Unfortunate Traveller*. Since he is an ironic discourser himself, however, Jack's comparison lacks integrity: it is a fake, producing intellectual caricatures of Erasmus and More so as to 'prove' each guilty for opposite reasons, insisting only on their incrimination. The equivocations of Erasmus are ingeniously misrepresented as the political manoeuvrings of a time server: '*Erasmus* in all his speeches seemed so much to mislike the indiscreof Princes in preferring of parasites and fooles, that he decreed with himselfe to swim with the stream, and write a booke forthwith in commendation of follie' (ii. 245). On the other hand More's *Utopia*, written in the same equivocating mode as *The Praise of Folly*, is

[29] *Thomas Nashe*, p. 153.

[30] Lucian; *Satirical Sketches*, trans. Turner, p. 279.

deliberately misunderstood as a testimony to the dangerously subversive opinions of its author. Jack quotes More as maintaining that 'principalities were nothing but great piracies . . . maintained by private vndermining and bloudshed' (ii. 245–6) whereas the words are in fact those of Raphael 'Nonsenso', a traveller as untrustworthy as Jack himself.[31]

Jack's narrative dissolution of the temporal and social distances between the historical figures he meets serves the menippean purpose of allowing images or caricatures of ideas (here, variations on the humanist ideal of oratory producing 'virtus') to encounter one another freely, as it were in dialogue with one another.[32] In menippean fiction, fantasy has the intellectual purpose of stripping away the protective layers of historical and social context and exposing fundamental attitudes to the experience of opposition. The dialogic presentation of consciousness is essential to menippean satire: every mode of perception is interrupted and challenged by what it necessarily excludes. The authorial voice itself is fractured and the autonomy of subjectivity denied by the adoption of different styles of discourse (as in Jack's narrative) or by a continual reminder of the presence of other, irreconcilable and interrupting voices. Lucian relates a long dream which he is about to expound for our benefit when he interrupts himself: 'While I was telling you all this, I heard one of you say: Good Lord, what a very long and boring dream!'[33] Nashe is constantly undermining his authorial status in the same way, transgressing the conventionally polite and didactic relationship of the Elizabethan writer to his reader in the anticipation of the abusive reactions of a far from tractable reading public: 'Whilst I am thus talking, me thinks I heare one say, What a fop is this . . .' (i. 240), or 'I dare say thou hast cald me a hundred times dolt for this senseles discourse' (i. 239). In *Have With You to Saffron Walden* Pierce Respondent is constantly being mocked and interrupted by his interlocutors: 'O, what do you meane to hinder my Proclamation?' he asks indignantly, interrupted in mid-flow by Bentivole's disbelief, 'I did, I did . . .' (iii. 130). His writing is always in mocking dialogue with itself, either as embodied by the person of a fool (such as Will Summers, who constantly exposes the dramatic strategies of *Summers Last Will*) or by the printed discourse itself, which develops in mocking relation to what precedes

31 See More, *Utopia*, p. 130.

32 See Bakhtin, *Dostoevsky's Poetics*, p. 94.

33 Lucian, *Satirical Sketches*, trans. Turner, p. 29.

on the page. Typographical conventions provide media for mocking dialogue: when Pierce becomes a fool in *Pierce Penilesse* he stops using marginalia as didactic pointers and brings them into farcical relation with his text, indicating, for example, a passage about the devil's blackness with the note 'The diuell a Great Tobacca taker' (i. 181).

The idea of the lying traveller or the untrustworthy narrator is another of the features that Nashe's fiction shares with its menippean antecedents. This motif is of course merely a variant of the 'testament' delivered by one who is no longer concerned to conceal his strategies. The untrustworthy narrative is typically signalled by such an equivocatingly frank introduction as we find in Lucian's *True History*: 'In this one respect, however, I shall be a more honest liar than my predecessors . . . Let this voluntary confession forestall any future criticism . . . mind you do not believe a word I say.'[34] Here the genre—history—depends absolutely for its validity on the credibility of the narrator. The same is true, in English popular tradition, of the ballads advertised as the latest 'news' to be sung by 'Tom-Tell-Truth' which turn out to be nonsense rhymes of the 'Hey diddle diddle, the cat and the fiddle' variety.[35] Obviously travellers are, like historians, charged with a particular responsibility towards the reader, so that the figure of the lying traveller becomes another staple of menippean fiction. More's Raphael 'Nonsenso' (who gains ironic credibility by being coupled with Amerigo Vespucci) is one of those when he reports on his experiences abroad.[36] In one early Elizabethan dialogue, William Bullein's *Dialogue Against the Fever Pestilence* (1564), we find a Lucianic traveller named Mendax who behaves like the lord of an English May game, dressed in a 'greene Kendall coate' like Robin Hood, playing the cittern and dancing festive jigs.[37] Nashe remembers both Bullein and More in his own most topical dialogue, *Have with You to Saffron Walden*. The motif of the lying traveller from the New World (Bullein's 'Mendax') reappears in the introduction of Mercury, who comes from 'Wingan-decoy' or Virginia, and sports several sets of wings 'like a fooles coate with foure elbowes',

34 Ibid. 250.

35 See Baskervill, *Elizabethan Jig*, pp. 62–3. For an example of the type see *Roxburghe Ballads*, viii, p. 425.

36 *Utopia*, pp. 38 and nn., 135.

37 William Bullein, *A Dialogue Against the Fever Pestilence* (1564), ed. M. W. and A. H. Bullen, p. 94.

warning us not to be 'too rash or too slow of beleefe' in reading this history (iii. 23–4). As Nashe's concern here is to make a mockery of Harvey's obsession with print as a publicity machine, his equivocation turns on the tantalizing illusion of topical reality produced by his predecessors—More's mixing of real and feigned speakers, or Bullein's anagrammatic transformation of the real Dr Burcot into the 'fictional' Dr Tocrub. He warns us that he has framed the 'whole Booke in the nature of a Dialogue much like *Bullen* and his Doctor *Tocrub*' (iii. 20) but backhandedly removes the implication by not wishing to imply that 'all these personages are fained, like *Americke Vesputius*, & the rest of the *Antwerpe* speakers in *Sir Thomas Moores Vtopia*' (iii. 21).

As his acknowledgement in *Have With You to Saffron Walden* suggests, Nashe was aware that in adopting these menippean strategies his writing was participating in the Lucianic tradition which came to him through Erasmus and More. Yet he used these strategies for intellectual and aesthetic purposes of his own, often, indeed, for dismantling assumptions about the nature and purpose of writing which humanist menippea had been instrumental in disseminating. It was the humanists who placed such faith in the profits of reading (which we must understand in their terms to be a form of self-creation, of producing in oneself the capacities of memory and imaginative power for future discourse). When humanist writers play the game of the untrustworthy narrator, therefore, it is not infrequently with the aim of stimulating the intellectual productivity of the reader. Thus when Rabelais jokingly equivocates about the 'real presence' of an allegorical sense hidden within the fictions of Ovid and Homer, he is not cancelling out the possibility of interpretation and intellectual significance, but requiring the reader to find the power of interpretation within himself, directing him back to the surface of the text where, as Terence Cave points out, its 'potential productivity' for meaning is stored.[38] Erasmus is likewise undaunted by the prospect of destroying the credibility of such textual authorities as Pliny, Plutarch, Hesiod, or Homer. While he encourages students of rhetoric to lend credibility to their discourse by appealing to the authority of their analogical sources, he himself tends rather to undermine the credit of exemplary 'authorities' so as to draw attention to,

[38] Rabelais, *Gargantua and Pantagruel*, p. 38. See also Cave, *Cornucopian Text*, pp. 99–100.

among other things, their flexibility as discursive source material.[39] At such moments pleasure in comic energy and virtuosity carry the reader over the mild sense of shock at the discovery that his trust in the analogy was misplaced. What the discourse appears to lose in straightforward credibility, therefore, it makes up by conveying to the reader a new sense of intellectual potential, of new possibilities in the handling of discursive material. Erasmus encourages the use of comparisons which are ironic and deliberately ill-fitting or analogies which are downright fantastic and incredible so long as their use does not utterly preclude the opening up of intellectual significance: as models to be followed he cites Lucian's *True Histories, Icaromenippus,* and Apuleius' 'story of an ass'.[40]

Reading the *Adages* and the *De copia* of Erasmus, one would imagine that the Lucianic use of the ironic comparison would be a staple feature in the rhetoric of the Elizabethan student. While this was certainly the case in the context of the schoolroom exercise, it was by no means so in the public arena of print for reasons that I have outlined in Chapter 3. Here the Lucianic and Erasmian technique of opening out new ways of meaning through ambiguous comparisons had, in the course of time, grown politically suspect.[41] Linked through the Marprelate episode with puritan dissent, and more generally with the spread of atheism and scepticism, Lucianic irony was by the 1590s regarded as a deliberately subversive mode, employed by those whose object was to undermine the political indivisibility of Church and Crown. The commercial development of the English press in response to humanist ideals of self-education through profitable reading created different kinds of pressures on the author who wished to go into print. His book became part of a political and social transaction which, narrowly interpreted, tautologically increased his own and his patron's authority and credit to the extent that it bestowed 'profitable' knowledge on the commonweal. When Nashe decides to play the game of the untrustworthy narrator in the text of *The Unfortunate Traveller* he does not copy irrelevant humanist concerns but focuses on social pressures which affect his own art, parodying

[39] Compare Erasmus's pedagogical precepts in *De copia*, pp. 68–9, 90, with his own sceptical use of exemplary material in amplifying the adage 'Scarabeus aquilam quaerit', *Erasmus on his Times*, ed. and trans. M. M. Phillips, pp. 58–9.

[40] Erasmus, *De copia*, pp. 86–7.

[41] See Duncan, *Lucianic Tradition*, pp. 77–96; also M. M. Phillips, 'Erasmus and Propaganda', p. 4.

the page's obligatory promise to give service and profit to the commonweal. His book explicitly says that its pages are 'waste' paper which 'cannot doe theyr countrie better seruice' than to dry and kindle tobacco or wrap velvet pantoffles (ii. 207). This kind of material debasement of an obsolete approach to the text clearly resembles the aforementioned Prologue to *Gargantua*, in which Rabelais compares the excavation of allegorical significance to the pleasure of 'tasting the sustaining marrow after the long and diligent labours of sucking and gnawing at a bone'.[42]

In *Lenten Stuffe* Nashe is responding to a different kind of pressure on the author: the pressure of political interpretation with its consequent threat of censorship which marked the final years of Elizabeth's reign.[43] As a result the work makes use throughout of the kind of mock accuracy we find in fantastic travelogues such as Lucian's *True History*, concerning itself with precise measurement and dates so as to give the illusion that its obscurity is a cover for something worth investigating: 'From that moment to this sextine centurie', he begins, and then pretends to consternation at his sloppy inaccuracy, 'or let me not be taken with a lye, fiue hundred and ninetie eight, that wants but a paire of yeares to make me a true man' (iii. 160). Hints like the anxiety about being 'taken with a lye' or the ostentation of suppressing a particular comparison for fear it should be 'a theame displeasant' (iii. 159) are in fact tantalizing mock indications of a subversive significance. *Lenten Stuffe* puts all its inventive energy into denying the possibility of interpretative activity by undermining the very intellectual power of the ironic comparison on which the mock-encomium is built. The figure of comparison itself, of course, was indispensable to the humanist way of thinking, not only for epideictic rhetoric (the invention of praise) but for the very invention of persuasive knowledge itself.[44] Humanist discourse relied heavily on the 'opening out' of topics by means of comparison (simile or analogy) with a stock of memorized *exempla*. 'Whatever needs to

[42] Rabelais, *Gargantua and Pantagruel*, p. 38.

[43] See G. B. Harrison, 'Books and Readers 1599–1603'; A. Patterson, *Censorship Interpretation*, pp. 40–7.

[44] On the importance of comparison in epideictic rhetoric (ironic or straightforward) see Burgess, *Epideictic Literature*, pp. 121–5. On the 'comparative disposition' of humanist thought in general, and the emphasis on invention in both rhetoric and dialectic, see Baxandall, *Giotto and the Orators*, p. 32; Trousdale, *Shakespeare and the Rhetoricians*, pp. 22–38; Cave, *Cornucopian Text*, pp. 9–34; Jardine, 'The Place of Dialectic Teaching in Sixteenth-Century Cambridge', pp. 50–2.

be established', wrote Rudolph Agricola, 'must acquire credibility from something else.'[45] Relying on comparison to such an extent in the general 'proving' of knowlege through discourse inevitably opened up possibilities for irony (in comparisons which promote uncertainty rather than credibility) on a vast scale. Erasmus makes this abundantly clear in the *De copia* when he shows such a disregard for the truth as opposed to the moralizable potential of his discursive material, or when he suggests doubling the potential productivity of exemplary material by using the same figurative comparisons to praise 'versatility' as a moral virtue that one would employ to illustrate and condemn the vice of 'inconstancy'.[46] Such a privileging of potential significance over morality obviously calls the whole comparative basis of rhetorical proof into question; or at least makes it possible to do so, should one wish to pursue the Erasmian method beyond the precincts of the student's manual. Nashe, I think, does choose in *Lenten Stuffe* to make polemic out of the self-defeating productivity of comparative proof, thereby defying the very expectations of ironic (and hence politically subversive) significance that the comparative dynamic of mock-encomium would arouse in his rhetorically trained readers.

This, I believe, is why *Lenten Stuffe* baffles twentieth-century critics who read the clues of Nashe's debt to Erasmus's *Praise of Folly* or Lucian's *Phalaris* and other works in the same tradition:

> This is a light friskin of my witte, like the prayse of iniustice, the feuer quartane, Busirus, or Phalaris wherein I follow the trace of the famousest schollers of all ages whom a wantonizing humour once in their life time hath possesst to play with strawes, and turne mole-hils into mountains. (iii. 151)

Turning from this to the work itself, they expect to encounter that heady sense of intellectual relativity that ironic comparison is capable at its best of producing. What they find instead is non-sense, made more distasteful by an impression of deliberate goading, and the existence of a real-life satiric target. Nashe's 'joy in pure invective militates against any sustained irony'[47] writes one critic, but in fact this is far from being the case. The very suggestion that a subversive significance might be teased out of Nashe's ironic comparisons by someone in the know is itself a mockery; the paradoxes are impenetrable as they are suggestive. Ingeniously conforming to the

[45] Quoted by Trousdale, *Shakespeare and the Rhetoricians*, p. 35. See also Ong, *Ramus, Method*, p.117.

[46] *De copia*, pp. 93–7.

[47] M. Geraldine, 'Erasmus and the Tradition of Paradox', p. 60.

sophisticated rules of the ironic encomium, their substitution of mockery where praise is expected and vice versa is designed to frustrate the politic reader and to lead him nowhere at all. For example, after evaluating the Yarmouth fleet through a series of heroic comparisons, the writing seems suddenly to switch direction and to comment reflexively upon the relationship between honour and substance, between epithets and 'true' aristocracy:

> Small thinges we may expresse by great, and great by smal, though the greatnesse of the redde herring be not small (as small a hoppe on my thumbe as hee seemeth). It is with him as great personages, which from their high estate and not their high statures propagate the eleuate titles of their Gogmagognes . . . (iii. 185–6)

Here the tone is one of playful apology. An apparent defence of lineage aristocracy alerts one's suspicions in the pointedly ambiguous distinction between the propagation of physical inadequacies (smallness of stature) and the inheritance of political power (high estate). But neither this suggestion nor its further anti-aristocratic implications (that 'high estate' arbitrarily creates the category of 'great personage') has a chance to develop before the whole thing collapses in the epithet 'Gogmagognes'. This apparently superlative tribute to nobleman's grandeur cannot but remind us of Gogmagog, the famous buckram-filled giant of the Guildhall pageants; all the teasingly political potential of the comparison thereby disintegrates into an intellectually innocuous equation of great men with men of straw.[48]

In *Lenten Stuffe,* then, the figure of comparison itself breaks down, as if unwilling to disclose the ironic significance it seems to be hinting at. Are we then therefore to accept the conclusion of past critics that *Lenten Stuffe*'s debt to Erasmus is superficial, and that Nashe was incapable of using the strategies of mock praise to direct attention towards the rhetorical structures of thought? Surely not; surely we must rather conclude that the significant irony of *Lenten Stuffe*, as of Nashe's other writings, unfolds through the text's very frustration of Elizabethan habits of 'profitable' or interpretative reading. Instead of being flattered by the productivity of his own interpretation, his ability to find 'vnder the shaddowe of greene . . . leaues . . . a further meaning closely comprised' (i. 28), the attentive reader finds himself inadvertently participating, like a fool, in a series

[48] F. W. Fairholt, *Gog and Magog: The Giants in the Guildhall*, p. 58.

of inconsequential verbal pastimes. Yet when Nashe admits that the whole text is nothing but insignificant pastime—'playing with a shettlecocke, or tossing empty bladders in the ayre' (iii. 225), he says, recalling Erasmus riding on his hobby horse in the *Praise of Folly*[49] —he scarcely expects his legal minded critics to believe him and to abandon their search for subversive meaning. Years before, in *Summers Last Will and Testament*, Nashe had played a similar game of calculated insignificance, allowing Will Summers to mock the pedagogic anxiety of Summer at the 'wit ill spent' and the 'bad words, bad wit' (iii. 243 and 249) of his careless stewards. Here, too, the stewards are burlesque versions of the dangerous ironic discourser or the sceptical pyrrhonist, defending their natural seasonal attributes as if these were subversive paradoxical opinions. The joke is on Summer who, like Ascham's Schoolmaster, distrusts the waste and fears the political consequence of such verbal intemperance.[50] The years intervening between *Summers Last Will* and *Lenten Stuffe*, however, had turned the mockery of such anxieties from a politically conservative to a politically radical gesture. In the context of Whitgift's learned household, Will Summers's scorn for 'moralizers' and 'deepe reaching wits' who 'wrest a neuer meaning out of euery thing' (iii. 235) could be sure of a reception on its own terms as an innocuous blow against scholarly interpretation. In *Lenten Stuffe*, by contrast, the mockery of such moralizing reading habits becomes a plea for the aesthetic integrity of the text and the author's intention—an attempt to resist the appropriation of all meaning by those in political power. Although his own works were soon to be expressly forbidden as part of a general panic over topical reference in contemporary satire, Nashe reverses the usual identification of the satiric author as one who 'bites' and defames contemporaries. His images suggest that texts are harmless by comparison with the legal interpreters who get their teeth into them. He fully expects himself to be 'mangled and torne in mennes mouthes about this playing with a shettlecocke, or tossing empty bladders in the ayre' (iii. 225). The literary text may in-

[49] p. 58.

[50] See Ascham, *Schoolmaster*, p. 74. Note how Ver and Bacchus irresponsibly praise carnal excess, how Orion follows Sextus Empiricus the sceptic philosopher in his praise of dogs (iii. 255), and how Winter's dispraise of learning burlesques another sceptical work, Cornelius Agrippa's *De incertitudine et vanitate scientiarum*. The imaginative possibilities opened up by pyrrhonic scepticism seem to have appealed to Nashe; see iii. 332 and his sceptical remarks on the dreaming imagination in *The Terrors of the Night*, i. 355–7.

sult or injure as the fool's bladder strikes random blows at the carnival crowd, but the effects are probably innocuous, given that the bladder is 'empty' and the shrovetide shuttlecock merely made of feathers. The author, however, does not get off so lightly; Nashe's image strikingly anticipates what happened to one author whose work had the misfortune to precipitate the edict of 1599. This was John Hayward, who found himself having to defend his *Life of Henry IV* from the charge of treasonous intent which Sir Edward Coke's scrutinous examination of the text made difficult to avoid. Well practised in the Elizabethan habit of applying the exemplary potential of a text, Coke's detailed notes profess to explore Hayward's 'secret drift' from under the 'outward pretence' of his history.[51] That other readers remained sceptical of this secret drift scarcely mattered: 'everything is as it is taken' remarked John Chamberlain.[52] Hayward escaped with his life from the charge of treason, but the ban on history and satire that followed ended Nashe's career. Not surprisingly, in this context, critics are inclined to draw the conclusion that Nashe was an author with a secret drift, a contemporary referent: 'Had his satirical revenge been deciphered?' asks one scholar.[53] But perhaps the implications can be taken another way. It could be that Nashe's texts were suddenly considered controversial not because they could be moralized or 'mangled' by interested readers who wished to find contemporary referents, but because their Lucianic mockery of such approaches to the printed text had itself come to be a political matter.

[51] M. Dowling, 'Sir John Hayward's Trouble over his *Life of Henry IV*', pp. 212–24, 215.

[52] Harrison, 'Books and Readers 1599–1603', p. 13.

[53] A. L. Scoufos, 'Nashe, Jonson and the Oldcastle Problem', p. 318.

# Part II: The Texts

# 8

# Wasting Time in *Summers Last Will and Testament*

'WHAT can be made of Summers last will & Testament?' asks the fool Will Summers, and answers derisively, in good festive spirit: 'Such another thing as *Gyllian* of *Braynfords* will, where shee bequeathed a score of farts amongst her friends' (iii. 235). But Will Summers is being misleading here; Summer's testament bears no resemblance whatsoever to the grotesque mocking testimonies of popular festival fools. Summer is no self-confessed sinner, merrily bequeathing his past crimes and excesses to the audience for their mockery and recreation. On the contrary he is, as Will Summers goes on to remark in the same breath, a master and a judge, one who must: 'call his officers to account, yeeld his throne to Autumne, make Winter his Executor, with tittle tattle Tom boy' (iii. 235). Will's dismissive 'tittle tattle Tom boy' implies, as C. L. Barber observed, that 'the scheme is familiar'.[1] But which scheme? From the outset, it seems, a playful tension is established between two entirely different dramatic conventions arising from the concepts of 'bequest' and 'inheritance'. In the festive scheme of things, the occasion of Summer's falling sick of excesses and yielding up sovereignty to his seasonal heir would be one of boisterous antagonism, one in which Summer would freely render up his body and goods for the re-creation of the new season. What we in fact encounter in Nashe's show, however, is a Summer lord who is filled with reluctance and anxiety concerning the disposal of his wealth and being. He is suspicious of the motives and character of his respective heirs, Autumn and Winter; will they make good use of what he has gathered on their behalf? 'Had I some issue . . .', he laments, envisaging the security of an inheritance transferred intact and built upon by generations after his death. There is no chance of such a future, however, being realized in his dissipated heirs:

[1] Barber, *Shakespeare's Festive Comedy*, p. 59. For the date and circumstances of the show's performance see ibid. 79–86; B. Nicholson in *The Complete Works of Thomas Nashe*, ed. A. B. Grosart, vol. vi, pp. xxvi–xxix; McKerrow, iv. 416–19.

when perforce these must enioy my wealth,
Which thanke me not, but enter't as a pray,
Bequeath'd it is not, but cleane cast away. (iii. 272)

The casting away of wealth should not be of concern to the festival lord who is, after all, re-created by the free dispersal of his stale riches; here, the Summer lord's characteristic licence has been exchanged for the careful providence of protestant humanism. We are incongruously transported back into a mid-century world of thrifty fathers anxious to build up a heritage of virtuous industry to be increased and furthered by the labours of their sons. Summer's request bears less resemblance to festive testimonies than it does to the provident words of Ascham in dedicating his *Schoolmaster* to his sons: 'Seeing at my death I am not like to leave them any great store of living, therefore in my lifetime I thought good to bequeath unto them in this little book . . . the right way to good learning, which if they follow . . . they shall very well come to sufficiency of living'.[2] Ascham's bequest expresses hope for the possibility of progress, increase in industry and *virtus* built upon the preceptual foundations of good learning and self-government. But with these hopes come fears, the dread of a lifetime's provident labour dissipated and brought to nothing through the prodigal tendencies of youth. For all the providence, the great 'cost and charge' invested in their sons' futures, anxious fathers frequently, says Ascham, reap nothing but 'the fruit of grief and care'.[3] Nashe made his own glibly conventional nod to the sufferings of the provident father in *The Anatomie of Absurditie* where he rebuked prodigal young men for 'casting that away at a cast at dice, which cost theyr daddes a yeares toyle' (i. 33). This is the same as the moralizing vein absurdly stuffed into the mouth of a summer slowly ripening into autumn:

I must depart, my death-day is set downe:
To these two must I leaue my wheaten crowne.
So vnto vnthrifts rich men leaue their lands,
Who in an houre consume long labours gaynes . . . (iii. 237–8)

Fear that the hard-won foundations of reform and learning would be incontinently consumed by the precocious inexperience of a second generation was the staple of mid-sixteenth-century prodigal son drama. The bourgeois fathers of Gascoigne's *Glasse of Governement* express their hopes that, having 'heaped up sufficient store'

[2] Ascham, *Schoolmaster*, p. 11.

[3] Ibid. 40.

by 'continuall payns and travayle', something of lasting value may be achieved; for virtuous sons may 'by learning aspire unto greater promotion, and builde greater matters uppon a better foundation'.[4] In the terms established by prodigal son drama the father's bequest becomes a monument to the achievements of the nation's past and an investment in its glorious future; the possibilities opened up by education turn the festive idea of dissipating the last generation's wealth into a threat to erase its history.

The solemn strains of the prodigal son discourse break through the context of seasonal merriment in *Summers Last Will*, its pragmatic awareness of the grave implications of material loss coexisting in a peculiar tension with the reckless gaiety of self-consuming festivity. What results is a quite extraordinary blend (as C. L. Barber observed) of pathos and irony, creating a sense of the physical frailty of human life quite beyond the reach of either its didactic or its festive antecedents.[5] For example, when Summer first appears lamenting the brevity of joy—'What pleasure alway lasts? no ioy endures' (iii. 237)—he is echoing the familiar plaint of Acolastus, the prodigal son, on finding his substance consumed in youthful riot, 'howe quite and cleane is it gone . . . excesse of fleshely pleasures . . . hath taken awaye . . . all that euer I had'.[6] Summer's anxieties in relation to the prodigality of his 'sons'—Harvest, Autumn, etc.—should be needless; he ripens into them, 'Haruest and age haue whit'ned my greene head', but darkly interprets this natural process as certain effacement by his enemies, 'Needs must he fall, whom none but foes vphold' (iii. 237). All the prodigal vices of Acolastus, who is glossed in the schoolboy drama as 'a stroy good, a begger, wantynge temperance in his diete, wantinge meane and measure, wantonly inclyned to bodily lustes, and one that wyll endure no correction: all whyche conditions may appere in this comedye . . .',[7] find themselves freely acknowledged in Nashe's own comedy as the prodigal attributes of Summer's servants and heirs, none of whom appears in the least perturbed by the provident cares of their paternal master. Ver is a beggar, Bacchus wants temperance in his diet, Sol is a 'Lasciuious and intemperate' courtier, wantonly inclined to bodily lusts, while Solstitium tediously upholds the virtues of mean and measure which

[4] Gascoigne, *Works*, ii. 90.

[5] See Barber, *Shakespeare's Festive Comedy*, p. 78 n.

[6] Acolastus, *Comedy*, trans. J. Palsgrave, p. 159.

[7] Ibid. 13.

the others pointedly lack. It becomes clear that far from standing in antagonistically festive relationship to one another, Nashe's seasons all assume the posture of prodigal servants being called to account by their master Summer. Rather than presenting occasion for ironic bequests from the Summer lord, the seasons face trial as provident stewards of his time and wealth: 'In presence of this Honourable trayne . . . Meane I to make my finall Testament', says Summer, 'But first Ile call my officers to count/*And of the wealth I gaue them to dispose/Known what is left, I may know what to giue*' (iii. 238, my italic). In this way, of course, Nashe's Summer lord game makes a mockery of another aspect of the prodigal son discourse: its tendency to regard young men as investments of time and precious talent, answerable to the judgement of God and his exacting earthly representatives.

This discourse is based on the parable (Matt. 25: 14–30) of the kingdom of heaven as a wealthy master who entrusted his talents to servants, one of whom invested wisely and was himself rewarded with mastery over a great multitude, while another, unprofitably burying his talent, was cast into outer darkness and the place of wailing and gnashing of teeth. Prominent in the writings of Protestant reformers (it is retold, for example, in Robert Crowley's 'Voyce of the laste trumpet', a didactic treatise on the duties of several vocations), this story and the values it implies are ironically present throughout Nashe's comedy, confounding themselves in it by definition.[8] As a master of art, Nashe is incriminated from the start in the parable's terms, since the very writing of such a trivial pastime is a 'waste' of the talent entrusted to him by his Divine Master. According to Gascoigne, any author who 'is (by the highest God) endued with anye haughty gifte, hee ought also to bestowe and employe the same in some worthie and profitable subiecte or travayle. Least in his default, he deserue the name of an unprofitable and carelesse Stewarde when his accoumpt is strictly cast.'[9] *Summers Last Will and Testament* can hardly be called a 'profitable subject or travail', worthy of the 'haughty' gift of God Gascoigne describes. This much is freely acknowledged in the voice of the fool Will Summers, who berates the author of the present work for 'making himselfe a publike laughing stock' by writing it. Nashe thus

[8] See *The Select Works of Robert Crowley*, ed. J. M. Cowper, pp. 60–3.
[9] Gascoigne, *Works*, ii. 212.

appears to mock at himself for not keeping his 'haughty' talent in reserve, like other '*Magisterij*' whose inuention is farre more exquisite'. But then the superiority of these worthy art-masters seems to arise from the fact that they are so anxious not to waste their God-given talent that they are 'content to sit still and doe nothing' (iii. 234). In mocking the prodigality of his author, therefore, Will Summers turns the whole discourse of profitable and unprofitable servants on its head. It is the provident ones who wastefully bury their talents.

Throughout the comedy the whole idea of language being answerable to a final judgement, being brought to account in columns of profit and loss, is joyfully mocked in Summer's misguided probings for returns of moral edification in the improvised word games of his prodigal servants. High-flying gifts of eloquence were all very well, wrote Gascoigne in the preface just quoted, but they should be employed to do more than play for the aesthetic gratification of the writer; invention for its own sake, as a pleasurable activity, 'might perhappes content a vayne desyre, but the profit or commoditie would scarcely quyte his coste'.[10] It is the internalized guilt present in the notion of examining one's own exertions as a 'cost' which has to be 'quyted' before an arbitrating conscience, which is dramatized in the ludicrous concept of Summer playing arbitrator and God to other seasons which are no more answerable to him for their 'wealth' and 'talents' than he is to them. Vitality is lent to the seasons by powers beyond Summer's intervention; Ver, who is 'Spring', replies that he has spent his wealth 'prodigally':

> Troth my Lord, to tell you playne, I can giue you no other account: *nam quae habui, perdidi;* what I had, I haue spent on good fellowes; in these sports you haue seen, which are proper to the Spring, and others of like sort (as giuing wenches greene gownes, making garlands for Fencers, and tricking vp children gay) haue I bestowde all my flowry treasure and flowre of my youth. (iii. 240–1)

'Is this th'account and reckoning that thou makst?' demands Summer after the dancing; Ver, he decides, has been badly brought up, an 'vnciuill nurturde boy' (iii. 240). But Ver's 'account' is both loss and having all at once; although it is spent and lost as soon as

[10] Ibid.

had (*nam quae habui, perdidi*) yet in its very 'loss' is the 'gain' of the comedy in the sports which Ver occasions. He *is* Spring, and this activity is 'proper to the spring', so while it seems like the loss of wealth, his 'flowry treasure' is a wealth bestowed by loss, the only mode in which it can be said to exist. Acknowledging time as a 'wealth' in itself, regardless of what may be gained by it, is impossible for Nashe's Summer, who continues to demand a reckoning of all his deputies as if their times were his own. 'With all thy hunting', he asks Orion, the hunter, 'how are we inricht?' (iii. 256), and when the dog star answers, 'hunters doe hunt for pleasure, not for gaine/While Dog-dayes last the haruest safely thriues', Summer, nonplussed, can only retort that Orion is an 'ill-gouern'd starre' (iii. 256–7). It is Harvest himself who finally reminds Summer that the wealth which he is so anxious to account for is not in fact his at all; far from being answerable to Summer for his treasure, Harvest points out that Summer and all the rest are dependent on him; he distributes himself to create wealth, 'vsury for your mony, thousands for one: what would you haue more?' (iii. 261). Harvest's appeal to the providence of seasonal time merrily explodes the social and psychological pressures created by the concept of man as autonomous master of his 'own' circumstantial and spiritual resources.

While festive apprehension of time irresponsibly liberates people from the past, the doctrine of reform naturally advocated retrospection, examining the past for the profits it had yielded, the gains of time well spent. Endings should provide opportunity not for mockery and abuse but for taking stock; such was the lesson instilled into young boys in grammar schools of the mid-century. At Winchester the boys were told by their tutor that as their holidays drew to a close they should remember Cicero's words in *De senectute* that all things come to an end.[11] Cato the Elder, as Cicero renders him in *De senectute*, becomes the obvious model for a satisfactory 'reckoning' of time well spent; as Erasmus says he did not fear old age, for 'he left to posterity monuments of his virtue and industry'[12]. Nashe's Summer pathetically looks back for monuments to the industrious investments of his allotted time, but all in vain, he has dispersed all his time, that is, him*self*, in the carefree

[11] Baldwin, *Small Latine & Lesse Greeke*, i. 333.
[12] Erasmus, *Colloquies*, p. 67.

becoming of one festival after another. Cicero's Cato blames the miserable endings of others on their 'youthful dissipation',[13] their inability to keep to a mean. But all Summer's deputed selves, from Ver to Bacchus, exist in dissipation, except for the tedious Solstitium, who is praised in accordingly moralizing terms by Summer:

> I like thy moderation wondrous well;
> And this thy ballance, wayghing the white glasse
> And blacke with equall poyze and stedfast hand,
> A patterne is to Princes and great men . . . (iii. 245)

It has been suggested that in Solstitium Nashe was attempting to present 'a positive ideal of moderation' which was simply a dramatic failure, despite 'Summer's unqualified approval'.[14] But surely this threadbare moralizing shows that the unqualified approval of such a decrepit old pedant as Summer is, in the play's terms, a joke; Summer speaks a completely inapplicable moral language which disintegrates in the parody of his buffoon Will Summers. It is Will Summers who turns Summer's stale stocktaking to material 'profit' in comic terms by making a mockery of the whole weighing-up process. Where Summer shows an acquisitive desire to wrest profitable meanings from the words of his stewards, Will Summers energetically participates in them, making them accessible as the material of laughter. Thus while Summer conducts his own deluded self-examination, calling his temporal officers to account, Will Summers subjects each one simultaneously to his own unofficial trial by mockery, proving what pleasure the time can yield. The abstract idea of temperance and moderation, which seems to Summer to yield so much profit and edification, is completely incomprehensible and inaccessible to Will Summers, who accordingly transforms Solstitium's 'scales'—signifying an outlook able to distinguish between time profitably spent and time lost—into the game of 'cales' or skittles, which of course represent time as irresponsible pleasure: 'What haue we to do with scales and hower-glasses . . . ? I cannot tell how other men are addicted, but it is against my profession to vse any scales but such as we play at with a boule' (iii. 247). Will's response encapsulates the creative method of the pastime as a whole. It is by effecting an encounter of two totally incompatible ways of thought—the reformed and the

13 Cicero, 'Cato the Elder on Old Age', in *Selected Works*, trans. M. Grant, p. 224.
14 Hibbard, *Thomas Nashe*, p. 97.

festive—that Nashe ensures a rich reserve of antagonistic meanings which break each other down into pleasurable material. Nashe's predecessors in prodigal son drama had made provident use of recreational and saturnalian precedents for their reforming uses. As John Dover Wilson observed, the whole Terentian machinery of bawds, slaves and pandars was incorporated into the didactic drama of the *Acolastus* type. Similarly, at Winchester in 1564, one tutor wrote a special shrovetide morality which made use of the Carnival occasion to *teach* the folly of feasting before a fast (*Acolastus*, incidentally, had been the performance of the previous Christmas). Gascoigne in his *Glasse of Governement* specifically distinguished his didactic drama from the licentious 'Italian toyes' and 'Terence phrase'; the time of the 'deformed shewes' of Saturnalia was past, he wrote, 'reformed speeche doth now become us best'.[15] But Nashe is reacting against an overdose of reformed speech; he turns language back from meaning into laughing-stocks, 'deforming' the discourse of morality. After all, he does not have to *teach* his audience anything; to attempt to do so would be presumptuous in a mere university graduate, writing for the distinguished entourage of the Archbishop of Canterbury. These are the men, if any are, who set the rules and precepts for mere art-masters: 'To make you merry, that are the *Gods of Art* and *guides vnto heauen* . . .', the epilogue explains, 'hammer-headed clownes . . . haue set their deformities to view, as it were in a daunce here before you' (iii. 294, my italic). Perhaps this explains the reckless freedom with which Nashe's pageant wastes and dissipates the resources of moralized invention. Whereas Lyly in 1580 felt compelled to reassure the Blackfriars audience of his *Campaspe* that they would receive edification with their pastime: 'We haue mixt mirth with counsell, and discipline with delight, thinking it not amisse in the same garden to sowe pot-hearbes, that we set flowers',[16] Nashe's prologue simply abandons any promises of that sort: 'As the *Parthians* fight, flying away, so will wee prate and talke, but stand to nothing that we say' (iii. 235). Authors and actors are incoherent delight makers, prepared to 'shame ourselues to make sport' for their learned audience; even the exemplary records of men's intellectual labours are turned into precedents for pastimes, 'odde trifles' such as the experiments of

[15] Gascoigne, *Works*, ii. 6. See also Baldwin, *Small Latine & Lesse Greeke*, i. 329–30; J. D. Wilson, 'Euphues and the Prodigal Son'.

[16] Lyly, *Works*, ii. 315.

mathematicians, 'daunsing balles, an egge-shell that shall clyme vp to the top of a speare' (iii. 235).

The prologue defies the providence of such 'moralizers' as would attempt to gather profitable meanings from their evening's entertainment in a way that is dramatized throughout the show by the futility of Summer's magisterial interrogation of his temporal deputies. Summer's anxiety about the credit and truth of the words he encounters relates his careful husbandry of time and land to a reformed distaste for wasted language. For him, Ver's rhetorical virtuosity in praise of beggary is a prodigal expenditure of resources: 'O vanitie it selfe! O wit ill spent!' he exclaims melodramatically (iii. 243). Will Summers finds the oration equally offensive, not, however, because it is 'vain' and empty of profit, but because it is too stale and uninventive to yield a 'belly-full' (iii. 244) of laughter; he parodies Summer's moral distaste for idle beggars by magnanimously offering to provide so impoverished an imagination with themes to set it to work: 'Well, rather then he shall haue no imployment but licke dishes, I will set him a worke my selfe, to write in prayse of the arte of stouping . . . Repayre to my chamber, poore fellow, when the play is done' (iii. 244). And so the show goes on with Summer constantly fearful of losing something by being given vanities for profitable truth. ('I must giue credit vnto what I heare', he protests, 'for other then I heare, attract I nought', while Harvest immediately rejoins with a parody of Summer's own prudent morality: 'I, I; nought seeke, nought haue:/An ill husband is the first steppe to a knave', iii. 260–1.) Will Summers, meanwhile, is busily applying his own criteria as auditor of words which may be worth listening to. He is no respecter of persons either: Summer's overlordship does not exempt him from the obligation to provide merriment. 'But let vs', he invites the audience, 'heare what Summer can say for himselfe, why hee should not be hist at' (iii. 237).

Will's criteria of pleasure from words is shared by Summer's deputies who constantly deflect their master's rational pursuit of information into gestures towards the sharing of song and dance and refreshment. 'Knowst thou the reason why I sent for thee?' demands Summer of Ver. But reasoning does not affect Ver:

> If you will daunce a Galliard, so it is: if not,
> Falangtado Falangtado, to weare the blacke and yellow:
> Falangtado Falangtado, my mates are gone, Ile followe.
>
> (iii. 239)

he replies, irrelevantly. The demand for reasonable words, words that secure a store of knowledge, is confounded by words active in the improvisation of a moment's pleasure just as, in spectacular terms, Summer's request for visual evidence of temporal profit is met by songs, hobby-horsing and morris dancing; the vitally present activity which is, as Ver says, the only 'grand capitall summe' (iii. 240) to be expected. Encountering Harvest, Summer's demands for substantial knowledge of gains and losses prove equally fruitless. He enquires after his possessions:

> Haruest, the Bayly of my husbandry,
> What plenty hast thou heapt into our Barnes?
> I hope thou hast sped well, thou art so blithe

But Harvest's blithe aspect is unaffected by success or failure; the occasion demands festivity, not reckoning:

> Sped well or ill, sir, I drinke to you on the same:
> Is your throate cleare to help vs sing *hooky*, *hooky*?
> [Heere they all sing after him
>
> (iii. 259)

The point being made is not just that the odds are rather obviously against Summer finding any 'profit' in the grotesquely disintegrating time and language of his own demise; it is more generally a humbling reminder that the provident husbanding of one's resources and investing of one's talents, though undoubtedly effective and productive of *virtus*, is nevertheless no guarantee against the ephemerality of the human condition. Monuments of virtue and industry look wan in the context of plague and harvest failure. Though articulated in festive terms, the *memento mori* aspect of the play has decidedly Christian overtones; Harvest's mockery reminds Summer that he deludes himself in thinking to 'own' the wealth yielded by his land, in a manner reminiscent of the mid-century preachers against enclosing landlords.[17] But mockery of the delusions of ownership and mastery is also made in less explicitly Christian terms through the re-creation of communicative language. The point of the play is its impertinence; through the uninhibited re-appropriation of Summer's censorious words for their own improvised sport the stewards avoid being judged for failures beyond their control, and 'prove' themselves more resourceful than

[17] See above, Ch. 4.

their provident master, who proves nothing but loss upon loss. Summer's painstaking attempts to force the drunken Bacchus to grasp the importance of statistics for the grape harvest: 'I would about thy vintage question thee:/ How thriue thy vines? hadst thou good store of grapes?' are met with verbal antics from Bacchus, an improvisation on the word vintage, switching into mock lament:

> Our vintage was a vintage, for it did not work vpon
> the aduantage, it came in the vauntgard of Summer,
> & winds and stormes met it by the way . . .
> And made it cry, Alas and welladay. (iii. 265–6)

Summer reaps no benefit from this kind of game, and doggedly pursues his point, 'That was not well, but all miscaried not?' (ii. 266). Bacchus' verbal dramatization of unavoidable material loss is characteristic of the improvisatory instinct, the capacity to derive pleasure from whatever rudiments are available, which differentiates the ephemeral fools from their conscientious master. Like Auden's birds and flowers, Bacchus and his fellows do not use language to 'assume responsibility for time', but to survive in its thrall as best they can. Thus Harvest, like Bacchus, makes verbal comedy of his poor returns:

> My oates grew like a cup of beere that makes the brewer rich . . . my barley, euen as many a nouice is crossebitten as soone as euer hee peepes out of the shell, so was it frost-bitten in the blade, yet pickt vp his crummes agayne afterward, and bade, Fill pot, hostesse, in spite of a deare yeere. (iii. 262)

The resilience of the 'crossebitten' (i.e. tricked, doublecrossed) barley which manages to provide for carousing in spite of its impoverishment, reflects the resourcefulness of Harvest himself, in reacting so stoutly to adversity. Although allusions to loss of substance recur, the festive characters' tendency to materialize and animate this loss provides the 'substance' which Summer tries to gather in vain. Learned paradoxes, arguments spun out of puns and double meaning similarly derive their nourishment from confusions and ambiguities, the lacunae of accurate verbal expression. Exuberant song, dance, and wordplay are dramatizations of physical prosperity; they represent a triumph over ephemerality and morality. The only way, however, that one can assess or profit by such displays of substance and prosperity is to engage in them as Will

Summers does, indulging in and parodying antic and sophistry. Summer's efforts to wrest profit from land and time which do not, in the comedy's terms, 'belong' to him is linked to the way in which his officious executors, Autumn and Winter, insist on treating the other dependants as hirelings, mere answerable labour. Not that this seems to bother him; when Autumn tries to get Harvest to answer 'direct' to his master Summer's demands, Harvest defiantly reminds Autumn that he is no employee: 'Answere? why, friend, I am no tapster, to say Anon, anon, sir' (iii. 259). Threatening to 'mow' off Autumn's leaves, Harvest is rebuked for mocking and 'mowing' at his peers by Winter. The officiousness of Winter and Autumn, and the general level of respect they attempt to exact from Summer's dependants, suggests, in the comic friction it creates, a small-scale dramatization of the kind of social changes disclosed in *King Lear* where the capacity of the old-style household to contain its own unruly, subversive energies is displaced unwittingly by Lear's claims to absolute possessive authority; thereafter his daughters help to usher in the new style of household, more private, more civilized, maintained by servants whose well-spoken officiousness indicates the relation of paid employee to employer.

In the old-style household the status of 'servants' was somewhat different; they were not so much employees as dependants, god-children, or the children of neighbours or tenants, maintained by the lord in accordance with codes of loyalty and protection of his territorial affinities.[18] Respect and obedience demanded by the new-style relations of lordship and service correspond to the more authoritarian relations of father to son, pedagogue to pupil, magistrate to commonality which were a general result of the educational revolution of the sixteenth century.[19] Elsewhere Nashe remarks ironically on magisterial intolerance of the laughter and mockery of social inferiors; it does seem as though the Tudor reform and centralization of authorizing institutions like the Justices of the Peace involved a certain simplification and sharpening of social stratifications, subordinating all local loyalties and privileges to the representation of the Crown, which could brook no

[18] See James, *Family, Lineage and Civil Society*, pp. 183–4; *Cyuile and Vncyuile Life*, sig. F2$^{v}$; also C. Hill, *Society and Puritanism in Pre-Revolutionary England*, p. 462.

[19] See F. F. Foster, *The Politics of Stability*, p. 89; James, *Family, Lineage and Civil Society*, pp. 96–107; Helgerson, *Elizabethan Prodigals*, p. 23.

disrespect. Laughter at social superiors became a political matter;[20] Nashe makes a joke about one over-zealous Justice of the Peace who, when the populace began to laugh at Tarlton on stage, set about them with his staff of office 'in that they, being but Farmers & poore countrey Hyndes, would presume to laugh at the Queenes men, and make no more account of her cloath in his presence' (i. 188).

The uninhibited mockery dispensed by the country hinds of *Summers Last Will* draws attention to itself as the dramatization of a dying social phenomenon; ten years later a group of summer revellers faced charges in the court of the Star Chamber for casting mocking aspersions on the local lord.[21] Not that Nashe was taking any such risks in his pastime; indeed it seems rather as though the mocking freedom with which Summer's dependants deflect him from his profit-gathering purposes and remind him of his festival obligations, makes some kind of reference to the old-fashioned style in which Archbishop Whitgift kept open house on festival days at Croydon. Whitgift was not, apparently, one of those who followed the new fashion of entertaining only friends of his own social rank; he kept house in the old style, open to dependants and strangers. The open lifestyle of the old household was not just metaphorical, but architecturally evident in the great hall with its open hearth.[22] It was only gradually in the course of the sixteenth and seventeenth centuries that properties were built with privacy in mind, relegating servants to special quarters and providing room to entertain only close relatives and friends. Whitgift's first biographer makes large claims for his open housekeeping: 'He had a desire alwayes to keepe a great and bountifull house; and so he did . . . And at Christmasse, especially, his gates were alwayes open, and his Hall set twice or thrice ouer with strangers.'[23] A household like this would be an appropriate context for mockery of the more possessive and individualistic aspects of reformed attitudes to poverty and social responsibility. At the same time it is clear that Nashe's celebration of hospitality is no absolutist fantasy of organic social

20 See K. Thomas, 'The Place of Laughter in Tudor and Stuart England'; also J. W. Allen, *A History of Political Thought in the Sixteenth Century*, pp. 408–10.

21 O'Conor, *Godes Peace and the Queenes*, pp. 83–7.

22 James, *Family, Lineage and Civil Society*, p. 187.

23 Sir George Paule, *The Life of the Most Reverend . . . John Whitgift*, p. 77. For Whitgift's contention with the aristocracy's despoliation of church wealth see also C. Hill, *Economic Problems of the Church*, p. 31.

harmony, such as Jonson depicts in *To Penshurst*. To Jonson the natural wealth of the country estate seems miraculous: the earth yields herself for her masters' consumption without requiring city costs. Household dependants are simply aspects of this golden age, dumbly offering themselves as produce to an estate which already rejoices in total possession:

> But all come in, the farmer and the clowne;
> And no one empty-handed, to salute
> Thy lord and lady, though they have no sute.
> . . . . . . . . .
> But what can this (more then expresse their loue)
> Add to thy free prouisions, farre aboue
> The neede of such? whose liberall board doth flow
> With all that hospitalitie doth know![24]

Jonson has recourse to a traditional ideal of hospitality to affirm exactly what Nashe uses the same ideal to deny: the tendency to regard other human beings as the speechless limbs of an organic body politic, whose harmonious identity is imposed by the consciousness of its master. For Jonson, people become seasonal tributes, 'saluting' and increasing their master's estate with handfuls of provision. For Nashe the tributary seasons are empty-handed but mocking and vociferous in their denial of the absolute mastery of any lord. At one point it even seems that Summer's comic delusions of temporal mastery and possession are being parodied in a direct ironic reference to Whitgift's lordship and 'ownership' of the material environment. When Ver's morris dancers are active in presenting their time-wasting 'reckoning' to the scandalized Summer, Will Summers warns them not to be too enthusiastic about wasting land as well as time: 'You, friend with the Hobby-horse, goe not too fast, for feare of wearing out my Lords tyle-stones with your hob-nayles' (iii. 240). Holiday-time may belong to no one, and harvest's bounty be the gift of the earth, but 'my Lord's tyle-stones' are evidently his own. In fact the whole comedy of modern economics, with its faith in the enclosure and exploitation of a material and temporal environment, is ludicrously parodied in Nashe's circumstantial drama of the vulnerable human body, desperately striving to immunize itself against the disintegrating forces of time. To be a 'banckrout asse' in these terms is not to be morally irresponsible, but simply to be 'weather-beaten', ravaged

[24] Ben Jonson, 'To Penshurst', in *Works*, viii. 95.

by time (iii. 273). If Whitgift's Christmas household is boldly open to strangers, Nashe's is more circumspect, and his fears that indiscriminate open house will undermine his wealth and social dignity are expressed in ludicrously concrete terms: 'Say I keepe hospitalitie, and a whole faire of beggers bid me to dinner euery day, what with making legges, when they thanke me at their going away, and setling their wallets handsomly on their backes, they would shake as many lice on the ground as were able to vndermine my house, and vndoe me utterly' (iii. 285).

In a society which was beginning, with the encouragement of government poor law legislation and the exertions of local magistrates, to espouse the virtues of bourgeois individualism, mendicancy was foregrounded as a real social menace and the 'able-bodied beggar' a threat to all good government.[25] With the materializing comic genius that is the gift of all Summer's buffoonish dependants, Christmas here makes a mockery of the cautious reservations of society against the undermining powers of sturdy beggars. The provident enclosure by which he lives is expressed (like Harvest's incessant self-expenditure) in grotesque bodily terms as constant battle for survival against the weathering expenditure of existence:

> *Liberalitas liberalitate perit*; loue me a little and loue me long: our feete must haue wherewithall to feede the stones, our backs walles of wooll to keepe out the colde that besiegeth our warme blood; our doores must haue barres, our dubblets must haue buttons. Item, for an olde sword to scrape the stones before the dore with, three halfe-pence: for stitching a wodden tanckard that was burst–These Water-bearers will empty the conduit and a mans coffers at once. (iii. 286–7)

The body becomes a household, fighting for solvency against encroachment by the cold, but this insistence on the vulnerability of the flesh serves to mock and undermine the ideology of possessive individualism for which it acts as a ludicrous analogy. Thus from Christmas's pragmatic saw 'Liberalitas liberalitate periit' (liberality undoes itself) we move to the absurd: 'our feete must haue wherewithall to feede the stones', with its overtones of an opposite

25 See F. G. Emmison, *Elizabethan Life: Disorder*, pp. 202–31; J. Pound, *Poverty and Vagrancy in Tudor England*, pp. 3, 25–36. For the comments of Elizabethan JPs on vagrancy see Thomas Harman, *A Caveat . . . for Common Cursitors* (1566), in *The Elizabethan World*, ed. A. V. Judges; also William Lambarde's addresses to the sessions in *William Lambarde and Local Government*, ed. C. Read, p. 173.

injunction, in the words of Christ against individual providence: 'Therefore take no thought, saying . . . Wherewithal shall we be clothed?' (Matt. 6: 31). Summer's preoccupation with making the best gains and securing the future of what wealth he has dispensed is reduced to farce in Christmas's fanatical determination to keep every item of his 'wherewithal' from erosion; his discourse degenerates into a list, reducing life to the futile effort of restricting its expenditure. In fact erosion ironically costs money in a sword required to scrape stones, while the money needed to repair a burst vessel seems to burst incontinently from a broached coffer.

To turn again to Will's opening provocation, 'What can be made of Summers last will & Testament?' (iii. 235) the answer from the audience's point of view would be 'nothing substantial, nothing profitable for the future, only mockery'. All the show ultimately does is bequeath the old moral language of providential responsibility for time, in all its grotesque inapplicability, to re-create a household sheltering from plague, and celebrating the time of harvest. As an artefact rather than an evening's entertainment, however, the comedy turns its mockery of the prodigal ideology to unusual aesthetic achievement. Nashe's widely celebrated lyric of farewell is, perhaps, the most intense moment of the comedy's haunting sense of the tenacious frailty of human endeavour, of physical existence. The peculiar tone of *Adieu*, *farewell earths blisse*, its devastatingly inconsequential resignation, could not have been achieved, I think, without the play's ironic purging of a didactic tendency present in the usual sixteenth-century dramatization of material loss. The *ubi sunt* element of Nashe's comedy does not descend directly from a medieval dance of death heritage;[26] it comes via a more pragmatic sixteenth-century discourse of the frailty of fleshly pleasures whose end is to urge the values of foresight, circumspection and industry. But it is precisely the comedy's embodiment and ridicule of these values that gives its own lament for ephemerality such stark and aching beauty. Moralizing on the theme is simply forbidden; Will Summers translates *memento mori* as 'remember to rise betimes in the morning' when he exhorts young boys to follow the example of the household dog in working diligently in a God-given vocation (iii. 258). If Acolastus' lament for

[26] For medieval lyrics in the *ubi sunt* tradition see P. Dronke, *The Medieval Lyric*, p. 69.

the vanishing of luxury and wealth ('Where be now these chopped meates, dressed with spyce and herbes . . . where [is become] the wyne beinge meruaylously of swete sauour?')[27] begins to be perceptible in the opening of the dirge for Summer:

> All good things vanish, lesse then in a day,
> Peace, plenty, pleasure, sodainely decay

yet its potential edification is cut off by the bleak sorrow of the song's refrain:

> Goe not yet away, bright soule of the sad yeare;
> The earth is hell when thou leau'st to appeare. (iii. 236)

Similarly, the grotesque embodiment, in Christmas, of the new morality of possessive individualism discloses, through its irony, the pathetic vulnerability of the human body, while Ver's mock-prodigality renders urgent and intelligible the concept of life as a 'flowry treasure'.

The acknowledgement of a need for forgiveness in Nashe's lyrics covers everyone: '*Lord haue mercy on vs*' (iii. 283). There is no hint of the meritocratic doctrine of simultaneous moral and social improvements implied by a distinction between good and bad uses of time, profitable and unprofitable servants. The providential belief that 'tyme is the greatest treasure which man may here on earth receive', one which ought therefore always to be employed 'that profitte may thereof be gathered',[28] is firmly routed by the epilogue which ironically apologizes to the grave divines of the audience for 'offence' in 'purloyning some houres out of times treasury, that might have beene better imployde' (iii. 293). For these men, though they be 'of the grauer sort' (iii. 292), are not to be allowed to stand in, like pedagogues and magistrates, for the God of the judgement day. No one is guilty, everyone needs forgiveness; the plague and the cold are common conditions, not moral categories. No matter how this time has been employed, Summer's death-day is at hand: 'Ah, who shall hide vs from the Winters face?' (iii. 292).

[27] Acolastus, *Comedy*, trans. Palsgrave, p. 159.
[28] Gascoigne, *Works*, ii. 27.

# 9
# *Pierce Penilesse*, the Bankrupt's Carnival

RHODES has left us in no doubt about the impact that Nashe's prose style made on contemporaries. It stimulated Jonson's particular genius for creating images of social utterance, it enabled Shakespeare to embody the comedy of linguistic subversion in Falstaff. And we know that this generative prose style, the hallmark of 'Pierce a Gods name' (iii. 152), made its first appearance in 1592 with the innovatory publication of *Pierce Penilesse his Supplication to the Divell.* But this, given modern critical accounts of the pamphlet, is puzzling. How can we reconcile the experimentalism that contemporaries found with modern apologies for Nashe's commercially expedient conservatism? Formalism offers no solution. Scholars are baffled by the pamphlet's lack of the formal or thematic coherence proper to satire. McKerrow argued that Nashe's main complaint against avarice was obscured by 'scarcely relevant satire' (v. 18). This irrelevance was vaguely defended by Hibbard who found that the pamphlet's 'apparent disorder . . . was one of its main attractions'.[1] Hibbard found a classical precedent for Nashe's disorder in Juvenal's 'farrago libelli' but he admitted that the moral inconsistency of *Pierce Penilesse* derived neither from Juvenal nor from the homiletic tradition of Langland. Nashe's lack of moral commitment must be due (Hibbard decided) to lack of topical relevance, since his topics were merely well-worn 'charges of preachers, poets and pamphleteers . . . since the fourteenth century' with jest-book anecdotes lamely thrown in 'to meet the demand for variety'.[2]

*Pierce Penilesse* certainly is disorderly, and full of second-hand morality, but this in itself is more topical and more dynamic than Nashe's critics suggest. Unlike ethical or homiletic satire, Nashe's menippean prose works by mimicry, by echoing worn-out professions of moral indignation, and by irresponsibly reversing moral commonplaces. His model is as much festive as it is literary; for all his urbanity he derives a great deal from the popular mockery of dying attitudes in seasonal games. He inverts the mid-century social com-

[1] Hibbard, *Thomas Nashe*, pp. 61–2.

[2] Ibid. 63–4, 75–6.

plaint typified by the 'supplication' of the plain-speaking 'Piers Plowman' figure whose radical humanist message against the commercial exploitation of a crumbling feudal structure had spawned the economic reformation of Elizabeth's reign.[3] These reforms (as we have seen) transformed the essentially ethical basis of the criticism voiced by the humanists and the 'commonwealthsmen' of the mid-century into a system of economic privilege, originally designed to patent new industries and to control habits of intemperance, thus improving productivity 'within the realm'. No one could seriously object, in retrospect, to the fact that the Utopian vision of the radicals had to be transformed into the pragmatic, productive morality of thrift and providence; this was simple necessity if England were to survive within a commercially advanced Europe. What seems (and must have seemed) so demoralizing about the process, however, was the rapidity with which the system of patents and monopolies (economic privileges and standardizing controls designed to encourage responsible and productive members of the commonweal to realize their provident, resourceful vision) was transformed into a source of economic and social privilege, a simple replacement for the lineage-based privileges of a feudal aristocracy.

This, the economic self-interest concealed by a bland humanist discourse of morality and temperance, was casually revealed to contemporaries by its negative paradigm, a Pierce/purse emptied out of the usual financial motives and ethical pretensions.

In order to appreciate the full impact of this sceptical revelation we have to imagine it appearing in all the sacred authority of print. For the printed text was recognized as the proof of its author's ability to govern his resources; it appeared to be the very means by which English humanist education had shifted the rewards and responsibilities of government from aristocratic lineage to the aristocratic patronage of talent and magisterial potential among the educated. Saying things in print was simply not the same as saying them in more informal ways; Nashe had mocked at the supposedly magisterial responsibilities of authorship in *Summers Last Will,* but that was in

[3] An early example of the Piers Plowman figure urging economic reform is *Piers Plowmans exhortation unto the lordes knightes and burgoysses of the Parlyament-house*; more admonitory is T.F.'s *Newes from the North, otherwise called the conference between Simon Certain and Pierce Plowman (1585)*. On the radical legacy of *Piers Plowman* see D. Norbrook, *Poetry and Politics in the English Renaissance*, pp. 43–90.

performance before a select audience of authors and magistrates, hosted by none other than the head of the High Commission, the Archbishop of Canterbury. In such a context it was possible to acknowledge that literary talent might devote itself to pleasure without displeasing God and demoralizing the commonweal. But not in print: dissipation in print would carry the implied authority of its magisterial privilege. We have to recapture the sense of novelty and shock with which *Pierce Penilesse* appeared on the scene, apparently endorsing this magisterial ideal by masquerading as the conventional probing of moral abuses for the reform of the commonweal except, of course, that it claimed this moral and economic authority from a diabolic buffoon.

That this was a novel approach is well attested by the difficulties that attended Nashe in publication. His intention was that this book should open abruptly, with a parodic echo of the typical address of the reformed author to reformed patron, 'lookyng backe' to the 'recklesse race' of youth, or the 'lost time of my youth mispent' and anxious to reap the 'fruites of repentaunce' in a discourse which would double as public exculpation and public service, some 'seryous travayle' which would both 'beare witnesse' to the author's reformation and 'generally become profitable unto others'.[4] The prefaces of Gascoigne's moral satires (from which these quotations are taken) endlessly recapitulate such professions of repentance for a youth misspent, which in themselves become an interesting test case for sublimation of patronage relations in the humanist identification of the author as reforming magistrate. For Gascoigne seems to find himself unable to articulate his dependence on aristocratic patronage without undermining the necessary humanist emphasis on his authorial qualifications; his '*virtus*' or his 'ability' to command resources for the profit of the commonweal. The only way he can get around the acknowledgement of aristocratic dependence is by suggesting that his previous 'inability' to profit the commonweal (through the poetry and fiction for which he is now remembered) was entirely due not to lack of patronage, but to a moral lack in himself.[5] The problem of homage in the dedication is resolved by the need to repent from past immorality; dedications thus become professions of moral reformation which assert the author's substance and 'ability' as

[4] Gascoigne, *Works*, ii. 135, 211.

[5] See especially the dedication to *The Steele Glas*, ibid. 135–6.

well as tacitly paying tribute to the real power and authority of his patron.

In this context Nashe's abrupt opening takes on a comically subversive look. Expecting the authoritative flourish of a dedicatory epistle, endorsing the poet's repentance as his claim to the economic privileges of magistracy, the reader instead finds himself listening to the naïve confidences of a disgruntled bankrupt, who refuses to sublimate the history of his own authorial failure: 'Hauing spent many yeeres in studyng how to liue, and liu'de a long time without money: hauing tired my youth with follie, and surfetted my minde with vanitie,' Pierce explains blandly, 'I began at length to looke backe to repentaunce & adresse my endeuors to prosperitie' (i. 157). The enormous, unspoken burden of meaning hidden behind the whole discourse of repentance in dedicatory epistles and moral satires moves into an embarrassing prominence—'prosperitie'. For that is what 'repentance'—as patronage, as a place in the administration of the commonweal, as the right to claim a living from searching out the moral and economic 'abuses' of common people—had by this time come to mean.

From then on the parodic intention of Nashe's text becomes clearer and clearer. Pierce finds that repentance is no longer a step on the ladder to promotion; undismayed, he tries frustration and rages with nice precision 'in all points' (i. 157) like a madman. Passionate complaint, however, is not his style, so he abandons the discourse of malcontent for that of fool: reversing complaint against the diabolic condition of the times, he turns the devil into his patron and lavishes all the typographic display of a dedicatory epistle (i. 165—unfortunately not reproduced in the Penguin edition) on his new-found source of discursive ability and aesthetic release. The magisterial ideal becomes a dummy, something from which linguistic pleasure (if not profit) may legitimately be claimed—without repentance.

Having said that, though, it would be misleading to give the impression that the indulgent, carnivalesque impetus of *Pierce Penilesse* is consistently evident. If we have misread Nashe's mockery of the moral pretensions of Elizabethan satire, we are not the first readers to do so. Part of the problem is inconsistency within Nashe's own conception; he *is* occasionally in earnest (as for example, when he is defending the contribution of poetry to the credibility of the state). Another, less obvious basis for our misreading may originate in a confusion which goes back to the pirated edition in which Nashe's parodic violation of reading conventions first appeared before the reading public.

It seems that Nashe originally entrusted the publication of his book to an unpretentious printer named Abell Jeffes who had agreed to present it without any prefatory apology, or authorizing dedication (Plate III). There was to be nothing before Pierce's abrupt confession of failed repentance except an unusually stark title page, bearing only the title and the device *Barbaria grandis habere nihil* from Ovid's *Amores*, III. viii (translated by Marlowe as 'Wit sometimes was more precious then gold / Now poverty great barbarism we hold'). This conspicuous lack of information would certainly have struck contemporary readers as odd. Without any of the usual promises of delight mixed with edification, or any explanation of how the manuscript fell accidentally into the publishers' hands, or any countenance of authority and nobility, or even any reassurance of a moral purpose behind the diabolic supplication, what was a reader to expect? But Nashe wanted above all to avoid setting out the book's whole intent in a prefatory epistle, because the whole intent of the book was to shock readers into thinking for themselves. The idea was that the reader should have to make his way unaided through the text before receiving any direct address from its author. Like Sterne after him, Nashe playfully thwarted reader expectations by putting his prefatory epistle and dedication at the end of the book: 'Gentle Reader *tandem aliquando* I am at leasure to talke to thee' (i. 239). His tone is characteristically familiar, abusive, unapologetic. The implication is that any reader who can survive the disorientating tactics of the supplication must deserve more critical respect than the sycophantic preface of a publisher trying to satisfy general expectations. Just as the parodic supplication to the devil laid bare the commercial interests behind a pervasive literary discourse of moral and patriotic zeal, so Nashe's inverted 'preface' was intended to expose the tawdry publishing interests behind the 'long *Circumquaque* to the Gentlemen Readers' (i. 240) that solemnly prefaced the trashiest moralizing pamphlets.

Unfortunately, this design was a bit too unconventional to escape being toned down by the very publishing interests it intended to expose.[6] Abell Jeffes was arrested by the High Commission for

[6] The following account of Nashe's publishing troubles is based on the findings of C. T. Wright, 'Mundy and Chettle in Grub Street', pp. 131–3.

publishing certain ballads that did not meet with government approval and in his absence, it appears, Nashe's manuscript was purloined by a certain Richard Jones. This unscrupulous publisher had business sense enough both to appreciate the potential popularity of Nashe's witty reversal of convention, and to judge that readers would need some kind of introductory apology to give them confidence to persevere with it. Accordingly he provided a coy '*Circumquaque*' of his own invention, to reassure Gentlemen Readers that the 'preposterous' (or back-to-front) composition of the book was in fact both rational and artfully 'conceited' (Plate I). There is no need to fear that the book lacks all the necessary authorizing features of the epistle, proem, and dedication:

The Printer to the Gentlemen
*Readers.*

Gentlemen: In the Authours absence, I haue been told to publish this pleasant and wittie Discourse of *Pierce Penilesse his Supplication to the Diuell*: which Title though it may seem strange, and in it selfe somewhat preposterous, yet if you vouchsafe the Reading, you shall finde reason, as well for the Authours vncouth nomination, as for his vnwonted beginning without Epistle, Proeme, or Dedication: al which he hath inserted conceitedly in the matter; but Ile be no blab to tell you in what place. Bestow the looking, and I doubt you, but you shalle find Dedication, Epistle, & Proeme to your liking.

Yours bounden in affection:
R. I.

R. I.'s affectionate concern for the reader's welfare did not end there. In his anxiety to reassure the public of moral profits to be had, he transformed Nashe's title page, effectively blurring its parodic purpose. His title page (Plate II) advertised the work as:

Pierce Penilesse his
Supplication to the
*Diuell.*

Describing the ouer-spreading of
*Vice*, and the suppression of
*Vertue.*

Pleasantly interlac't with variable delights: and pathetically intermixt
*with conceipted reproofes.*

Written by *Thomas Nash Gentleman.*

The Printer to the Gentlemen *Readers.*

GEntlemen: In the Authours abſence, I haue been bold to publiſh this pleaſaunt and wittie Diſcourſe of *Pierce Penileſſe his Supplication to the Diuell*: which Title though it may ſeeme ſtrange, and in it ſelfe ſomewhat prepoſterous, yet if you vouchſafe the Reading, you ſhall finde reaſon, aſwell for the Authours vncouth nomination, as for his vnwonted beginning without Epiſtle, Proeme, or Dedication: al which he hath inſerted conceitedly in the matter: but Ile be no blab to tell you in what place. Beſtow the looking, and I doubt not, but you ſhall finde Dedication, Epiſtle, & Proeme to your liking.

Yours bounden in affection:
*R. I.*

A 2

I. Printer's introductory epistle to the first (pirated) edition of *Pierce Penilesse* (1592)

Pierce Penileſse his
Supplication to the
*Diuell*,

Deſcribing the ouer-ſpreading of
*Vice*, and ſuppreſsion of
*Vertue*.

Pleaſantly interlac't with variable delights: and pathetically intermixt
*with conceipted reproofes.*

Written by *Thomas Naſh* Gentleman.

*LONDON*,
Imprinted by *Richard Ihones*, dwelling at
the Signe of the Roſe and Crowne,
nere Holburne Bridge.
1592.

II. Title page of the first edition of *Pierce Penilesse* (1592)

Pierce Penileſſe
HIS SVPPLICATION
to the Diuell.

Barbaria grandis habere nihil.

Written by *Tho. Naſh*, Gent.

LONDON,
printed by Abell Ieffes, for
I. B. 1592.

III. Title page of the second edition of *Pierce Penilesse* (1592)

All this prefatory caution blunted the intended shock of the original. Nashe was forced, in a second edition, to compromise by affixing a letter to the printer (Abell Jeffes, who by this time was released) explaining that he had never wanted to give his book such a 'long-tayled Title' or to advertise the moral efficacy of its contents with such a 'tedious Mountebanks Oration to the Reader' (i. 153).

It seems fair to say that had Nashe been able to ensure that *Pierce Penilesse* appeared as he had intended, its netherworld confessional aspect would have been much clearer. Pierce is brought on as a bankrupt fool, ingenuously confessing the emptiness of the moralizing posture on which a successful bid for patronage depends, going on to turn the frustration of this knowledge into carnival pleasure by openly acknowledging his patron as the devil, and bequeathing him, in something like the itemized form of a mock-testament or a ragman's roll, all the irrelevant stock phrases under which individual profit masquerades as moral reformation.

Under the banner of moral reformation were produced endless discourses on the various 'abuses' and 'deceits' of English manufacture, or the over-consumption of foreign luxuries (particularly in 'proud' apparel), on gluttony in meats and drinks, and vicious idleness of frequenting taverns, theatres, and other places of recreation. Pierce's use of the seven deadly sins is less like homage to the homiletic tradition than like a grotesque dismemberment of the political reclassifying of deadly sins in the interests of economic individuality.[7] Categories such as Pride and Gluttony sound as hopelessly inadequate and ludicrous in the context of Pierce's supplication as they must have done to contemporaries who heard them invoked in homiletic propaganda on behalf of the political Lent for fishmongers, or in vehement chastisement of starched ruffs and social mobility by earnest moralists such as Philip Stubbes.[8]

It is important to appreciate that the basic format of moral satire, whether classified according to social 'abuses' such as the deceits of various tradesmen (the lawyer, the tailor, the tanner, etc.) or according to deadly sins, had been positively done to death in published versions from the 1560s to the 1590s. Originality was not considered a virtue in the composition of moral satire and treatments of the topics had always been extremely derivative. Whetstone's *Mirour for Magestrates of Cyties* (1584) was basically a reworking of Elyot's

[7] e.g. Hibbard, *Thomas Nashe*, p. 64.

[8] See above, p. 1.

*Image of Governaunce* (1541),[9] while Greene's *Quip for an Upstart Courtier* (1592) and the *Defence of Conycatching* (usually attributed to him) are witty recapitulations of the economic abuses long ago exposed in Thynn's *Debate between Pride and Lowliness* (*c.*1570). The *Quip* is also indebted to Stubbes's *Anatomy of Abuses* (1584) which is in turn heavily indebted to official homilies and to the mid-century sermons of Latimer.[10]

Lack of originality is not always a serious accusation against sixteenth-century literature, but Nashe was right to see in this case the absurdity of the consequences. As the moral and satiric argument of these discourses became more and more derivative, so they lost touch with the rapid processes of social and economic change taking place in their immediate environment. Latimer's remarks on the abuses in clothmaking could hardly be appropriate in the context of the economic success of the New Draperies, nor could they be compatible with arguments against the prodigality of wearing English-made woollens and worsteds. More important, however, were the effects of economic privilege—patents and monopolies—in destroying the credibility of a magisterial discourse on the need to seek out 'abuses' and to impose a moral reformation. In the early to mid years of Elizabeth's reign the high displeasure of Almighty God and the imminent decay of the poor of this realm could be invoked with conviction as the likely consequence of tolerating parasites who ate meat throughout Lent, or attired themselves in 'monstrous' hose made by the imported silks and velvets, or turned a blind eye to 'deceits' and 'abuses' in English manufacture. As the economy improved with the stimulus of patents and penalties, however, the more stringent of these morally justified economic controls (such as standardization against 'deceit' in cloth manufacture, or the obligation to cultivate hemp for the navy) became redundant and even oppressive. Their chief justification now was the lucrative incomes they afforded those who gained the right to the fines they yielded. Other moral prohibitions—against the exportation of unwrought wool for example—had always been subject to interference by powerful interests. Moral ex-

[9] As Izard notes, *George Whetstone*, p. 149.

[10] Compare *The Life and Works of Robert Greene*, ed. A. B. Grosart, xi. 217–94, with Thynn, *Debate*. See also J. Carey, 'Sixteenth- and Seventeenth-Century English Prose', p. 367, and compare Stubbes, *Anatomy*, pt. I, pp. 52–3 with Burghley's proclamation of 1574 on apparel, *Tudor Royal Proclamations*, ii. 381–9; also compare Stubbes, *Anatomy*, pt. I, pp. 55–67 with *Two Books of Homilies*, ed. Griffiths, pp. 308–17. Stubbes recalls Latimer, *Anatomy*, pt. II, pp. 9, 28.

hortations to justices of the peace to punish offenders in 'apparell . . . and excessyve abundance of wynes'[11] must have been known to be futile in view of the fact that the vintners readily paid enormous dues to overcome the import regulations, to the gain of such noblemen as the Earl of Leicester, who held the customs farm of sweet wines.[12]

In other words, what was persistently represented in discourse as a moral crusade in the interests of reforming the commonweal, was increasingly becoming in practice a major source of income for the magistrates and noblemen who implemented it.[13] In 1577, for example, one John Leake 'prepared his diatribe against "abuses" in clothmaking'[14] in order to secure himself the right to collect the penalties involved. A proclamation of 1592, inveighing sternly against the 'deceits' and 'deceitful mixing' of woollen cloths, was shortly followed by the granting of a lucrative office to Simon Bowyer, magistrate, as sole informer to compound with violators of this proclamation.[15] Despite the increasing dependence of magistrates on profits gleaned from the dispensation of wealthy violators, they nevertheless persisted (with a righteous indignation worthy of Justice Adam Overdo) in searching out the petty 'enormities' of the poorer sort, and ascribing to these the general decay of the commonweal. As late as 1598 JP William Lambarde exclaimed at the sessions:

> What multitudes of unlicensed alehouses be daily raised, what abundance of barley is continually malted, what excessive strong drinks be yet still brewed, how licentiously is flesh devoured, how obstinately starch is yet continued, and how many other wastes are now in this penury committed which even in the greatest plenty were not to be abiden and suffered by us![16]

Prohibiting the unlicensed manufacture of starch, a royal proclamation justifies the granting of a monopoly to courtier Richard Young as a charitable measure towards alleviating the sufferings of the poor in the years of dearth: 'And whereas her majesty hath already, by her said letters patent, granted to one of her loving subjects the making of starch to be made of bran only, to the end that the poorer sort may be

[11] *TED* ii. 45.

[12] See G. D. Ramsay, *The City of London*, pp. 56–7; Youngs, *Proclamations of the Tudor Queens*, p. 44.

[13] See W. H. Price, *The English Patents of Monopoly*, p. 9; Thirsk, *Economic Policy*, pp. 51–97; Youngs, *Proclamations of the Tudor Queens*, p. 144; and M. G. Davies, *The Enforcement of the English Apprenticeship 1563–1642*, pp. 30–8.

[14] Davies, *Enforcement*, p. 126.

[16] *William Lambarde*, ed. Read, p. 130.

relieved'.[17] Yet the real motive for the monopoly turns out not to be the relief of the poor at all (monopolizing starch in this way simply ruined the less well-off starchmakers) but as the Crown's means 'towards the satisfaction and payment of a certain debt due to us by Richard Yung, deceased'.[18]

Courtiers made their request for revenue in the unmistakable idiom of the reforming idealism, pleading the profit of the commonweal for every device dreamed up for their own enrichment. Requesting a lucrative patent on the licensing of gaming houses, a courtier in 1591 explains implausibly how by this means, 'deceitful playing may be suppressed, many young gentlemen kept from spoil, many poor men driven from unlawful exercises to live upon lawful labour, much other wickedness reformed'.[19] Consumers and producers whose activities offered scope for magisterial 'reform' of this kind were typically referred to as 'idle', 'unlawful', 'disorderly', or 'parasitical' in official discourse; in reality, as one economic historian has argued, it was the magistrates themselves who lived like 'parasites on the unwieldy and growing body of penal statutes'.[20]

The anomaly of an idealistic discourse of productivity and thrift being transformed in this way as the instrument of a monopolistic oppression of manufacturers by magistrates is perfectly expressed in the grotesque comedy of the economy (or 'housekeeping') run by the improbable partnership of Greedinesse and Dame Niggardize (i. 166–8). Their household is kept so bare, Pierce confides to the devil, that no edible or workable material is left lying around for unofficial consumers ('Rattes and mise', i. 168) or producers ('spiders and dustweauers', i. 168) to exploit. The irregularly employed, the casual spiders who were once 'wont to set vp their loomes in euery window', now find themselues 'decayed and vndone' by vigorous spring-cleaning, just as in actual fact many clothworkers had been forced, by over-zealous exactions of forfeitures and penalties against their 'deceits', to forsake their trade 'to the great decay of clothmaking . . . and utter undoing of great numbers of poore people'.[21] Pierce's spiders have recourse to remoter regions, emigrating to the country to be 'out of the reach of the broome and the wing' (i. 168). Again this

[17] *Tudor Royal Proclamations*, iii. 166.

[18] Ibid. 188. See also Thirsk, *Economic Policy*, pp. 88–90; Youngs, *Proclamations of the Tudor Queens*, p. 146; Price, *English Patents of Monopoly*, pp. 15–16.

[19] *CSPD 1591–4*, cct/iii, Oct. (?) 1592, p. 284.

[20] Davies, *Enforcement*, p. 31.

[21] *Tudor Royal Proclamations*, iii. 53.

appealing fantasy represents economic fact: Joan Thirsk has shown that it was indeed by receding further into the country that small-time manufacturers managed to escape the over-enthusiastic cobweb-sweeping of courtly informers. This practice was a common feature of what she classifies as the 'scandalous phase' of Elizabethan economic projects, during which, under moral cover of controlling and reforming the 'deceits' and 'abuses' of manufacture, magistrates and holders of office roamed the country, harassing the poorer, more irregular manufacturers.[22] Exploitation masqueraded not only as moral 'government' for the profit of the commonweal, but (under the patronage system) as a social right, the due of lordship and the increase of honour. The nuances of these incompatible languages—one expressing moral righteousness in terms of productivity and government, the other social pride in aristocratic status—are nicely captured by Pierce Penilesse doing heraldic duty for the modern magistrate:

> All malcontent sits the greasie son of a Cloathier, & complaines (like a decaied Earle) of the ruine of ancient houses: whereas the Weauers loomes first framed the web of his honor, & the lockes of wool, that bushes and brambles haue tooke for toule of insolent sheep, that would need a striue for the wall of a fir bush, haue made him of the tenths of their tar, a Squier of low degree; and of the collections of their scatterings, a Justice, *Tam Marti quam Mercurio*, of Peace. (i. 168–9)

While the hierarchy of honour is in fact built on a commercial system (its governors are 'greasie' with their inheritance from the cloth-making boom of the 1550s[23]) and while it promotes its own interests through the exploitation of penal controls (tolls collected from the wool irregularly 'manufactured' by disorderly sheep), the language volved nevertheless uses aristocratic codes of honour and revenge which we noted as underlying Gascoigne's Preface to the *Steele Glas* (interestingly enough *Tam marti quam mercurio* was Gascoigne's motto). The wool is removed from sheep for their 'insolent' refusal to observe etiquette (taking the wall of a fir bush!) much as the poorer sort are condemned in magisterial discourse for their insolence in the independent manufacture and acquisition of a wanton variety of consumer goods.

As the incompatible alliance of morally productive and aristocratically exclusive attitudes underlying Elizabethan social mobility is

[22] Thirsk, *Economic Policy*, pp. 117–18.

[23] See Thomas Wilson, *A Discourse upon Usury*, ed. R. H. Tawney, p. 96.

made palpable in Pierce's mock testament, so its governing economic impulses are paraded in the grotesque marriage of a couple of carnival-type effigies. The reforming ideals of productivity and thrift, realized in the successful promotion of economic projects, are transformed into a target of popular abuse—Dame Niggardize, figure of avarice and filth. Ballads and records of popular festivity frequently direct blows and curses at the vendors of stale or rotten wares; in the May games at Wells in 1607 old 'Grandam Bunche' (whom Nashe mentions in connection with 'slimie ale', i. 173) was trundled through the town 'in a wheele barrowe' with a pot full of the 'fylthye gutt' with which she bolstered out her stale puddings.[24] Another slatternly pudding wife, in the ballad of 'seldome cleanly', thriftily saves candle ends which 'helpe to make her puddings fat, / With the droppings of her nose'.[25] Dame Niggardize, the epitome of English thrift and prudence, belongs to this illustrious family, as she sits 'barrelling vp the droppings of hir nose, in steed of oyle, to saime wooll withall' (i. 167). The reference is to an ingenious project for the making of woollen goods within the realm. The New Draperies faced crisis in 1568–70 when the Spanish oil used for seaming wool became an undesirable import on account of the war and an escalation in price.[26] Projectors and politicians searched about for suitable alternatives until in 1576 one of Burghley's researchers urged the benefits of hempseed oil which, as a by-product arising from the cultivation of hemp for sacking and canvas, would provide more employment for idle poor and encourage landowners to invest more in the drainage of otherwise useless fen land, drained fen being especially suitable for hemp production. Hemp thereby became a creator of numerous resources, a crop 'more gainful to the owners . . . of land than any corn'.[27] The 'hempen raile' which Dame Niggardize has thriftily improvised as a shawl for herself 'borrowed of the one end of hop-bag' (i. 167) indicates yet another way in which the versatile hemp seed helped to realize England's dreams of economic independence. In the 1560s and '70s import prices for hops and for sacking thread rose alarmingly; the growing and spinning of hemp then became important as supporting industries when projects for the production of English beer from English hops were seriously undertaken in the

[24] 'The Wells May Game', in *Lost Plays of Shakespeare's Age*, ed. C. J. Sisson, p. 180.
[25] *Roxburghe Ballads*, ii. 513–19.
[26] The following discussion is taken from Thirsk, *Economic Policy*, pp. 68 ff.
[27] Thirsk, *Economic Policy*, p. 69.

1580s. The satisfying interdependence of all these productive pursuits is grotesquely caricatured in the composition of Niggardize, whose very skirt is made of fenland sedge, suggesting that under her domestic economy, no material (from unprofitable marshland to nose droppings) need ever go to waste.

Incongruously yoked to the fanatically productive Niggardize of England's economic projects is the remorseless exploitation of their profits under the pretext of moral control by the magisterial Greedinesse. For this carnival king the 'sariants mace'—symbolic of the legal power to enforce statutes—turns into the food which he devours 'night and day' (i. 167). The ingenuity that characterized monopoly-hunting courtiers of the 1590s, 'ceaseless' as one historian writes, 'in the invention of new devices whereby the Queen might be served, the commonwealth benefited—and the suitor enriched',[28] materializes in Greedinesse's sharp-toothed shoes, which snarl 'at the stones . . . in the street, because they were so common for men, women, and children to tread vpon, and he could not deuise how to wrest an odde fine out of any of them' (i. 166–7). It was indeed the commonness of the commodities exploited by grants of monopoly that laid such an intolerable burden on poor households; patents prohibited the unlicensed production of saltpetre, vinegar, cloth, soap, oil, and starch, while the notorious monopoly on the making of common salt 'digs in every mans House'[29] as one MP was later to complain, unconsciously echoing Nashe's image of Greedinesse digging in the streets. Fashioned out of offcuts ('the lists of Broadcloths') Greedinesse's breeches are further expressions of a legal rather than productive ingenuity, indicating the security of the monopolist's privilege to collect these lists 'by letters pattents assured him and his heyres, to the vtter ouerthrowe of Bowcases and Cushin makers' (i. 166). While the existence of entire industries manufacturing cushions and cases for fiddlesticks might seem to hang rather precariously on free access to the collection of broadcloth remnants, it scarcely, in fact, exaggerates the monopolistic situation. In 1592, for example, one John Spilman who held letters patent to collect linen rags for paper-making requested the Privy Council to enforce stricter 'restraincte and punishement'[30] of unlicensed persons who went

[28] W. T. MacCaffery, 'Place and Patronage in Elizabethan Politics', in *Elizabethan Government and Society*, ed. Bindoff *et al.*, p. 119.

[29] Sir Simonds D'Ewes, *Journals of all the Parliaments during the Reign of Queen Elizabeth*, p. 653.

[30] *APC* xxiv, Feb. 1592, p. 72.

about salvaging the rags that his industry relied upon. Such legal security clothes and warms Greedinesse: his 'Capouch of written parchment buttond downe before with Labels of wax' suggests both the proverbial hypocrisy of the hooded capuchin and the snug comfort of legal privilege written on *parchment* (sheepskin) securely soldered up with royal wax against the chill of political or economic uncertainties.

Nashe's grotesque tableau of the household of Niggardize and Greedinesse, assembled as it is out of the scraps of official discourse on the reformation of the commonweal, emerges as surprisingly uninhibited, and irreverent in its comic debasement. The vaguely patriotic materializes as the sordidly domestic, and phrases normally implemented to determine economic privilege become the assortment of tatters which both create and mock these verbal effigies. This translation of the instruments of power into the materials of their own mockery is typically carnivalesque; the characteristic phrase, the trademark of an attitude becomes a blow against itself. At Wells in 1607, when two local kill-joys (a grocer and a pewterer) were caricatured in the aforementioned May game, it was their *trademarks* which made up the rough music and the blows: a pewter basin struck with a hammer providing the din, while grocer's scales were filled with 'graynes & other trashe' to fling about 'in mens necks & faces'.[31] So the kernels of moral and economic discourse are strewn, like holiday trash, through Pierce Penilesse's printed May game.

Setting *Pierce Penilesse* in the context of carnivalesque improvisation helps us to see the form of Nashe's work; how Pierce's triumph over the ineffectual role of malcontent within a bankrupt discourse designed both to facilitate and suppress social mobility, is achieved by his carnivalesque transformation of that discourse into the materials of its own mockery. Pierce's initial reaction to the failure of his education to secure him government office is predictably to fall into the position of a malcontent; but this posture is 'empty' in as much as the malcontent is defined by the values of a society in which he is denied a place. In this discontented humour Pierce's discourse remains penniless; it can only be articulated in the borrowed, moralistic moralistic terms of a discourse of social complaint which locates the problem as being the fault of those 'upstarts' and 'droans' to whom the speaker bears an envious, competitive relation. Success could not

[31] 'The Wells May Game', p. 173.

alter the terms of this discourse in the slightest, as Nashe makes clear in a shift from Pierce's envious fulminations into the complacent moralizing of his socially successful antagonist. Pierce blames the short-sightedness of an older generation who, having gained office through commercial success, refuse to promote their successors:

This is the lamentable condition of our Times, that men of Arte must seeke almes of Comorantes . . . thinking belike, that, as preferment hath made themselues idle, that were earst painefull in meaner places, so it would likewise slacken the endeuours of those Students that as yet striue to excell in hope of aduauncement. (i. 159–60)

If a similar policy had been in operation when they were young, concludes Pierce enviously, there would have been fewer drones occupying lucrative offices. The voice of the older generation, however, cuts in with exactly the same complaint: too many drones and upstarts are being advanced to undeserved office.

I, I, weele giue loosers leaue to talke: it is no matter what *Sic probo* and his pennilesse companions prate, whilest we haue the gold in our Coffers: this is it that will make a knaue an honest man, and my neighbour *Cramptons* stripling a better Gentleman than his Grandsier. O it is a trim thing when Pride, the sonne, goes before, and Shame, the father, follow after. Such presidents there are in our Common-wealth a great many; not so much of them whome Learning and Industry hath exalted . . . as of Carterly vpstarts . . . (i. 160)

Distinctions collapse and lose their meaning in a discourse which identifies promotion with *virtus*, yet defines all others who are promoted as 'upstarts' and 'droans'. Pierce comes to recognize that it is not he who is morally bankrupt and lacking in discursive 'abilitie' but the resources of discourse themselves which are exhausted and unable to articulate the social situation.

The only way out of the tautological impotence of this inherited moral attitude is by deliberate parody, mocking these definitions to the extent of making a material effigy out of them, and so transforming them into a significant indictment of their own inappropriateness. This is the solution Pierce hits on when he composes his devil out of commonplace social 'abuses'; the ineffectuality of complaint becomes positive verbal re-creation as Pierce rifles through proverbs and adages to find out where the devil is hiding, 'Masse, thats true: they say the Lawyers haue the Diuell and all . . .' he muses (i. 162). Here 'the devil and all' simply means having a lot of business; but Pierce rejects this evidence of the devil's presence among the lawyers on the authority of another saying that 'he must needs run whom the devil drives'. Legal proceedings are not notorious for alacrity: 'Fie, fie, the Diuell a driuer in Westminster hall? it can neuer be', decides Pierce on second thoughts (i. 162).

So Pierce goes on hedonistically re-creating himself through the resources of language. And as he does this he discovers that his purse is far from empty; the theme of Avarice can yet yield him a rich discourse for the purposes of recreation, if no longer for profitable admonition. Contemplating the possibilities of a diabolic composition, Pierce finds a plenitude of material; 'manifest coniectures of Plentie, assembled in one common-place of abilitie' (i. 161). The 'full belly' of complaints on the theme of Avarice provides Pierce with a 'full hande' (i. 161) of material, ripe for creation. The incoherence of Pierce's supplication merely exaggerates the senile disintegration of an idealistic discourse designed to promote economic and social reforms. Pierce identifies gluttony as excessive meat consumption in a diatribe against carnivoracity: 'Nay, we are such flesh-eating Saracens, that chast fish may not content vs, but we delight in the murder of innocent mutton, in the vnpluming of pullerie, and quartering of Calues and Oxen' (i. 201). The rape, murder and desecration of corpses that we call butchery is, Pierce concludes, 'horrible and detestable, no Godly fishmonger that can digest it' (i. 201). The interests of fishermen and those of Almighty God were identified by the homily which preached fasting for 'policy'[32] and indeed, as the Privy Council noted during the Lent of 1592, 'fishmongers are willing to . . . take paines in the reformation of these abuses more exactlie then in former times'.[33]

Informers and monopolists, however, were not the only members who had an interest in adopting a magisterial attitude against particular enormities; by the beginning of the 1590s almost the entire publishing industry was dependent on the production of moralized discourse against the abuses of excess and intemperance. Pierce's mimicry of the godly fishmonger's diatribe against the gross habits of gluttony finds its publishing equivalent in parodic echoes of 'sin-washing' poets who profit from their fulminations against all the 'abuses' of consumerism, from starch to stage plays. Mockery of the sin-washing poets is, in fact, close to the polemical heart of Pierce's

[32] *Two Books of Homilies*, ed. Griffiths, pp. 277–307.
[33] *APC* xxii, Mar. 1591–2, p. 374.

supplication. In his frank exposure of the commercial interest which actually motivates the publication of so much moral and admonitory writing Pierce puts authors (ideally conceived of as provident guardians of the commonweal) on a level with the 'deceitful' manufacturers whose abuses they pretend to expose. Typical of such moral satire is its indictment of tradesmen who pass off as new materials that are worn and threadbare; the haberdasher notoriously 'trims vp olde felts and makes them very faire to the eie, and faceth & edgeth them neatly'.[34] Pierce, however, turns this satire against the satirists themselves, who are nothing more than hasty refurbishers of threadbare classical *exempla*, able at best to set 'a new English nap on an old Latine apothegs' (i. 199). Leatherworkers and tanners are another manufacturing group whose 'abuses' were a source for much moral castigation;[35] Pierce caricatures the repetitiveness and irrelevance of this satire in the nostalgia of the antique dealer, who will 'fall a retayling *Alexanders* stirrops, because (in veritie) there is not suche a strong peece of stretching leather made now adayes' (i. 182). Where the moralizers are obliged to set up their profitable discourses as the retail shops of authorial commonplace selling 'the choycest Writers extant for cues a peece' (i. 196), Pierce proudly boasts the originality of his unauthorized recreation. Against women's cosmetics a moralizer dredges up the old adage, 'farre fetched and deare boughte is good for Ladyes, they say';[36] but Pierce, instead of railing, turns the very concept of cosmetic excess into the resource of his artistic ability: 'I need not fetch colours from other countries to paint the vglie visage of Pride, since her picture is set forth in so many painted faces here at home' (i. 180). These sinful painters become models for Pierce's own fantastic improvisation, as they draw their facial colours from the most unlikely sources:

> Their lips are as lauishly red, as if they vsed to kisse an okerman euery morning . . . so that if a Painter were to drawe any of their Counterfets on a Table, he needes no more but wet his pencill, and dab it on their cheekes, and he shalle haue vermillion and white enough to furnish out his worke, though he leaue his tar-boxe . . . behind him. (i. 180–1)

34 *The Life and Works of Robert Greene*, ed. A. B. Grosart, xi. 286–7.

35 See e.g. Gascoigne, *Works*, ii. 171; Thynn, *Debate*, p. 32; Stubbes, *Anatomy*, pt. II, p. 36; Greene, *Works*, xi. 260–2. For efforts to reform the tanning and currying of leather see L. A. Clarkson, 'The Organization of the English Leather Industry in the Late Sixteenth and Early Seventeenth Centuries', pp. 245–6.

36 Stubbes, *Anatomy*, pt. I, pp. 33, 64.

From being the most idle and parasitical member of the commonweal (a poet), Pierce thus transforms himself into a productive creator of resources 'within the realm' of his own invention and its immediate environs. Rather than 'seek abroad' for materials, Pierce searches about resourcefully for the alternative raw materials which lie about unregarded; 'I need not fetch colours from other countries', he writes (i. 180), and 'it is enough for me to licke dishes here at home, though I feed not mine eyes at any of the *Romane* feasts' (i. 199). Given this almost projector-like ability to create resources and employment out of the idle scraps and offcuts of the London scene, it is appropriate that when Pierce comes to the most heinous of the sins in the homily book—idleness—he reverses expectation and celebrates the unthrift and the vagrant at the expense of the Elizabethan ideal of the productive, responsible, houseowning citizen. The gadabout poet wins over his master, the stationary stationer. The implications of this inversion are interesting and intellectually innovative, both in publishing terms and in social terms, running counter as they do to an increasing tendency in Elizabethan thought to assume the moral superiority of the private and self-sufficient householder, relegating more public and unpropertied styles of life to the margins of respectability.[37] The paternalism of London's aldermen and the country magistrates did not, apparently, extend to the vagrant poor—'After all, they were not citizens'.[38] The problem of London's homeless became acute in the 1590s, when unpaid, disbanded soldiers from the Netherlands converged upon the capital. Vagrant soldiers faced execution without trial if caught by the Provost Marshall; for ordinary vagrants the penalty was still branding, although by the end of the century the invocation of martial law was not unknown in civilian cases.[39] The city fathers, a close wealthy community, were committed to the relief of householders and citizens; their solution to the problem of vagrancy, however, was to drive offenders into the suburbs.[40] Pierce hopes on the disgorging of their wealth that 'Saint Peter would let them dwell in the suburbes of heauen' since at that moment their oligarchic monopoly forces 'poore Scholers and Souldiers' to 'wander in backe lanes and out-shiftes of the Citie' (i. 204).

[37] On this subject see Emmison, *Elizabethan Life: Disorder*, pp. 202–31; F.F. Foster, *The Politics of Stability: A Portrait of the Rulers in Elizabethan London*, pp. 115–23.

[38] Foster, *Politics of Stability*, p. 91.

[39] See L. Boynton, 'The Tudor Provost Marshall', pp. 451–3; F. Aydelotte, *Elizabethan Rogues and Vagabonds*, p. 69.

[40] Foster, *Politics of Stability*, p. 91; Ramsay, *City of London*, pp. 41–3.

Pierce attributes the evils of vagabondage and the growing problem of London's slum suburbs to the exclusiveness of the city itself. The very category of vagabondage is created, and the underworld to some extent defined, by the magisterial assumption that all social benefit and productive labour derives from the private well-to-do household. With their constant allusion to the biblical injunction 'in the sweat of thy brows shalt thou eat thy bread',[41] magistrates and ministers give the impression that it is *activity* that defines and validates man's labour, but in fact any labouring activity that drew a man into highways and public places of resort was almost equally inevitably defined as 'idleness'. It was enough that the masterless and the infirm could receive charity at home, said JP William Lambarde, without 'suffering them to gad abroad for their living'.[42] And if the popular entertainments of a traditional lifestyle—May games, church ales and mummings—had been condemned as idle and wasteful of productive time, how much more pernicious was the emergence of entertainment on a commercial basis in theatre and tavern. Theatres, wrote Stubbes, maintain 'a great sort of ydle Persons, doing nothing but playing and loytring, hauing their lyuings of the sweat of other mens browes, much like vnto dronets devouring of the sweet honie of poore labouring bees'.[43] Pierce begins by endorsing this moralist argument with the barest hint of of parody. As it is the duty of everyone to 'prouyde for theyr necessarye lyuynge' so providence is the great task master of idleness: 'the nurse of this enormitie (as of all euills) is Idleness, or sloth, which, hauing no painfull Prouidence to set himselfe a worke, runnes headlong, with the raines in his owne hand, into all lasciuiousnesse and sensualitie that may be . . .' (i. 208). He begins to sketch a scenario involving various stereotyped idlers—a drunkard, a lecher, and a gambler—but abruptly abandons this traditional conception of idleness for the devil and prurient moralizers to investigate: 'betwixt you and their soules be it, for I am no Drawer, Box-keeper, or Pander, to be priuie to their sports' (i. 209). For if by the argument of productivity, thrift, and providence, all gadding about and pastime must be dismissed as idle and sinful, how are London's citizens to be employed? On a commercial basis thriftless pastime forms the basis of London's thrift; the gallants and tearaways provide employment for the substantial virtuous citizens. Thus Pierce turns opinion on its

41 *William Lambarde*, ed. Read, p. 173.

42 Ibid. 181.

43 Stubbes, *Anatomy*, pt. I, p. xi.

head and argues that true idleness is not a 'gadding about' quality at all; redefined as 'sloth' it comes to resemble the great Elizabethan ideal of solvency and thrift. Pierce's vagrant and restive imagination roams the streets in search of these housebound idlers: 'If I would raunge abroad, and looke in at sluggards key holes, I should finde a number lying a bed to saue charges of ordinaries . . .' (i. 209). If, as it is commonly conceded, the most profitable member of the commonweal is he who provides for the livings of others, then the self-expenditure of the unthrift must carry it away over the stingy caution of the private citizen: 'The vnthrift abroad exerciseth his bodie at dauncing schoole, fence schoole, tennis, and all such recreations: the vintners, the victuallers, the dicing houses, and who not, get by him' (i. 209–10).

In publishing terms, of course, the same distinction between 'profitable' and 'idle' discourses operated in favour of the moralizers, encouraged by an entrepreneurial approach to publication. Original, imaginative writing, less reliable in its marketing appeal, was easily dismissed on a moral basis as 'idle' and unprofitable to the reader. Sin-washing ballads were what the public seemed to like, and what the stationers (who ran the publishing industry on an entrepreneurial basis, employing printers, booksellers, and authors as labour) paid writers to produce.[44] Nashe was well aware that publishers preferred news reports to original inventions. In 1596 he wrote to William Cotton that it was no good hoping for any money from the press: all the publishers were 'gaping' for the news ballads of the Essex voyage and would scarcely be interested in any invention he had to offer (v. 194). Not that 'news' here means factual reportage; the old humanist criteria of providence and profitability required that the reader be able to benefit from a moralized rendering of historical events which would bring the 'news' into stereotyped line with every exemplary discourse on a similar topic.[45]

The polemic against this inhibiting, publishing-house definition of a 'profitable' discourse which underlies the whole of *Pierce Penilesse*

[44] See R. B. McKerrow, 'Booksellers, Printers and the Stationers' Trade', in *Shakespeare's England*, ii. 212–39; E. H. Miller, *The Professional Writer in Elizabethan England*, p. 166. On the organization of the publishing industry see G. Unwin, *Industrial Organization in the Sixteenth and Seventeenth Centuries*, pp. 108–9; on the publishing preference for sermon literature see A. F. Herr, *The Elizabethan Sermon*, pp. 67, 70–1.

[45] M. A. Shaaber, *Some Forerunners of the Newspaper in England 1476–1622*, pp. 204–21.

is brought to a climax in Pierce's comic and radical redefinition of 'idleness', the root of all evil, as the capitalist dictator of English publishing, the idle stationer:

If were to paint Sloth . . . I would drawe it like a Stationer that I knowe . . . who if a man come to his stall and aske him for a booke, neuer stirs his head, or looks vpon him, but stands stone still and speakes not a word: onely with his little finger points backwards to his boy, who must be his interpreter . . . (i. 209)

Adapting the conventions of the patronage system as well as a debased version of the humanist doctrine of the profitability of discourse, publishers had developed an ideal format which made it almost impossible for a writer to stimulate rather than satisfy reader expectations, as we saw from Nashe's lack of success when he attempted to bypass the usual apology to the gentle reader. This is what the fool Pierce conveys when he identifies moralizing authors with the commercial abuses they repeatedly expose. If they were really concerned about commercial abuse they would not go on selling wares which, in the festive terms appropriate to a seasonal market-place, would infect the customer with disease and decay. According to Pierce, the publishing industry is as rotten and disreputable as Grandam Bunche for contaminating the good air with filthy old guts and stale giblets: 'Looke to it, you Booksellers and Stationers, and let not your shops be infected with any such goose gyblets or stinking garbadge, as the Iygs of newsmongers . . .' (i. 239). Instead of producing fresh inventions, the best-selling hacks and moralizers bolster out pudding-like compilations which betray their rotten entrails, boasting 'no inuention but heere is to bee noted, I stoale this note out of *Beza* or *Marlorat*' (i. 192). An improvised discourse like that of *Pierce Penilesse*, by contrast, offers itself as a fresh experience to the reader: 'Newe Herrings, new, wee must crye, euery time wee make our selues publique, or else we shall bee christened with a hundred new tytles of idiotisme' (i. 192). The associations of 'new' with tawdry consumer novelty have confused critics into taking this as Nashe's admission that he was a hack, 'a commercial writer who had to please'[46] by churning out endless sensation. In fact the claim being made here is quite the opposite: in the context of the sixteenth-century market-place the cry of 'new herrings' would be understood to refer to freshly-caught fish, herrings that were neither red (dried) nor rotten. The distinction

[46] e.g. Hibbard, *Thomas Nashe*, p. 75.

is important, for dried and stale foodstuffs have ludicrous associations in the seasonal system of imagery. Elderton's ballad of 'Lenten stuff', for example, warns that the cry of fish, 'newe, at every tyde',[47] may be a hoax; some of the herrings so advertised are neither dried nor fresh, but stale: 'Herrynge, herrynge, whyte and red, / Seeke owt suche as be rotten'.[48] Vendors who try to 'set to sale / Suche baggage as ys olde and stale'[49] will be mocked when their subterfuge is discovered. Indeed, the purveyor of rotten wares will find himself the 'stale' of public merriment, re-created for general amusement in improvised ballads, and 'christened' as Pierce anticipates, 'with an hundred new tytles of idiotisme'. Pierce, in fact, credits the public with imagination, with the capacity to participate actively in the reception of any discourse. Any writer who wants his inventions to survive without being re-created as the materials of mockery against him has to be sure that they are fresh enough to recreate his readers. As an approach to the publishing market this is altogether more sophisticated than the old condescendingly magisterial promise of eloquent edification. The readership that Nashe writes for is past being passively 'impressed' by the wisdom of the orator.

In making sense of *Pierce Penilesse* in terms of its recreative mockery of outworn assumptions and outworn modes of discourse, I am aware that I have had to ignore an entire aspect of Nashe's work which is not concerned with the re-creation of admonitory topics at all, but with the question of patronage, with the relation of discursive 'abilitie' to social mobility. A tension is evident in this aspect of the work, arising from the fact that despite its radical subversion of the discourse which founded government qualification on the 'having and use of virtue', *Pierce Penilesse* nevertheless basically identifies the aim of poetry as rhetorical praise (i. 193) and clearly envisages the eventual advancement of its author through his praise of a virtuous patron (i. 195). Gascoigne had once described poetic ability as a falcon, a 'high flying Hawke' which must be employed not only to soar for the owner's pleasure but to stoop to 'such Quarries as are both pleasant and profitable'[50] to all. When Pierce, however, laments the neglect of this same 'high towring Faulcon' by an avaricious nobility he conceives of it less in terms of a general asset than of

[47] 'A new ballad entytuled Lenton stuff', in *Songs and Ballads*, ed. Wright, p. 189.
[48] Ibid. 188.
[49] Ibid. 189.
[50] Gascoigne, *Works*, ii. 212.

a function of aristocratic rapine 'wont . . . to dryue whole Armies of fearefull fowle before her to her maisters Table' (i. 179), indistinguishable, in fact, from the ravenous pursuit of honour elsewhere derided as the envious hunger of courtiers 'ready to bite at euery Dog that hath a boane giuen him besides themselues' (i. 185).

Nashe's final attempt to render his ironic discourse serviceable by dedication to a member of the nobility (i. 245) cannot but be undermined by its earlier re-creation of discourse established to facilitate the social mobility of those with magisterial ability. Social mobility, he argues again and again, necessarily involves a physical production of the self through the exercise of talent; given the chance of promotion, writers will 'make a ladder of cord of the links of their braines' to climb to it (i. 180), the soldier will 'fight himselfe out of his skinne' (i. 178). Only spurious nobility is achieved by filching the core or the *virtus* of another; by flattering a Spaniard you may 'commaund his heart out of his belly' to make yourself a nice bit of bacon to lard and warm your own heart (i. 176), but flattery is the short-cut of untalented men who 'filche themselues into some Noble mans seruice' and ascend with lightning speed (i. 175). Commerce accelerates another breed of spurious nobility, a spontaneous generation of gentry out of deceits practised in trade—'butchers by fli-blown beefe' and so forth (i. 174). The magisterial ideal, the *vir virtutis* in whom the heart of manhood is fully realized, is thus reduced in the terms of Pierce's mockery to 'collections of . . . scatterings' (i. 169), a bloodless amalgam of insects, weeds, and other rapidly sprouting organisms. In the terms of Pierce's own ironic confession nothing worth having is to be gained through the praise and patronage of contemporary aristocracy.

# 10
# Gabriel Harvey and the Politics of Publication

If, as I have argued, Nashe meant the opening scene of *Pierce Penilesse* to read like a parody of the penitent and profitable biographies of promotion-hungry authors, how ironic it is that we should take our cue in reading it now from one contemporary on whom this joke was obviously lost: that is, of course, Gabriel Harvey. By accident or design, Harvey succeeded in misunderstanding Nashe's parodic critique to the extent of taking the caricature for the real thing. In Harvey's account, the Menippus-figure of Pierce Penilesse becomes a projection of his author, as deliberately composed to gain public credit as the rhetorical 'Harvey' who conducts a multi-voiced (and at times incoherent) appeal to the reader of his *Foure Letters and certaine Sonnets* (1592).

Harvey evidently read Pierce Penilesse—or at least its opening pages and the libel against his brother—in Richard Jones's pirated edition. Taking the profession of the title page to heart, he ironically commends the book for being 'pleasantlie interlaced with diuers new-founde phrases of the Tauerne: and patheticallie intermixt with sundry dolefull pageantes of his own ruinous, & beggerlie experience'.[1] Assuming an avuncular tone, Harvey remonstrates with the author for being so unwise as to give discursive proof of nothing but ineffectual despair, and advises him to project himself as a talent more worthy of preferment: 'either gallantlie aduance thy vertuous self, maugre Fortune: (what impossible to aspiring industry?) or mightilie enchant some magnificent Mecoenas, (for thou canst doe it) to honour himselfe in honouring thee'.[2]

This obstinately biographical reading seems to show Harvey to be some twenty years out of step in his assumptions about the function of publication. (Gascoigne's *Posies*, the classic statement of Harvey's argument, were published in 1575.) Whatever Harvey's

[1] Harvey, *'Foure Letters and certaine Sonnets'*, in *Works*, ed. Grosart, i. 195. See above, Chapter 3 for a brief outline of the quarrel between Harvey and Nashe.

[2] Ibid. 196–7.

retardedness in the appreciation of literary developments, however, the textual strategy of his response in the *Foure Letters* shows that he was by no means insensitive to changes in the political reception of these developments. It does seem as though, once again, as in the 1570s, the publication of unauthorized fiction was being regarded by the government as a threat, not, this time, a threat to its policies of economic and social reform, but a threat to its own religious and political authority.[3] In the early years of Elizabeth's reign poets had been obliged to adopt a posture of penitence for past literary 'prodigality' in order to achieve public office without undermining the status of the printed word as an agent of social, economic and educational reform. The educational and economic improvements of the 1580s, however, spawned their own problems in increased competition for government office and, inevitably, more openly expressed dissatisfaction with the monopolies of economic, political and religious authority exercised by Crown patronage. War with Spain exacerbated fears that Puritan dissension from within the nation would lay England open to attack from her Catholic enemy; throughout the 1590s there were alerts to port towns about the possibility of Spanish invasion, and Catholics and Puritans alike were being imprisoned for possessing 'traiterous' books.[4] Ironic discourse and unauthorized publication became a specific focus of government anxiety; the precedent set by Martin Marprelate could not be dismissed. Once again it became crucial for authors to identify their appearance in print with the interests of an influential patron. This time, however, the aristocratic countenance signified not hopes of preferment, but anxieties about conformity. Without an epistle dedicatory, the author was liable to be under suspicion of 'singularity' (individualism), his work thereby openly inviting all kinds of subversive political interpretations. One writer who felt particularly called upon to respond to the growing trend of individualism which he perceived in both the religious and secular handling of the press was the Revd Richard Harvey, brother of Gabriel. In 1590 he published a collection of his sermons with a preface (reproduced in McKerrow, vol. v) which was designed to draw attention to his own exemplary conformity as one who had secured a patron through the proper channels before presuming to

[3] See Helgerson, *Elizabethan Prodigals*, pp. 14–15.

[4] *CSPD 1591–4*, ccxliv, 6 Jan., 25 Feb., 24 Mar., 6, 7, 26 Apr. 1593, pp. 305–45.

appear before the public in print. Only thus, he intimated, could discourse have the right to claim the authority of the press, for print elevates discourse above partiality and individualism into public speech on behalf of the entire body politic. In the terms of Harvey's preface, it is patronage rather than rhetorical skill which gains him the attention and credit of his reader, and defines his utterance as 'infallible':

To the fauourable or indifferent

*Reader.*

Now so worthy a Lord hath vouchsafed the honourable patronage of this Treatise, I presume the rather you will vouchsafe me the fauourable or indifferent reading of the same. My meaning is good, and respecteth a godly end: only my desire is, to be well vnderstood and wel taken where I intend well. It is not my purpose to confute or controwle, but in declaring the infallible and inuincible truth, I am driuen to touch some vnchristian opinions, partly contrary and partly repugnant to our christian iudgement. Ours, I say, as not mine in seuerall, but ours in common; and only mine as the dutifull subscription of one smal member to the most authenticall and soueraigne doctrine of the whole body, euen that catholick body, whereof the Lamb is the head. (v. 176)

By applying the image of Christ's mystical body, the Church, to the political state, Harvey was attempting to deny the authenticity of discourse which could not claim to proceed from the government's mouth. He invests the dedicatory epistle—proof that the text has been 'countenanced' by an influential member of the government—with a power which entirely eclipses that of the discourse itself. By virtue of the patron's credit the author's words gain an authority beyond the dreams of oratory: they become the authentic words of the body politic. Initially, the political patronage of authorship had been a means of advancing the policies of reformation, functioning only incidentally as a check on authorial originality. But Richard Harvey, responding in 1590 to a fearful vision of Church and State crumbling before unchecked assaults of satire and mockery, deliberately brought out the notion of surveillance latent in patronage, presenting it as a form of censorship. How, after all, could an author hope to speak without guilt, if merely to publish were to make a claim for the credit of one's words on behalf of the whole state? And then, to affirm the truth of one's discourse without the sanction of patronage might by implication be construed as a claim to patronage by the higher authority of divine inspiration. This was the kind of construction that the bishops were putting on the words of dissenters and separatists in the years 1592–3. John Udall, still in prison in the spring of 1593, had originally been convicted because of his assertion that he spoke the undoubted truth of God.[5] In 1593 John Penry was executed 'upon the statue made against *seditious words and rumours uttered against the Queen*'.[6] The month before his execution had seen the trial and execution at Tyburn of two other dissenters, Barrow and Greenwood, who, as Strype reports, 'were condemned at the sessions without Newgate, for writing seditious books and pamphlets tending to the slander of Queen and government'.[7] In November of the same year Nashe found himself relegated among these violators of the body politic for similarly claiming divine (rather than aristocratic) authority for his denunciation of a secular authority. The aldermen of the City of London took umbrage at the insinuations made against their management of plague funds in the text of *Christes Teares* and summoned Nashe to appear 'at the nexte Sessions of Gaiole delyvrye of Newgate to be houlden for the Citty of London . . . Read ye to make answere to all such matters as shal be obiected against him on her Majesties behalf.'[8] The timely interference of George Carey, bearing Nashe away with him to the Isle of Wight to spend Christmas, prevents us from knowing what would otherwise have been the outcome of this incident.[9] In itself, however, the action of the city fathers affords evidence of their increasingly rigorous interpretation of what might constitute a seditious discourse, and their increasing readiness to take punitive action on their own behalf as government representatives. If the authorities particularly resented the direct defiance of their dissenting critics' claims to divine inspiration, they were no less suspicious of the more indirect threat implied in the adoption of an ambiguous or ironic mode of discourse. Marprelate, of course, could be made to represent the connection between dissent and ironic discourse, and numerous prefaces confronted the readers of the 1590s with the hypothesis that Lucian, Rabelais, Aretino, and

[5] Collinson, *Elizabethan Puritan Movement*, p. 407. See *CSPD 1591–4*, p. 325.

[6] John Strype, *The Life and Acts of John Whitgift*, ii. 176. See also Loades, 'Theory and Practice of Censorship', pp. 153–5.

[7] Strype, *Whitgift*, ii. 186.

[8] See L. Hutson, 'Thomas Nashe's "Persecution" by the Aldermen in 1593', *N&Q*, NS 232 (1987), 199–200.

[9] See C. G. Harlow, 'Nashe's Visit to the Isle of Wight and his Publications of 1592–4'.

other ironic discoursers were in fact responsible for stimulating the disregard for authority which Marprelate and now other authors were readily disseminating.[10] Richard Harvey was one proponent of this line of thought: '*Rabelays* is no good reformer of Churches and States,' he wrote, 'if Saint *Augustine* be vnsufficient, *Lucian* is more vnmeete' (v. 178). Providentially-minded authors tended to offer lists of these ironic discoursers as *exempla* of divine vengeance in the moments of their horrible and unrepentant deaths; soon enough another writer of the early 1590s, Christopher Marlowe, qualified to take his place among the Lucianic scoffers when he died in a brawl in 1593.[11] In order to identify themselves on the side of unity and authority in Church and State, certain authors seem to have been almost anxious to point out the individualistic tendencies of others. Such, at least, was Richard Harvey who, in his anxiety to dissociate himself from the taint of Marprelatian singularity, started off the entire Harvey–Nashe dispute. In the preface already cited he unprovokedly singled out the younger author as an instructive example of recent Marprelatian trends in literary criticism. Nashe's crime, it seems, had consisted in having the temerity to publish an unsolicited review (his own opinions) of the contemporary state of English literature, without the auspices of a patron. This 'famous obscure' Thomas Nashe ('one whome I neuer heard of before', wrote Richard Harvey pointedly) had apparently acted 'in ciuill learning, as *Martin* doth in religion' (v. 179–80). Such acts of individualism it seems could not be tolerated if the printed word were to be instrument of divine and civil authority within the state. Government anxiety about its own representation in unauthorized publications must have been exacerbated in the 1590s when the dissenting voices from the puritan presses were joined by the voices of the poets who in more favourable circumstances might have been its patronized upholders. Adopting the pose of satirist or malcontent, these writers aimed directly at individuals in power. Burghley, for example, was in 1591 explicitly satirized both in Thomas Lodge's *Catharos* and in Spenser's bitter beast fable, *Mother Hubbard*. Catholics abroad took careful note of these literary developments as signs of growing disaffection; in 1592 one Richard Verstegan mocked the fear of censorship that made English poets veil their

10 See Duncan, *Lucianic Tradition*, pp. 77–96.

11 See Thomas Beard, *The Theatre of Gods Iudgements* (1597), sigs. K3, K5$^{r}$.

criticism of Burghley in a '*Mother Hubberds* tale, of the false fox and his crooked cubbes'.[12] In England the new fashion for beast fable as a form of satire was, like the ironic stance adopted by certain puritan critics, traced back to the evil influence of the usual group of sceptics: Rabelais, Lucian, and Aretino.[13]

In such a political climate it is perhaps scarcely surprising that Gabriel Harvey should choose to misunderstand Nashe's Lucianic mockery of the patronage conventions which had been forcing authors into repentant biographical strait-jackets, reinterpreting this mildly subversive critique as an act of impolitic self-exposure on the part of a 'malcontented' author. We must not think, however, that Harvey himself was averse to the fantastic ironies of Aretino or Lucian. He approved of them above all things, but only as rhetorical strategies by means of which an author might retain his public credit and innocent reputation while working secretly to destroy and discredit his (or his patron's) enemies. In fact, if we look closely, we can see how Harvey himself used what he thought of as Lucianic irony and fantasticality of invention while explicitly disavowing these (disavowal was part of the ironic strategy) in the *Foure Letters* which contain his libel against Robert Greene. In the opening of these letters he employs the casual, off-hand manner suitable to the genre to imply that his mission against Greene occurred as a trivial parenthesis between more pressing patriotic duties. Having laid this patriotic foundation, Harvey goes on to conflate the notions of personal defamation and political subversion so as to imply that a published attack on the Harveys falls not far short of a violation of the whole patronage system which holds together the 'body' politic: 'they perillously threaten the Commonwealth, that goe-about to violate the inuiolable partes thereof'.[14] Nashe and Greene are identified with the trend that produced Spenser's *Mother Hubbard*, a book in which the playful spirit of the *Faerie Queene*, according to Harvey, went too far and 'wilfully ouer-shott her malcontented selfe'. This phenomenon is predictably enough linked back to the licentious precedents of Lucian and other ironic discoursers.

[12] Quoted by A. G. Petti, 'Beasts and Politics in Elizabethan Literature', p. 80. See also Helgerson, *Elizabethan Prodigals*, pp. 105–6.

[13] See e.g. T.B.'s Epistle to the Reader in Pierre de la Primaudaye, *The Second Part of the French Academie*, sig. B4v; also Innocent Gentillet, *A discovrse vpon the meanes of wel governing*, trans. Simon Patericke (1608), sig. *3v.

[14] Harvey, *'Foure Letters', Works*, i. 165.

Oratours haue challenged a speciall Liberty: and Poets claimed an absolute Licence . . . Inuectiues by fauour haue bene too bolde . . . I ouerpasse *Archilochus*, *Aristophanes*, *Lucian*, *Iulian*, *Aretine*, and that whole venemous and viperous brood, of old & new Raylers.[15]

All this seems orthodox enough; Harvey at least at this point is clearly trying to gain credibility by identifying his own libelling enemies with the general trend towards unauthorized satire which he reads as potentially subversive. When it comes to analysing the actual text in which one of these libels is contained, however, he seems to change tack. The text in question is, of course, *Pierce Penilesse*, and the libelling episode part of a digression on the sin of wrath which takes an incidental swipe at Richard Harvey's *Astrologicall Discourse*:

wherein (as if hee had lately cast the Heauens water, or beene at the anatomizing of the Skies intrailes in Surgeons hall) hee prophecieth of such strange wonders to ensue from stars destemperature and the vnusuall adultrie of Planets, as none but he that is Bawd to those celestiall bodies could euer discry. (i. 196)

In a passage like this attention is deflected from serious consideration of Richard Harvey towards the farcical development of the 'celestial bawdy' joke. Its effects as libel are therefore difficult to assess, for while it certainly damages the credibility of Richard Harvey (if he still had any after the original publication of the *Astrologicall Discourse*) it does so in the posture of the clown, sacrificing the credibility of the author to the pleasures of his impertinent wordplay. It is this episode that Gabriel Harvey fastens on, but not, as one might expect, in order to defend his brother, so much as to admonish its author for approaching the thing the wrong way. Far from being too bold in his invention ('licentious' in the political sense) Gabriel Harvey argues that Nashe has been insufficiently venomous, discrediting himself rather than destroying his enemy (i.e. he has been too 'licentious' in the imaginative sense). As a representation of brother Richard, Nashe's libel is too fantastic, too comic, too blatantly unreasonable to gain the reader's credit. As such it fails the aims of rhetoric which, even when it is ironic, should always operate to gain credit for the writer:[16] 'Euen Lucians true

[15] Ibid. 164.

[16] Ibid. 200. See also Erasmus, *De copia*, p. 86.

tales are spiced with conceit', Harvey points out, recalling Erasmus and Vives. Nashe's fault is this neglect of his own credit as an author, which, according to Harvey, renders his otherwise considerable talent completely ineffective. Credibility is all: 'Vnreasonable fictions palpably bewray their odious grosnesse: and hee that will be a famous deuiser . . . must be content . . . not to be credited, when he auoweth a trueth.'[17] Harvey does not attack Nashe, nor does he give the younger author up for lost. In fact his drift is that Nashe might pick up a thing or two from a libel against Robert Greene in which it is ably demonstrated how the tactics of 'Lucians true tales' may be adopted against one's enemy without damaging one's own credit at all. Turning to the libel against Greene it becomes obvious that this is one place in which Harvey's much disputed admiration for Lucian and Aretino (testified privately by quantities of marginal notes) has borne rather dubious fruit.[18]

Before we condemn the crudeness of Harvey's attitude we have to take into consideration his view of print as a medium. So far as he was concerned, print was a technical extension of rhetoric and both were ways of 'inventing' (i.e. disclosing, making publicly intelligible) an otherwise invisible self. In thinking like this Harvey was not unusual in his time; indeed, in reserving the act of publication peculiarly for such writings as related to the public self, the restitution of damaged credit, he followed the illustrious example of Sir Philip Sidney, who intended the *Defence of Leicester* alone of all his writings (so far as we know) for publication.[19] But Harvey went further than this. For him not only publication but also such rhetorical embellishments as irony or fiction were themselves superfluous to a composition unless they functioned as authorizers —ways of gaining credit—for the writer and his writing as a whole. This explains his predilection for the rather outmoded convention of the prefatory epistle, a popular strategy which excused the author's presumption by constructing a fictional history of how his work either fell into the hands of the printer without knowledge, or was

[17] Harvey, *'Foure Letters', Works*, i. 165.

[18] For Harvey's admiration of Aretino see E. Relle, 'Some New Marginalia and Poems of Gabriel Harvey', p. 415. Relle refutes earlier views that Harvey had changed his mind about Aretino, and shows him to have admired the satirist privately even while writing against Nashe's 'Aretinism' in public. Harvey's marginalia on the strategic importance of irony are noted by V. Stern, *Gabriel Harvey*, pp. 160, 183.

[19] Sidney, *Miscellaneous Prose*, p. 124.

urged from him by the request of importunate friends.[20] Fictions like these, full of 'verie probable occurences' in Harvey's words, were useful inasmuch as they served to 'countenance and authorize'[21] the more licentious aspects of the work. Writing is all a matter of tactical manoeuvre. In his own *Foure Letters* Harvey employs the authorizing device of the fictional correspondence, stretching it to its utmost limits in the setting out of his social credibility. He then uses it to pass off as fact what is actually a wildly improbable account of Greene's dying circumstances. Fiction is here subservient to rhetorical attack, the effect of the libel. While Harvey is not sparing of squalid circumstantial detail (twice in the space of a page the reader is reminded that Greene has lice) he is equally careful to dissociate himself from the charge of originating the description, which he repeatedly ascribes to the 'ascertayned reportes' of his more callous acquaintances which he himself has been 'ashamed, to heare'.[22] Most outrageous of all, he even tries to imply that only as licentious a perpetrator of fictions as Greene could ever be 'Lucianicall' enough to turn such pathetic circumstances to his authorial advantage: 'O what notable matter were here for a greene head, or Lucianicall conceit: that would take pleasure in the paine of such sorry distressed creatures?'[23]

Having thus done the necessary demolition work on the character and morals of that notorious libeller Robert Greene, Harvey blithely resumes his innocent unassuming persona and bids goodbye to his fictional correspondent:

> Let the worlde deale with simple men (i.e. Gabriel Harvey) as it pleaseth: I loath to be odious to any: and would be loth to bee tedious to you. The next weeke, you may happily haue a letter of such . . . other intelligences, as the credible relation of inquisitiue frendes . . . shall acquaint me withall.[24]

The portrait of Greene is then turned into a warning, an *exemplum* for the admonitory profit of such authors as have 'neither hability to help, nor witt to pittie themselves':[25] Thomas Nashe, take warning.

This mask of moral concern did not conceal Harvey's libelling

[20] On this phenomenon see J. W. Saunders, 'The Stigma of Print: A Note on the Social Bases of Tudor Poetry', pp. 140–56.

[21] Harvey, *Works*, i. 200. For Harvey's fondness for the fictional epistle see his comments on Gascoigne, *Works*, ii. 96. See also above, Ch. 3, p. 70.

[22] Harvey, *'Foure Letters', Works*, i. 168–70.

[23] Ibid. 172.

[24] Ibid. 174.

[25] Ibid. 193.

tactics from Nashe, who made exuberant mockery of Harvey's rhetorical pose as a patriotic news correspondent by replying in the parodic format of a sensational news pamphlet, advertising *Strange Newes, of the intercepting certaine Letters, and a convoy of Verses, as they were going Priuilie to victuall the Lowe Countries.* Intercepted letters were a valuable news item: Nashe thus exposes the absurdity of Harvey's professions of patriotic concern by relegating him to the rank of a publisher's hack, along with Greene and the other commercial writers who were supposed to present such a dire threat to the stability of the government.[26] Nashe's defence presents Robert Greene's commercial attitudes to the press as capable of subverting Harvey's assumptions about publication as a way to win political credit: 'Hee made no account of winning credite by his workes, as thou dost . . . his only care was to haue a spel in his purse to coniure vp a good cuppe of wine with at all times' (i. 287). It would be a mistake, however, to assume that Nashe's praise of Greene is unequivocal, or that Nashe identified himelf in *Strange Newes* with Greene's attitude to authorship. As a commercial author who regarded the press as an employer, Greene was a perfect trickster figure, a perfect agent of mockery against Harvey. Nashe avoided passing any aesthetic judgement on a skill which was sufficiently validated by its commercial rates, 'glad was that Printer that might bee so blest to pay him deare for the very dregs of his wit' (i. 287). Carefully dissociating his own attitudes to authorship from both Greene's and Harvey's Nashe was left with a problem which *Strange Newes* could not solve.

*Pierce Penilesse* had oriented itself against the uninventive literary productions perpetuated by a commercial adherence to the conventions of an outworn morality. One of these conventions had been the assumption that fiction exists to be read as a rhetorical strategy—a 'biography' to facilitate the author's projection of himself as a credible figure. By stubbornly refusing to understand and appreciate the aesthetic point made by Pierce Penilesse, Harvey plunged Nashe into an authorial dilemma. Harvey had represented him to the world as a shiftless, penniless beggar. How was he to refute this accusation except by 'answering' Harvey in print, a tactic which could only undo the progress he had made towards breaking

[26] For an interesting appreciation see K. Friedenreich, 'Nashe's *Strange Newes* and the Case for Professional Writers'. Nashe did not, however, identify himself with the professionals to the extent that Friedenreich suggests.

down assumptions about the rhetorical role of publication? He attempted to pour scorn on Harvey's misunderstanding of *Pierce Penilesse*, drawing attention to the distance between himself and his fictional protagonist. 'God and Dame Fiction knows thou art farre wide of thy ayme', he protested to Harvey (i. 303), explaining how he had set the discourse to the devil in motion by introducing 'a discontented Scholler vnder the person of *Pierce Pennilesse*, tragicallie exclaiming vpon his partial-eid fortune, that kept an Almes boxe of compassion in store for euery one himselfe' (i. 306). However, when it came to redeeming his personal reputation from the damage done by Harvey's *Foure Letters*, Nashe was beset by the contradiction of his position. The easy irony of his defence of Greene and the professionals could not be pressed into service where his own good name was concerned, and *Strange Newes* degenerates at such points into splutteringly impotent invective. On one occasion he collars Harvey, demanding instant satisfaction.

> Answere me *succinctè & expeditè*, what one period any way leaning to licentiousnes, canst thou produce in *Pierce Pennilesse*? . . . For the order of my life, it is as ciuil as a ciuil orenge; I lurke in no corners, but conuerse in a house of credit, as well gouerned as any Colledge, where there bee more rare quallified men and selected good Schollers than in any Noblemans house that I knowe in England.
>
> If I had committed *such abhominable villanies, or were a base shifting companion*, it stoode not with my Lords honour to keepe me, but if thou hast saide it, & canst not proue it, what slandrous dishonor hast thou done him, to giue it out that he keepes *the committers of abhominable villanies and base shifting companions,* when they are farre honester than thy selfe.
>
> If I were by thee, I woulde plucke thee by the beard, and spit in thy face, but I would dare thee, and vrge thee beyonde all excuse, to disclose and prooue for thy heart bloud, what villanie or base shifting by mee thou canst . . . (i. 329–30)

Obviously, the task is impossibly self-contradictory. Nashe's attempt to reinstate his lost credit by means of a printed appeal to the honour of his erstwhile patron simply amounts to an endorsement of Harvey's belief that publication exists as part of the would-be courtier's rhetoric of self-promotion, and that skilful use of creative language is a subordinate issue. Nashe needed to find a new format which would allow him to make out the case for appealing to the reader's mind through the pleasures of metaphor and fiction, thereby ridding himself for ever of the whole tedious question of truth, libel, and limits of rhetorical licence in published discourse.

He did not find a suitable format until four years later. The result was *Have With You to Saffron Walden*, a book which made fun of all the usual pretensions to factual accuracy which a century of fierce religious dispute conducted in print had made familiar to every reader. (*Strange Newes* had conformed to these conventions as far as possible, making efforts to quote the antagonist's words accurately before replying to them in a contrasting typeface.[27]) An obsession with accuracy and the limits of rhetorical licence in the embellishment of historical fact, and a fanatical concern with the defamatory powers of publication, emerge from *Have With You* as carnival effigies, the mock-heroes of a fiction about the issues of publication. The book is introduced dramatically as a 'solemn' attempt at redress for the damaged reputation of a well-known author called Thomas Nashe. Readers are invited to imagine it all taking place:

> In some nooke or blind angle of the *Black-Friers* you may suppose (if you will) this honest conference to bee held, after the same manner that one of these *Italionate* conferences about a *Duell* is wont solemnly to be handled, which is when a man, being specially toucht in reputation, or challenged to the field vpon equall tearmes, calls all his friends together, and askes their aduice how he should carrie himselfe in the action. (iii. 21)

The reluctant subject of all this is Nashe, who models himself on the conventional figure of the self-effacing author, bullied into publication (as Harvey repeatedly claims to be) by the 'importune requestes'[28] of friends. These importunate friends have their farcical embodiment in Nashe's overbearing companion and adviser Signor Importuno, whose volubility on the subject of reputation and public credit singles him out as Harvey's equal. Importuno is obviously a man after Harvey's own heart when it comes to the politics of publication and rhetorical self-presentation; he even speaks Harvey's language, to the bemusement of his interlocutors. Other companions represent opposing assumptions about the relation of publication and creative language; Don Carneades de boone compagniola has the re-creative mind of a poetic trickster, combustible enough to replenish the world, should it ever run out, with an entirely new supply of apothegms and *exempla* 'out of his affluent capacitie' (iii. 23). He stands for the strategy of *Have With You*

[27] On this convention see Rosenberg, *Leicester*, p. 195.

[28] Harvey, *'Foure Letters', Works*, i. 221.

itself which aims to 'recreate and enkindle' the 'decayed spirites' of the readers in Paul's Churchyard by enabling them to encounter Harvey's unintelligible productions as creative substance (iii. 30). Carnivalesquely embodied in Signor Importuno are all the criteria of courtesy literature on which Harvey had modelled his public persona and by which he conducted his complicated literary manoeuvres. Foremost is the anxious dependence of identity on the 'voyce and opinion abroad'. Signor Importuno externalizes and makes comic the threat of public opinion, of the obliteration of the self by a damaging blow to what Gascoigne called 'the ramparts of my poore credite'.[29] The lost credit of the idle prodigal becomes a fictional bogey:

IMPORT. Tush, tush you are all for iest, & make him be more careles of his credit than he wold be, by thus contemning and debasing his Aduersarie. Will you heare what is the vnited voyce and opinion abroad? Confidently they say, he is not able to answere him, he hath deferd it so long . . . though I, for mine owne part, know the contrarie, & will engage my oath for him (if need be) . . . Often enough I told him of this, if he would haue beleeu'd me; but at length I am sure he findes it, and repents it all too late. In no companie I can come, but euerie minute of an howre . . . they still will be tormenting me with one question or another, of what he is about, what means he to be thus retchles of his fame . . . whether he be dead or no, or forbidden to write . . ? whereto I answere nothing else, but that he is idle and new fangled . . . (iii. 26)

In a magnificent exaggeration of Harveyesque principles, physical injury pales into insignificance beside the injury of defamation. 'Many will sooner loose their liues, then the least Iott of their reputation',[30] Harvey portentously claimed. 'Spittle', intones Signor Importuno likewise,

may be wip't off, and the print of a broken pate . . . quickly made whole and worne out of mens memories, but to be . . . imprinted at London the reprobatest villaine that euer went on two legs, for such is Gabriell Scurueies . . . witles malicious testimony of thee . . . is an attainder that will sticke by thee for euer. (iii. 27)

Print's physical durability is comically—yet ambivalently—contrasted with the ephemeral consequences of assault. But there are worse threats in store. What about Nashe's reputation in the minds of the generations to come? What if all posterity believes Harvey's equation of Tom Nashe with the vagabond Pierce? Even if no one

[29] Gascoigne, *Works*, i. 8.

[30] Harvey, *'Foure Letters'*, *Works*, i. 165.

buys Harvey's books, argues Importuno, there is nothing to stop them being handed down as a printer's heirloom: 'while Printing lasts, thy disgrace may last, & the Printer (whose Copie it is) may leaue thy infamie in Legacie to his heyres, and his heyres to their next heyres successiuely to the thirteenth and fourteenth generation, Cum Priueligio . . . (iii. 27–8). Between them, in the dialogue of fool and pedant, Importuno and Pierce Respondent embody and farcicalize the issue of print, posterity, and personal reputation. The absurdity of Importuno's pedagogic lecturing is made palpable when Pierce identifies it with the 'graue fatherly Forasmuches', typical of Harvey's proclamatory style. A weighty burden of authorial responsibility towards generations not only unborn but unfurnished as yet with cradles can thus be merrily dismissed:

Yet this I must tell you, sir, in the way of friendship twixt you & mee, your graue fatherly forecasting *Forasmuches*, and vrging of posteritie and after ages whose cradle-makers are not yet begot, that they may do this, and they made doo that, is a stale imitation of this heathen *Gregorie Huldricke*, my *Antigonist*. (iii. 31)

*Have With You* challenges the assumption that the press is an instrument of the patronage system, and that the credit of the author is dependent on his power to invoke suitably authoritative names. The rhetorical practice of authorizing discourse by recourse to the credibility of *exemplum* and precedent had been transformed by Harvey into an unsubtle technique of name-dropping:

The truth is, I stande as little vpon others commendation, or mine owne titles, as any man in England whosoeuer . . . but being so shamefully and intollerably prouoked in the most villanous termes of reproch, I were indeede a notorious insensate asse, in case I should eyther sottishly neglect the reputation of soe worthy fauorers or vtterly abandon mine owne credit. Sweet Gentlemen, renowned knightes, and honorable Lordes, be not ashamed of your Letters, vnprinted, or written . . . I speake not onely to M. Bird, M. Spencer, or Monsieur Bodin . . . but to M. Thomas Watson, a notable Poet; M. Thomas Hatcher a rare Antiquary; to M. Daniel Rogers of the Court . . .[31]

The series becomes self-perpetuating since naming is the only effective gesture in a scheme where fame alone confers value. Only the suppression of names could be a more eloquent indicator of social standing. Profuse with prefatory thanks to all who make up his vast network of friends and supporters, Harvey regretfully

[31] Id. 'Pierces Supererogation', *Works*, ii. 83.

restrains himself from mentioning them all individually, 'till the Print be better acquainted with their names'. Nashe ridicules this substitution of nominative power for real wealth and variety of rhetorical invention. In the opening pages of *Have With You* he mimics Harvey by apostrophizing his nobody of a patron (Dick) with relentless mock determination to dispel all possible doubts about his identity and nomination: 'Acute & amiable Dick, not *Dic mihi, Musa, virum* . . . nor *Dic obsecro* . . . nor Dick swash, or Desperate Dick (iii. 5). The point, as he informs his 'patron' and 'authorizer', is to make sure that everyone is aware how much more powerful for discursive proof are names than any figure of speech 'to shew the redundance of thy honorable Familie, and how affluent and copious thy name is in all places, though *Erasmus* in his *Copia verborum* never mentions it' (iii. 6).

Credit, reputation and security as a writer were in no small degree dependent upon the ability to identify one's own name with the more influential name of a patron. A reading public attuned to this idea would naturally assume the right to interpret, to search out *à clef* references to famous names in publications which obscured their origins and begged the question of their identity by refusing to affiliate themselves to any authority. The libels and beast fable satires of the late 1580s and early '90s encouraged the reader to employ his invention in the ingenious discovery of these famous names under 'devices'. Readers (as Nashe complained in *Lenten Stuffe,* iii. 212–14) were often more interested in tracking down and deciphering libellous references to public figures than in exercising any critical appreciation of the writings of their contemporaries. *Have With You* is a work which deliberately sets out to frustrate the reader's impulse to identify and evaluate a published discourse according to its topical reference. It incidentally mocks the kind of reader who assumes that what is no longer current news is automatically invalid as reading material ('Say, what are you reading? *Nashe* against *Harvey*. Fo, thats a stale ieast', iii. 18). From the outset, Nashe tries to unsettle the all too common impulse to seek gratification in the security of recognizing references instead of activating one's imagination through metaphor.

Whatever else *Have With You* may be about, it is definitely not concerned with reinstating the 'good name' of Thomas Nashe. No attempt to dissociate Thomas Nashe from the taint of Pierce Penilesse is ever made. The issue is deliberately confused by Nashe's inclusion of himself among his fictional interlocutors as 'Pierce Respondent' while Signor Importuno hails him as 'Tom' (iii. 25). In the ensuing dialogue the distinction is shrugged off as immaterial after all. The crucial question of personal reputation is thus irreverently swept aside and its place taken by the mockery of reader expectation in all its hunger for finality and satisfaction. Bentivole personifies this feeling. 'I am very glad, for thy credits sake, that thou perseuerst', he replies, when Pierce confirms that he is composing an answer to Harvey, 'but more glad would I bee to see it abroad and publisht' (iii. 31–2). The fetish of the 'final product' never appears; we have to be content with the experience of a work in progress, work in dialogue with itself, reminding us of the arbitrary nature of its prescribed form, jolting us out of a facile acceptance of the reader's role. The treatment of fictional readers within the work unsettles a real reader's sense of identity and location. Nashe's fictional readers want a preview of the answer to Harvey. 'I pry thee', says one, 'if thou hast anie of the papers of thy Booke about thee, shew vs some of them, that, like a great Inquest, we may deliuer our verdit before it come to the *Omnigatherum* of Towne and Countrey' (iii. 32). Pierce replies that he has already read the dedicatory epistle to the barber. As 'real' readers we have been told in an intervening epistle of the fictional nature of these other readers, yet at this point they echo our dissatisfaction about the unresolved identity of the barber patron: 'I, to the Barber: such a thing I well remember, but what Barber it was, or where he dwelt, directly thou neuer toldst vs' (iii. 33).

Harvey assumed that authorial power to move belief was dependent on the nomination and identification of a source of real power: a famous name. Having proved the question of power to be irrelevant beside that of creative capacity, Nashe is at liberty to distort both Harvey's discourse and his biography without being guilty of violating the true identity of his antagonist. Accuracy becomes another pseudo-issue. Nashe introduces the selected highlights of Harvey's book as the 'cleare repurified soule of truth, without the least shadow of fiction' (iii. 42), but Importuno is concerned at the lack of reference for the purposes of accurate verification: 'I wonder thou setst not downe in figures in the margent, in what line, page & folio a man might find euerie one of these fragments, which would haue much satisfied thy Readers' (iii. 44). As Nashe's purpose is far from wishing to satisfy his readers, however, he pours scorn on this suggestion, drawing attention instead to the pleasurable texture of his inaccurate composition.

Turning from the discursive to the biographical representation of *Have With You*'s antagonist, we find the words of Greene's libeller turned like weapons against him. As Harvey passed off his viciousness towards Greene as an admonitory *exemplum*, so Nashe's companions solemnly declare that Harvey's jest-book biography will serve them as 'an ensample, for since the raigne of *Queen Gueniuer* was there neuer seene worse' (iii. 102). The transparent fraudulence of Harvey's appeal, throughout his libellous account, to 'ascertayned' and 'credible' authorities is travestied throughout Nashe's mock biography by the wild ambiguity of the author's attempts to authenticate his story. The vexed question of rhetorical licence is referred with mock solemnity to the precedents of historians. Documentary proof is only another strategy interchangeable, if the reader finds it hard to swallow, with the sop of rhetorical licence as practised by sycophantic historians:

> In sadnes I would be loath to discourage ye, but yet in truth . . . the coppie of his Tutors Letter to his father I will shew you, about his carriage and demeanour; and yet I will not positiuely affirme it his Tutors Letter neither . . . and what you list not beleeue, referre to after Ages, euen as *Paulus Iouis* did in his lying praises of the House of *Medices*. (iii. 64)

*Have With You* abandons every last vestige of the protestant-humanist assumption that publication and literary skill are mere accessories to the rhetorical propagation of true doctrine amongst the ignorant. As representations of the truth cease to be even nominally at stake in certain kinds of published discourse, so the whole question of allowing for rhetorical licence disappears. It is impossible to go on maintaining, as Harvey tried to do, that a 'licentious' and 'unauthorized' fantasticality of invention could somehow represent a subversive threat to the political state. At one point in his attack Harvey labels Nashe 'Apuleius', associating his Lucianic fantasy with the licentiousness of change and innovation in the political sense. In *Have With You* Nashe pretends to be affronted by the imputation, regarding it as a libel against one Apuleius: 'ho: hath *Apuleius* euer an Attorney here? One Apuleius (by the name of *Apuleius*) he endites to be an engrosser of arts and inuentions, putting down *Plato, Hippocrates, Aristotle*' (iii. 118). His companions, however, advise him not to get too excited about what is, after all, nothing but a rhetorical figure of amplification.

Nashe is mortified: 'Rhetorical figure? and if I had a hundred sonnes, I had rather haue them disfigur'd & keep them at home as cyphers than send them to schoole to learn to figure it after that order' (iii. 120).

He is right of course. Rhetorical figures do have the power to disfigure and damage identity, so long as freewheeling fiction is repressed, and the press remains through censorship the organ of official power and a form for the creation of public reputation. The most ingenious dramatization of this problem, however, was not *Have With You* but the confession of the lying page known as *The Unfortunate Traveller*.

# 11
# Credit for the Page of *The Unfortunate Traveller*

Fellows of Jack Wilton, king of the pages, must make his acquaintance by way of an induction which asks them to swear to the articles of his mock-sovereignty:

> *Memorandum*, euerie one of you after the perusing of this pamphlet is to prouide him a case of ponyardes, that if you come in companie with anie man which shall dispraise it or speak against it, you may straight crie *Sic respondeo*, and giue him the stockado. It stands not with your honours (I assure ye) to haue a gentleman and a page abused in his absence. Secondly, whereas you were wont to swere men on a pantofle to be true to your puisant order, you shall sweare them on nothing but this Chronicle of the king of Pages hence forward. Thirdly, it shall be lawful for anie whatsoeuer to play with false dice in a corner on the couer of this foresayd Acts and Monuments. (ii. 207–8)

These articles indicate that what follows involves a retreat into holiday time and space. 'Many speciall graue articles more had I to giue you in charge', the induction goes on,'but let this suffice for a tast to the text.' The text, however, is apparently going to be a festive occasion, the communally produced experience of a story-telling: 'Heigh passe, come aloft: euerie man of you take your places and hear Iacke Wilton tell his own tale' (ii. 208). The history that follows intermittently recalls the ambiguity of its medium, now consciously dissolving the respectful distance of the conventional author–reader relation: 'Gentle Readers (looke you be gentle now since I haue cald you so), now insisting on the emotional identification aroused by oral narrative: 'Oh my Auditors, had you seene him how he stretcht out his lims, scratcht his scabd elbowes at this speach' (ii. 218–19). Both modes are disquieting, the one reminding the reader that politeness towards him serves the page's own rhetorical interests, the other unexpectedly implicating him in the sordid means by which this coney-catching style of history achieves its morally edifying ends. The invitation to the reader to hear the king of pages tell his own tale signals the beginning of the holiday king's confessional abdication in a narrative revelation of the pursuit of credit which characterizes his operations in print. For print, as I have suggested, was ideally supposed to operate within the confines of the Elizabethan systems of patronage and censorship. The patronage system, with its altruistic origins in the policies of moral and economic reform, insisted on the printed page's revelation of a profitable and patriotic discourse which would advance the author's political ambitions and increase his patron's credit as a furtherer of the reformation. Crucial to this patriotic yoking of interests was the obligation that the text in question yield profit to the reader, if not by the straightforward truthtelling of a technical discourse, then at least by inviting the reader to moralize and discover the profitable application of its verbal devices and narrative inventions. The page was, in other words, devoted to rhetorically pursuing the reader's credit so as to authorize itself; all the histories, fictions, and verbal devices it could discover would be idle unless offering the reader matter for interpretation or persuasions to secure political conviction. At the same time this obligation to pursue conviction or yield interpretative matter meant that the printed page was rarely out of danger of censorship, for to be denied the right to tell a tale without offering to profit the reader laid the page open to unforeseen political interpretations, while claiming to speak an absolute truth not explicitly identified with the interests of a patron risked the recrimination of magistrates who would be sure to discover seditious implications in the page's claim to have direct access (unmediated by the Church of England) to the truth of God. The page of a printed history was thus obliged both to hunt political credit, the source of which was the court and patronage, and to expend its narrative energy in proving the admonitory profit of every tale it had to tell.

Something of the intellectual and moral contradictions involved in these incompatible obligations can be illustrated by the credit-seeking and profit-yielding services rendered to discourse first by the political patronage and then by the political history of the Earl of Essex in the 1590s. Essex, as we saw in the last chapter, provided Richard Harvey with all the credit his page required to authorize his claim to speak truth on behalf of God and the State, without risking unfavourable interpretation (v. 176). On Essex's death, however, the Earl's political credit was nil, and his unfortunate history was swiftly turned into a profitable discourse by his secretary, who discovered in writing 'the life and end of the most noble Robert Earl of Essex' many admonitory aphorisms that could be usefully applied to his own ambitions and interests.[1]

Nashe's page, being chronicler of its own unfortunate history, reveals the moral hypocrisy and aesthetic impoverishment of narratives thus obliged to sacrifice everything and everyone in the interests of credit and profit. The page becomes historian of itself, a narrator whose narrative can only be the disclosure of rhetorical strategy after rhetorical strategy, page after page pretending to secure credit for itself, pretending to make its history 'profitable' to readers. In the process of course the narrative renders itself incapable of persuading the reader, or of unfolding any more profit from its pages than might be contained in a printer's napkin (ii. 207). All the knowledge the reader gains is inevitably to the discredit of the page. He—the page, that is, otherwise known as Jack Wilton—begins by exposing the dependence of his credit upon the court and its system of patronage: 'I, *Iacke Wilton*, (a Gentleman at least,) was a certain kind of an appendix or page, belonging or appertaining in or vnto the confines of the English court; where what my credit was, a number of my creditors that I cosned can testifie' (ii. 209). Frankly admitting his debt to a corrupt system, the page warns us against looking for coherence in his narrative or consistency in Jack's character. The lack of integrity that has so troubled critics of *The Unfortunate Traveller* is in fact a measure of its integrity: for it is only by disclosing the lies and contradictions on which they depend that these pages can begin to reveal the truth about themselves. The page, therefore, is committed to being a liar.

We can begin to make fictional sense of these lies, however, by trusting to Jack's own revelation of how his credit works. Military companies, he explains, offer creditors of all kinds:

> Those companies, lyke a greate deale of corne, do yeeld some chaffe; the corne are cormorants, the chaffe are good fellowes, which are quickly blowen to nothing wyth bearing a light heart in a lyght purse. Amongest this chaffe was I winnowing my wittes to liue merrily, and by my troth so I did: the prince could but command men spend their bloud in his seruice, I could make them spend al the mony they had for my pleasure. (ii. 210)

All the characteristic strategies which will subsequently be developed in the disclosure of the page's deceits are present in this short extract. For simplicity's sake we may distinguish these as three.

[1] Quoted by Trousdale, *Shakespeare and the Rhetoricians*, p. 148.

First, by bringing himself into explicit comparison with the warring king ('the prince could but command men spend their bloud in his seruice, I could make them spend al the mony they had for my pleasure') Jack not only breaks down the expected *virtus/* prodigality opposition, exposing the king as a grosser spendthrift than himself, but, more important, reveals the relationship of page and prince to be an emulative, competitive one, dependent for power upon the current, liquid nature of their resources. The narrative goes on to discover in Jack's relations with the cider merchant how court patronage, idealized as the mutual dependency of page and peerage, actually involves a fierce struggle for the monopoly of such liquid currency as the court affords. Dedicatory epistles do not honour the aristocracy but promote the credit of the page at the patron's expense (an example is Gascoigne's dedication of *The Steele Glas* to his patron Lord Grey). In Nashe's text political credit is made equivalent to oratorical fluency, which is comically embodied in images of vital liquids—tears, cider, blood.[2]

The second authority claimed by Jack in his division of creditors into corn and chaff is a pretension to divine sanction on the pragmatic basis of the Tudor morality of thrift and providence. The moralistic distinction between provident and improvident lifestyles is, of course, a fundamental tenet of Tudor thought; one thinks of Ascham's opposition of 'light' and 'grave' wits: 'Quick in wit and light in manners be either seldom troubled or very soon weary in carrying a very heavy purse', so that they are seldom 'fortunate for themselves or very profitable to serve the commonwealth'.[3] Jack's parody identifies his own material interests with those attributed to the commonweal, since provident cormorants are more serviceable to him than unthrifty chaff. What makes this parody of magisterial discourse so shocking, however, is the revelation of its underlying moral pragmatism through a near-blasphemous echo of divine sanction in the corn and chaff metaphor of the Last Judgement. In fact, as we have seen, similar pretensions to divine authority are latent throughout the Tudor discourse of reform: Crowley's 'Voyce of the laste trumpet' encourages thift and diligence in the commonweal by citing the biblical preferment of the profitable servant who invested his talents. Jack's punning transformation of these profit-

[2] The importance of these images of liquid and currency was noted by M. Ferguson in her excellent article 'Nashe's *The Unfortunate Traveller*: the "Newes of the Maker" Game'.

[3] Ascham, *Schoolmaster*, p. 22.

able servants into 'cormorants', however, identifies them with the hoarders and investors who are condemned by John the Baptist's prophecy of the Last Judgement, when God is figured as the thresher of humanity, the winnower of corn from chaff, of Pharisees, hypocrites, and profiteering governors from true servants: 'he will thoroughly purge his floor, and gather his wheat into the garner; but he will burn up the chaff with unquenchable fire' (Matt. 3: 12). John the Baptist's prophecy is directed against the Pharisees, that 'generation of vipers' (Matt. 3: 7), and it is no coincidence that Nashe took this prophecy as part of his text against the hoarding City governors in *Christes Teares Over Jerusalem* ('his Fan is in his hande to purge his Floore', ii. 15; and see ii. 111–12, 158–61). *The Unfortunate Traveller* reflexively comments on the internal contradictions of a presumptuous and apocalyptic satire like *Christes Teares* (in which Nashe actually assumes the voice of Christ in judgement) by disclosing the spurious providence which compels every Tudor page to moralize and to 'invent'any narrative as moral proof of divine judgement. This compulsion to moralize, and to disclose divine providence, is of course one of the things that runs the printed page into danger, as was evident enough in the spring of 1593, when no fewer than three Puritans—Penry, Barrow, and Greenwood—were executed under the laws against seditious writing, for claiming scriptural authority for their opposition of the magistrates.[4] No doubt discourses were soon penned to profit from the deaths of these men as the *exempla* of divine judgement against Anabaptistical rebels. Thus, in *The Unfortunate Traveller*, all events, whether brought about by Jack himself in his initial posture of coney-catcher, or witnessed by him thereafter as moralizing chronicle, are regularly sacrificed to our edification as admonitory proofs of that same 'unfallible rule' of divine retribution which, according to Ralegh, it was 'the end and scope of all History . . . by examples of times past' to reveal to the present.[5] What this moralizing compulsion implies, of course, is the obliteration of all further becoming and sequential development as every new departure in the narrative flattens into an admonition of its own punishment; finally there is no choice but for the narrative to take vengeance upon itself, and end.

[4] See *The Examinations of Henry Barrowe, John Greenwood and John Penrie before the High Commissioners* (1593).

[5] Sir Walter Ralegh, *The History of the World* (1614), p. 458.

The third strategy which we can distinguish in operation in this extract is the means by which the first two were brought to our attention. By this of course I mean Jack's characteristic mode of parody. In this instance two kinds of discourse are recognizable in parodic form, one being the pragmatic Tudor discourse of prodigality and profitable state service, the other being a prophetic discourse of apocalyptic judgement. What is even more important to notice, however, is how Jack's rhapsodic idiom relentlessly parodies the comparative proofs of rhetorical discourse, the Erasmian techniques which properly served to enable discourse to be as copious—as intensely persuasive and as morally generative—as possible. Robert Lanham was probably nearer the mark than he realized when he condemned *The Unfortunate Traveller* as a 'bankrupt' narrative which could bring us neither 'profit' nor 'delight'.[6] What appeared to him as the book's rhetorical defect was actually a measure of its artistic strength and subtlety. Although not, perhaps, a novel in any other sense, Nashe's book arrives through parody at a novelistic recognition of the relativity of all viewpoints, all discourses, a recognition of the fact that 'every discourse has its own selfish and biased proprietor; there are no words with meanings shared by all, no words "belonging to no one" '.[7]

A tendency to classify Jack as a satirist and to regard *The Unfortunate Traveller* as the vehicle of his satiric comment leads attention away from what is surely the most important point: it is not a society that is the object of representation in Jack's narrative, but the way in which society is currently 'set forth' in discourses of all kinds, not least in Jack's own. These discourses are objectified and materialized in all their biased, proprietorial expediency by Jack's aptitude for mimicry. We find discourses of all kinds forcing their materiality on our attention, not only through the caricaturing of stylistic properties (as, for example, in the Arcadian parody, ii. 271–8) but also in the imagery that materializes the 'property' of discourse itself as credit, as power to command the resources of others. Thus for the pander, Petro de Campo Frego, linguistic mastery becomes portable property; he carries 'halfe a dosen seueral languages in his purse' (ii. 255); the orator Vanderhulke is ready to

[6] R. A. Lanham, 'Tom Nashe and Jack Wilton: Personality as Structure in "The Unfortunate Traveller" ', p. 215.

[7] M. Bakhtin, *The Dialogic Imagination*, ed. M. Holquist, p. 401.

ready to 'vncaske' his 'orificiall rethorike' from its safe treasury the 'bard hutch' because he knows his liquid investment in the Duke's welcome will be adequately compensated by the 'beaue princely bloud' flowing in his patron's veins (ii. 248). Liquids, like rhetoric, however, are not always so politically potent; the Duke's princely blood has to suffer some harmless dilution by the rosewater and rainwater of 'a very learned or rather ruthfull oration' delivered by Wuittenburg's university orators 'emptying their phrase bookes' while 'the world emptied his intrailes' (ii. 246). Even the most modest discourses are materialized in liquid terms as being conscious of the credit they will purchase; the 'extemporal dity' which bursts from Surrey at the sight of Geraldine has pretensions to an inky immortality: 'Never be drie these my sad plaintiue lines' (ii. 254).

Conceiving of rhetorical mastery in terms of ready money is, of course, a commonplace. Erasmus recommends the gathering of exemplary resources as a way of turning buried riches into current money by 'accustoming' the reader 'to utilizing the riches of your reading. For there are those who hold a great many things in their minds, as though stored up in the earth, although in speaking and writing they are wonderfully destitute.'[8] The very etymology of *copia*, as Terence Cave writes, involves the domain of material riches in *ops*, and 'confidently asserts the values of affluence, military power, and rhetorical fluency'.[9] The achievement of linguistic mastery through a struggle to emulate and outdo one's authorities was, moreover, figured by Quintilian, Erasmus, and others as a process of mental digestion. The discourse of ancient authors must be learned by heart, 'reduced . . . almost to a state of liquefaction' the better to be committed to the memory for 'subsequent imitation'.[10] In the first episode of *The Unfortunate Traveller* we have an image of the dependence of rhetorical fluency on affluence and military power through various transactions of sustaining liquids that dramatize Jack Wilton's relations with the aristocratic cider merchant. The 'liquid alleageance' exacted by Jack from his 'vnthrifte subiects' (ii. 210) has run dry and in pursuit of more the page approaches a peer of the realm who has a monopoly of such resources, 'a License to furnish the Campe with syder and such like prouant' (ii. 214). Apostrophizing this magistrate in the

8 Erasmus, *De copia*, p. 89.

9 Cave, *Cornucopian Text*, p. 3.

10 Quintilian, *Institutio oratoria*, x. i. 19.

terms of a dedicatory epistle, the page is clearly parodying the inappropriate discourse of honour, service, and mutual increase which could hardly articulate the real relations between ambitious authors and noblemen who derived their incomes from exploiting economic controls. His lordship having drunk to Jack, the page responds:

> I . . . discourst vnto him what entire affection I had borne him time out of minde, partly for the high descent and linage from whence hee sprong, and partly for the tender care and prouident respect he had of pore souldiers, that, whereas the vastitie of that place . . . might humble them to some extremitie . . . he vouchsafed in his owne person to be a victualler to the campe (a rare example of magnifisence and honorable curtesy). (ii. 211)

The point here is not, as some critics have suggested, that Nashe is getting cheap laughs by conflating a merchant with a nobleman but that he is portraying the competitive dependence of both page and patron on the same limited pool of economic privileges commanded by the Crown.[11] Jack's oratorical resources are replenished by drink supplied by his credulous auditor. Even his feigned oratorical inability is fed by cider: 'by this drinke it grieues me so I am not able to repeate it' (ii. 212–13). The strain of grief could also be interpreted, as Quintilian put it, by means of another liquid; that of tears. 'Again, it is a most effective device to confess in the peroration that the strain of grief and fatigue is overpowering, and that our strength is sinking beneath them, as Cicero does in his defence of Milo: "but here I must make an end: I can no longer speak for tears." '[12] Nashe's page indulges in hyperbolic caricature of this particular oratorical device:

> Why (quoth I), my selfe that am but a poore childish well-willer of yours, with the verie thought that a man of your deserte and state by a number of pesants and varlets shoulde be so iniuriously abused in hugger mugger haue wepte all my vrine vpwarde. The wheele vnder our cittie bridge carries not so much water ouer the citie, as my braine hath welled forth gushing streames of sorrow: I haue wepte so immoderatly and lauishly that I thought verily my palat had bin turned to pissing Conduit in London. My eyes haue bin dronke, outragiously dronke, wyth giuing but ordinarie entercourse through their sea-circled Ilands to my distilling dreriment. What shal I say? (ii. 213)

But for all this fluency and fluidity the resources which actually

[11] See e.g. Lanham, 'Tom Nashe and Jack Wilton', p. 210.

[12] Quintilian, *Institutio oratoria*, XI. iii. 173.

sustain and are sought after by the orator are not (as they are in Rabelais for example) identifiable with the generative imagination itself but rather with the Crown, to which all power and influence must answer. There is possibly a pun at work here between cider (or syder) and desire; Jack misquotes Ovid, '*Tendit ad sydera virtus*, thers great vertue belongs . . . to a cup of sider', especially as 'authorized' by a lord (ii. 210). The source of this, Ovid's 'tendit in ardua virtus', occurs significantly enough as part of a plea to a friend to use his influence and oratorical skill to temper Caesar's wrath against the poet.[13] Ovid's suggestion is that the very difficulty of the oratorical task will inspire his friend to plead effectively to Caesar on his behalf; Nashe's subversion makes it clear that the Elizabethan page's oratorical success depends on the exploitation of cider/desire which defines itself as a sordid political dependence on the king's monopoly of credit. To the lord, Jack's discourse becomes a 'so much desired relation' (ii. 212) because it threatens to cut off his patent on cider by claiming to tap its royal source—credit with the king. Investing lies and rumour with all the political currency that royal patronage can command, the page has aristocracy itself silent, weeping out all last week's cider in a 'hell of suspense' (ii. 213). Reports given credit by the king are death warrants:

> that which malice hath saide is the meere ouerthrow and murther of your daies . . . It is buzzed in the Kings head that you are a secret frend to the Enemie, and vnder pretence of getting a License to furnish the Campe with syder . . . you haue furnisht the Enemie, & in emptie barrels sent letters of discouerie and corne innumerable. (ii. 213–14)

Again, in the burlesque suggestion of supplying the enemy with resources (information) in cider barrels, we have another instance of the liquid/discourse-as-portable-property series of images. At the same time it is plain that the power of discourse means political power: fictitious letters to the enemy, malicious rumours reported by the page. All that matters is making these rumours credible enough to seem like a reality; the pathetic vulnerability of the cider lord resembles the vulnerability of the body politic itself as represented by government legislation against the printing and circulating of 'lewd and seditious tales' and 'malicious rumours'.[14] As an orator Jack reduces his authorizing patron of cider to a state of

[13] Ovid, *Tristia, Ex ponto*, trans. A. L. Wheeler, II. 2. 113.

[14] See e.g. Loades, 'Theory and Practice of Censorship', p. 144.

liquefaction; the demand is not just for cider but for lifeblood: 'Nay (quoth I), you shall pardon me, for I haue spoken too much alreadie; no definitiue sentence of death shall march out of my well meaning lips; they haue but lately suckt milke and shall they so sodainly change their food and seeke after bloud?' (ii. 214–15). Sentences become death sentences; the lord is 'readie to hang himselfe for the ende of the full point' (ii. 213). Having sent the lordly tapster into a trance-like state of fear with his appalling words, Jack exacts a final drink as if wringing him after execution: 'I was verie loath mine hoste and I should part with drye lips . . . I met him halfewaies and askt his Lordship what hee meant to slip his necke out of the collar so sodainly' (ii. 214).

In this instance it is the page's pursuit of credit which translates the body of a peer from a state of liquid replenishment (his very garments 'larded' with 'daintie liquor', ii. 210) into a dismembered pulp. A later episode, however, finds the page's credit cast in doubt by the authority of a nobleman, and it is Jack's own body which is threatened with imminent dissolution. Jack has been living in high style on Diamante's money and the credit that accrues to him by claiming to be the Earl of Surrey, when his patron returns unexpectedly in the middle of a lavish banquet.

> sitting in my pontificalibus with my curtizan at supper, lyke *Anthonie* and *Cleopatra*, when they quafte standing boules of Wine spiced with pearle together, he stole in ere we sent for him, and bad much good it vs, and askt vs whether wee wanted anie gests. If he had askt me whether I would haue hanged my selfe, his question had bin more acceptable. Hee that had then vngartered me might haue pluckt out my heart at my heeles. (ii. 267)

The very doubt cast upon his credit dissolves the page's power; words become, as for the cider merchant, the equivalents of execution. The counterfeits, Diamante and Jack, are ready to disintegrate for sheer terror: 'A trembling earthquake or shaking feauer assailed either of vs; and I thinke vnfainedly, if he, seeing our faint heart agonie, had not soone cheered and refreshed vs, the dogs had gone together by the eares vnder the table for our feare-dropped lims' (ii. 267–8).

Characteristically even the dogs are involved in the emulative struggle for power and increase, going together 'by the ears' like the ambitious male combatants of Shakespeare's *All's Well that Ends Well*:

KING. The Florentines and Senoys are by th'eares,
Haue fought with equall fortune, and continue
A brauing warre.

1 LORD DUMAINE. So tis reported sir.

KING. Nay tis most credible

(lines 229–32 [I. ii. 1–4])

Interestingly enough, Shakespeare's play, concerned as it is with the question of credit and the rhetorical nature of male virtue (*virtus*), shares with Nashe's fiction the figure of the army captain whose lack of credibility is indicated by his being a creature made up of lendings; garments which do not 'belong'. Like Parolles trailing his lists and scarves, Jack's captain companion depends for his authority on the nobility's cast-offs, acquiring from Jack, 'One of my Lords cast veluet caps, and a weather-beaten feather, wherewith he threatned his soldiers a far off, as Iupiter is said with the shaking of his haire to make heauen & earth to quake' (ii. 217). So tenuous, however, is this captain's command of the credit of authority (as the Olympian travesty indicates) that, once cornered by the enemy, he is unable to justify himself with any plausibility: 'Questiond of the perticular cause, he had not a word to blesse himselfe with, yet faine would he haue patcht out a polt-foot tale, but (God knowes) it had not one true leg to stand on' (ii. 223). Obviously, a 'true leg' here means a creditable counterfeit such as Jack himself, with his mastery of exemplary and comparative 'proofs', had employed in the preceding pages to persuade the captain to this extremity. Discredited thus, and without any language to sustain him, the captain's body becomes forfeit to the French, 'none there but was ready to rent him in pieces' (ii. 224). However, the usual economy operates; the French hope to translate this unfortunate body into a viable currency, asking him 'what of the King of Englands secrets (so aduantageable) he was priuy to' (ii. 224). The captain is unable to invest his discourse with a court-derived authority; 'in good honesty', as Jack ambiguously relates it, 'they were lies which he had not yet stampt' (ii. 224). And the page goes on to report the torture of the captain's body as if it were no more than he deserved for such an incoherent unprofitable discourse.

Obviously this sequence of images involving sustaining liquids and 'stampt' or current languages is repeatedly invoked to suggest that the credibility of printed pages is dependent on the countenance of magisterial authority; the patronage that endorses a book's claim to speak infallible truth, the king's face stamped upon the true coin of the realm. What gives the King's countenance its authority is in turn the liquid currency—blood of subjects—it can command. This is the economy in which the lying page must operate, exercising power until its credit, gradually depleted, runs out and leaves it prey to the bloodthirsty exactions of further moralizing pages, just as the Earl of Essex was prey to the moralizing of his biography.

This is not, however, to say that Nashe's *Unfortunate Traveller* communicates entirely on the level of poetic imagery, however subtle. The biased and proprietorial nature of discourse is made palpable in another sense through the reflexive nature of the page's autobiographical narrative. As the page is both subject and object of its own discourse, so it is constantly presenting objectified images of its own lying rhetoric. Changing places with Surrey, for example, provides the page not only with opportunity to mimic Surrey's wonted rhetoric with its military 'march' of magisterial 'precepts of grauetie & modestie' (ii. 245) but also to represent Jack's own rhetorical pranks and divine pretensions in the counterfeit speeches of Tabitha and the disguised Earl of Surrey. First, at the revelation of Tabitha's and Petro de Campo Frego's dastardly plot against his life, Jack, disguised as Surrey, assumes a fitting countenance of authority and justice replete with precepts:

> I very mildly and grauely gaue him audience; raile on them I dyd not after his tale was ended, but sayde I would trie what the lawe could doe. Conspiracy by the custome of their countrie was a capitall offence, and what custome or iustice might affoorde they should bee all sure to feele. I could, quoth I, acquite my selfe otherwise, but it is not for a straunger to be his owne caruer in reuenge. (ii. 257)

The scrupulousness with which the magisterial 'Surrey' distinguishes between custom, law, and self-seeking revenge is emphasized by the switch to direct speech, weighty with the authority of adage ('I could, quoth I . . .'). However these scruples turn out to be spurious. Jack goes on to relate how, as Surrey, he received Tabitha's counterfeit rhetoric:

> Not a word more with Tabitha, but die she would before God or the deuill would haue her: shee sounded and reuiued, and then sounded again, and after she reuiued againe, sighed heauily, spoke faintly and pittifully, yea, and so pittifully, as if a man had not knowen the prankes of harlots before,

> he would haue melted to commiserations. Tears, sighs, and dolefull tuned wordes coulde not make anie forcible claime to my stonie eares. (ii. 257–8)

The excellence of this is the subtlety with which the narrator mocks the figures of speech he reports; 'Not a word more with *Tabitha*, but die she would before God or the deuill would haue her' is achieved by the condensation of several idioms which might be employed for passionate effect. It could be 'before God I'll not speak another word', or 'I'll die before I speak a word more', or 'Devil take me if I', etc. As it stands, of course, the phrasing is nonsensical, and it is important to see that this is the significance of the narrative process. It is the narrator who deprives rhetoric of its credibility by exposing such credit-seeking exclamations as part of a bag of rhetorical tricks. This technique is a reflexive one; when Jack goes on to try and gain the reader's credit for his own version of events by the same means a few lines later—'O falsehood in faire shewe', for example (ii. 258)—his words do not sound authentic. The 'tears, sighs, and dolefull tuned wordes' he caricatures in Tabitha are all familiar to us from his own repertoire. Caricature is thus always self-caricature. The page's magisterial disdain for the melting 'prankes of harlots' is a credible counterfeit of his master Surrey, until he turns out to be unassailable not by virtue of having memorized 'sterne precepts of grauetie & modestie' but because he hopes to profit materially from Tabitha's guilty confession: 'It was the glittering crownes that I hungred and thirsted after, & with them for all her mocke holy-daie iestures she was faine to come off, before I condescended to anie bargaine of silence' (ii. 258). Whether this is 'Jack' or 'Surrey' whose voice we now hear is immaterial; either way the page mocks its own relentless seeking of credit. This time, however, the coin it exacts is no current money, and as the result of giving credit to Tabitha's counterfeit coin, Surrey and Jack are imprisoned in 'the master of the mintes house' (ii. 258) for conspiracy. At this point the page indulges in a shameless display of indignation which is recognizably of the same counterfeit stamp as that used long ago to dupe the cider merchant: 'I could drinke for anger till my head akt, to thinke howe I was abused', 'I, silly milkesop, mistrusting no deceit', 'O falsehood in faire shewe', etc. (ii. 258).

While the page thus continues to discredit its own rhetoric by repetition and self-quotation, it also casts further doubts upon its moralizing pretensions. Earlier in this same episode, Jack relates how Tabitha approached Surrey (disguised as Jack himself) with a plot to kill his supposed master. The prose switches back and forth between Tabitha's words and Jack's commentary; when it comes to paraphrasing Surrey's reply, however, the result is decidedly unlike any idiom in which Surrey has spoken so far: 'He verie subtilly consented to her stratageme at the first motion; kill me hee would, that heauens could not withstand, and a pistol was the predestinate engine which must deliuer the parting blow' (ii. 256). The page is here representing Surrey's imitation of himself, Jack Wilton, as moralizer of his own inventions. This identification of the page with divine providence ('kill me he would, that heauens could not withstand' and the pistol as 'predestinate engine') is familiar to us from Jack's very earliest introduction of himself as the instrument of divine justice. In subsequent episodes the claim to godlike authority becomes as familiar as pretensions to be in credit with the aristocracy. Thus when, still in the army camp, Jack takes his revenge on the officious clerks who keep back dead-pays and refuse to give credit in advance to spendthrift soldiers, he justifies his actions as the predestined will of God: 'My masters, you may conceaue of me what you list, but I thinke confidently I was ordained Gods scourge from aboue for their daintie finicalitie. The houre of their punishment could no longer be proroged, but vengeance must haue at them at all a ventures' (ii. 226). And yet the claim is discredited in its very making: 'you may conceaue of me what you list', the page confides to its readers. So far as the divine will is concerned, the page simply cannot compel belief; Jack's self-mockery stimulates the reader into awareness that it is his own responsibility to be critical of the printed word.

But surely Jack's assurance of being 'ordained Gods scourge from aboue' (ii. 226) contradicts his claims to political credit? For as God is above the king, so his appointed scourge is above wanting to be countenanced and authorized by any earthly magistrate. True, yet if there is a contradiction in Jack's position it is a contradiction already implicit in Tudor political doctrine which formulated the relationship between the magistrate and the rebel as a kind of economy of mutual retribution. The sovereign magistrate (God's representative on earth) acts as a divine scourge to the rebellious subject, and vice versa. Thus Thomas Wilson's *Rule of Reason* in 1552 cited 'God himself, or els the ordinaunce of God' as the first efficient cause of the magistrate and 'unquiet people, rebelles, disobedient people' as the second.[15] The magistrate existed to keep

[15] See Trousdale, *Shakespeare and the Rhetoricians*, p. 28.

order and subdue the rebel, but if the magistrate became a tyrant he usurped his divine ordinance and to punish him 'then suffereth God the Rebel to rage'.[16] One form of tyranny was invasive war, as Robert Crowley wrote in his apocalyptic lesson for the magistrate in the 'Voyce of the laste trumpet':

> . . . If thou do invade
> And get by force commoditie
> The same shal certenly be made
> A scorge to thy posteritye.[17]

Henry VIII's war at the beginning of *The Unfortunate Traveller* was an invasive one; a truly providential history would be obliged to discover some kind of retribution in the sequel. What Jack's history enacts instead, however, is the double-edged nature of this concept of the providential scourge. On the one hand Tudor writers were inclined to moralize the activities of rebels and foreign enemies as divinely ordained chastisements for their own (and their sovereign's) sins;[18] commenting on the lax moral attitudes of the 1560s, Ascham explains rebellious attitudes as 'God's just plagues . . . brought justly upon us for our sins'.[19] On the other hand no amount of divine ordination could exculpate rebels from the charge of being usurpers themselves, impiously coveting 'the office of a King and consequently the office of God'.[20] As St Paul conveniently articulated it, the magistrate was the only *officially* sanctioned scourge of God: 'Let every soul be subject unto the higher powers. For there is no power but of God: the powers that be are ordained of God. Whosoever therefore resisteth the power, resisteth the ordinance of God: and they that resist shall receive to themselves damnation' (Rom. 13: 1–2). So there is no way out of the retributive economy. First, the over-ambitious magistrate receives his 'scourge' through the agency of the rebel, then the rebel receives a scourge to his own ambition. For rebellion in Tudor political thought came about through the sin of ambition; both recusant and puritan nonconformists were persistently chastised by the authorities for their

[16] See W. R. D. Jones, *The Tudor Commonwealth 1529–1559*, p. 49.

[17] Crowley, *Select Works*, p. 99.

[18] See J. R. Hale, 'Sixteenth-Century Explanations of War and Violence', p. 8; P. Jorgeson, 'Theoretical Views of War in Elizabethan England', p. 476; and id., 'Elizabethan Religious Literature for Time of War', pp. 6–10.

[19] Ascham, *Schoolmaster*, p. 44.

[20] J. W. Allen, *A History of Political Thought in the Sixteenth Century*, p. 136.

Lucifer-like ambition.[21] It is clear that Tudor doctrine, despite its apparent rejection of vengeance as an illegal usurpation of magisterial power, actually underwrites the authority of the powers that be in terms indistinguishable from those of illegal revenge. Indeed, St Paul goes on to define 'the minister of God' as he who 'beareth not the sword in vain . . . a revenger to execute wrath upon him that doeth evil' (Rom. 13: 4). Distinctions between the rebel and credit-claiming king of the pages were certainly blurred in 1593 when dissenters were being put to death for asserting in writing the imminence of God's vengeance upon his earthly magistrates. John Penry, in a treatise published in 1590 proving that those who favoured reformation were not enemies to the Queen and State, openly challenged such magistrates 'as beare chiefe authority vnder hir majesty' to acknowledge that 'in fighting against vs they labor . . . to aggrauat & hasten their owne damnation', reminding them that although God 'ruleth by the ciuill magistrate', yet civil magistrates will be answerable when God 'shall in the daye of judgement put an ende vnto this regiment'.[22] Nashe was prosecuted for prophesying judgement against a more modest level of magistrate in 1593, when he took as his text Matt. 23, in which Christ preaches against the Pharisees 'that were the Princes of the People' (see ii. 20 and 111–12). Against the city fathers he thus implicitly set Christ's radical statement 'Call no man your father upon the earth: for one is your father, which is in Heaven' (Matt. 23: 9). Nevertheless, even the heavenly Father as he is portrayed in *Christes Teares* is only to be known through his avenging scourge, the plague; indeed Nashe takes as his text 'The Lord is knowne by executing iudgement' (ii. 15). This inability to conceive of authority in other than powerful terms causes *Christes Teares* to be full of ambivalence; Nashe utters his scourging rhetoric fully aware of its own ambitious culpability. His admonition contains a diatribe against the 'bodie-wasting industry' of 'vild double-fac't Oratory' (ii. 89) and prefaces itself with an equivocal renunciation of the usurping ambition which defines itself as authorship: 'Farre be from me any ambitious hope

[21] See e.g. *The Works of John Whitgift*, ed. J. Ayre, i. 106–10; C. Read, 'William Cecil and English Public Relations', in *Elizabethan Government and Society*, ed. Bindoff *et al.*, p. 24.

[22] J. Penry, *A Treatise Wherein is Manifestlie Proved that Reformation and Those that Sincerely Fauor the Same, are unjustly charged to be Enemies vnto her Majestie and the State* (1590), sigs. *3$^{v}$, 22$^{v}$, F2$^{r}$.

of the vaine merite of Arte . . . Mine owne wit I cleane disinherite' (ii. 15).

In *The Unfortunate Traveller* all words are thus trapped into a usurpation of unrighteous authority, either by claiming credit with the king or by pretending to bypass and subvert aristocratic power through a direct warrant from God; usually the page claims both at once. In 1593 John Udall was writing to Burghley pleading for release from an imprisonment which had lasted since 1590 when Whitgift and the ecclesiastical authorities had considered his profession to speak 'the undoubted truth of God' too dangerous to allow him to go free, lest he should 'buzz into the people's ears such a conceit'.[23] At this time comparison with the Anabaptists of Munster was familiar in Whitgift's and Bancroft's denunciation of puritan dissenters.[24]

It seems hardly surprising that Jack Wilton should chronicle the delusions of the Anabaptists in similar terms; 'Why inspiration was their ordinarie familiar, and buzd in their eares like a Bee in a boxe euerie hower what newes from heauen, hell, and the land of whipperginnie' (ii. 233). But there is no real difference between Jack the rebel of Leiden and Jack Wilton, counterfeit king of the pages. If Anabaptists show a readiness to wreak revenge with divine authority—'displease them who durst, he should haue his mittimus to damnation *ex tempore*' (ii. 233)—this is no more than the page himself had pretended, in his extemporal inventions of 'divine' vengeance against the corrupt officers of the army camp. The page's irony in chronicling the absurdities of the Anabaptists begins, in fact, to proliferate uncontrollably: 'Verie deuout Asses they were, for all they were so dunstically set forth, and such as thought they knew as much of Gods minde as richer men' (ii. 233). Scorn directed against 'devout Asses' collapses in the irony of comparison with the devotion of 'richer men', but after all by whom have the Anabaptists been 'dunstically set forth' but by the narrator himself? For it is Jack Wilton whose saturnalian idiom creates the equivocal terms in which the Anabaptists seem to be condemned. Thus the page makes a mockery of the orthodox charge against Jack of Leiden as a usurper of magisterial power, the power that bears not the sword in

23 Collinson, *Elizabethan Puritan Movement*, p. 407.

24 Bancroft, *Suruay of the pretended Holy Discipline*, sig. B1$^r$; Whitgift, *Works*, i. 106.

vain. None of the Anabaptists will bring a blade into battle, mocks Jack:

It was not lawfull, said they, for anie man to draw the sword but the Magistrate; and in fidelitie (which I had welnigh forgot) *Iack Leiden*, their Magistrate, had the image or likeness of a peece of a rustie sword, like a lustie lad, by his side: now I remember mee, it was but a foyle neither, and he wore it to shewe that he should haue the foyle of his Enemies. (ii. 233)

The disingenuous mock-accuracy of the chronicle is emphasized by ambivalent qualification: 'in fidelitie (which I had welnigh forgot)'. In treating the rising as an apocalyptic charivari[25] Jack's chronicling narrative actually invites us to link the episode to his grotesque rhetorical invention of the social and medical horrors he witnessed (ii. 227–31) in England. The switch from Jack's coney-catching subversions of society in the army camp to his new role as chronicler of society is signalled by his insistence on a more direct 'signiorie ouer the Pages' than hitherto (ii. 227) in the guise of providential historian: 'For your instruction and godly consolation, bee informed' (ii. 227). What follows at this point is a description of his own courtly attire in a series of improvised base comparisons; a description, in fact, in the grotesque mode in which the Anabaptists were 'set forth' as subverters of the rational order. England in the grip of sweating-sickness, overrun by vagabonds and returning soldiers, is portrayed grotesquely as a world-upside-down. Jack's invention of the 'order of passing into the Court' (ii. 227) disturbingly conflates such social conseqences of war as the rash of knighthoods distributed after Essex's campaigns in France with the imposition of martial law upon disbanded soldiers who were troubling her Majesty during the plague of 1593.[26] Jack dubs the knights with the 'armes Passant', that is, brands them as vagabonds: 'we set a red marke on their eares, and so let them walke as authenticall' (ii. 228). Subsequent descriptions of the sweating-sickness and 'honorable wars in christendome' (ii. 241) reach their grotesque climax at Munster where the providential historian abandons responsibility altogether. 'This tale must at one time or other giue vp the ghost' (ii. 241), he says, as it struggles towards the semblance of a moral.

The decisive authority in the Munster episode, of course, is not

[25] See Rhodes' interesting observations, *Elizabethan Grotesque*, pp. 93–9.

[26] For Essex's knights see L. Stone, *Crisis of the Aristocracy*, pp. 73–4; for vagabonds see *CSPD 1591–4*, ccxliv, 7 Apr. 1593, p. 342.

the divine ordinance of the rebellious scourge, nor the ordinance of the magistrate *per se* but the Jove-like authority of the imperial canon, the 'great Ordinance' which with 'hailing thunder' dismembered and 'dissoule-ioyned' the people (ii. 241). Imperial justice, as critics have commented,[27] is portrayed as being highly ambivalent. If the Anabaptists are guilty of 'desires of reuenge and innouation' (ii. 239) their punishment is nothing but 'stearne reuenge' (ii. 240). Not only are the punitive fathers scarcely distinguishable from their innovative sons but, in the polarization of all action into vengeful retribution for vengeful innovations, the possibility of any non-masterful communication (the possibility of pity or love) is denied. Thus, although Jack chastises the Anabaptists for their ambitious attempts to penetrate heaven with invective ('They followed their God as daring him', ii. 239), what he then offers as the exemplary mode of following Christ is not humility and love but rape: 'Amor est mihi causa sequendi', words expressing Apollo's pursuit of Daphne (who became his laurel) in the *Metamorphoses*.[28] Ambitious desire for glory (laurel crowns or 'glittering crownes', ii. 258) thus emerges as the only impulse of action; any other kind of love is an effeminate yielding, melting and dissolving 'into commiseration' (ii. 258), failing in *virtus* and mastery. The imperial forces achieve victory because 'drums and trumpets sounding nothing but stearne reuenge in their eares, made them so eager that their handes had no leasure to ask counsell of their effeminate eyes' (ii. 240). It is this rejection of non-powerful conceit as 'effeminate' that creates the incessantly retaliatory movement of profit and credit-seeking discourse. Curiously ill-fitting quotations from Ovid define the Anabaptist 'rape' of ecclesiastical power as deriving from the ambition of churchmen such as Wolsey who first 'gelt religion' (ii. 238) by depriving the Church of financial power. Cardinal Wolsey was frequently presented as an *exemplum* of ambition; the effect in this context, however, is to present the whole Anabaptist rebellion as part of a deterministic, almost mechanical law of retribution. When the Anabaptists follow God as daring him, God hears their prayers and 'Quod petitur poena est' (ii. 239) they pray for their own punishment, 'receive to themselves damnation'. Wolsey has a similar history, being 'in suas poenas ingeniosus', clever in securing his

27 See e.g. Ferguson, ' "Newes of the Maker" Game', p. 177.
28 Ovid, *Metamorphoses*, trans. M. M. Innes, p. 42.

own eventual punishment (ii. 238).[29] The obligation to moralize is itself a scourge, and act of vengeance, every ambitious action proves its own admonition 'a scorge to . . . posteritye'. Submerged Ovidian references give an ironic slant to the Anabaptist episode. As the narrative goes on to examine and comment on the relation of various authors and monarchs, the situation of the exiled poet of the *Amores* becomes almost paradigmatic. Referring Ovidian citation back to its context provides the reader with another underlying narrative in which the act of political censorship is represented as inevitable retribution, the punitive reaction of a wrathful deity. Wolsey's moral 'qui in suas poenas ingeniosus erat' actually comes from a key poem in Ovid's *Tristia* which addresses itself to Caesar in the form of a legal defence, pleading the innocence of Ovid's poetry. Ronald Syme has drawn attention to the ambiguous emphasis, kept up throughout Ovid's plea, on the God-like wrath of Caesar ('Caesaris ira, Iovis ira, ira dei', etc.).[30] According to Syme's reading, Ovid represents himself as just as helplessly victimized as one of his own poetic subjects in the *Metamorphoses*. This posture of what appears to be utter subservience is in fact a way of implying that Caesar's action was arbitrary and unjust, 'ira' conveying the desire for vengeance commonly associated with an offended deity rather than a responsible governor. The ambivalence of Ovid's plea in the second book of the *Tristia*, arising from the double-bind of an imperial power which seems to demand poetic texts that magnify it without displaying any ambitious desire to partake of its secrets, becomes highly appropriate for the story of the page in *The Unfortunate Traveller*. If *The Unfortunate Traveller* portrays the dilemma of published discourse in Elizabethan England as the page's inescapable drive towards censorship by those very institutions which seem to insist on its culpability, the suggestion of a connection with Ovid, or indeed with the victims of divine rape and vengeance in the *Metamorphoses,* is surely not accidental.[31] Ovid, for example, playfully suggests in the *Tristia* that the reason for his fault in Caesar's eyes is his wantonness in having chosen to write

[29] Both these phrases come from Ovid, *Tristia*, ii. 342. 3; v. 2. 77.

[30] R. Syme, *History in Ovid*, p. 223. For the *Tristia* as a piece of forensic oratory see R. J. Dickinson, 'The *Tristia*: Poetry in Exile', in *Ovid*, ed. J. W. Binns, pp. 170–4.

[31] Picking up Ovidian references in *The Unfortunate Traveller* produces an interesting reading of almost every passage; through the narrative as a whole runs the sense of an inescapable guilt, connected with the secrets of divine authority.

love elegies instead of imperial panegyric. But this ironically points up his innocence of the charge of ambition; his point is that he has not, in writing, imitated the ambitions of those rebellious giants who, piling Mount Pelion upon Mount Ossa, were punished by Jove for trying to climb to Olympus. Epic and imperial panegyric are much more ambitious forms than love poetry. Ovid uses the figure of the giants again when he writes from exile to a friend that he had never been ambitious enough to imagine that 'should Ossa uphold Pelion, my hand could touch the bright stars'; an explicit disavowal of the poetically 'ambitious' ending of the *Metamorphoses* where he defied the anger of Jove itself to prevent his fame from soaring 'far above the stars'.[32] In its repeated acts of self-censorship, its repeated scourgings of its own rhetorical claims to political credit, Jack's narrative seems to be replaying the ironies of Ovid's suffering at the hands of a Caesar on whom he had bestowed a kind of poetic immortality. Ovid's figure of culpably ambitious discourse—the rebellious giants—is everywhere in *The Unfortunate Traveller*. Borrowing the admonitory idiom of *Christes Teares*, Jack prophesies vengeance against religious reformers, for 'whosoever seekes by headlong meanes to enter into Heauen and disanull Gods ordinance, shall, with the Gyaunts that thought to scale heauen in contempt of *Iupiter*, be ouer-whelmed with Mount *Ossa* and *Peleon*, and dwell with the diuell in eternal desolation' (ii. 235–6). In *Christes Teares* itself divine retribution is claustrophobically inescapable in a theology which presents all individual action as ambition, and all ambition as rebellion against the absolutism of providence: 'if . . . as distrusting his prouidence) we shall grow in mislike with him and reuolt to Ambition, his enemy, and betray him . . . wil hee euer after acknowledge vs?' (ii. 86–7). This God 'lyke a wise Prince that will trust no Traytours' behaves no differently from Jove the thunderer: 'As soone as euer they are come neere hym, downe the hyll they climbed vp to him shall hee headlong reuerse them' (ii. 87). This consideration makes Nashe aware of the ambiguity of his own venture: 'Euen in thys dilatement against Ambition, the deuill seekes to sette in a foote of . . . popular fames Ambition in my stile, so as hee incited a number of Phylosophers (in times past) to prosecute theyr ambition of glory in writing of glories contemtiblenesse' (ii. 87).

[32] Ovid, *Tristia*, ii. 323–34; *Ex ponto*, II. ii. 9–10; *Metamorphoses*, trans. Innes, p. 357.

Once again the orator 'disinherits' the mastery and affluence of eloquence; whatever may 'pierce or profite' readers he attributes to the power of Christ and not to the power of his own rhetoric (ii. 87). Explicit self-effacement of this kind is not, however, a possibility with the State whose Church and Prince control the patronage system towards which the page ultimately aspires. The poets and orators of *The Unfortunate Traveller* are thereby trapped into incessant climbing up the hill of ambition, incessantly exercising ingenuity to bring about their own overthrow. Even a discourse in praise of poverty can be made to resemble ambitious designs upon the basis of sovereignty; thus Jack explains absurdly how philosophers in times past 'plotted . . . how to make their pouertie better esteemed of than rich dominion and souereigntie' (ii. 237). The self-sufficiency of Diogenes, coining his money in his own little cell (ii. 237), suggests the independence of the affluent orator, rich in a never failing currency of his own minting; indeed, Quintilian describes the ideal orator as one who is surrounded by affluence—'For he that has reached the summit has no more weary hills to scale'.[33]

Encountering Surrey and removing with him to academe, the narrative indulges in a slightly more light-hearted consideration of the counterfeits and rebellions of discourse. This all-too-palpable flattery of the Wittenberg orators hardly threatens the Duke; it simply affords him with 'ironicall occasion' for mirth (ii. 249). The innovative discourse one might expect from Martin Luther is equally impotent; nothing but a tedious pastime which offers nothing, as Jack comments, 'to make a man laugh' (ii. 250). His treatment of other poets and orators, however, does not allow for such a light dismissal of their desires of revenge and innovation. One is reminded that 1593 was the year of Christopher Marlowe's death, the year in which Harvey's *New Letter of Notable Contents* linked Nashe with Marlowe, the 'Lucianic blasphemer'.[34] It seems as though Nashe's reaction to Harvey has found its way into Jack's ambiguous treatment of the two poets, Surrey and Aretino.

It was Marlowe, of couse, who translated the *Amores*, in which Ovid playfully announces his abandonment of an epic perspective in verse that has been 'slacked' under the influence of Love.[35] The

[33] Quintilian, *Institutio oratoria*, XII. x. 78.

[34] Harvey, *Works*, i. 37.

[35] See Marlowe, *Complete Poems and Translations*, ed. S. Orgel, p. 113. Interestingly enough Nashe uses Marlowe's translation of the *Amores* at ii. 238.

Surrey whose temperance and solvency would initially have seemed to be exemplary (Jack praises him as 'a good purse-bearer', ii. 243, and an utterer of profitable precepts, ii. 245) has in fact, when we encounter him, been morally emasculated, 'Metamorphozed' by love (ii. 243). For Surrey, as for Ovid, this new master is one who subverts the imperial power of Caesar; Surrey has vowed allegiance henceforth to 'one that proclaimes himselfe sole King and Emperour of pearcing eyes, and cheefe Soueraigne of soft hearts' (ii. 243).[36] (Incidentally, this formula 'sole King' echoes Jack's own introduction of himself as 'sole king of the cans' and 'keisar' of 'liquid alleageance' (ii. 209–10), relegating Henry VIII to the position of 'true subiect of Chronicles', ii. 209.) Surrey's travels through Italy, while posing no threat to his sovereign, seem to have been undertaken without the king's authority; after winning the tournament Surrey is censored, his fame 'quit cut off by the shins' by a king who orders him back to England against his own desire that Florence should have the 'maidenhead of his chiualrie' (ii. 279). The tournament itself seems to re-enact, in the frivolous, highly stylized mode of courtly combats and revels, the same relations of rebellious ambition and authoritarian oppression that were bloodily witnessed in the Anabaptist episode. The most extravagant and ludicrous of all the knightly *imprese* is nothing less than a representation of frustrated desire expressed in terms of the giants' rebellion:

> The seuenth had, lyke the giants that sought to scale heauen in despight of *Iupiter*, a mount ouerwhelming his head and whole bodie; his bases out-laid with armes and legges which the skirtes of that mountaine left vncouered. Vnder this did he characterise a man desirous to climbe to the heauen of honour, kept vnder with the mountaine of his princes command, and yet had he armes and legs exempted from the suppression of that mountain. The word, *Tu mihi criminis author* (alluding to his Princes command), thou art the occasion of my imputed cowardise. His horse was trapped in the earthie strings of tree rootes . . . (ii. 275)

Even on this burlesque level the echoes from Ovid lend a slightly sinister air; '*Tu mihi criminis author*' are the words of Myscelus, trapped into guilt by the conflicting commands of the law and the god Hercules who loved him above all the rest of his generation.[37] While Surrey might not be so obedient to his sovereign as first appeared, discourses of Petrarchism and Arcadian chivalry provid-

[36] Compare Marlowe's translation of the *Amores*, I. ii (*Poems*, p. 115) where Cupid regards Caesar as his 'kinsman'.

[37] Ovid, *Metamorphoses*, xv. 40.

ing modes in which his ambitious desires might be legitimately expressed,[38] we are nevertheless prepared for quite another kind of anti-monarchism when Jack encounters the other major poet-figure, Aretino. Aretino apparently represents the epitome of free speech:

> He was no timerous seruile flatterer of the commonwealth wherein he liued. His tongue & his inuention were forbourne; what they thought, they would confidently vtter. Princes hee spard not, that in the least point transgrest. His lyfe he contemned in comparison of the libertie of speech. (ii. 265)

In Aretino independence appears to confer an aesthetic, even spiritual excellence; his style is the 'spiritualitie of artes', more derivative writers are 'meere temporizers' (ii. 264). At the same time, however, this independence implies absolutism: Aretino is 'determined to tyrannize' (ii. 264). Moreover, for all his pretensions as the scourge of princes, he is as involved in the patronage stakes as any subservient flatterer. Not only is his tongue chained by the chain of gold tongues sent to him by Francis I, but the very power which enables him to rescue Surrey derives, like Surrey's power, from the authority of Henry VIII. For it is by virtue of the 'pension of foure hundred crownes yerely', for which he is 'beholding to the king of England' (ii. 264), that Aretino is ready to 'straine the vtmost of his credit' to get Jack and Surrey off the charge of conspiracy. The great subverter of society behaves just like a salaried civil servant.

The narrative casts aspersions on other discoursers; Erasmus and More are caricatured in the ironic terms of their own writings, and the example of Erasmus is extended into a mocking testimony to the humanist ideal of the Christian orator. Cicero, classical exemplar of moral and oratorical *virtus*, is the man Erasmus desires to witness in action in Agrippa's magic glass (ii. 252). The case he requests is the notoriously difficult *Pro Roscio Amerino* in which Cicero was called upon to get his client off the charge of parricide, the most unthinkable of crimes in the Roman Republic, and not without significance in the context of *The Unfortunate Traveller*. So well did

[38] For a discussion of Surrey's Petrarchism see D. Jones, 'An Example of Anti-Petrarchan Satire in Nashe's "The Unfortunate Traveller" '. The social implications of Petrarchism at Elizabeth's court in the 1590s are admirably discussed by L. Foster, *The Icy Fire*, pp. 122–47, and by A. Marotti, ' "Love is not love": Elizabethan Sonnet Sequences and the Social Order'. K. Duncan-Jones drew attention to Arcadian pastiche in 'Nashe and Sidney: the Tournament in "The Unfortunate Traveller" '. The 'social tropes' of such combat are analysed by F. Whigham, *Ambition and Privilege*, pp. 78–82.

Cicero carry it away, Jack relates, that 'all his auditours were readie to install his guiltie client for a God' (ii. 252). The capitalization of 'God' and the references to Cicero's 'soule-stirring iestures' and 'exaltation of spirit' are clear indications that the inspiration associated with ambitious Puritans and the blasphemous self-sufficiency attributed to such subversive mockers as Lucian, Aretino, and Marlowe is here indistinguishable from the oratorical *virtus* displayed by that moral paradign of the Renaissance, Marcus Tullius Cicero. In Florence, with the encounter of Surrey and Aretino over the question of gold crowns, counterfeit or otherwise, the identification of sovereign power with currency became quite explicit. By the time the narrator reaches Rome, however, even this last vestige of a distinction between the legitimate and the illegitimate collapses. Rome is a graveyard of monuments to the pursuit of glory, in which the only unquestionable authority left is the plague (ii. 279–80, 286). One scourge authorizes another: while God punishes covetous Rome with stifling cormorant-like clouds (ii. 286) he provides scope for the bandetto *Esdras of Granado* to 'breake into those riche mens houses in the night where the plague had most rained' (ii. 287). Jack, finding himself in a house which Esdras has marked out for invasion, is comically impotent to alter the situation; his pistol is 'vncharged' (ii. 287), his offers of money redundant: 'I cride out, Saue her, kill me, and Ile ransome her with a thousande duckets: but lust preuailed, no prayers woulde be heard' (ii. 287).

Through the dialogue that ensues between Heraclide and Esdras the narrative witnesses a continual collapsing of distinction between all recognized forms of power: divine retribution, legally authorized punishment and private blood lust and revenge. Esdras is associated with divine power, arriving as he does in the plague, 'during this time of visitation' (ii. 287), but he is also a *legal* figure 'authorised by the pope' (ii. 287). Heraclide interprets his attack as a deserved punishment, a divine ordinance: '. . . art thou ordained to be a worse plague to me than the plague it selfe?', but ambiguity creeps in: 'haue I escapt the hands of God to fal into the hands of men?' (ii. 288). For escaping the hands of God carries its own suggestion of moral impunity as Esdras himself points out: Heraclide cannot frighten him with the threat of divine retribution because of the thousand perils he has passed through: 'What plague canst thou name worse than I haue had? whether diseases, imprisonment, pouertie, banishment, I haue past through them all' (ii. 291).

Heraclide and Esdras are thus caught in bandying of authoritative counters; to her he is 'deaths vsurper' (ii. 288) since she escaped death by the plague, but he insists on a 'charter aboue scripture' (ii. 288–9). She responds with a vision of self-induced retribution with which the narrative is obsessed—the huge mountains of Ossa and Pelion, mountains of presumptuous sin ready to pash the sinner into pieces: 'A man that hath an vneuitable huge stone hanging only by a haire ouer his head' (ii. 289). But the power of her words collapses. The stone is God's hand; God's hand is the plague; the plague, however, concludes weakly as the representative of an arbitrary legal power: 'what is the plague but death playing the Prouost Marshall, to execute all those that will not be called home by anie other meanes?' (ii. 289). The scene concludes farcically, with the menacing frown and overhanging sword of divine retribution which Heraclide desperately invokes (ii. 289) travestied in the unmoved figure of Esdras on his 'chaire of state'. . . 'leaning his ouer-hanging gloomie ey-browes on the pommel of his vnsheathed sword' (ii. 290). In the failure of her alternate intercessions and attempts to threaten Esdras with a divine retribution of which she makes her own infected breath the agent, Heraclide provides Jack/the narrative with its final witness of the self-destructive dilemma of discourse. Chameleon-like persuasive oratory, alleging whatever it hopes will authorize its own desires, vies with an equally deceitful providential discourse, which inevitably falls back on locating moral power within itself. Realization of this creates the moral void, the absence of any authenticating power which (as it is figured in Heraclide's rape) produces the final violation and collapse of identity. What Jack reports to us as her 'subdued resons discourse' (ii. 293) is in fact an accurate representation of the dilemma: 'Sue, plead, intreate; grace is neuer denied to them that aske. It may be denied; I maie be a vessell ordained to dishonor' (ii. 294). The 'guilt' of the raped woman, 'a vessell ordained to dishonor', is paradigmatic of the inescapable guilt of the page in a system which demands and censors its complicity, 'tu mihi criminis author'. Thus, as the wrath of God becomes indistinguishable from the sin itself, the suicide or vengeance of the self upon the self emerges as the only option: 'The onely repeale we haue from Gods vndefinite chastisement is to chastise our selues in this world' (ii. 294).

Heraclide's desire to escape from her guilty reflection in the mirror (ii. 294) anticipates the intolerable multiplication of reflections set up by the 'vndefinite chastisement' of murder by revenge. Indeed it seems at this point that the story might have done better to proceed directly to the vengeance that Heaven (according to Jack's unreliable interpretation) takes against Cutwolfe for having taken vengence against Heraclide's rapist—but it does not. Instead the narrative delays over a sequence of exaggerated physical chastisement in which it is Jack's body—the body of the narrative itself—that continually risks obliteration. This all but final episode reads very much like a last ditch attempt on the part of *The Unfortunate Traveller* to turn itself back into profitable discourse by trying to prove that the page is a prodigal son who has finally 'consumed his substance in riotous living'.

Heraclide's death provokes the comic resurrection of her husband, and the narrative's belated and unconvincing attempt to moralize itself. 'Here beginneth my purgatorie', announces the page (ii. 295), escaping the hangman's noose and inevitable profitable repentance ('I . . . had made a Ballad for my Farewell in a readines, called *Wiltons Wantonnes*', ii. 295) only through the intervention of another moralizing force, the 'graue fatherly aduertiser' (ii. 303) who attempts at this late stage to salvage the credit of the page. As well as invoking all the usual *exempla* of Cain, Icarus, Ulysses, the old man includes among the traveller's ills the consumption of resources by harlots and usurers:

> That wit which is thereby to be perfected or made staid, is nothing but *Experienta longa malorum*. . . The experience that such a man lost his life by this folly, another by that: such a yong Gallant consumed his substaunce on such a Curtizan: these courses of reuenge a Merchant of *Venice* tooke against a Merchant of *Ferrara*. (ii. 299)

Escape from the tedious predictability of the moral launches Jack straight into experience of all these commonplaces; he chooses to moralize upon himself, 'God plagud me for deriding such a graue fatherly aduertiser' (ii. 303). The commonplace of 'falling' into danger of the law Jack experiences quite literally by tumbling into the cellar of the usurer Zadoch who decides to retain him as a bondman as 'it was then the law in *Rome*' (ii. 304). In *Christes Teares* 'none but the Vsurer is ordained for a scourge to Pride and Ambition' (ii. 98) and it is the 'ryot and misgouernment' of young gentlemen 'that must deliuer them ouer into theyr hands to be deuoured' (ii. 96). *The Unfortunate Traveller* does its best to conform to this pattern of retribution by delivering Jack first into the hands of Zadoch and Zacherie who intend to bleed him to death, and thence into the clutches of Juliana, the Pope's concubine, by whom he is 'consumed and worne to the bones' (ii. 314). The acceleration of the narrative, and the deliberate dovetailing of usurer/courtesan episodes, mimics the switchback ride of recrimination set up by providential admonitions. Jack moves straight from one scourge to another: 'The first ground I toucht after I was out of *Zacharyes* house was the Countesse *Iulianas* chamber' (ii. 308). While from Juliana's stripping of Jack we flip back to the parallel of Zadoch's sexual assault on Diamante:

> Not too much of this Madam Marques at once; let me dilate a little what *Zadoch* did with my curtizan, after he had sold me to *Zacharie*. Of an ill tree I hope you are not so ill sighted . . . to expect good fruite: hee was a Iew, and intreated her like a Iew. Vnder shadow of enforcing her to tell how much money she had . . . hee stript her, and scourged her . . . (ii. 309)

The reader is invited to expect the stereotypes of harlot and Jew; 'I hope you are not so ill-sighted . . . to expect' anything else, writes Jack, and goes on to connect this Jewish behaviour with a popular moral 'ballet of the whipper' (ii. 310). In order for the page to remain unconsumed by the false ending towards which he is now tending, the reader must be allowed to witness the sadistic licensed scourging of admonitory history for what it is. The appalling lingering of the narrrative over the tortures experienced by Zadoch closes abruptly without a moral. One stereotype of evil (the harlot who 'rapes' and 'consumes' male *virtus*) has simply won out against another (the scourging Jewish usurer): 'Triumph, women, this was the end of the whipping Iew, [of ballad fame], contriued by a woman, in reuenge of two women' (ii. 316).

What takes place thereafter is the obliteration of the narrator altogether in his witness to the discourse of Cutwolfe, which itself opens out into a potentially infinite sequence of retribution. When, in *Christes Teares*, the Saviour despairs of his efficacy as redeemer of Jerusalem, the old law in effect replaces the new and Abel's blood cries out again for vengeance (ii. 24). As an agent of the old law of blood vengeance, Cutwolfe takes revenge on Esdras for the murder of his brother Bartoll. *Ira Caesaris* and *ira dei* apparently meet in Cutwolfe, who claims to possess the soul of Julius Caesar by reversion (ii. 320). Jack, however, professes to interpret the law's punishment of Cutwolfe as divine vengeance for the rape and suicide of Heraclide:

> Strange and wonderfull are Gods iudgements, here shine they in their glory. Chast Heraclide, thy bloud is laid vp in heauens treasury, not one drop of it was lost . . . Murder is widemouthd and will not let God rest till he grant reuenge. Not onely the bloud of the slaughtred innocent, but the soul, ascendeth to his throne, and there cries out & exclaimes for iustice and recompence. Guiltlesse soules that liue euery houre subiect to violence, and with your dispairing feares doe much empaire Gods prouidence, fasten your eies on this spectacle that will adde to your faith. Referre all your oppressions, afflictions & iniuries to the euen ballanced eie of the Almightie; he it is, that when your patience sleepeth, will be most exceeding mindfull of you. (ii. 320)

The narrative's attempt to moralize itself here become blatantly self-contradictory. For taking vengeance on her own life, Heraclide's prayers have forfeited any hope of credit with the deity: yet Jack persists in seeing her blood as having gained oratorical interest on her behalf. The only effective orator, then, is blood or murder 'wide-mouthd' seeking more murder.

Jack steps aside at this point: his discourse is but 'a glose upon the text', which is Cutwolfe's, who, refusing to be meekly obliterated, 'crusht in peeces' (ii. 320) by authority without pleading his own defence, concludes that murder is, in fact, the fulfilment of all the law and the profits of Renaissance glory and providential morality:

> Reuenge is the glorie of armes, & the highest performance of valure: *reuenge is whatsoeuer we call law or iustice*. The farther we wade in reuenge, the neerer come we to the throne of the almightie. To his scepter it is properly ascribed; *his scepter he lends vnto man when he lets one man scourge an other*. (ii. 326, my italics)

All along the page has used duplicity and deceit to imply, but avoid the downright identification of, godly magistrate and God-imitating outlaw; now that Cutwolfe has uttered the truth the only response is complete disintegration. Nothing is omitted in the account of Cutwolfe's dismemberment: 'no lim of his but was lingeringly splinterd in shiuers' (ii. 327). The page produces a perfunctory moral about the unsearchable book of destiny and hastens back, repentant, to the safe confines of the English court, ready to regain credit with the king of England who has remained in the background throughout the narrative as the ultimate practical source of effective discursive power.

*The Unfortunate Traveller* reveals how a literature which is obliged to conform to criteria of rhetorical effectiveness and providential 'profit' on a simultaneously political and moral level inevitably operates to curtail its own freedom, and to obliterate *itself* in order to exculpate itself from the crimes of wanton amorality or political subversion. Stephen Greenblatt once suggested that if Foxe's *Acts and Monuments* (1563) 'dwelt lovingly' upon the tortures of martyrs this was a way of revealing the hollowness of the Catholic Church's claim to consensual unity: 'a consensus held together by threats of torture . . . is no consensus at all'.[39] Perhaps we can regard *The Unfortunate Traveller*'s insistence on testifying to the excruciating martyrdom and torture of its own moral histories as a way of revealing, in a not dissimilar fashion, the often cruel contradiction inherent in the combined authority of Church and State's insistence that discourse should not be published unless it spoke 'unfallible truth' or was 'profitable' to the State. Such an obligation all too often laid the author open to the charge of flat Anabaptism, if he escaped being suspected (in Jack's words) of intending a Lucianic 'two-hand Interpretation' (ii. 233). A text obliged to render itself 'true' and 'profitable' by the threat of censorship is bound to lie.

[39] S. Greenblatt, *Renaissance Self-Fashioning*, p. 79.

# 12

# Patronage as the Red Herring of *Lenten Stuffe*

LENTEN STUFFE is Nashe's last and perhaps most baffling work. Apparently inexhaustible for sheer invigoration of latent metaphor, the pamphlet offers a linguistic experience unsurpassed in its kind in English literature. Reading it for fun is exhilarating, but only in short bursts; at length the extraordinary resistance of Nashe's language to any sustained interpretation becomes exasperating, even intolerable. This fact is in itself a curious feature, given the extravagant claims Nashe's language generally makes for the stimulus and pleasure it so freely affords. *Lenten Stuffe* professes no other end than to provide entertainment for a host of hungry readers. Then why should it, of Nashe's writings, prove so indigestible, so intractable to any impulse to interpret as well as experience its linguistic plenitude? So opaque is its drift that scholars have come to mutually contradictory conclusions about what it is trying to say. One assumes the piece to be 'a sort of bread and butter letter' to the people of Yarmouth, who had offered Nashe hospitality when his fiery denunciations had brought down on him a temporary exile.[1] Another suggests that its 'lenten' association indicates a repentant gesture towards the offended London authorities from whom he was seeking refuge in Yarmouth.[2] Obviously there is some kind of plea, or remonstration, or gratification to be inferred from the work's connection with Nashe's exile by the authorities, but what? He himself repudiates the bread and butter theory from the outset: '*Nashes Lentenstuffe*: and why *Nashes Lentenstuffe*? some scabbed scald squire replies, because I had money lent me at Yarmouth, and I pay them againe in prayse of their towne and the redde herring . . . but thou art a Ninnihammer; that is not it' (iii. 151).

Appeasement of the London authorities would seem equally

[1] M. Geraldine, 'Erasmus and the Tradition of Paradox', p. 59. See also McKerrow, iv. 372 and v. 29–34.

[2] Hibbard, *Thomas Nashe*, p. 236.

clearly to be out of the question; praising a rival port for its hospitality is hardly the most tactful way of reconciling oneself with the government of the city from which one has been exiled. There is another possibility, of course; *Lenten Stuffe* might conceal its meaning *à clef*. Alice Scoufos has made a case for the entire work's being a satiric attack on a member of the Privy Council, Henry, Lord Cobham, who had recently been involved in hostilities against the commercial players.[3] She bases her theory on the fact that the Cobham family are elsewhere satirically referred to as herringcobs, gudgeons, miller's thumbs, and other diminutive fish, and finds references to such small fry throughout Nashe's work, often blatantly suggestive of a Cobham connection. Although all the supporting evidence makes this explanation seem plausible enough, it is curiously belied in the experience of reading *Lenten Stuffe*. Any reading of the work as a masquerade of tendentious meaning would have to come to terms with its appalling inefficiency in satiric terms; the attack simply goes on far too long. And if this loose, digressive quality is because, as Scoufos claims, 'Nashe's disjointed fables' are intended as mutual cover-ups, to 'cast shadows for each other',[4] surely this betrays satiric inefficiency in another sense, since no amount of verbiage is going to conceal the glaring reference to a certain noble family in tracing the herring ancestry of 'cobbing countrey chuffes which make their bellies and their bagges theyr Gods' and are called 'riche Cobbes' (iii. 211). Without wishing to deny the possibility of interpreting Nashe's language as satiric reference to specific individuals, I would suggest that it is this very activity—the activity of inventing language in such a way as to create such references—that is, if anything, the satiric focus of linguistic energy in *Lenten Stuffe*.

If censorship is part of the fiction of *The Unfortunate Traveller*, it is part of the reality of *Lenten Stuffe*. The work is entered to Cuthbert Burby in the Stationers' Register 'vpon Condicon that he gett yt Laufully Aucthorised' (iii. 141). This external evidence of a problematic relation with the authorities is directly corroborated within the work itself, which includes a lengthy and impassioned diatribe against the inventive abilities of Inns of Court graduates, who, with an eye to the main chance, are ready to subject any piece of contemporary writing to political interpretation:

[3] A. L. Scoufos, 'Nashe, Jonson and the Oldcastle Problem', pp. 310–18.

[4] Ibid. 318.

Talke I of a beare, O, it is such a man that emblazons him in his armes, or of a woolfe, a fox, or a camelion, any lording whom they do not affect it is meant by. The great potentate, stirred vppe with these peruerse applications, not looking into the text it selfe, but the ridiculous comment, or if hee lookes into it, followes no other more charitable comment then that, straite thunders out his displeasure, & showres downe the whole tempest of his indignation vpon me, and, to amend the matter, and fully absolue himselfe of this rash error of misconstruing, he commits it ouer to be prosecuted by a worse misconstruer then himselfe, *videlicet*, his learned counsaile. (iii. 214)

It is, of course, the materiality of copious language, its densely figurative nature, that gives it the capacity to 'shadow' any number of meanings. Nashe caricatures the ease with which political meanings can be invented out of innocent figures of speech:

out steps me an infant squib of the Innes of Court, that hath . . . scarce warmed his Lawyers cushion, and he, to approue hymselfe an extrauagant statesman, catcheth hold of a rush, and absolutely concludeth, it is meant of the Emperour of Ruscia, and that it will vtterly marre the traffike into that country if all the Pamphlets bee not called in and suppressed, wherein that libelling word is mentioned. (iii. 213)

The usual proverbial association of straws and legal pedantry ('to go to law for the wagging of a straw') is submerged and new sense created by the transformation of the 'straw' into the 'rush' which is at once both an organic material to be clasped, and the verbal material out of which a momentous figurative significance may be drawn. What is so ingenious about this caricature is the way in which the revitalization of the proverb has made 'superficial' linguistic activity (the unexpected transition from 'rush' to 'Russia') seem so satisfying and rich as to preclude the reader's desire for any further 'depth' of significance. Indeed the search for a 'deeper' meaning emerges by comparison as a superficial activity, mocked by the material density of the linguistic surface itself. This tendency to 'palpabrize' linguistic activity,[5] a tendency evident throughout Nashe's writing, is here in *Lenten Stuffe* most fully realized for this very purpose. Thus, for example, in relating the difficulties experienced by Yarmouth's people after the disastrous plague of 1348 when they found themselves unable to afford the stone necessary to complete the expensive alterations of their church, Nashe concludes: 'nowe they haue gone a neerer way to the woode, for with wooden galleries in the Church that they haue, and stayry

[5] See Rhodes, *Elizabethan Grotesque*, pp. 25–6.

degrees of seates in them, they make as much roome to sitte and heare as a newe west end would haue done' (iii. 166). The submerged proverbial phrase 'there are more ways to the wood than one', with its obvious connotation of resourcefulness, becomes, through the play on 'wood' as destination and material, a linguistic celebration of that improvisatory genius which thrives on having to use the materials that lie to hand. Immediately one senses the analogy with Nashe's linguistic resourcefulness; sheer creative energy reanimates these facts through the material of common proverbs, providing a bonus in the happy coinage 'stayry' with its suggestion of 'starry' heights.

Throughout *Lenten Stuffe* this kind of metaphoric density challenges the inventive capacity of the reader just to keep making sense of it all. John Carey puts this best when he writes of *Lenten Stuffe* that Nashe's 'loving cultivation of the commonplace renovates experience for us'.[6] But this renovation of experience through language has its own polemic purpose. It pleads on behalf of the figurative power of the English language, that it may be developed by contemporary poets, without being interpreted or expounded out of existence. The 'poverty' of *Lenten Stuffe*, as all critics, and indeed the work itself, would agree, is its continual harping on the same subject: 'Alas, poore hungerstarued Muse . . . was it so hard driuen that it had nothing to feede vpon but a redde herring?' (iii. 225). This too, however, is part of the same polemic, expressing as it does the poverty and reductionism of assuming exposition to be all that is involved in reading literary texts. *Lenten Stuffe* relentlessly puts readers through their paces in moralizing. No extraordinary invention is required once you get the hang of it; the moral kernel unwrapped by every fable, concealed under every leaf, shadowed in every trope, is none other than a red herring. Thus the application of Midas and his gold poses no problem; 'that fable of *Midas* eating gold had no other shadow or inclusive pith in it, but he was of a queasie stomacke and nothing hee coulde fancie but this newe found guilded fish' (iii. 193). On the heels of this helpful exposition comes the true meaning fabled in the story of Dionysius and Jupiter's golden coat: 'Follow this tract in expounding the tale of *Dionisius* and *Iupiter*, and you cannot goe amisse. No such *Iupiter*, no such golden coated image was there; but it was a plaine

[6] J. Carey, 'Sixteenth- and Seventeenth-Century English Prose', in *English Poetry and Prose 1540–1674*, ed. C. Ricks, pp. 376–7.

golden coated red herring, without welt or garde' (iii. 194).

This in turn is followed by the oldest of love stories, the story of Hero and Leander, immortalized as fish. Exhausting the possibilities of this tale, Nashe plunges into a beast fable of birds and fishes which he leaves unmoralized for 'some *Alfonsus*, *Poggius*, or *Aesope* to vnwrap, for my penne is tired in it . . .' (iii. 203). To crown all these rich amplifications of the same Lenten moral is an which is distinguished for making absolutely no sense at all, disclosing not even a red herring. It reads remarkably plausibly, superbly poised upon the tantalizing suggestion of intelligibility:

> There was a Herring, or there was not, for it was but a Cropshin, one of the refuse sort of herrings, and this herring or this cropshin, was sensed and thurified in the smoake, and had got him a suit of durance that would last longer then one of Erra Paters Almanacks or a cunstables browne bill. (iii. 216)

The cropshin goes a-wooing Lady Turbot with 'whole hecatombs and a twoo-hand-sword'; but she refuses him:

> This speech was no spireable odor to the *Achelous* of her audience; wherefore she charged him by the extreame lineaments of the Erimanthian beare, and by the priuy fistula of the *Pierides* to committe no more such excruciating sillables to the yeelding ayre, for she would sooner make her a French-hood of a cowsharde and a gowne of spiders webbes, with the sleeues drawn out with cabbages . . . (iii. 217)

Although completely fake, this reads with considerably more liveliness than much contemporary political allegory. Nashe, however, makes the point of it quite clear: 'O, for a Legion of mice-eyed deciphers and calculaters vppon characters, now to augurate what I meane by this: the diuell, if it stood vpon his saluation, cannot do it' (iii. 218). Surely the problem with urging the Lord Cobham or indeed any nobleman as the satiric referent concealed by *Lenten Stuffe* is that such a hypothesis relegates all readers to the ranks of mice-eyed decipherers, which is clearly what the text itself is trying to discourage. The predictability with which the herring is dredged up out of the depths of every verbal configuration ought to caution us against reducing *Lenten Stuffe* to a sequence of 'disjointed fables' which merely 'cast shadows for each other'.The praise of Yarmouth, which such an interpretation seeks to dismiss as merely one more of these covering fables for the red herring, is, in any case, nearly a third of the whole book. Its invention must have some other motive than that of satiric smoke screen. If, like the latter half of the book, it is making some kind of statement on behalf of literary language, then it is to aesthetic intelligibility rather than satiric expediency that we must direct our attention.

This is not to say that external referents are unimportant; a work like *Lenten Stuffe* cannot be separated from the context of political censorship that made it necessary to write. Literary activity in *Lenten Stuffe* is stimulated by the consciousness of censorship as its unavoidable destiny. It is the struggle with the threat of oblivion that yields the author his text, thereby restoring him temporarily to consciousness and fame before engulfing him once and for all. Meaninglessness and oblivion threaten the very fame and eloquence they nourish in the ambivalent figure of the sea which is at once a source of food and figurative meaning (as it is so often in Renaissance texts) and at the same time a predator, insatiable and tempestuous, ready to swallow the author who ventures into its element. The angry sea of unintended meaning is figured towards the end of the pamphlet in the nobleman who interprets the entire text as an insult to his name, and 'straite thunders out his displeasure, & showres downe the whole tempest of his indignation vpon me' (iii. 214). Such an anticipation of misinterpretation ('this rash error of misconstruing', iii. 214) recalls the circumstances from which the text itself declares that it arose, in the aftermath of 'tempestes . . . astonishing outragious and violent' (iii. 153–4) which brewed in London on the performance of Nashe's offensive comedy, *The Isle of Dogs*.

We obviously cannot reconstruct *The Isle of Dogs*, and it is quite possible that it too suffered from being 'mangled . . . in mennes mouthes' in order to provoke such hostile government reactions. What we can do, however, is retrace briefly the circumstances of its offence. It seems that the period 1596–7 was a bad time for the players, the balance of Privy Council opinion being finally tipped in favour of the civic authorities, who had long campaigned against the tolerance of commercial theatres in the city. In a letter to the MP William Cotton in 1596, Nashe speaks of being disappointed in his own schemes of playwriting by recent changes of policy towards the theatres:

> an after haruest I expected by writing for the stage & for the presse, when now the players as if they had writt another Christs tears, ar piteously persecuted by the L. Maior & the alder men, & howeuer in there old Lords

tyme they thought there state setled, it is now so vncertayne they cannot build vpon it. (v. 194)

The civic authorities, always hostile to plays, appear to have increased their offensive; Nashe indicates the severity of the campaign in a characteristically personal and sympathetic evocation of the players' misery 'as if they had writt another Christs tears'. It seems that the death of Henry Carey, Lord Hunsdon ('there old Lord') in 1596, and his replacement on the Privy Council by William, Lord Cobham, altered the Council's balance of opinion in such a way as to give support to the municipal authorities, thus precipitating the move to suppress theatres throughout the City.[7] It was perhaps the death of William, Lord Cobham and his replacement as Chamberlain by George Carey, Lord Hunsdon, in 1597 which lifted the ban temporarily; unfortunately, that 'lewd' and 'sclanderous' play *The Isle of Dogs* brought down even severer restraint against playhouses. Jonson was committed to prison; Nashe fled, his vacated lodgings being searched for incriminating papers by the government's agent Topcliffe.[8]

Given then, that the anti-theatrical Privy Council and city fathers had plenty of reason to be offended with Nashe, any utterance on his own behalf was a fairly presumptuous undertaking, as he himself acknowledged in the opening pages of *Lenten Stuffe*:

Too inconsiderate headlong rashnesse this may be censured in me, in beeing thus prodigall in aduantaging my aduersaries, but my case is no smoothred secret, and with light cost of rough cast rethorike it may be tollerabley playstered ouer, if vnder the pardon and priuiledge of incensed higher powers it were lawfully indulgenst me freely to aduocate my owne astrology. (iii. 154)

The pun in 'smoothred', which could be 'smoothered' (suppressed) or, as rough-cast would suggest, 'smooth-read' (meaning that his story cannot but arouse indignation), indicates a certain self-assertiveness beneath this apparently obsequious gesture towards 'incensed higher powers'. But how, even if it were 'lawfully indulgenst', can *Lenten Stuffe* be read as any kind of 'advocate' for Nashe's cause? How can we read a description of the 'first Procreation and Increase of the towne of Great Yarmouth' as a plea

[7] Chambers, *Elizabethan Stage*, i. 297; iv. 321.

[8] McKerrow, v. 31; *APC* xxvii, 15 Aug. 1597, p. 333; Chambers, *Elizabethan Stage*, iv. 323.

on behalf of the freedom to produce and the freedom to enjoy figurative language?

The 'first procreation' of Yarmouth is like the slippery origin of the text of *Lenten Stuffe* itself; neither are attributed to the honour and glory of a patron or procreator: both town and text exist as part of an ongoing process of self-defence and self-creation. The text's unlikely, unauthorized origins, 'out of drie stubble to make an after haruest, and a plentifull croppe without sowing, and wring iuce out of a flint, thats *Pierce a Gods name* and the right tricke of a workman' (iii. 152), correspond to those of a town kept above water only by the 'vncessant inestimable expence of the Inhabitantes' (iii. 156) and patronized by nothing other than the sandy material of which it is made:

> Forth of the sands thus struglingly as it [Yarmouth] exalteth and liftes vp his glittering head, so of the neyboring sands no lesse semblably . . . it is so inamorately protected and patronized, that they stand as a trench or guarde about it in the night, to keep off their enemies. (iii. 157)

Paradoxically, the very force which originally congregated the sands thus as Yarmouth's patrons and protectors is none other than the tempestuous sea from which the town required protection: 'The Northerne winde was the clanging trumpetter, who, with the terrible blast of his throate, in one yeallow heape or plumpe, clustred or congested them togither' (iii. 160). As Nashe's authorial identity is restored by his creation of this vehicle of self-expression, so Yarmouth sands, arising from tempests, gather themselves into self-sufficient existence:

> A towne it is . . . out of an hill or heape of sande, reared and enforced from the sea most miraculously, and, by the singular pollicy and vncessant inestimable expence of the Inhabitantes so firmely piled and rampierd against the fumish waues battry, or suying the leaste action of recouerie, that it is more coniecturall of the twaine, the land with a writ of an *Eiectione firma* wil get the vpperhande of the Ocean, then the Ocean one crowes skip preuaile against the Continent. (iii. 156)

The figure for the triumph of Yarmouth's existence is the head rising above water: 'Forth of the sands thus strugglingly as it . . . liftes vp his glittering head' and, a few pages further on, '*Caput extulit vndis*, the sands set vp shop for themselves, and from that moment . . . they would no more liue vnder the yoke of the Sea, or haue their heads washt with his bubbly spume or Barbers balderdash, but clearely quitted, disterminated and relegated themselves from his inflated Capriciousness of playing the Dictator ouer them' (iii. 160).

Following Manship's history of Yarmouth which describes the town as originally a mere bank of sand, indistinguishable from any other, 'being contynuallye under water and over flownen with the sea',[9] Nashe dramatizes the town's emergence as a combat with the buffoonishly pedantic legal power of the ocean (compare his remarks later on about the ugliness of legal language and absurdity of its dictatorial presumption over artists like himself, iii. 215–16). Throughout the pamphlet, head-washing figures as a carnivalesque image of humiliation and defeat. The phrase appears to have been metaphoric: in *Have With You* Nashe spoke of the youthful Harvey as unwilling to endure a rebuff: 'he would not haue giuen his head for the washing' (iii. 73). In *Lenten Stuffe* Ascham's insult to the dignity of Yarmouth's small, low vessels which deserve 'small commendation for any cunning sailing at all' (iii. 181) is ostentatiously refuted by Nashe, who insists that in the activity of chasing after herring these humble boats 'will not giue their heads for the washing, holding their owne pell-mell in all weathers as roughly as vaster timber men' (iii. 181). Images like this, and that of the sands' refusal to have 'their heads washt' with the pompous sea's incoherent legalistic balderdash, both express and displace the real threat that hostile political interpretation poses to the 'head' (discursive power, literary identity, consciousness itself) of an author who figures his own state as 'so tost and weather-beaten that it hath nowe no anchor-holde left to cleaue vnto' (iii. 156) and who is prepared therefore in one last 'plunge aboue water' (iii. 153) to wrest his identity from oblivion: 'Famam peto per vndas' (iii. 145).

Transforming the mundane activities of Yarmouth's fishermen into a carnivalesque combat of knights errant with 'no trustier lances then their oares' against the monstrous belching throat of the sea (iii. 183) figuratively reproduces Nashe's strategies against hostile interpretation: the sea becomes a carnival buffoon, a senile oppressor whose torn up body yields the herring that makes Yarmouth's hospitality possible.

Nashe likewise exploits his own anticipation of censorship for the

[9] Henry Manship, *A Book of the Foundacion and Antiquitye of the Towne of Greate Yermouthe*, ed. C. J. Palmer, p. 5.

buffoonish welter of metaphor it affords to feed and fool his readers; we have already seen how copy is made out of the kind of teasing digression that we still call a 'red herring'. Ultimately, of course, the herring becomes an ambiguous patron, both in discursive and in economic terms mocking the assumption of protection and provision that 'patronage' implies by suggesting that the need for protection is itself the creation of a patronage system. The anachronism of patronage is brought home more than once in economic terms in the image of Yarmouth's wealth-generating product—the herring—as her great 'well meaning *Pater patriae*, & prouiditore and supporter' (iii. 191), but the history of Yarmouth's commercial relations with London may be significant in other ways too. As Nashe says, Yarmouth sands 'set vp shop for themselues'; Yarmouth's free acknowledgement of the commercial sources of her prosperity implies a criticism of the sublimated discourse of honour, patronage and moral obligation through which London's governors negotiated their lucrative economic privileges. The Merchant Adventurers were at this time particularly oppressive in their determination to maintain trading privileges at the expense of provincial port towns; the retaliation of the provinces would be felt soon enough in James I's parliaments, but in the meantime the company insisted that all trading outside its own privilege was illegal and 'disordered'.[10] The traders of Yarmouth and King's Lynn consistently opposed these 'merchaunt venturers' that 'restrayneth all men'.[11] It is possible that praising Yarmouth in itself signified an act of withdrawal from the exploitative 'patronage' of city and court which formed the basis of London's economy; Nashe declares that his raising of Yarmouth's 'head' is an admonishment to those that 'aduaunce their heades aboue all others' (iii. 156). Certainly, since the death of Thomas Howard in 1572, Norfolk's patronage relations with London and the court had not been easy. In a striking affirmation of Nashe's metaphor of Yarmouth's sands uniting in resistance to the sea, a modern historian writes of Norfolk at this time: 'It is likely that reaction against interference from London and Court interests proved the greatest single factor in developing cohesion within the country.'[12]

[10] See *APC* xxvii, Apr. 1597, p. 50. For an account of retaliation against the Merchant Adventurers see R. Ashton, *The City and the Court 1603–1643*, pp. 84 ff.

[11] A. Hassel-Smith, *County and Court: Government and Politics in Norfolk 1558–1603*, p. 11.

[12] Ibid. 16.

A general polemic against the monopolizing of wealth through the anachronism of patronage in a commercial economy has its bearing on the question of writing as a professional act which defies any official monopoly on interpretation. The Merchant Adventurers' denial of free-trading corresponds for an artistic 'workman' (iii. 153) like Nashe to the refusal of the city fathers (no doubt some of them were Merchant Adventurers) to allow commercial theatres in the city and liberties. *Lenten Stuffe* ridicules the London definition of prosperity as the acquisition, accumulation and protection of its own freedoms and privileges, figured in the long-winded excuses with which fortune-hunting courtiers greet the writers they undertake to patronize (iii. 148). The point about these privileged groups is the extraordinary vulnerability of their wealth; despite their lands and revenues, their endless husbanding of resources, they seem, absurdly, to be threatened by a few mendicant authors. Yarmouth, on the contrary, is the image of a wealth that creates itself by expenditure of energy, without being able to rely on accumulated resources. In 1611 John Speed remarked on the economic disadvantages peculiar to Yarmouth: not only did the town lack a landed revenue, but merely in order to survive it was at the continual expense of preventing the encroachment of the sea: 'It maintaineth a Peere against the Sea at the yeerly charge of fiue hundred pound, or thereabout: yet it hath no possessions, as other Corporations.'[13] Manship also remarks on this, commending the resourcefulness of a people, 'whose charges have alwaies ben verye greate, and their Landes and Revenwes verye smalle, for theye doe live onelie by there trades unto the Seas'.[14] Nashe celebrates Yarmouth's lack of landed revenue: 'not a beggers noble' do they get by their 'barraine sands', but 'their whole haruest is by Sea' (iii. 171). This implicitly contrasts the City of London, which, for all its monopolistic command of the nations' best resources, protests itself unable to provide for the crowds of strangers encouraged by the theatres, with an unprivileged Yarmouth which seems to rejoice in the hospitable provision for strangers. The order for tearing down playhouses in 1597 had been given to prevent 'confluence' of strangers to London,[15] and the argument of the city fathers had long long been that the playhouses encouraged 'mvltitudes of people for

13 John Speed, *The Theatre of the Empire of Great Britaine* (1611), p. 35.

14 Manship, *Book of Greate Yermouthe*, p. 1.

15 *APC* xxvii, July 1597, pp. 313–14.

whome we shall not be able to make prouision of vitale, fewell, an other necessaries at any reasonable prises'.[16] Nashe draws attention to Yarmouth's capacity to provide in this respect, despite her remarkable lack of natural privileges. He remarks pointedly on his wonder that a town 'of it selfe so innumerable populous and replenished, and in so barraine a plot seated, should not onely supply her inhabitants with plentifull purueyance of sustenance, but prouant and victuall moreouer this monstrous army of strangers' (iii. 158). Victual and fuel remain at reasonable prices for the whole duration of the fair: 'in all that while the rate of no kinde of food is raised, nor the plenty of their markets one pint of butter rebated' (iii. 158). The town, in fact, apparently revels in the very presence of the 'rabble rout' (iii. 158) that the London government was always trying to marginalize and exclude from the city. Since the herring fair was a commercial event this 'great concourse of people' drawn to it did, as Speed wrote, make 'the Towne very much the richer all the yeere'.[17] In the terms of Nashe's text, however, it is the welcoming of crowds themselves which enriches the town: Yarmouth is populated and 'replenished' where London is oppressed and threatened by humanity. Crowds become a source of vitality for the imagination in *Lenten Stuffe*, the work is packed with throngs of all kinds. Nashe declares his 'prime pleasure' in Yarmouth to have been that of watching the fleet conglomerate after a storm, when the ships 'lay close pestred together as thicke as they could packe; the next day following, if it were faire, they would cloud the whole skie with canuas' (iii. 158). The ships which replenish the sea and sky are, in another image, freighted with food; their sea-rolling ('wallowing') becomes a comically sensuous expression of repletion: 'If all her Maiesties fleet at once should put into their bay, within twelue days warning with so much double beere, beefe, fish, and bisket they would bulke them as they could wallow away with' (iii. 158).

In the imagination of their appreciative beholder, crowds beget images of crowds. The concourse of people at the autumn herring-fair inspires a description of the festive hoards of pilgrims who crossed the seas in the bad old days of Catholicism:

> I neuer crouded through this confluent herring faire, but it put me in memory of the great yeare of Iubile in *Edward* the thirds time, in which . . .

[16] Chambers, *Elizabethan Stage*, iv. 281.
[17] Speed, *Theatre of Great Britaine*, p. 35.

three hundred thousand people romed to Rome for purgatorie pils and paternal veniall benedictions, and the waies beyond sea were so bunged vp with your dayly oratours or *Beads-men* and your crutchet or croutchant friers or crosse-creepers and barefoote penitentiaries, that a snaile could not wriggle in her hornes betwixt them. (iii. 185)

As in the reference to writers as vagrants ('frier mendicants') Catholicism here carries the associations of idleness and disorder. But there is not a shred of the usual disapproval that goes with this view; Nashe's materializing mockery of Catholic beliefs (i.e. in 'purgatorie pils') is celebratory. The sheer density and vitality of the crowd (suggested in the congestion of consonants) is offered as a liberating conception.

True to the independent, anti-aristocratic spirit of *Lenten Stuffe,* Nashe's history of Yarmouth departs from the usual Renaissance tradition of immortalizing great men and setting up monuments to the glory of past governors. Instead, history becomes an extended tribute to the resilient vitality of crowds of 'strangers'—of vagrant humanity unconcerned about tracing its origins back to Brute, determined only to accommodate itself and survive on Yarmouth's shores. Early merchants and migrants arrive as heterogeneously as crowds to a play, 'thronging theaters of people (as well Aliens as Englishmen) hiued thither about the selling of fish and Herring' (iii. 162). Their thriving industry requires no monopolies, no umbrella protection from disorderly outsiders; only the elements need to be fended off with 'sutlers booths and tabernacles, to canopie their heads in from the rhewme of the heauens, or the clouds dissoluing Cataracts' (iii. 162). The festive-pilgrim motif appears again with the Bishop of Norwich's concern to provide a church for the 'gangs of good fellowes that hurtled and bustled thither, as thicke as it had beene to the shrine of Saint *Thomas* a *Becket* or our Ladie of Walsingham' (iii. 162). Nashe's idiosyncratic history immortalizes neither Yarmouth's great men nor their great works but the toughness and adaptability of the townspeople. Focusing on the wonder and comedy of human resilience, his 'monuments to posterity' are at once curiously indiscriminate and specific in their reference. Thus another bishop of Norwich in King John's time decides to pull down the existing chapel and build a church not because (as the source says) he observes the extent to which Yarmouth's buildings have expanded, but because he sees 'the numbrous increase of soules of both kindes that there had framd their nests, and meant not to forsake them till the soule Bell towld' (iii. 163). The usual historical criteria—great deeds, individual greatness—are abandoned for an emphasis on the tenacity and inventiveness of all creaturely souls who couple and nest. The source credits the bishop and the 'devotion' of the people with building the church;[18] Nashe specifies the return of the fishermen with 'nets full' (iii. 163) as the real founders and builders. Typically, the edifice tries to achieve monumental status; Nashe mocks it for forgetting the origins of its grandeur, 'verie queasie it admits any haylefellow well met' (iii. 163). Disaster is recorded with a complex combination of pathos and humour. During the plague of 1348 'seauen thousand and fifty people toppled vp their heeles' (iii. 165); the appalling precision of the statistics contrasts oddly with the cartoon-like animation of the colloquialism. Such records cannot be rendered in tragic terms because it is not great men whose deeds have enriched Yarmouth by this account, but all the people—'whole tribes of males and females' (iii. 163)—whose corporate energy has given Yarmouth an identity which communicates itself to the rest of the country.

The point, however, is more than a simple analogy between Yarmouth's resourcefulness and that of her orator. What is taking place through the ironic comparison of Yarmouth with London is a redefinition of the concept of prosperity itself; prosperity emerges as an activity, something that only exists in so far as it is communicated. Yarmouth provides the model, for, unlike the 'oystermouthd pouches' (iii. 156) of monopolistic London, she does not merely swallow up profit with ever-increasing rapacity, but 'communicats' her 'common good . . . to the whole state' (iii. 169). While parsimony and protection would seem to be the surest form of affirming and increasing oneself, Nashe's *Lenten Stuffe* proves the opposite case; it is in fact by dispersal and communication to others (in the act of writing) that one creates a self and realizes one's own capacities as a producer of prosperity. Thus, as Yarmouth gets her head above water economically by realizing those waters as a source of commerce and hospitality in the herring, Nashe raises his head above the poverty of distress and complaint by communicating his pleasure in Yarmouth's hospitality. When he first arrives in Yarmouth he has been deprived by exile from London of the means

[18] Manship, *Book of Greate Yermouthe*, p. 9.

to provide for himself, 'sequestred . . . from the woonted meanes of my maintenance' (iii. 153). Unnourished, he is unproductive, a creature 'not able to liue to my selfe with my owne iuice' (iii. 154). Through Yarmouth's hospitality, however, he is more than restored, he turns into a restorative, a source of food, capable of affording hospitality to others. The very crumbs of Yarmouth's generosity to him, 'like the crums in a bushy beard after a greate banquet, will remaine in my papers to be seene when I am deade and vnder ground; from the bare perusing of which, infinite posterities of hungry Poets shall receiue good refreshing' (iii. 154).

Nashe offers his words as contributions to creation and the creativity of other poets; the very reading of his text involves invention and re-creation; it is in itself a poetic activity. Even the sensations excited by Yarmouth are communicated as food for the imagination, 'that which especiallest nourisht the most prime pleasure in me' (iii. 158) and 'the delectablest lustie sight and mouingest object' (iii. 157).

As the antitype of monopolistic London is fair-time Yarmouth, so the inversion of the courtly patron and protector (who turns so easily into wrathful persecutor) is the 'King of good felowshippe' (iii. 149), the morris-dancing Humphrey King. As crowds generate wealth in a commercially based economy, so the wealth afforded by playful, figurative, and unpretentious eloquence can only be increased by being shared in joking dialogue. Nashe's only request from Humphrey King is that he should respond re-creatively to Nashe's words, giving 'good words' in return: 'Giue mee good words I beseech thee, though thou giuest me nothing else, and thy words shal stand for thy deeds; which I will take as well in woorth, as if they were the deedes and euidences of all the lande thou hast' (iii. 149). For Nashe and his generous patron the reciprocal expenditure of genius and good words becomes a way of increasing wealth and realizing prosperity; the landed courtier, on the other hand, suffers expenditure as a drain on resources which he is pitifully unable to make up. Nashe parodies the long-winded excuses of the fortune hunter embarking for Ireland: 'before God, money so scatteringly runnes heere and ther uppon vtensilia, furnitures, ancients and other necessary preparations' (iii. 148), and goes on to suggest (in a sketch anticipatory of Restoration comedy) that the expense which actually threatens the courtier's considerable revenues is in fact the fashionable demands of urban life (iii.148). The wealth that runs away from the courtier ('By S. Loy, that drawes deepe', iii. 148) can never escape the morris dancer and his orator, since dancing, like the improvisatory eloquence of *Lenten Stuffe*, is prosperity realized in the moment of expenditure.

As the writer of *Lenten Stuffe* (which is itself conducted like a dance; see iii. 201) Nashe becomes an orator who, in Quintilian's words, is prosperous: free from the anxiety and impoverishment of cautious self-correction, he is 'opulent' (*locuples*) of speech, 'lord and master of all the resources of eloquence whose affluence surrounds him', having 'reached the summit' with 'no more weary hills to scale'.[19] The reason, of course, that he is for the moment *locuples* is that he has transformed the anxiety of self-correction and evasion into his *topos* in the image of the red herring, whose impositions may be ironically rendered as virtues and 'documentized most locupleatly' (iii. 173). Where the paradoxist usually stresses the perversity and ingenuity of his position, Nashe stresses its material resourcefulness; he repeatedly emphasizes the paradox in terms of its capacity to create further substance, to increase his material, to 'turne mole-hills into mountaines' (iii. 151). One of the ways in which the illusion of substance and plenty is achieved is by the rich and diverse associations which images accrete within the self-referring confines of pamphlet. The conventional definition of paradox as means of inflating the trivial, making 'mountains out of mole-hills', is thus associated in this context with Yarmouth's geological and commercial increase, which is in turn made analogous to Nashe's oratorical recovery and the procreativity which he attributes to metaphor. In fact it is through such dense analogical cross-reference that *Lenten Stuffe* 'proves' its case against the constitution of identity in terms of monopolistic possession (the possession of a single interpretation, of personal revenues) and begins to redefine identity and prosperity in terms of the reciprocal communication and regeneration of experience. Such a redefinition would be spurious were it not the case that reading *Lenten Stuffe* does in fact invigorate the reader's ability to think metaphorically and to experience the physical impact of every metaphor in such a way as to stimulate the imaginative intelligence. It is only by sympathetic analogy, by being forced into an almost physical appreciation of Yarmouth's material and financial erosion by the

[19] Quintilian, *Institutio oratoria*, XII. x. 77–8.

sea, that we arrive at any kind of imaginative awareness of the 'vncessant inestimable expence' involved in Nashe's unremittingly playful conception of the text itself. And it is not through statement, but through the conviction afforded by the experience of its linguistic freedom, that *Lenten Stuffe* is able to launch an uncompromising attack on the implications of patronage relations in a society which is increasingly founded on the market economy of supply and demand; a fact which is as readily acknowledged in the stench of Yarmouth's herring-fair as it is sublimated and distorted by the so-called 'patronage' of tradesmen and writers in fashionable London (iii. 148-9). At the beginning of this book, I argued that Elizabethan students of Latin would have acquired certain habits of moralizing or reading for 'profit' which were frequently expressed in a terminology similar to that in which the values of individualism —moral and financial solvency, more productive attitudes to the enviroment—were also gaining ground. As social values changed with the loosening of local loyalties and the spread of grammar-school education, the pre-literate expression of prosperity in the careless present of festive pastime gradually lost its power to communicate. I want to conclude this reading of *Lenten Stuffe* in a way that develops the implications of this characteristically Elizabethan respect for an exploitative, profit-seeking approach to experience, showing how Nashe has used the imagery and idiom of customary festive attitudes to open out an alternative way of calculating the 'profits' of life.

The subject of *Lenten Stuffe*—the gain brought in by the herring —along with its encomiastic structure, might invite a comparison with the contemporary economic discourse as it is recorded in the statutes, proclamations, and treatises of projectors. The writings of economic projectors are, in fact, encomia of one sort or another, setting forth with more or less sophistication the advantages to be had from any specific enterprise. Nashe's conception of the generous herring derives from one of these projects. The enthusiastic conjectures of subsidiary industries to be generated by the promotion of herring fishing in Robert Hitchcocke's *Politique Platt* provides the model for the Lenten patron who doles out work to 'Carpenters, Shipwrights, makers of lines, roapes, and cables dressers of Hempe, spinners of thred, and net weauers' (iii. 180).[20]

[20] See McKerrow, Supplement, v. 57.

In Nashe's travesty the two styles of discourse associated with economic treatise and mock encomium produce a kind of dialectic, debating the possibility of defining and locating the 'profit' of any activity. Mock encomia, for example, are heaped up not just as precedents, but in mockery of their economic unprofitability, as a 'catalogue of wast authors' (iii. 178). On the other hand the gains and industries stimulated by the herring are throughout praised as if they were pleasurable experiences rather than components of a profitable enterprise. There is a constant suggestion that the 'profitable' end result of any activity is actually negligible by comparison with the experience itself, just as the concealed meanings misguidedly clutched after by political readers are mocked for their impoverishment by the rich commerce of good words. Nobody, Nashe complains, as he endeavours once more to set out feelingly the true virtues of the herring, really appreciates and tastes his virtues: 'such is the obduracy & hardnesse of heart of a number of infidels in these dayes, they will teare herrings out of their skins as fast as one of these Exchequer tellers can turne ouer a heape of money, but his vertues, both exterior and interior, they haue no more taste of then of a dish of stockfish' (iii. 190). Pulling out meanings without conceiving imaginatively of verbal experience is 'hardnesse of heart'.[21] It is a kind of this-worldly asceticism, analogous to that represented by contemporary economic treatises, which are incapable of praising or rejoicing in their topic, other than in terms of profits it will yield at a future date. The economic treatise reads like an encomium in which the only trope or figure capable of moving the reader's hard heart is the trope of calculation, the translation of all present and sensuous experience into an eternal deferral, the statistic promising interest upon interest, profit on profit. Robert Payne's *Brief Description of Ireland*, for example, represents every aspect of that country in terms of an unexplored asset, in terms of the 'commodities' it might 'yield' or the expenses it might incur.[22] Hitchcocke's treatise on the herring industry praises every detail of the fishing process in terms of input and output, right down to a scheme for poor relief in which beggars will support themselves by 'conuertyng the benefite of their trauell to the increase of the same stocke';[23] the stock, that is, which has been

[21] For poetry as 'heart-ravishing' see Sidney, *Miscellaneous Prose*, p. 76.

[22] Robert Payne, *A Briefe Description of Ireland: Made in this yeare, 1589*, p. 8.

[23] Hitchcocke, *Pollitique Platt*, sig. C3r.

invested to supply them with employment. Profits themselves cease to be the end view, and are swallowed up as the components of further profitable enterprise. Nowhere are Weber's remarks about the tendency of all activity to translate into the rationale of enterprise more clearly exemplified. In such discourse, Weber observed, 'Everything is done in terms of balances: at the beginning of the enterprise an initial balance, before every individual decision a calculation to ascertain its probable profitableness, and at the end a final balance to ascertain how much profit has been made.'[24]

There is, of course, nothing wrong with the balancing outlook as a method, a way of planning, but it is clearly not a way of defining value itself in any terms that are intelligible outside the terms of balance. Confusing calculation with an intelligible definition of profit corresponds to the facile disparagement of idle words in favour of profitable meaning; for words, unlike calculations, make more sense of experience, render it more meaningful, in proportion to the complexity of the sensible experience which they themselves offer the imagination. Nashe suggests this in his communication of Yarmouth's economic commodities by conveying them not in terms of exchange or statistic, but as verbal recreations. The image of the herring-fair itself, with its connotations of business and commerce as a way of life, an ongoing recreation, is central to this conception. Thus in Nashe's praise of the industry, the 'fetching in' of the herring becomes a carnivalesque procession, like the fetching in of summer (iii. 185–6), while all prosperous, productive activities from the quest of catching the herring on 'wodden horses' (iii. 182) to the selling of meat by butchers 'out of their wits . . . haunted with continuall takings . . . from one Shroft-tuisday to another' (iii. 184) acquire similar carnival associations. Abstract economic relations are also carnivalized, celebrating themselves in the intoxication of verbal play. Where Thomas Wilson, for example, praises the Norwich stocking-knitters by statistic, 'accounts haueing been made yearly what children from 6 to 10 yeares have erned toward there keeping in a yeare',[25] Nashe compares for praise the Yarmouth net-braiders: 'or those that haue no cloathes to wrappe their hides in or breade to put in their mouthes but what they earne and get by brayding of nets' (iii. 169). The profits of the net-weaving industry

24 Max Weber, *The Protestant Ethic and the Spirit of Capitalism*, trans. Talcott Parsons, p. 18.

25 Thomas Wilson, *State of England*, p. 20.

come alive in the verbal relationships generated by image and assonance; nets appear to transform themselves into clothes as *braiding* miraculously produces *bread*. Moreover, Nashe presents this verbal comedy as a 'shew of netbrayders' (iii. 169) comparable to the emblematic tableaux of stocking-knitters at Norwich which in 1578 presented their prosperity to the Queen on progress.[26] But Nashe's 'shewe' is not allegorical or emblematic; it is a verbal re-creation of actuality just as Carnival is 'a pageant without a stage';[27] in other words, not an emblematic representation of life, but life itself lived holidaywise, experienced with a kind of intoxicating immediacy.

Economic and festive attitudes fuse in a similar carnivalized presentation of Yarmouth's natural advantages; a place, for example, to mend and dry fishing nets. Nashe indicates the exceptional capacity of this drying-place by telling us that there may be 'aboue fiue thousand pounds worth' of nets 'at a time vppon her dennes a sunning' (iii. 170). Calculation, which removes direct experience into the hypothetical realm of exchange ('fiue thousand pounds *worth*'), is transformed into sensuous participation by the verb 'sunning'. Rather than merely 'drying' for the convenience of industry, the nets bask sensuously in their own sufficient existence, like the old women of Nashe's spring song: 'Young louers meete, old wiues a sunning sit' (iii. 239). Enumeration of economic advantages constantly involves a sense of participation in holiday experience. The navigability of Yarmouth's quay is recommended for ships and bathers: 'A conuienient key within her hauen shee hath, for the deliuery of nets and herrings, where you may lie a floate at a lowe water, (I beseech you doe not so in the Thames)'(iii. 170).

Epideictic comparisons and economic evaluations of profit are both translated into boisterous activity, the assertive and self-mocking gestures and blows of carnival combat. Thus, as Yarmouth sands were said to challenge 'the vpperhande of the Ocean' (iii. 156), so, in the hypothetical rhetorical contest, the burgesses in Parliament challenge 'the vpper hand' of the superior revenues which Nashe claims for Yarmouth (iii. 174). Comparative commercial value ceases to be numerical abstraction, and becomes a market place free-for-all as '*Transalpiners* with their lordly *Parmasin* . . .

[26] Holinshed, *Chronicles* (1587), iii. 1290.

[27] Bakhtin, *Dostoevsky's Poetics*, p. 100.

shoulder in for the vpper hand' against the English cheese-makers (iii. 179).

Farmers and fishermen, rival nations and towns may argue about which of them produces the most valuable commodity, but it is authors themselves who quarrel by implication about how value and commodity can be compared and defined. The traditional invocation of burlesque precedents—praises of nuts, fleas, fevers, and baldness—in itself implies some kind of judgement about what is substantial and worthy of verbal rehearsal. Nashe turns his version of this traditional list into a kind of carnival combat by including much literature of a profitable, practical, and technical nature.[28] When earnest volumes setting out the advantages of the long bow or calculating the cornucopian commodities of keeping a cow ('what an aduantageable creature shee is, beyond all the foure footed rablement of *Herbagers* and grasse champers', iii. 178) are set beside insubstantial descants in praise of unworthy objects, distinctions are confounded and these ostensibly profitable treatises emerge as being as eccentrically devoted to the pleasure of rehearsing their own obsessions as their idle companions. The profitable maxims of Sir Hugh Plat, reduced to a memorable 'dozen of points', rub shoulders with Elderton's praise of drunkenness and the 'diuersitie of red noses' (iii. 177).[29] The zeal with which earthly pleasures are rejected for profitable 'points' of knowledge becomes the vigorous eccentricity of an author who 'sweeps behind the dore all earthly felicities, and makes Bakers maulkins of them, if they stand in competencie with a strong dozen of poyntes' (iii. 177). As throughout *Lenten Stuffe* dancing and singing figure prosperity as a form of ephemeral experience, so all Nashe's profitable and trivial authors are antics, dancing, and trumpeting their own idiosyncrasies. Homer 'heroquit it' about rats and frogs; sonneteers 'sing descant' in praise of a mistress's glove, philosophers 'come sneaking in' with unlikely propositions, while physicians like to 'deafen our ears' by employing the longest words they can find (iii. 176). French pornographers 'swarme euery pissing while' in imitation of their own sexual excitability; one English writer plays on the advantages of tobacco

28 Such as medical treatises, rules for tennis, and so forth. See McKerrow, Supplement, v. 55.

29 Compare Sir Hugh Plat, 'The Floures of Philosophy', *Censura Literaria*, ed. S. E. Bridges, vol. viii, no. xxix, with 'A Dozen of Points' in *Old Ballads*, ed. Rollins, pp. 315–19.

as if it were a trumpet, while another 'capers it vp to the spheares in commendation of daunsing' (iii. 177). *Terlerygincks*, elsewhere defined by Nashe as a clowne who 'libels in commendation of little witte very loftily' (i. 296) while dancing in a light-foot jig, here defines the song-and-dance substantiality, the freedom to please themselves, which is all these authors represent, whether or not they pretend their works are otherwise profitable: 'If all these haue *Terleryginckt* it so friuolously of they reckt not what, I may *Cum gratia & priueligio* pronounce it, that a red herring is wholesome in a frosty morning' (iii. 178).

The freedom to utter '*cum gratia & priueligio*' ideas which threaten or contravert the foundations of society and government is, of course, the object of paradox. Again, it is not so much that the trickster, the all-licensed fool, 'conceals' the truth in jest, but that by breaking down the normal bounds of comparative thought he creates terms in which ideas may be conceived with a new freedom. Ideas that were hitherto impossible to conceive become possible in the re-creation of definitions. *Lenten Stuffe* is about redefining prosperity as a kind of freedom of movement. In social terms this means the uninhibited commerce of the Yarmouth herring-fair rather than an accretion of profit through economic monopoly or dependence upon the competitive relations of patronage. In rhetorical terms oratorical affluence ceases to refer to the personal increase through the power to persuade and manipulate others, and redefines itself as a capacity to stimulate and be stimulated by words without having them manipulated against oneself. So Nashe is 'fed' by his Yarmouth experience, and 'feeds' us with the verbal recreation of it; ideally, like the poets who were to banquet on the crumbs left in this bushy beard, readers should then go on to realize this feeding through their own creative energy, communicating themselves to others. What Nashe anticipates, however, is readers who, looking to increase their personal power at the expense of others, will 'mouth' and 'missound' his free pronouncing and 'disioynt and teare euery sillable betwixt their teeth seuerally' (iii. 214–15). These are they who, fishing for hidden meanings, 'vse mens writings like bruite beasts' (iii. 215). We must not mistake the pugnacious tone of *Lenten Stuffe* for the fighting rhetoric of the satirist, for Nashe's antagonist is this powerful mouthing and swallowing up of men by means of words. His own battle is an ostentatious pretence at the tendentious meaning which this antagonist is bound to dredge up against him. His tongue only arms itself for survival against the whelming power of the sea, like Yarmouth which he describes as '*lingulam terrae*, a little tong of the earth', which 'sticks not to mannage armes and hold his owne vndefeasably against that vniuersall vnbounded empery of surges' (iii. 157). Even holding his own against the unbounded powers of censorship within the precincts of the pamphlet becomes a celebration of energy; having decided to suppress any tendentious comparisons between Yarmouth and other towns, the text rehearses the activity involved in 'unwinding' and omitting as part of its ongoing activity: 'Of that profligated labour yet my breast pants and labours: a whole moneths minde of reuoluing meditation I raueling out therin, (as raueling out signifies *Penelopes telam retexere*, the vnweauing of a webbe before wouen and contexted' (iii. 168). Similarly, the act of strewing about gudgeons and cobs and other small fish in an apparently satirical dismembering and devouring of Lord Cobham becomes in fact the gratuitous feeding of those readers who like to fish out morals and meanings: Nashe calls his fishy evidence a 'gudgeon dole': 'I haue destributed gudgeon dole amongst them, as Gods plenty as any stripling of my slender portion of witte' (iii. 213). The only way to defy in anticipation the charge of using language satirically to 'bite' those in power is to offer it to them as nourishing food. In our time the readers of *Lenten Stuffe* are likely to be scholars, critics, and professional writers who feel relatively free to engage in literary production, criticism, and interpretation and who are unlikely to have felt the pressure of what Nashe's texts were up against. Perhaps this has contributed to a tendency in academic circles to play down the implications of the official silencing of Nashe after *Lenten Stuffe*. McKerrow has suggested that the bishops' edict was not taken seriously, since *Summers Last Will and Testament* was published the following year (v. 34). This is true, but it may be relevant to note that the play's registration by the publisher makes no mention of Nashe's authorship, simply recording it as presented by 'William Sommers' (iii. 227). In a sense we endorse the silencing of Nashe by assuming that the fate of the texts and their author is a consideration beyond the scope of literary criticism, because such assumptions tend to impoverish our experience of Nashe's writing and deny us access to the subtlety of its intellectual challenge. Another kind of silencing, or rather a deafness, is the result of a more general critical reluctance to discern humanity and human relevance in fiction which does not dramatize individual human subjects. It is a mark of the historical and aesthetic achievement as well as the humanity of Nashe's writing, however, that it resists the very notion of the individual as a concept too easily made to serve a falsely moralizing system of representation. Nashe's writing is humane precisely because, by endowing contemporary economic, social, and discursive relations with fictional features and accents, it can render the otherwise invisible and mute operations of power accessible to the reader in the form of imaginative pleasure and laughter.

# WORKS CITED

## PRIMARY SOURCES


Acolastus, *The Comedy of Acolastus,* trans. from the Latin of Fullonius [G. Gnapheus] by John Palsgrave (1540), ed. P. L. Carver. London: EETS, os 202, 1937.

*Advice to a Son,* ed. L. B. Wright. Ithaca, NY: Cornell Univ. Press, 1962.

*Ancient Christmas Carols MCCC to MDCC,* ed. Edith Rickert. London: Chatto & Windus, 1928.

Anon., *Pyers Plowmans exhortation unto the lordes knightes and burgoysses of the Parlyamenthouse.* London: Antony Scoloker, 1549.

Anon., *Cyuile and Vncyuile life.* London: Richard Jones, 1579.

Anon., *The debate and Stryfe betwene Somer and Wynter,* ed. J. O. Halliwell. London: 1860.

Anon., *The Wyll of the Deuyll and Last Testament,* ed. F. J. Furnivall. London: Ballad Soc., 1871.

Aretino, Pietro, *Tutte le comedie,* ed. G. B. de Sanctis. Milan: Grande Universale Mursia, 1968.

Ariosto, Ludovico, *Tutte le opere,* 5 vols., ed. Cesare Segre. Milan: Arnoldo Mondadori, 1974.

Ascham, Roger, *The Schoolmaster* (1570), ed. Lawrence V. Ryan. Ithaca, NY: Cornell Univ. Press, 1967.

Awdeley, John, *The Fraternitye of Vacabondes,* ed. F. J. Furnivall. London: EETS, 1868.

Bancroft, Richard, *Dangerous positions and proceedings.* London: John Wolfe, 1593.

_____ *A Suruay of the pretended Holy Discipline.* London: John Wolfe, 1593.

Beard, Thomas, *The Theatre of Gods Iudgements.* London: Adam Islip, 1597.

Bullein, William, *A Dialogue against the Fever Pestilence* (1564), ed. Mark W. and A. H. Bullen. London: EETS, ES, 1888.

Chettle, Henry, *Kind-Hartes Dreame* (1592), ed. G. B. Harrison. London: Bodley Head, 1923.

Cicero, *Selected Works,* trans. Michael Grant. Harmondsworth: Penguin, 1960.

_____ *Murder Trials,* trans. Michael Grant. Harmondsworth: Penguin, 1975.

Coffey, Michael, *Roman Satire*, London: Methuen, 1976.

Copland, Robert, *Jyl of Brentford's Testament,* ed. F. J. Furnivall. London: Ballad Soc., 1871.

Crowley, Robert, *Select Works,* ed. J. M. Cowper. London: EETS, ES, 1872.

D., E., *The Prayse of Nothing.* London: H. Jackson, 1585.

Deloney, Thomas, *The Novels,* ed. Merrit E. Lawlis. Bloomington, Ind.: Indiana Univ. Press, 1961.

D'Ewes, Sir Simonds, *The Journals of all the Parliaments during the Reign of Queen Elizabeth.* London: Paul Bowes, 1682.

Dolman, John, *Those Fyue Questions which Marke Tully Cicero disputed in his manor of Tusculanum.* London: Thos. Marshe, 1561.

*Early English Carols,* ed. R. L. Greene. Oxford: Clarendon Press, 1935.

Elderton, William, 'New Merry News', *Fugitive Tracts,* 2nd ser., vol. ii, ed. William C. Hazlitt. London: Chiswick Press, 1875.

Elyot, Sir Thomas, *The Boke Named the Gouernour* (1531). London: Dent, 1907.

_____ *Four Political Treatises,* introd. Lillian Gottesman. Gainesville, Fla.: Scholars' Facs., 1967.

_____ *A Preservatiue Agaynste deth.* London: 1534.

Erasmus, *Erasmi Rotterdami Moriae encomium & Ludus L. Annae Senecae de Morte Claudii Caesaris.* Basle: 1515.

_____ *On Copia of Words and Ideas* [*De utraque verborum ac rerum copia*], ed. and trans. D. B. King and H. D. Rix. Milwaukee, Wis.: Marquette Univ. Press, 1963.

_____ *The Colloquies of Erasmus,* trans. Craig R. Thompson. Chicago, Ill.: Univ. of Chicago Press, 1965.

_____ *Erasmus on his Times: A Shortened Version of the Adages of Erasmus,* ed. and trans. Margaret Mann Phillips. Cambridge: Cambridge Univ. Press, 1967.

_____ *Praise of Folly,* trans. Betty Radice. Harmondsworth: Penguin, 1971.

F., T., *Newes from the North, Otherwise called the conference between Simon Certain and Pierce Plowman.* London: Edward Allde, 1585.

Fetherston, Christopher, *A Dialogue agaynst light, lewde, and lascivious dauncing.* London: Thos. Dawson, 1582.

Gascoigne, George, *Works,* 2 vols., ed. J. W. Cunliffe. Cambridge: Cambridge Univ. Press, 1910.

_____ *A Hundredth Sundrie Flowres.* London: Richard Smith, 1573.

_____ *The Posies of George Gascoigne Esquire. Corrected, perfected and augmented by the author.* London: Richard Smith, 1575.

Gentillet, Innocent, *A discovrse upon the meanes of wel governing*

. . . *against Nicholas Machiavel,* trans. Simon Patericke. London: Adam Islip, 1608.

Golding, Arthur, *The Fyrst Fower Bookes of P. Ouidius Nasos worke intituled Metamorphosis.* London: William Seres, 1565.

Googe, Barnabe, *The Popish Kingdome.* London: H. Denham, 1570.

Gosson, Stephen, *The School of Abuse.* London: T. Woodcocke, 1579.

Greene, Robert, *Life and Works,* 12 vols., ed. A. B. Grosart. London: 1881–3.

Guilpin, Everard, *Skialethia or A Shadow of Truth in Certaine Epigrams and Satyres,* ed. D. Allen Carroll. Chapel Hill, NC: Univ. of North Carolina Press, 1974.

Hake, Edward, *Newes Out of Powles Churchyarde* (1579), ed. Charles Edmonds. London: Henry Southern, 1872.

Harvey, Gabriel, *Works,* 3 vols., ed. A. B. Grosart. London: 1884.

_____ *Letter Book of Gabriel Harvey A.D. 1573–1580,* ed. Edward J. Scott. London: Camden Soc., 1884.

_____ *Gabriel Harvey's Marginalia,* G. C. Moore-Smith. Stratford-upon-Avon: Shakespeare Head Press, 1913.

Hitchcocke, Robert, *A Pollitique Platt.* London: John Kyngston, 1580.

Jonson, Ben, *Works,* 11 vols., ed. C. H. Herford, P. Simpson and E. Simpson. Oxford: Clarendon Press, 1925–52.

Judges, A. V. (ed.), *The Elizabethan Underworld.* London: Routledge & Kegan Paul, 1965.

Lacy, John, *Wyl bucke his Testament.* London: Wyllam Copland, n.d.

Lambarde, William, *William Lambarde and Local Government,* ed. Conyers Read. Ithaca, NY: Cornell Univ. Press, 1962.

Latimer, Hugh, *Seven Sermons before Edward VI,* ed. E. Arber. London: English Reprints, 1869.

Lever, Thomas, *Sermons* (1550), ed. E. Arber. London: English Reprints, 1895.

Lucian, *Works,* 8 vols. with Eng. trans. by A. M. Harmon. Cambridge, Mass.: Harvard Univ. Press (Loeb), 1913–67.

_____ *Satirical Sketches,* trans. Paul Turner. Harmondsworth: Penguin, 1961.

Lupton, Thomas, *A Moral and pitieful Comedie, Intituled All for Money.* London: Roger Warde, 1578.

Lyly, John, *Complete Works,* 3 vols., ed. R. W. Bond. Oxford: Clarendon Press, 1902.

Machyn, Henry, *The Diary of Henry Machyn 1550–1563,* ed. J. Gough Nichols. London: Camden Soc., 1848.

Manship, Henry, *A Book of the Foundacion and Antiquitye of the Towne of Greate Yermouthe,* ed. Charles John Palmer. Great Yarmouth: Sloman, 1847.

Marlowe, Christopher, *Complete Poems and Translations,* ed. Stephen Orgel. Harmondsworth: Penguin, 1979.

Marprelate, Martin (pseud.), *The Marprelate Tracts, 1588, 1589,* ed. William Pierce. London: James Clarke, 1911.

Middleton, Thomas, *Works,* 5 vols., ed. Revd Alexander Dyce. London: Edward Lumley, 1840.

More, Thomas, *Utopia,* trans. Paul Turner. Harmondsworth: Penguin, 1965.

_____ *Yale Edition of the Complete Works.* New Haven, Conn., and London: Yale Univ. Press, 1963– . Vol. 3, pt. 1: *The Translations of Lucian,* ed. Craig R. Thompson, 1974; vol. 8, pt. 1: *The Confutation of Tyndale's Answer,* ed. Louis Schuster *et al.,* 1973.

Nashe, Thomas, *Complete Works,* 5 vols., ed. A. B. Grosart. London: The Huth Library, 1883–4.

_____ *Works,* 5 vols., ed. R. B. McKerrow, rev. F. P. Wilson. Oxford: Basil Blackwell, 1966.

_____ *The Unfortunate Traveller and Other Works,* ed. J. B. Steane. Harmondsworth: Penguin, 1972.

North, Sir Thomas (trans.), *The Diall of Princes,* ed. K. N. Colville. London: Philip Allan & Co., 1919 (selections).

Northbrooke, John, *A Treatise Wherein Dicing, Dauncing, Vaine Playes or Enterludes . . . are reproued.* London: George Byshop, 1577.

*Old English Ballads, 1553–1625,* ed. Hyder E. Rollins. Cambridge: Cambridge Univ. Press, 1920.

Ovid, *Tristia, Ex Ponto*, with Eng. trans. by A. L. Wheeler. Cambridge, Mass.: Harvard Univ. Press (Loeb), 1925.

_____ *Metamorphoses,* trans. Mary M. Innes. Harmondsworth: Penguin, 1955.

Paule, Sir George, *The Life of the Most Reverend . . . John Whitgift, Lord Archbishop of Canterbury.* London: Thomas Snodham, 1612.

Payne, Robert, *A Briefe Description of Ireland: Made in this yeare, 1589.* London: Thomas Dawson, 1589.

Penry, John, *A Treatise Wherein is Manifestlie Proved that Reformation and Those that sincerely Fauor the Same, are unjustly charged to be Enemies vnto hir Majestie and the State.* 1590.

_____ *The Examinations of Henry Barrowe, John Greenewood and John Penrie before the High Commissioners.* 1593.

Perkins, William, *The Works of the Famous and Worthie Minister . . . M. William Perkins.* Cambridge: John Legat, 1609.

Petrarch, 'On his own ignorance and that of many others', repr. in *The Renaissance Philosophy of Man,* ed. Ernst Cassirer *et al.* Chicago, Ill.: Univ. of Chicago Press, 1948.

Plat, Sir Hugh, 'The Floures of Philosophie' (1572), in *Censura Literaria,* ed. Samuel Egerton Brydges, vol. viii, no. xxix. London: 1808.

Plautus, *Works,* with Eng. trans. by Paul Nixon, 5 vols. Cambridge, Mass.: Harvard Univ. Press (Loeb), 1932.

Primaudaye, Pierre de la, *The French Academie,* trans. T. B. London: George Bishop, 1589.

____ *The Second Part of the French Academie,* trans. T. B. London: G. B. 1594.

Puttenham, George, *The Arte of English Poesie,* ed. Gladys Doidge Willcock and Alice Walker. Cambridge: Cambridge Univ. Press, 1936 (repr. 1970).

Quintilian, *Institutio oratoria,* trans. H. E. Butler, Cambridge, Mass.: Harvard Univ. Press (Loeb), 1922.

R., B. [Barnabe Rich?], *Greenes Newes both from Heaven and Hell* (1593), ed. R. B. McKerrow. London: Sidgwick & Jackson, 1911.

Rabelais, François, *The Histories of Gargantua and Pantagruel,* trans. J. M. Cohen. Harmondsworth: Penguin, 1955.

*Remains of the Early Popular Poetry of England,* 4 vols., ed. William C. Hazlitt. London: 1864.

*Roxburghe Ballads,* ed. W. M. Chappell. London: Ballad Soc., 1871.

Roy, William, and Barlow, Jerome, *Rede me and be nott wrothe,* ed. E. Arber. London: English Reprints, 1871.

Seneca, *The Apocolocyntosis,* trans. J. P. Sullivan. Harmondsworth: Penguin, 1977.

Sextus Empiricus, *Works,* 4 vols., with Eng. trans. by R. G. Bury. Cambridge, Mass.: Harvard Univ. Press (Loeb), 1933.

Shakespeare, William, *Complete Works,* original-spelling edn., ed. S. Wells and G. Taylor. Oxford: Clarendon Press, 1986.

Sidney, Sir Philip, *Miscellaneous Prose,* ed. Katherine Duncan-Jones and Jan van Dorsten. Oxford: Clarendon Press, 1973.

____ *The Countess of Pembroke's Arcadia (The Old Arcadia),* ed. Jean Robertson. Oxford: Clarendon Press, 1973.

____ *The Poems of Sir Philip Sidney,* ed. W. A. Ringler. Oxford: Clarendon Press, 1962.

Sisson, C. J., *Lost Plays of Shakespeare's Age.* Cambridge: Cambridge Univ. Press, 1936.

Smith, Sir Thomas (attrib.), *A Discourse of the Commonweal of this Realm of England,* ed. Mary Dewar. Charlottesville, Va.: Univ. of Virginia Press, 1969.

*Songs and Ballads, Chiefly of the reign of Philip and Mary,* ed. Thomas Wright. London: J. B. Nichols for the Roxburghe Club, 1860.

Speed, John, *The Theatre of the Empire of Great Britaine.* London, 1611.

Spenser, Edmund, *Poetical Works,* ed. J. C. Smith and E. de Selincourt. London: Oxford Univ. Press, 1912.

Stowe, John, *The Annales or General Chronicle of England,* London: Thomas Adams, 1615.

Stubbes, Philip, *The Anatomy of Abuses in England in Shakespeare's Youth* (1584), ed. F. J. Furnivall. London: New Shakespeare Soc., 1877–9.

Studly, John, *The Eyght Tragedie of Seneca entituled Agammemnon.* London: Thos. Colwell, 1566.

Tarlton, Richard, *Tarlton's Jests and News Out of Purgatory,* ed. J. O. Halliwell. London: Shakespeare Soc., 1844.

Thynn, Francis, *The Debate Between Pride and Lowliness* (1570), ed. J. Payne Collier. London: 1867.

Transcript of the Registers of the Company of Stationers of London (1544–1640), 5 vols., ed. E. Arber. London: 1875.

Tudor Economic Documents, 3 vols., ed. R. H. Tawney and E. Power. London: Longman, Green & Co., 1924.

*Tudor Royal Proclamations,* 3 vols., ed. Paul L. Hughes and James F. Larkin. New Haven, Conn.: Yale Univ. Press, 1969.

Turner, William, *A newe Dialogue wherin is conteyned the examination of the Messe.* London: 1548.

*Two Books of Homilies Appointed to be Read in Churches,* ed. J. W. Griffiths. Oxford: Oxford Univ. Press, 1859.

Udall, Nicholas, *Ralph Roister Doister,* in *Four Tudor Comedies,* ed. W. Tydeman. Harmondsworth: Penguin, 1984.

Whetstone, George, *The Rocke of Regard* (1576), ed. J. Payne Collier. London: 1867.

_____ *The Right Excellent and Famous Historye of Promos and Cassandra.* London: R. Jhones, 1578.

_____ *A Mirour for Magestrates of Cyties.* London: Richard Jones, 1584.

Whitgift, John, *Works,* 3 vols., ed. John Ayre, Parker Soc. Cambridge: Cambridge Univ. Press, 1851–3.

Wilson, Thomas, *The Art of Rhetorique.* London: R. Grafton, 1553.

____ *A Discourse Upon Usury,* ed. R. H. Tawney. London: G. Bell & Sons, 1925.

____ *The State of England Anno Dom 1600,* ed. F. J. Fisher, Camden Miscellany, 16. London: 1936.

## SECONDARY SOURCES

Allen, John W., *A History of Political Thought in the Sixteenth Century*. London: Methuen, 1928.

Altman, Joel B., *The Tudor Play of Mind*. Berkeley and London: Univ. of Calif. Press, 1978.

Appleby, Joyce Oldham, *Economic Thought and Ideology in Seventeenth-Century England*. Princeton, NJ: Princeton Univ. Press, 1978 (pbk. 1980).

Ashton, Robert, *The City and the Court 1603–1643*. Cambridge: Cambridge Univ. Press, 1979.

Aydelotte, Frank, *Elizabethan Rogues and Vagabonds*. London: Frank Cass, 1967.

Babcock, Barbara A. (ed.), *The Reversible World*. Ithaca, NY: Cornell Univ. Press, 1978.

Bakhtin, Mikhail, *Rabelais and his World,* trans. Hélène Iswolsky. Cambridge, Mass.: MIT Press, 1968.

____ *Problems of Dostoevsky's Poetics,* trans. R. W. Rotsel. USA: Ardis, 1973.

____ *The Dialogic Imagination,* ed. Michael Holquist, trans. Caryl Emerson and Michael Holquist. Austin, Tex.: Univ. of Texas Press, 1981.

Baldwin, Thomas W., *William Shakespere's Small Latine & Lesse Greeke,* vol. i. Urbana, Ill.: Univ. of Illinois Press, 1944.

Barber, Cesar L., *Shakespeare's Festive Comedy*. Princeton, NJ: Princeton Univ. Press, 1959 (pbk. 1972).

Baskervill, Charles Read, *English Elements in Jonson's Early Comedy*. Bulletin of the Univ. of Texas, 178, 1911.

____ 'Dramatic Aspects of Medieval Folk Festivals in England', *SP* 17 (1920), 19–87.

____ *The Elizabethan Jig and Related Song and Drama*. Chicago, Ill.: Univ. of Chicago Press, 1929.

Baxandall, Michael, *Giotto and the Orators*. Oxford: Clarendon Press, 1971.

Best, Michael, 'Nashe, Lyly and Summers Last Will and Testament', *PQ* 48 (1969), 1–11.

Bindoff, Stanley T., *et al., Elizabethan Government and Society: Essays Presented to Sir John Neale*. London: Athlone Press, 1961.

Bindoff, Stanley T., *et al.*, 'Clement Armstrong and his Treatises of the Commonweal', *Ec. HR* 14 (1944), 64–73.

Boyce, Benjamin, 'News from Hell: Satiric Communications with the Netherworld in English Writing of the Seventeenth and Eighteenth Centuries', *PMLA* 58 (1943), 402–37.

Boynton, Lindsay, 'The Tudor Provost Marshall', *EHR* 77 (1962), 437–55.

Burgess, Theodore C., *Epideictic Literature.* Chicago, Ill.: Studies in Classical Philology, III, 1902.

Burke, Peter, *Popular Culture in Early Modern Europe.* London: Temple Smith, 1978.

Campbell, Oscar J., *Comicall Satyre and Shakespeare's 'Troilus and Cressida'.* San Marino, Calif.: Huntington Library Publications, 1933.

Carey, John, 'Sixteenth- and Seventeenth-Century Prose', in *English Poetry and Prose 1540–1674,* ed. Christopher Ricks. London: Sphere, 1970.

Cave, Terence, *The Cornucopian Text.* Oxford: Clarendon Press, 1979.

Chambers, Edmund K., *The Elizabethan Stage,* 4 vols. Oxford: Clarendon Press, 1923.

—— *The English Folk Play.* Oxford: Clarendon Press, 1933.

Clark, Peter, *English Provincial Society from the Reformation to the Revolution.* Hassocks, Sussex: Harvester Press, 1977.

Clarkson, L. A., 'The Organisation of the Leather Industry in the Late Sixteenth Century', *Ec. HR,* 2nd ser. 8 (1955–6), 280–95.

Colie, Rosalie L., *Paradoxia Epidemica: Renaissance Tradition of the Paradox.* Princeton, NJ: Princeton Univ. Press, 1966.

Collinson, Patrick, *The Elizabethan Puritan Movement.* London: Jonathan Cape, 1967.

Conley, Carey H., *The First English Translators of the Classics.* New Haven, Conn.: Yale Univ. Press, 1927.

Cornford, Francis M., *The Origins of Attic Comedy.* Cambridge: Cambridge Univ. Press, 1934.

Crane, William G., *Wit and Rhetoric in the Renaissance.* New York: Columbia Univ. Press, 1937.

Crewe, Jonathan, *Unredeemed Rhetoric: Thomas Nashe and the Scandal of Authorship.* Baltimore, Md.: The Johns Hopkins Univ. Press, 1982.

Davies, Margaret Gay, *The Enforcement of the English Apprenticeship.* Cambridge, Mass.: Harvard Univ. Press, 1956.

Dewar, Mary, 'The Authorship of the "Discourse of the Commonweal" ', *Ec. HR,* 2nd ser. 19 (1966), 388–400.

Dickinson, R. J., 'The *Tristia*: Poetry in Exile', in *Ovid*, ed. J. W. Binns. London: Routledge & Kegan Paul, 1973.

Dorsten, Jan van, 'Mr Secretary Cecil, Patron of Letters', *English Studies,* 50 (1969), 545–53.

Dowling, Margaret, 'Sir John Hayward's Trouble over his *Life of Henry IV', The Library,* 4th ser. 11 (1930–1), 212–24.

Dronke, Peter, *The Medieval Lyric.* London: Hutchinson Univ. Library, 1968.

Duncan, Douglas, *Ben Jonson and the Lucianic Tradition.* Cambridge: Cambridge Univ. Press, 1979.

Duncan-Jones, Katherine, 'Nashe and Sidney: The Tournament in "The Unfortunate Traveller" ', *MLR* 63 (1968), 3–6.

_____ 'Philip Sidney's Toys', *PBA* 66 (1980), 161–78.

Eliade, Mircea, *The Myth of the Eternal Return,* trans. Willard R. Trask. London: Routledge & Kegan Paul, 1955.

Elliot, Robert C., *The Power of Satire.* Princeton, NJ: Princeton Univ. Press, 1960 (pbk. 1966).

Elton, Geoffrey R., 'An Early Tudor Poor Law', *Ec. HR* 6 (1953), 55–67.

_____ 'Reform and the "Commonwealth-men" of Edward VI's reign', in *The English Commonwealth 1547–1640,* ed. Peter Clark *et al.* Leicester: Leicester Univ. Press, 1979.

Emmison, Frederick G., *Elizabethan Life: Disorder.* Chelmsford: Essex County Council Record Office, 1970.

Fairholt, Frederick W., *Gog and Magog: The Giants in the Guildhall.* London: 1859.

Fehrenbach, Robert J., 'Recent Studies in Nashe (1968–1979)', *ELR* 11 (1981), 344–50.

Ferguson, Arthur B., 'The Tudor Commonweal and the Sense of Change', *Journal of British Studies,* 3 (1963), 11–35.

Ferguson, Margaret, 'Nashe's *The Unfortunate Traveller*: the "Newes of the Maker" Game', *ELR* 11 (1981), 165–82.

Fisher, Frederick J., 'The Development of London as a Centre of Conspicuous Consumption in the Sixteenth and Seventeenth Centuries', *TRHS,* 4th ser. 30 (1948), 37–50.

Forster, Leonard, *The Icy Fire.* Cambridge: Cambridge Univ. Press, 1969.

Foster, Frank Freeman, *The Politics of Stability.* London: Royal Historical Society, 1977.

Friedenreich, Kenneth, 'Nashe's *Strange Newes* and the Case for Professional Writers', *SP* 71 (1974), 451–72.

Gaignebet, Claude, 'Le Combat de Carneval et de Carême de P. Brueghel (1559)', *AESC* 27 (1972), 313–45.

García de Diego, P., 'El Testamento en la Tradición', *Revista de Dialectología y Tradiciones Populares,* 9 (1953), 603–66.

Geraldine, Sister M., 'Erasmus and the Tradition of Paradox', *SP* 61 (1964), 41–63.

Gibbons, Sr Marina, 'Polemic, the Rhetorical Tradition, and *The Unfortunate Traveller', JEGP* 63 (1964), 408–21.

Golding, Louis T., *An Elizabethan Puritan: Arthur Golding.* New York: R. R. Smith, 1937.

Gomme, Alice B., *The Traditional Games of England, Scotland and Ireland* (1894–8). London: Thames & Hudson, 1984.

Greenblatt, Stephen, *Renaissance Self-Fashioning from More to Shakespeare.* Chicago, Ill.: Univ. of Chicago Press, 1979.

Hale, John R., 'Sixteenth-Century Explanations of War and Violence', *P&P* 51 (1971), 3–26.

Harlow, C. G., 'Thomas Nashe, Robert Cotton the Antiquary, and "The Terrors of the Night" ', *RES,* NS 12 (1961), 7–23.

—— 'Nashe's Visit to the Isle of Wight and his Publications of 1592–4', *RES,* NS 14 (1963), 225–42.

Harrison, George B., 'Books and Readers 1599–1603', *The Library*, 4th ser. 14 (1934), 1–34.

Hassell-Smith, A., *County and Court: Government and Politics in Norfolk 1558–1603.* Oxford: Clarendon Press, 1974.

Haynes, Jonathan, 'Festivity and the Dramatic Economy of Jonson's "Bartholomew Fair" ', *ELH* 51 (1984), 645–8.

Helgerson, Richard, *The Elizabethan Prodigals.* Berkeley, Calif.: Univ. of Calif. Press, 1976.

Herford, Charles H., *Studies in the Literary Relations of England and Germany in the Sixteenth Century.* Cambridge: Cambridge Univ. Press, 1886.

Herr, Alan F., *The Elizabethan Sermon* (1940). New York: Octagon Books, 1969.

Hibbard, George R., *Thomas Nashe: A Critical Introduction.* London: Routledge & Kegan Paul, 1962.

Hill, Christopher, *Economic Problems of the Church.* Oxford: Clarendon Press, 1956.

—— *Society and Puritanism in Pre-Revolutionary England.* London: Secker & Warburg, 1964.

Homans, George C., *English Villagers of the Thirteenth Century.* Cambridge, Mass.: Harvard Univ. Press, 1942.

Hoskins, William G., *The Age of Plunder: King Henry's England 1500–1547.* London: Longman, 1976.

Hulme, Edward W., *The Early History of the English Patent System.* Boston, Mass.: Little, Brown & Co., 1909 (repr. from *Law Quarterly Review,* 1896–1902).

Hutson, Lorna, 'Thomas Nashe's "Persecution" by the Aldermen in 1593', *N&Q*, NS 232 (1987), 199–200.

Izard, Thomas C., *George Whetstone: Mid-Elizabethan Gentlemen of Letters*. New York: Columbia Univ. Press, 1942.

James, Mervyn E., 'The Concept of Order and the Northern Rising of 1569', *P&P* 6 (1973), 49–83.

James, Mervyn E., *Family, Lineage and Civil Society: A Study of Society, Politics and Mentality in the Durham Region 1500–1640*. Oxford: Clarendon Press, 1974.

Jardine, Lisa, 'The Place of Dialectic Teaching in Sixteenth Century Cambridge', *Studies in the Renaissance*, 21 (1974), 31–62.

Jefferson, Ann, and Robey, David (eds.), *Modern Literary Theory: A Comparative Introduction*. London: Batsford, 1982.

Jones, Ann Rosalind, 'Inside the Outsider: Nashe's *Unfortunate Traveller* and Bakhtin's Polyphonic Novel', *ELH* 50 (1983), 61–81.

Jones, Dorothy, 'An Example of Anti-Petrarchan Satire in Nashe's "The Unfortunate Traveller" ', *Yearbook of English Studies*, 1 (1971), 48–54.

Jones, Emrys, *The Origins of Shakespeare*. Oxford: Clarendon Press, 1977.

Jones, Whitney R. D., *The Tudor Commonwealth 1529–1559*. London: Athlone Press, 1970.

Jorgeson, Paul A., 'Theoretical Views of War in Elizabethan England', *JHI* 13 (1952), 469–81.

____ 'Elizabethan Religious Literature for Time of War', *HLQ* 37 (1973–4), 1–17.

Jung, Carl G., *Four Archetypes*, trans. R. F. C. Hull. London: Routledge & Kegan Paul, 1972.

Kerényi, Karl, 'The Trickster in Relation to Greek Mythology', in *The Trickster: A Study in American Indian Mythology*, ed. Paul Radin. London: Routledge & Kegan Paul, 1956.

Kolve, Verdel A., *The Play Called Corpus Christi*. Stanford, Calif.: Stanford Univ. Press, 1966.

Lanham, Richard A., 'Tom Nashe and Jack Wilton: Personality as Structure in "The Unfortunate Traveller" ', *Studies in Short Fiction*, 4 (Newberry, SC, 1966), 207–16.

Latham, Agnes, 'Satire on Literary Themes and Modes in Nashe's "Unfortunate Traveller" ', *ES* (1948), 85–100.

Lewis, Clive S., *English Literature in the Sixteenth Century*. London: Oxford Univ. Press, 1954.

Loades, David M., 'The Theory and Practice of Censorship in Sixteenth-Century England', *TRHS*, 5th ser. 24 (1974), 141–57.

Lytle, Guy Fitch, and Orgel, Stephen (eds.), *Patronage in the Renaissance*. Princeton, NJ: Princeton Univ. Press, 1981.

McKerrow, Ronald B., 'Booksellers, Printers, and the Stationers' Trade', in *Shakespeare's England,* ii. Oxford: Clarendon Press, 1916.

Malloch, A. E., 'The Techniques and Function of the Renaissance Paradox', *SP* 53 (1956), 191–203.

Mares, Frances, 'The Origin of the Figure Called "Vice" in Tudor Drama', *HLQ* 22 (1958–9), 11–29.

Marotti, Arthur, ' "Love is not love": Elizabethan Sonnet Sequences and the Social Order', *ELH* (1982), 396–428.

Miller, Edwin H., *The Professional Writer in Elizabethan England.* Cambridge, Mass.: Harvard Univ. Press, 1959.

Neale, John E., 'The Elizabethan Political Scene', *PBA* (1948), 97–117.

Nef, John U., *Cultural Foundations of an Industrial Civilization.* Cambridge: Cambridge Univ. Press, 1958.

Nelson, William, *Fact or Fiction: The Dilemma of the Renaissance Storyteller.* Cambridge, Mass.: Harvard Univ. Press, 1973.

Nicholl, Charles, *A Cup of News.* London: Routledge & Kegan Paul, 1984.

Norbrook, David, 'Panegyric of the Monarch and its Social Context under Elizabeth I and James I'. D.Phil. thesis, Oxford, 1978.

—— *Poetry and Politics in the English Renaissance.* London: Routledge & Kegan Paul, 1984.

O'Conor, Norreys J., *Godes Peace and the Queenes.* London: Oxford Univ. Press, 1934.

Ong, Walter J., *Ramus, Method and the Decay of Dialogue.* Cambridge, Mass.: Harvard Univ. Press, 1958 (repr. 1983).

—— *Rhetoric, Romance and Technology.* Ithaca, NY: Cornell Univ. Press, 1971.

—— *Interfaces of the Word.* Ithaca, NY: Cornell Univ. Press, 1977.

Owst, G. R., *Preaching in Medieval England.* Cambridge: Cambridge Univ. Press, 1926.

—— *Literature and Pulpit in Medieval England.* Oxford: Basil Blackwell, 2nd rev. edn., 1961.

Parkin, Charles, *The History and Antiquities of Yarmouth.* London: 1776.

Patterson, Annabel, *Censorship and Interpretation: The Conditions of Writing and Reading in Early Modern England.* Madison, Wis.: Univ. of Wisconsin Press, 1984.

Payne, F. Anne, *Chaucer and Menippean Satire.* Madison, Wis.: Univ. of Wisconsin Press, 1981.

Pease, Arthur S., 'Things Without Honour', *Classical Philology,* 21 (1926), 27–42.

Peter, John, *Complaint and Satire in Early English Literature.* Oxford: Clarendon Press, 1956.

Petti, Anthony G., 'Beasts and Politics in Elizabethan Literature', *ES* 16 (1963), 68–90.

Phillips, Margaret Mann, 'Erasmus and Propaganda', *MLR* 37 (1942), 1–17.

Phythian-Adams, Charles, 'Ceremony and the Citizens: The Communal Year at Coventry 1450–1550', in *Crisis and Order in English Towns 1500–1700,* ed. Peter Clark and Paul Slack. London: Routledge & Kegan Paul, 1972.

____ *Local History and Folklore.* London: Bedford Square Press, 1975.

____ *Desolation of a City: Coventry and the Urban Crisis of the Late Middle Ages.* Cambridge: Cambridge Univ. Press, 1979.

Popkin, Richard H., *The History of Skepticism from Erasmus to Descartes.* London: Harper & Row, 1964.

Pound, John, *Poverty and Vagrancy in Tudor England.* London, 1971.

Price, William Hyde, *The English Patents of Monopoly.* London: Constable, 1906.

Prouty, Charles T., *George Gascoigne.* New York: Columbia Univ. Press, 1942.

Ramsay, George D., *The City of London in International Politics at the Accession of Elizabeth Tudor.* Manchester: Manchester Univ. Press, 1975.

Relle, Eleanor, 'Some New Marginalia and Poems of Gabriel Harvey', *RES,* NS 23 (1972), 401–16.

Rhodes, Neil, *Elizabethan Grotesque.* London: Routledge & Kegan Paul, 1980.

Ringler, William, *Stephen Gosson.* Princeton, NJ: Princeton Univ. Press, 1942.

____ 'The First Phase of the Elizabethan Attack on the Stage 1558–1579', *HLQ* 5 (1942), 391–418.

Rollins, Hyder E., 'William Elderton: Elizabethan Actor and Ballad-Writer', *SP* 17 (1920), 199–245.

Rosenberg, Eleanor, *Leicester, Patron of Letters.* New York: Columbia Univ. Press, 1955.

Salingar, Leo G., *Shakespeare and the Traditions of Comedy,* Cambridge: Cambridge Univ. Press, 1976.

Saunders, J. W., 'The Stigma of Print: A Note on the Social Bases of Tudor Poetry', *EC* 1 (1951), 139–64.

Scoufos, Alice Lyle, 'Nashe, Jonson and the Oldcastle Problem', *MP* 65 (1968), 307–24.

Shaaber, M. A., *Some Forerunners of the Newspaper in England, 1476–1622.* New York: Octagon Books, 1966.

Siebert, Frederick S., *Freedom of the Press in England 1476–1776.* Urbana, Ill.: Univ. of Illinois Press, 1952.

Skinner, Quentin, *The Foundations of Modern Political Thought,* vol. i. *The Renaissance.* Cambridge: Cambridge Univ. Press, 1978.

Smith, R. S., 'A Woad Growing Project at Wollaton in the 1580s', *Transactions of the Thoroton Society,* 65 (1961), 27–46.

Sontag, Susan, *Illness as Metaphor.* New York: Farrar, Straus & Giroux, 1978.

Stern, Virginia, *Gabriel Harvey: His Life, Marginalia and Library.* Oxford: Clarendon Press, 1979.

Stone, Lawrence, 'The Educational Revolution in England, 1560–1640', *P&P* 28 (1964), 41–80.

—— *The Crisis of the Aristocracy.* Oxford: Clarendon Press, 1965.

Strutt, Joseph, *The Sports and Pastimes of the People of England,* ed. J. C. Cox. London: Methuen, 1903.

Strype, John, *The Life and Acts of John Whitgift, D. D.,* 4 vols. Oxford: Clarendon Press, 1822.

Syme, Ronald, *History in Ovid.* Oxford: Clarendon Press, 1978.

Thirsk, Joan, *Economic Policy and Projects: The Development of a Consumer Society in Early Modern England.* Oxford: Clarendon Press, 1978.

—— *The Rural Economy of England: Collected Essays.* London: Hambledon Press, 1984.

Thomas, Keith, 'The Place of Laughter in Tudor and Stuart England', *TLS,* 21 Jan. 1977, pp. 77–81.

Thompson, Craig R., *The Translations of Lucian by Erasmus and St. Thomas More.* Ithaca, NY: Cornell Univ. Press, 1940.

Thompson, Edward P., 'Time, Work-Discipline and Industrial Capitalism', *P&P* 38 (1967), 56–97.

—— ' "Rough Music": Le Charivari anglais', *AESC* 27 (1972), 285–312.

Trousdale, Marion, *Shakespeare and the Rhetoricians.* London: Scolar Press, 1982.

Unwin, George, *Industrial Organization in the Sixteenth and Seventeenth Centuries.* Oxford: Clarendon Press, 1904.

Weber, Max, *The Protestant Ethic and the Spirit of Capitalism,* trans. Talcott Parsons. London: Allen & Unwin, 1930.

Wells, Stanley, 'Thomas Nashe and the Satirical Stance', *Cahiers E.* 9 (1976), 1–17.

Whigham, Frank, *Ambition and Privilege: The Social Tropes of Elizabethan Courtesy Theory.* Berkeley, Calif.: Univ. of Calif. Press, 1984.

Wiles, David, *The Early Plays of Robin Hood.* Cambridge: D. S. Brewer, 1981.

Wilson, John Dover, 'Euphues and the Prodigal Son', *The Library,* NS 10 (1909), 337–61.

Wright, A. R., *Moveable Festivals,* British Calendar Customs, ed. T. E. Lones, vol. i. London: Folklore Soc., 1936.

Wright, Celeste Turner, 'Mundy and Chettle in Grub Street', *Boston University Studies in English,* 5 (1961), 129–38.

Wright, Louis B., *Middle Class Culture in Elizabethan England.* Chapel Hill, NC: Univ. of North Carolina Press, 1935.

Youngs, Frederick A., *The Proclamations of the Tudor Queens.* Cambridge: Cambridge Univ. Press, 1976.

# INDEX